More Wiley Concise Guides to Mental Health

W9-BYE-026

Books in the *Wiley Concise Guides to Mental Health* series feature a compact, easy-to-use format that includes:

- A practical approach that emphasizes real-life treatment over theory
- Vignettes and case illustrations
- Resources for specific readers such as clinicians, students, or patients

ISBN-10: 0-471-68991-2
ISBN-13: 978-0-471-68991-1
Paper • $34.95 • 336 pp.
February 2006

Wiley Concise Guides to Mental Health: Substance Use Disorders guides you through the entire continuum of addiction care and presents the latest scientific understanding of substance use and abuse. This informative reference provides a complete overview of diagnosis, treatment, research, emerging trends, and other critical information about chemical addictions while covering some of the most cutting-edge topics in the field.

ISBN-10: 0-471-70513-6
ISBN-13: 978-0-471-70513-0
Paper • $34.95 • 400 pp.
August 2006

Wiley Concise Guides to Mental Health: Posttraumatic Stress Disorder uses clear, highly accessible language to comprehensively guide you through PTSD and related issues. This informative reference provides a complete overview of the history of the field, diagnosis, treatment, research, emerging trends, and other critical information about PTSD. Examining both theory and practice, the text offers a multifaceted look at the disorder.

ISBN-10: 0-471-77994-6
ISBN-13: 978-0-471-77994-0
Paper • $34.95 • 256 pp.
March 2007

Wiley Concise Guides to Mental Health: Anxiety Disorders contains the most current, effective information about the treatment of anxiety disorders. This handy go-to reference includes an overview of anxiety disorders, assessment and treatment using cognitive behavior therapy, and coverage of special issues, such as treating anxiety in children and adolescents, group therapy with anxiety disorders, and supervision.

1807
WILEY
2007
BICENTENNIAL
wiley.com

The Wiley
Concise Guides
to Mental Health

Bipolar Disorder

The Wiley
Concise Guides
to Mental Health

Bipolar Disorder

Brian Quinn, L.C.S.W.,
Ph.D.

 John Wiley & Sons, Inc.

Library of Congress Cataloging-in-Publication Data

Quinn, Brian, L.C.S.W., Ph.D.
   Bipolar disorder / by Brian Quinn.
      p. ; cm. – (Wiley concise guides to mental health)
   Includes bibliographical references.
   ISBN: 978-0-470-04662-3 (pbk. : alk. paper)
   1. Manic-depressive illness. I. Title. II. Series.
      [DNLM: 1. Bipolar Disorder–diagnosis. 2. Bipolar Disorder–therapy. 3. Diagnosis, Differential.
WM 207 Q75p 2007]
   RC516.Q56 2007
   616.89'5–dc22

                                                                           2006037551

Printed in the United States of America.
10 9 8 7 6 5 4 3 2 1

CONTENTS

Series Preface   ix

Preface by S. Nassir Ghaemi, MD, MPH   xi

Acknowledgments   xv

Section One: Epidemeology, Phenomenology, and Diagnosis

INTRODUCTION   Bipolar Spectrum Illnesses: Common but Often
                   Misdiagnosed and Inappropriately Treated   3

CHAPTER 1   An Overview of Bipolar Disorder and Its Diagnosis   11

Section Two: Differential Diagnosis and Comorbidity

CHAPTER 2   Differentiating Unipolar from Bipolar Depression   37

CHAPTER 3   Differentiating Bipolar Illness from Organic Illnesses and
                   Other Psychiatric Disorders   59

CHAPTER 4   Comorbidity: Organic Illnesses, ADHD, Personality, Eating,
                   Anxiety, and Impulse Control Disorders   79

CHAPTER 5   Comorbidity: Alcohol and Drug Abuse   95

Section Three: Treatment

CHAPTER 6	Pharmacologic Treatment of Mania and Hypomania	129
CHAPTER 7	The Problem of Bipolar Depression	179
CHAPTER 8	Psychosocial Treatments	223
CHAPTER 9	Nonpharmacologic Approaches	241
CHAPTER 10	Identification and Management of Suicide Risk	261
CHAPTER 11	Child and Early Adolescent Bipolar Disorder: An Emerging Diagnosis by Carolyn Colwell, LCSW	275
CHAPTER 12	Bipolar Disorder in Older Adults by Colin Depp, Ph.D	309
CHAPTER 13	A Multidimensional Approach to Helping Patients with Bipolar Disorder	321
Index		337

SERIES PREFACE

The *Wiley Concise Guides to Mental Health* are designed to provide mental health professionals with an easily accessible overview of what is currently known about the nature and treatment of psychological disorders. Each book in the series delineates the origins, manifestations, and course of a commonly occurring disorder and discusses effective procedures for its treatment. The authors of the *Concise Guides* draw on relevant research as well as their clinical expertise to ground their text both in empirical findings and in wisdom gleaned from practical experience. By achieving brevity without sacrificing comprehensive coverage, the *Concise Guides* should be useful to practitioners as an on-the-shelf source of answers to questions that arise in their daily work, and they should prove valuable as well to students and professionals as a condensed review of state-of-the-art knowledge concerning the psychopathology, diagnosis, and treatment of various psychological disorders.

Irving B. Weiner

PREFACE

There is an old story about two medical students on graduation day where one turned to the other and said, "Well, from now on, we'll never be wrong; it'll only be a difference of opinion." There are certain things that doctors and clinicians in general do well: admitting they are wrong is not one of them. Unfortunately, bipolar disorder is a condition that is less well managed than other clinical pictures, and frankly, we clinicians are making enough mistakes that it would take generations to balance the Hippocratic scale of future benefit to outweigh past harm. Yet, with books such as this one, we may be heading in the right direction.

The clinical dilemma is not minor. It is likely that psychiatrists are more adept at diagnosing bipolar disorder than primary care physicians, for instance, but when about 60 percent of such patients are initially misdiagnosed in the hands of psychiatrists (Ghaemi, Boiman, & Goodwin, 2000), one is not dealing with good diagnostic methods versus bad: the difference is between bad and worse. Similarly low rates of accurate diagnosis and appropriate referral for treatment are seen in clinical psychology and social work settings.

Into this breach, with this book, steps Brian Quinn. With a doctorate in clinical social work, postgraduate training in psychoanalytic psychotherapy and a specialization in mood disorders and substance abuse for the past 15 years, he has observed poor diagnostic and treatment patterns both among psychiatrists and non-MD professionals. Often psychiatrists are too set in their ways to recognize their limitations; it takes colleagues from allied fields to point out our flaws. Dr. Quinn brings a great deal of clinical knowledge to educating all of us more about bipolar illness. In fact, he has lived through decades in which an intellectually honest person would have to admit that the mental health professions have been adrift (Ghaemi, 2003). Trained initially in a psychoanalytic model, he soon realized that the doctrines of that creed did not adequately explain the problems of many persons with biologically-based mood conditions. At first, it seemed that everything was depression and the cure for all was antidepressants (the Prozac-in-the-water solution), but unlike many colleagues who swallowed (and continue to swallow) this particular ideology, Dr. Quinn noted that many patients had peculiar reactions to antidepressants: they became hyper, agitated, even sometimes suicidal.

He did something too few clinicians do: he read the scientific literature and reexamined his assumptions. (William Osler once remarked that it was astonishing that one could practice medicine without reading the literature, but it was not astonishing how badly one might thus practice [Trede et al., 2003].) Reading more about bipolar illness, Dr. Quinn went back to the source of it all—to Emil Kraepelin (Bliss, 2002)—and by going back a century, he gained perspective that revealed the inadequacies of our age. He saw how community psychiatrists, enveloped in the depression paradigm, misdiagnosed bipolar disorder as depression, and how his own psychology and social work colleagues, living in their psychoanalytic houses, misdiagnosed bipolar illness as personality disorders.

Now he brings us his wisdom in written form, knowing full well that he too lives within a certain paradigm, that we all do, and that all our knowledge is limited and will change. But for now, there seems enough justification to do what he does here, to point out some of our current and recent errors in diagnosing and treating bipolar disorder, to offer some ideas about how to do a better job in the future, to review the state of the scientific literature at the present time, and to offer practical clinical advice to practitioners, patients, and their families.

No doubt he, and I, and all those who are taking this approach are getting some of it wrong. We raise more questions than answers, but it is scientific progress to realize that your old beliefs were false, even if you do not yet know what your new beliefs will be. This uncertainty may be uncomfortable, but it is a scientific uncertainty, one which nurtures a clinical caution that ultimately does more good than harm (Jouanna, 2001).

We must get beyond our clear errors so that we can get closer and closer to the truth. After all, as the American philosopher Charles Sanders Peirce put it, truth is nothing but corrected error (Peirce, 1958). In that spirit, knowing we are wrong, but hoping we are getting less and less wrong, I hope readers will take up this book and that we all get to work on better recognizing and managing this all too human affliction.

S. Nassir Ghaemi, MD MPH
Atlanta
October 2006

References

Bliss, M. (2002). *William Osler: A life in medicine.* Toronto: University of Toronto Press.

Ghaemi, S. (2003). *The concepts of psychiatry: A pluralistic approach to the mind and mental illness.* Baltimore: Johns Hopkins University Press.

Ghaemi, S., Boiman, E., & Goodwin, F. (2000). Diagnosing bipolar disorder and the effect of antidepressants: A naturalistic study. *Journal of Clinical Psychiatry, 61,* 804–808.

Jouanna, J. (2001). *Hippocrates.* Baltimore: Johns Hopkins University Press.

Peirce, C. (1958). What pragmatism is. In P. Weiner (Ed.), *Selected writings* (pp. 180–202). New York: Dover Press.

Trede, K, Salvatore, P., Baethge, C., et al. (2005). Manic-depressive illness: Evolution in Kraepelin's textbook, 1883–1926. *Harvard Review of Psychiatry, 13,* 155–178.

ACKNOWLEDGMENTS

I would like to acknowledge the sacrifices my children and especially my wife made in order to give me time to write this book. Running a household with active kids and working full-time while your husband is chained to the word processor is no easy task. I also appreciate my wife's editorial assistance.

It was my extreme good fortune to have Dr. S. Nassir Ghaemi, Director of the Bipolar Disorder Research Program at Emory University, agree to review my chapters on psychopharmacologic treatment. Dr. Ghaemi has given generously of his time and expertise.

I knew that Dr. Ghaemi was one of the world's foremost authorities on bipolar illness when I contacted him. What I did not know, until I began working with him on this book, was that he was also one of those rare individuals with both expertise in a particular field and a breadth of knowledge that has allowed him to think deeply about what it means to help others. He brings the kind of wisdom and perspective to our increasingly fractured field that it sorely needs.

I would like to acknowledge the contributions of my colleagues Carolyn Colwell and Colin Depp for helping me round out the content of this book with their contributions on pediatric bipolar illness and bipolar disorder in older adults.

I would also like to thank David Bernstein, Irving Weiner, and all the editors at Wiley for helping me through the difficult process of turning ideas into readable text.

Finally, I have to thank the inventors of the computer and the Internet. How did anyone manage to research and write anything in less than a lifetime without word processing software and electronic databases?

Brian Quinn
April 2007

Epidemiology, Phenomenology, and Diagnosis

THE WILEY
CONCISE GUIDES
TO MENTAL HEALTH

Bipolar
Disorder

Bipolar Spectrum Illnesses: Common but Often Misdiagnosed and Inappropriately Treated

Those who suffer from bipolar disorder in its extreme form have episodes of debilitating depression that alternate or mix with periods of mania, during which they talk incessantly, get along on little or no sleep for days at a time, spend money with abandon, and often abuse alcohol and other drugs. People with full-blown mania are obviously ill and often need to be hospitalized. But, in any given year, only 2 percent of the U.S. population has this form of bipolar illness, referred to as bipolar I disorder (Grant et al., 2005).

"The majority of bipolar patients are, however, not bipolar I," write Sachs and Graves (2005, p. 396). Most bipolar patients belong to a less dramatic, or *soft*, but still recognizable group of individuals with certain characteristic traits, which can include periodic disturbances in mood, energy level, productivity, and need for sleep. Manifestations of bipolarity run on a continuum or spectrum from patients with bipolar I disorder at one extreme to temperamentally normal individuals with varying degrees of extroversion, high energy, and creativity at the other.

Recent community and national population studies from several countries have shown that patients with soft or bipolar spectrum illnesses are quite common, probably as common as patients with unipolar depression. Judd and Akiskal (2003), for instance, in a reanalysis of data from a national survey of the United States population, found 5.1 percent of the population had soft forms of bipolar disorder. Moreno and Andrade (2005) reported a 6.6 percent prevalence of bipolar spectrum patients in a community sample from Brazil. Pini et al. (2005) found a similar prevalence rate of bipolar spectrum illnesses in a European sample. A report from Swiss researchers indicated a nearly 11 percent prevalence of individuals with soft bipolar disorder in a 20-year prospective community cohort study of young adults (Angst et al., 2003).

When *up*, the individuals in this soft bipolar spectrum often have a muted form of mania referred to as *hypomania* (from the Greek *hypo*, meaning under or below). The American Psychiatric Association's *Diagnostic and Statistical Manual of Mental Disorders*, text revision, 4th edition (2000), labels some patients with episodes of depression and hypomania as having bipolar II illness. Perugi, Ghaemi, and Akiskal (2006) estimate that over 90 percent of bipolar patients seen in clinical practice today are in the bipolar II spectrum.

Hypomanic episodes may be "sunny" or "dark" (Akiskal, Hantouche, & Allilaire, 2003). The pure *sunny* hypomanic individual is outgoing, cheerful, witty, charming, and able to function well with 6 hours or less of sleep per night for extended periods. He or she is unlikely to seek help when actively hypomanic, although irritability or impulsive behavior may prompt their spouse to *mandate* treatment.

"Dark" forms reflect a combination of depressive symptoms and some hypomanic traits (so-called bipolar II depressive mixed states). Such patients are typically moody, critical, irritable, demanding, controlling, and may have explosive tempers. They may be the most frequently seen patients with bipolar illness in outpatient practice today (Benazzi & Akiskal, 2005). In addition to an irritable or dysphoric mood, these individuals may have racing or crowded thoughts, display somewhat loud and pressured speech, and be distractible and hypersexual in spite of numerous symptoms of moderate to severe depression (unipolar depressed patients typically lose interest in sex).

A large proportion of patients with soft or bipolar spectrum illness have symptom pictures and course characteristics that may not meet *DSM-IV-TR* criteria for bipolar disorder. They may, for instance, have only a day or 2 of hypomania rather than the 4 days required by the *DSM-IV-TR* for a diagnosis of bipolar II. They may have just one or two hypomanic symptoms mixed in with their depression rather than the six hypomanic symptoms required by *DSM-IV-TR* for a diagnosis of mixed bipolar I illness. Or, they may feel physically agitated and have panic attacks along with symptoms of depression. Although these individuals have historically been classified as having agitated unipolar depression, it is now believed that most of them are actually bipolar (Koukopoulos & Koukopoulos, 1999). Many patients who seek help for what is apparently unipolar depression will, when carefully examined for markers of bipolarity, be found to have soft forms of bipolar illness (see, for instance, Manning et al., 1997).

Marneros and Goodwin (2005) have noted that the concepts of mixed states and forms of bipolar disorder that do not meet *DSM-IV-TR* criteria for bipolar illness are not new, but that awareness, interest, and research in them has only recently undergone a renaissance. "Some of [these] rediscovered psychopathological states," they write—although very well described—are still *terra incognita* and a source of confusion for many psychiatrists" (p. 2).

Of greater concern, however, is how easily bipolar spectrum illnesses can be overlooked and misdiagnosed by nonmedically trained clinicians in agency and private practice. Individuals with "soft" forms of bipolar illness often first seek the help of marriage counselors, psychologists, and social workers for the emotional pain and interpersonal problems caused by their mood dysregulation. These professionals are generally inadequately trained in the recognition of all but the most serious mental disorders. Even those in postgraduate psychotherapy institutes or university doctoral programs receive little or no training in the diagnosis of the various mood disorders. Instead, they are typically taught specialized forms of psychotherapy and/or research methodology.

Individuals with soft bipolar spectrum illnesses may be impulsive, angry, abuse alcohol and drugs, have very chaotic lives and stormy interpersonal relationships. When these individuals go for help, studies show that mental health professionals either fail to make any mood disorder diagnosis at all or misdiagnose them as having unipolar depression or personality disorders (Hantouche et al., 2006). Hirschfeld, Calabrese, and Weissman (2003) sent the Mood Disorder Questionnaire (MDQ), a validated screening instrument for bipolar I and II disorders, to roughly 128,000 people selected to represent the United States adult population. Approximately 85,000 subjects responded. When adjusted for bias introduced by nonresponders, only 20 percent of the individuals with positive screens for bipolar I or II disorders reported that they had previously received a diagnosis of bipolar disorder. A little more than 30 percent reported receiving a diagnosis of unipolar depression, while 49 percent said they had not received a diagnosis of either bipolar disorder or unipolar depression. Ghaemi, Saggase, and Goodwin (2006) have concluded that roughly one-half of bipolar patients seen in mental health treatment settings are misdiagnosed. This may well be a conservative estimate.

A study of members of the National Depressive and Manic-Depressive Association found that two-thirds of them were mistakenly first diagnosed as having either unipolar depression or schizophrenia (Hirschfeld, Lewis, & Vornik, 2003). What is even more alarming is that it took an average of 8 years from onset of first symptoms to accurate diagnosis for bipolar I patients. Ghaemi, Boiman, and Goodwin (2000) reported that, in a study of 54 bipolar outpatients with more subtle forms of the disorder, it took about 12 years before the patient got a correct diagnosis In the same study, Ghaemi and his colleagues reported that it took non-M.D. mental health professionals an average of 8.9 years to correctly diagnose bipolar patients. Psychiatrists did not do much better. Bipolar patients seeing psychiatrists were misdiagnosed for an average of 6.5 years.

There are several reasons why patients with bipolar disorder are often misdiagnosed as having unipolar depression. One is that clinicians are not aware of the unique markers that suggest the presence of bipolar depression. One marker, for instance, is child, adolescent, or young adult onset of major depression. Early onset is a marker for the later development of bipolar illness. Geller et al. (2001)

found, for instance, in a 10-year follow-up of children with depression, that more than 48 percent of them later developed bipolar I or II disorder.

Another reason bipolar patients are misdiagnosed as unipolar is because patients with the softer forms of bipolar disorder spend the vast majority of the time they are ill in the depressed phase of their illness (Judd et al., 2003). They generally seek help only when they are depressed and will not spontaneously mention any "up" periods they may have had because they view them as normal. If clinicians do not ask the right questions to uncover a history of hypomania or if they fail to interview family members for information, the proper diagnosis will be missed. Table I.1 summarizes the reasons for misdiagnosis.

Patients with bipolar depression who are misdiagnosed as having unipolar depression are often mistakenly prescribed antidepressant medication. Surprisingly, even when the patient is recognized as having bipolar depression, they are most often given antidepressants and not prescribed mood–stabilizing drugs (Ghaemi et al., 1999; Shi, Thiebaud, & McCombs, 2004). This is in spite of the fact that the use of mood–stabilizing drugs for patients with bipolar depression—not antidepressant monotherapy—is the current standard of care (American Psychiatric Association, 2002).

TABLE I.1

Reasons for Misdiagnosis of Bipolar Disorder as Unipolar Depression

Clinicians' reluctance to make the diagnosis of bipolar illness.

First episode of illness is often a depressive episode.

Requiring a previous history of hypomania for the diagnosis of bipolar illness.

Clinicians' lack of awareness of markers for bipolar depression.

Making the diagnosis of depression on the basis of symptoms of depression.

Clinicians' failure to probe for a history of hypomania.

Clinicians' focus on mood instead of behavioral activation when probing for hypomania.

Clinicians' failure to interview family.

Bipolar II patients spend vast majority of time ill in depressed phase.

Patients do not identify hypomania as illness and do not recall hypomanic episodes.

Hypomania can be adaptive, not disruptive.

Patients do not seek help when hypomanic.

The use of antidepressants runs the risk of causing a number of very serious problems in depressed bipolar patients. These include the induction of hypomania, rapid-cycling, and mixed, dysphoric, or agitated states and destabilization of the long-term course of the illness. The induction of hypomania occurs not just with older, tricyclic antidepressants but occurs, as well, in the latest generation of antidepressants such as Zoloft, Effexor, and Wellbutrin, even when patients are on mood-stabilizing drugs (Leverich et al., 2006). There is also evidence to suggest that some bipolar patients who have been treated with antidepressants may not respond as well to subsequent treatment with mood stabilizers (Koukopoulos, Kaliari, & Tondo, 1983; Winsberg et al., 2001).

There is, therefore, an urgent need for physicians, mental health clinicians, and patients to become aware of the dangers associated with the misdiagnosis and inappropriate treatment of individuals with bipolar spectrum illnesses. Proper diagnosis and treatment can spare patients months and even years of suffering. Recognizing the disorder in children is even more crucial since undiagnosed and inappropriately treated bipolar disorder can severely disrupt a youngster's psychosocial development and academic performance. In addition, early-onset bipolar disorder has been found to be associated with a less favorable long-term course and outcome (Goldstein & Levitt, 2006).

The longer correct diagnosis is delayed, the more likely it is that patients will continue to cycle between depression and hypomania. The greater the number of episodes, the less likely the patient is to respond to treatment (Nolen et al., 2004). In addition, uncontrolled bipolar illness may result in neurodegenerative changes. Kessing and Andersen (2004), for instance, reported that the risk of dementia increases with the number of episodes in major depressive and bipolar disorder.

The early chapters of this book are devoted to the foregoing descriptive and diagnostic issues. These chapters provide a brief history of the concept of the bipolar spectrum, describe the *DSM-IV-TR* diagnostic scheme for bipolar disorders and the problems associated with it, how unipolar depression can be distinguished from bipolar disorder, and how to differentiate bipolar disorder from medical and other psychiatric disorders including attention-deficit hyperactivity disorder and borderline personality disorder.

Even when properly diagnosed, patients with bipolar illness are challenging to treat. Medical problems and other serious psychiatric disorders, such as panic attacks, eating disorders, or posttraumatic stress disorder, along with substance abuse often complicate therapeutic efforts. Nearly 60 percent of bipolar I patients, for instance, abuse alcohol or drugs (Grant et al., 2005). Unrecognized and untreated substance abuse leads to a number of adverse outcomes in bipolar patients, including an increased risk of suicide.

The middle chapters will help clinicians broaden their knowledge of medical, psychiatric, and substance abuse comorbidity so that they can meet these patients' full range of treatment needs. Practical tips for nonmedically trained therapists on how to spot possible medical disorders mimicking the symptoms of depression or mania will be discussed.

Mental health professionals typically do not receive much training in identifying and dealing with substance abuse in their patients, so tools for recognizing and effectively managing patients abusing alcohol and drugs will be outlined.

The final chapters provide detailed information on the most recent pharmacologic treatment options for bipolar disorders. Information on the importance of making sure that patients, particularly older women, have optimal thyroid hormone levels is described, along with information on identifying patients at highest risk of suicide.

Research on psychological interventions for bipolar illness was relatively neglected until about 1990. Since then, an increasing number of controlled trials with a variety of psychosocial treatments have demonstrated the effectiveness of these approaches in improving the general course and outcome of bipolar illness and, in particular, reducing relapse rates (Scott, Colom, & Vieta, 2006).

Medication and psychotherapy are not the only effective interventions in bipolar illness. Electroconvulsive therapy (ECT) is an often maligned, misunderstood, and underutilized treatment for mood disorders. It also happens to be the most effective treatment in specific subgroups of patients and, in some cases, the safest one, as well. ECT, transcranial magnetic stimulation, and other potent nonpharmacologic interventions, such as manipulation of sleep, light, and dark, may be used to treat bipolar depression and mania. Information will also be provided on nutritional and biochemical approaches to bipolar illness with special emphasis on the latest research on the use of omega-3 fatty acids. Finally, the reader will find separate chapters on the diagnosis and treatment of bipolar disorder in children and older adults.

This book is geared toward the practicing clinician, those in training for the mental health or substance abuse treatment fields, and patients who want to learn more about their illness and its proper treatment. Clinicians and those in training will come away with practical information they can use immediately to help improve the lives of patients with whom they work. Patients and their relatives will learn valuable information that will enable them to intelligently discuss the best treatment options with their doctors and therapists and learn what they can do to improve their chances for getting and staying well.

References

Akiskal, H., Hantouche, E., & Allilaire, J. (2003). Bipolar I with and without cyclothymic temperament: "Dark" and "sunny" expressions of soft bipolarity. *Journal of Affective Disorders, 73*(1–2), 49–57.

Angst, J., Gamma, A., Benazzi, F., et al. (2003). Toward a re-definition of subthreshold bipolarity: Epidemiology and proposed criteria for bipolar-II, minor bipolar disorders and hypomania. *Journal of Affective Disorders, 73*(1–2), 133–146.

American Psychiatric Association. (2000). *Diagnostic and statistical manual of mental disorders* (text revision, 4th ed.). Washington, DC: Author.

American Psychiatric Association. (2002). *American Psychiatric Association practice guidelines for the treatment of patients with bipolar disorder* (2nd ed.). Washington, DC: Author.

Benazzi, F., & Akiskal, H. (2005). Irritable-hostile depression: Further validation as a bipolar depressive mixed state. *Journal of Affective Disorders, 84*(2–3), 197–207.

Geller, B., Zimmerman, B., Williams, M., et al. (2001). Bipolar disorder at prospective follow-up of adults who had prepubertal major depressive disorder. *American Journal of Psychiatry, 158*, 125–127.

Ghaemi, S., Boiman, E., & Goodwin, F. (2000). Diagnosing bipolar disorder and the effect of antidepressants: A naturalistic study. *Journal of Clinical Psychiatry, 61*, 804–808.

Ghaemi, S., Sachs, G., Chiou, A., et al. (1999). Is bipolar disorder still underdiagnosed? Are antidepressants over utilized? *Journal of Affective Disorder, 52*, 135-144.

Ghaemi, S., Saggase, J., & Goodwin, F. (2006). Diagnosis of bipolar depression. In R. El-Mallakh & S. Ghaemi (Eds.), *Bipolar Depression: A comprehensive guide* (pp. 3–33). Washington, DC: American Psychiatric Publishing.

Goldstein, B., & Levitt, A. (2006). Further evidence for a developmental subtype of bipolar disorder defined by age at onset: Results from the National Epidemiologic Survey on Alcohol and Related Conditions. *American Journal of Psychiatry, 163*(9), 1633–1636.

Grant, B., Stinson, F., Hasin, D., et al. (2005). Prevalence, correlates, and comorbidity of bipolar disorder and axis I and II disorders: Results from the National Epidemiologic Survey on Alcohol and Related Conditions. *Journal of Clinical Psychiatry, 66*(10), 1205–1215.

Hantouche, E., Akiskal, H., Azorin, J., et al. (2006). Clinical and psychometric characterization of depression in mixed mania: A report from the French National Cohort of 1090 manic patients. *Journal of Affective Disorders,* Jan. 18. (Epub ahead of print)

Hirschfeld, R., Calabrese, J., & Weissman, M. (2003). Screening for bipolar disorder in the community. *Journal of Clinical Psychiatry, 64*(1), 53–59.

Hirschfeld, R., Lewis, L., & Vornik, L. (2003). Perceptions and impact of bipolar disorder: How far have we really come? Results of the national depressive and manic-depressive association 2000 survey of individuals with bipolar disorder. *Journal of Clinical Psychiatry, 64*(2), 161–174.

Judd, L., & Akiskal, H. (2003). The prevalence and disability of bipolar spectrum disorders in the US population: Re-analysis of the ECA database taking into account subthreshold cases. *Journal of Affective Disorders, 73*(1–2), 123–131.

Judd, L., Akiskal, H., Schettler, P., et al. (2003). A prospective investigation of the natural history of the long-term weekly symptomatic status of bipolar II disorder. *Archives of General Psychiatry, 60*(3), 261–269.

Kessing, L., & Andersen, P. (2004). Does the risk of developing dementia increase with the number of episodes in patients with depressive disorder and in patients with bipolar disorder? *Journal of Neurology, Neurosurgery and Psychiatry, 75*(12), 1662–1666.

Koukopoulos, A., Kaliari, B., & Tondo, A. (1983). Rapid cyclers, temperament and antidepressants. *Comprehensive Psychiatry, 24*, 249–258.

Koukopoulos, A., & Koukopoulos, A. (1999). Agitated depression as a mixed state and the problem of melancholia. *Psychiatric Clinics of North America, 22*(3), 547–564.

Leverich, G., Altshuler, L., Frye, M., et al. (2006). Risk of switch in mood polarity to hypomania or mania in patients with bipolar depression during acute and continuation trials of venlafaxine, sertraline, and bupropion as adjuncts to mood stabilizers. *American Journal of Psychiatry, 163*(2), 232–239.

Marneros, A., & Goodwin, F. (2005). *Bipolar disorders: Mixed states, rapid cycling and atypical forms.* New York: Cambridge University Press.

Manning, J., Haykal, R., Connor, P., & Akiskal, H. (1997). On the nature of depressive and anxious states in a family practice setting: The high prevalence of bipolar II and related disorders in a cohort followed longitudinally. *Comprehensive Psychiatry, 38*(2), 102–108.

Moreno, D., & Andrade, L. (2005). The lifetime prevalence, health services utilization and risk of suicide of bipolar spectrum subjects, including subthreshold categories in the Sao Paulo ECA study. *Journal of Affective Disorders, 87*(2–3), 231–241.

Nolen, W., Luckenbaugh, D., Altshuler, L., et al. (2004). Correlates of 1 year prospective outcome in bipolar disorder: Results from the Stanley Foundation Bipolar Network. *American Journal of Psychiatry, 161,* 1447–1454.

Perugi, G., Ghaemi, S., & Akiskal, H. (2006). Diagnostic and clinical management approaches to bipolar depression, bipolar II and their co-morbidities. In H. Akiskal & M. Tohen (Eds.), *Bipolar psychopharmacotherapy* (pp. 193–234). West Sussex, England: Wiley.

Pini, S., de Queiroz, V., Pagnin, D., et al. (2005). Prevalence and burden of bipolar disorders in European countries. *European Neuropsychopharmacology: The Journal of the European College of Neuropsychopharmacology, 15*(4), 425–434.

Sachs, G., & Graves, M. (2005). Investigational strategies: Treatment of rapid cycling, mixed episodes, and atypical bipolar mood disorder. In A. Marneros & F. Goodwin (Eds.), *Bipolar Disorders: Mixed states, rapid cycling and atypical forms* (pp. 369–385). New York: Cambridge University Press.

Scott, J., Colom, F., & Vieta, E. (2006). A meta-analysis of relapse rates with adjunctive psychological therapies compared to usual psychiatric treatment for bipolar disorders. *International Journal of Neuropsychopharmacology, 20,* 1–7. (Epub ahead of print)

Shi, L., Thiebaud, P., & McCombs, J. (2004). The impact of unrecognized bipolar disorders for patients treated for depression with antidepressants in the fee-for-services California Medicaid (Medi-Cal) program. *Journal of Affective Disorders, 82*(3), 379–383.

Winsberg, M., DeGolia, S., Strong, C., & Ketter, T. (2001). Divalproex therapy in medication-naïve and mood-stabilizer-naïve bipolar II depression. *Journal of Affective Disorders, 67*(1–3), 207–212.

CHAPTER 1

An Overview of Bipolar Disorder and Its Diagnosis

Descriptions of mania and melancholia date back to the time of Hippocrates (circa 400 BC). The Greek physician Aretaeus (second century AD) is credited with being the first to suggest that mania was intimately connected with melancholia and to note the many forms of manic-depressive illness (Maneros & Goodwin, 2005):

> The development of mania is really a worsening of the disease [melancholia], rather than a change into another disease . . . the sadness [of melancholics] became better after various lengths of time and changed into happiness; the patients then develop a mania. (p. 6)
>
> Some patients with mania . . . laugh, play, dance day and night, and stroll through the market, sometimes with a garland on their head, as they had won a game . . . But others fly into a rage. The manifestations of mania are countless. (p. 5)

The idea that mania and depression are two manifestations of the same illness was written about extensively by French clinicians in the mid-nineteenth century. Jean-Pierre Falret introduced the term *folie circulaire* and Jules Baillarger the term *la folie a double forme* to describe the alternation of manic and depressive episodes that are the hallmark of classic bipolar disorder (Pichot, 2004). In 1854, Falret predicted that many depressed patients would eventually be recognized as actually belonging to the bipolar spectrum (Akiskal et al., 2006a). Many of the manifestations of bipolar spectrum illness that have been the subject of recent clinical attention were described by these French doctors (Haustgen, 1995).

The German psychiatrist Emil Kraepelin built on the work of the French and made careful long-term observations of a large number of manic-depressive patients during the late nineteenth and early twentieth centuries. In his 1921 edition of *Manic-Depressive Insanity and Paranoia*, he concluded, as had Falret before him, that many forms of depression are actually expressions of bipolar illness:

> Manic-depressive insanity . . . includes on the one hand the whole domain of so-called periodic and circular insanity, on the other hand simple mania, *the greater part of the morbid states termed melancholia* and also a not inconsiderable number of cases of [confusional or delirious insanity]. (p. 1; emphasis added)

It is clear, as well, from the following that Kraepelin was a proponent of the spectrum model:

> . . . we include here certain slight and slightest colorings of mood, some of them periodic, some of them continuously morbid, which on the one hand are to be regarded as the rudiment of more severe disorders, on the other hand pass without sharp boundary into the domain of personal predisposition. In the course of the years I have become more and more convinced that all of the above-mentioned states only represent manifestations of a single morbid process. (p. 1)

The idea that patients with both mania and melancholia might have an illness different from those patients who suffered with just melancholia did not begin to take shape until the last half of the twentieth century. A German physician, Karl Leonhard, came up with the concept of a monopolar-bipolar dichotomy. This distinction received some validation in the late 1960s when research showed there were clinical, familial, and course features that differentiated the two (Vieta et al., 2005). The separation of unipolar from bipolar disorder was not formally accepted, however, until the publication of the third edition of the American Psychiatric Association's *Diagnostic and Statistical Manual of Mental Disorders* in 1980.

There were categories for cyclothymia and atypical bipolar disorder in the *DSM-III*, but bipolar disorders not meeting criteria for bipolar I were often considered unipolar variants and treated as such. A number of studies have found many patients initially diagnosed with unipolar depression in a variety of settings actually have, upon closer examination, a bipolar disorder (e.g., Ghaemi et al., 2000; Hirschfeld et al., 2003; Lish et al., 1994; Manning et al., 1998). In the study by Ghaemi, 56 percent of subjects diagnosed initially with unipolar depression were subsequently found to have a bipolar spectrum illness upon more careful examination.

Some psychiatrists are now suggesting that the unipolar-bipolar distinction may be a false dichotomy and are urging a return to the unitary view of depression and mania. The effectiveness of treatments such as lithium, quetiapine, and electroconvulsive therapy in both the manic and depressive phases of the illness supports this view.

Even if the distinction between unipolar and bipolar disorder has some validity at the extremes (alternating manic and depressive episodes at one extreme and pure depression without manic or hypomanic episodes at the other), careful observation has revealed there are many patients in between these extremes who appear to belong to a broader spectrum of bipolar illness than that defined by the *DSM* criteria. In 1990, Goodwin and Jamison wrote that "... there is evidence individual patients exhibit varying degrees of loading for mania or depression—evidence that strongly suggests a continuum or spectrum model [of mood disorders]" (p. 70). A tendency to mood instability or mania may be expressed more readily when the patient is given antidepressants—something that has been happening increasingly since the debut of Prozac in the United States in 1989. A 5-year study of prescription claim information from a random sample of two million commercially insured patients under the age of 18 found that the use of antidepressants increased 49 percent from 1998 to 2002. For children ages 5 and under, the study revealed there was a 100 percent increase in use of antidepressants in girls and a 64 percent increase in use in boys (Delate et al., 2004).

Hagop Akiskal and a number of other psychiatric researchers (e.g., J. Angst, F. Benazzi, S. Ghaemi, F. Goodwin, A. Koukopolous, A. Marneros, G. Perugi) have revitalized and extended Kraeplin's ideas about the bipolar spectrum. They have written extensively on the connections between many forms of depression and bipolar disorder, the phenomenology of the bipolar spectrum illnesses, the misdiagnosis of bipolar disorder as unipolar depression, the problems of antidepressant monotherapy in bipolar depression, the temperamental foundations from which full-blown mood episodes later emerge, and how disorders such as substance abuse, cluster B personality disorders, and a number of impulse control problems are associated with bipolar illness. We may well be coming full circle back to the idea of a unitary manic-depressive illness.

The *DSM-IV-TR*

The *Diagnostic and Statistical Manual of Mental Disorders—DSM-IV-TR* (American Psychiatric Association, 2000)—describes four types of mood episodes (Table 1.1), which "cannot be diagnosed as separate entities [but] serve as the building blocks" (p. 345) for the mood disorder diagnoses, including the bipolar disorders.

A *major depressive episode* in adults is defined in the *DSM-IV-TR* as the presence of five or more of the following symptoms: depressed mood, loss of pleasure, changes in appetite and weight, insomnia or oversleeping (hypersomnia), psychomotor agitation or retardation, fatigue, feelings of worthlessness or excessive guilt, trouble concentrating or indecisiveness, suicidal ideation or recurrent thoughts of death. At least one of the symptoms has to be either (a) depressed mood or (b) loss of interest or pleasure. In addition, the *DSM-IV-TR* requires that "the symptoms cause clinically significant distress or impairment in social, occupational, or other important areas of functioning" (p. 356).

A *manic episode* in an adult is defined in the

TABLE 1.1

DSM-IV-TR Mood Episodes

- Major depressive
- Manic
- Mixed
- Hypomanic

DSM-IV-TR by "a distinct period of abnormally and persistently elevated, explosive, or irritable mood lasting at least 1 week (or any duration if hospitalization is necessary)" (p. 357). Three or more of the following symptoms (four if the mood is only irritable) must have persisted for at least one week and "been present to a significant degree" (p. 357): inflated self-esteem or grandiosity, decreased need for sleep, increased talkativeness or pressure to keep talking, flight of ideas or subjective experience that thoughts are racing, distractibility, increase in goal-directed activity (socially, at work or school, or sexually) or psychomotor agitation, excessive involvement in pleasurable activities that have a high potential for painful consequences (e.g., engaging in unrestrained buying sprees, sexual indiscretions, foolish business investments). In addition, the *DSM-IV-TR* requires that "the mood disturbance is sufficiently severe to cause marked impairment in occupational functioning or in usual social activities or relationships with others, or to necessitate hospitalization to prevent harm to self or others, or there are psychotic features" (p. 357).

A *mixed episode*, according to *DSM-IV-TR* criteria, is diagnosed when an individual meets criteria both for a manic episode and a major depressive episode nearly every day for at least a 1-week period. As is the case for a manic episode, the *DSM-IV-TR* also requires that a mixed episode "is sufficiently severe to cause marked impairment in occupational functioning or in usual social activities or relationships with others, or to necessitate hospitalization to prevent harm to self or others, or there are psychotic features" (pp. 362–363). As opposed to the euphoria and grandiosity seen in pure mania, mixed mania includes symptoms such as severe anxiety, agitation, hostility, irritable mood, somatic complaints, expressions of extreme distress, and cognitive impairment (Goldberg et al., 2000). I will describe mixed episodes in more detail later in this chapter.

A *hypomanic episode* is defined in the *DSM-IV-TR* as a distinct period of persistently elevated, expansive, or irritable mood lasting at least 4 days. This mood must be clearly different from the usual nondepressed mood. During the period of mood disturbance, three or more (four if the mood is only irritable) of the symptoms described previously for a manic episode have been present to a significant degree, have produced an unequivocal and uncharacteristic change in functioning, are observable by others, are not severe enough to cause marked impairment in functioning or hospitalization, and are not associated with psychotic features. Table 1.2 lists the *DSM-IV-TR* subtypes of bipolar disorder.

Bipolar I disorder in adults is characterized by episodes of major depression and mania. An individual may receive the diagnosis of bipolar I disorder in the *DSM-IV-TR* only if he or she currently has or has had at least one manic or

TABLE 1.2

DSM-IV-TR Bipolar Disorder Categories

- Bipolar I
- Bipolar II
- Cyclothymia
- Bipolar Disorder NOS (Not Otherwise Specified)

---

mixed episode. The current episode of bipolar I disorder, for those who have had a previous manic or mixed episode, may be described as hypomanic, manic, mixed, or depressed.

Bipolar II disorder is the second category listed in the *DSM-IV-TR* classification of bipolar disorders. In adults, it is characterized by episodes of major depression and hypomania. The most recent or current episode may be described as either hypomanic or depressed. The third category of bipolar disorder in *DSM-IV-TR* is *cyclothymia*. In adults, it is defined as the presence, over at least a 2-year period, of numerous hypomanic and depressive episodes that cause clinically significant distress or impairment of functioning. The person must not have been without the symptoms for 2 months and the depressions cannot meet diagnostic criteria for a major depressive episode during the first 2 years of the illness. After the initial 2 years, a diagnosis of both cyclothymia and bipolar I disorder is given if the person develops a manic episode, and a diagnosis of both cyclothymia and bipolar II disorder is given if the person develops symptoms of depression that meet diagnostic criteria for a major depressive episode.

The final *DSM-IV-TR* bipolar disorder category is *Bipolar Disorder Not Otherwise Specified*. This category is for mood disorders with bipolar features that do not meet criteria for any of the other three categories.

DSM-IV-TR Mood Disorder Symptom and Course "Specifiers"

The *DSM-IV-TR* lists a number of terms that may be used to describe the current symptom picture and the course of a mood disorder. These terms are referred to as specifiers. Five are key in understanding the symptoms and course of bipolar spectrum illnesses. These are listed in Table 1.3.

Psychotic Features

The presence of false beliefs (delusions) or false perceptions (hallucinations) does not necessarily imply a diagnosis of schizophrenia. As many as two-thirds of bipolar patients in a manic episode have delusions or hallucinations (Goodwin & Jamison, 1990). Bipolar patients in mixed and depressive phases of the illness may also have delusions or hallucinations. There are two types of psychotic features: mood-congruent and mood incongruent.

Mood-Congruent Psychotic Features According to the *DSM-IV-TR*, mood-congruent psychotic features are delusions or hallucinations "whose content is entirely consistent with either the typical depressive themes of personal inadequacy, guilt, disease, death, nihilism or deserved pun-

TABLE 1.3

Key *DSM-IV-TR* Symptom and Course Specifiers

- Psychotic features
- Rapid cycling
- Atypical features
- Seasonal pattern
- Postpartum onset

ishment" (p. 413) or "the typical manic themes of inflated worth, power, knowledge, identity or special relationship to a deity or famous person" (p. 415). An example of a depressive delusion of disease, for example, is the belief that one's insides are rotting. A belief one is Jesus Christ is an example of a manic delusion of grandiosity. A depressive hallucination would be hearing death's footsteps in the house each night. Hearing a voice telling you that you have been chosen by God to save the world is a manic hallucination. Hallucinations are typically auditory. Visual or olfactory hallucinations should prompt a search for organic illness.

Mood-Incongruent Psychotic Features   Mood-incongruent psychotic features are delusions or hallucinations that do not have typical depressive or manic themes. Mood-incongruent psychotic symptoms, according to the *DSM-IV-TR*, include the belief that one is being harassed, harmed, or targeted for harm by some person or organization (delusions of persecution), the experience that the thoughts of others are being inserted into one's mind (thought insertion), the experience that one's thoughts are being sent out to others or that others can perceive one's thoughts (thought broadcasting), and the belief one's mind or body is being controlled by others or some outside force (delusions of control).

The depressive or manic content of mood-congruent psychotic features may prompt clinicians to consider a mood disorder diagnosis, but mood-incongruent psychotic features often lead clinicians to quickly and mistakenly diagnose schizophrenia. Bipolar patients can, however, have mood-incongruent psychotic features.

Rapid-Cycling

DSM-IV-TR defines rapid-cycling as "at least four episodes of mood disturbance in the previous 12 months that meet criteria for a Major Depressive, Manic, Mixed, or Hypomanic Episode" (p. 428). Episodes must be separated "by partial or full remission for at least 2 months" or there must be "a switch to an episode of opposite mood episode" (p. 428). Patients with bipolar disorder may cycle much more often than four times a year, especially when exposed to antidepressants. Cycling can even occur on or within the same day, especially in children with bipolar disorder. This is referred to as *ultradian cycling*. I will discuss rapid-cycling in more detail later in this chapter.

Atypical Features

A depressed patient who loses his or her appetite, who has middle-of-the-night or early morning awakening, and whose mood is not reactive (his or her mood does not improve temporarily in response to positive events) is said to have typical symptoms of depression. *DSM-IV-TR* defines another set of symptoms as *atypical*. The term *atypical* does not imply unusual or rare. Atypical symptoms are common, especially in nonpsychotic, mildly to moderately depressed, female outpatients. A patient is said to have atypical symptoms when, during the most recent

2 weeks of a major depressive episode, his or her mood improves temporarily in response to positive events and when he or she has two or more of the following symptoms: increased need for sleep (hypersomnia); increased appetite or significant weight gain; heavy, leaden feelings in the arms and legs (leaden paralysis); and a "long-standing pattern of interpersonal rejection sensitivity (not limited to episodes of mood disturbance) that results in significant social or occupational impairment" (American Psychiatric Association, 2000, p. 422).

Depression with hypersomnia had the highest specificity for the diagnosis of bipolar II disorder of any of the atypical symptoms in a study by Benazzi and Rihmer (2000). However, clinicians should keep in mind that bipolar patients, when more severely depressed, may have the middle-of-the-night awakening typically seen in severely depressed unipolar patients (Goodwin & Jamison, 1990).

Seasonal Pattern

Patients who oversleep, crave carbohydrates, gain weight, and become lethargic in the fall and winter and then become more energetic in the summer are said to have seasonal affective disorder (SAD). A substantial number of patients with SAD have bipolar illness (Goodwin & Jamison, 1990; Rosenthal & Wehr, 1987). A small percentage of patients with SAD have summer depressions and winter euthymia or hypomania.

The *DSM-IV-TR* notes that the prevalence of the seasonal pattern increases with higher latitudes. Levitt and Boyle (2002) presented data showing there was no evidence to support an increase in prevalence with increasing latitude. However, their data was based on a survey of individuals spread across only eight degrees of latitude. The *DSM-IV-TR* also indicates that women make up 60 to 90 percent of individuals with a seasonal pattern of depression.

Postpartum Onset

The *DSM-IV-TR* defines postpartum onset of depression as a depressive episode that begins within 4 weeks of giving birth to a child. Postpartum mood episodes with psychotic features occur in 1 in 500 to 1 in 1,000 deliveries but occur more frequently in women with previous postpartum episodes, a prior history of mood disorder, and especially in women with a history of bipolar I disorder. They may also occur more frequently in women with a family history of bipolar disorder (American Psychiatric Association, 2000).

There is a strong association between postpartum psychosis and bipolar disorder (Chaudron & Pies, 2003). A woman seeking help for depression who has a history of postpartum psychosis should be suspected of having bipolar disorder.

Problems with the *DSM-IV-TR* Classification of Bipolar Disorders

Akiskal (1996) and others such as Benazzi (2006b), Angst et al. (2003), and Ghaemi et al. (2006) have pointed out that there are a number of problems with the *DSM-IV-TR* classification of bipolar disorders that lead to the under-diagnosis of bipolar spectrum illnesses. As Vieta et al. (2005) suggest, "current diagnostic criteria lack the sensitivity to detect the full range of conditions within the bipolar spectrum" (p. 89).

Shortcomings of the *DSM-IV-TR* classification of bipolar disorders include the following:

1. The *DSM-IV-TR* contains no criteria for differentiating unipolar from bipolar depression. More specifically, differences in symptoms (phenomenology), course and family history between the two are not described.

2. An episode may only be labeled *mixed* in *DSM-IV-TR* if the patient's symptoms meet the full criteria for both depression and mania. However, it is not uncommon, especially in outpatient practice, for clinicians to see patients with a major depressive episode who also have only a few manic symptoms. Benazzi (2001) has found that the presence of three hypomanic symptoms (agitation, irritability, and racing or crowded thoughts) clearly differentiates bipolar from unipolar patients. Agitated depression has typically been considered a unipolar variant. Koukopoulos and Koukopoulos (1999) have argued persuasively that agitated depression is, in fact, a type of mixed state.

3. *DSM-IV-TR* requires 4-day duration for an activated state to be considered a hypomanic episode. But Angst et al. (2003) have documented that the mean duration of hypomanic episodes is 1 to 3 days.

4. The sharp demarcation of Axis II personality disorders in general and antisocial, narcissistic, and borderline personality disorders in particular from Axis I mood disorders may not be warranted (Akiskal et al., 2006b). The fluidity of the boundaries between Axis I and Axis II was demonstrated in 1980 when depressive personality disorder was reclassified as an Axis I disorder and labeled dysthymia. The disorder had been thought to originate from trauma in the oral stage of development and the dynamic interplay between subsequent hostile impulses and the superego (Goldberg, 1975). But a number of lines of evidence indicated that depressive personality disorder had, in spite of its chronic course, a close biological connection to episodic major depressive disorder.

5. The *DSM-IV-TR* requirements for a diagnosis of atypical depression are overly strict. *DSM-IV-TR* requires that a patient have mood reactivity (mood improves in response to positive events) if his or her symptoms are to be labeled atypical. Benazzi (2005) asserts there is little empirical support for this requirement. He describes the study by Angst et al. (2002), which found that mood reactivity is no more important for the diagnosis of atypical depression than any of the other atypical features. A clinician's

index of suspicion for a bipolar depression should be raised if the patient is oversleeping, even if mood reactivity is not present.

6. *DSM-IV-TR* requires that an individual have a euphoric or irritable mood to be labeled hypomanic. But periods of overactive behavior and increased productivity are more reliable markers of hypomania (Akiskal, 2005). They are more easily remembered by the patient and his or her family than a change in mood.

7. *DSM-IV-TR* acknowledges that "some evidence suggests that there may be a bipolar 'diathesis' in individuals who develop manic- or hypomanic- or mixed-like episodes following somatic treatment for depression" (p. 359). But, as of now, in the absence of a previous history of mania or hypomania, manic patients who develop manic, hypomanic, or mixed episodes with somatic antidepressant treatments are not considered bipolar. Akiskal and Pinto (1999), however, have found that individuals with antidepressant-induced hypomania very often go on to develop spontaneous hypomania. Angst et al. (2003) discuss a number of other "minor forms" of bipolar disorder. Table 1.4 lists several of these minor or atypical forms of bipolar disorder. They are atypical in the sense that individuals with these forms have no prior history of hypomania.

The problem with widening the diagnostic criteria for bipolar disorder, of course, is the loss of specificity and the danger of overdiagnosis. As sensitivity to the subtle manifestations of bipolar disorder increases, specificity of the diagnosis decreases. While the risk of overdiagnosis should be kept in mind, clinicians need to be aware that the risk of misdiagnosis of bipolar depression as unipolar depression poses substantially greater potential for harm. Treatment of bipolar depression with antidepressants runs a number of serious risks including the induction of hypomania, mixed states, or rapid cycling or the worsening of preexisting agitation and rapid cycling.

TABLE 1.4

Atypical Forms of Bipolar Disorder (No History of Hypomania)

- Antidepressant-induced hypomania or mixed states
- Depression in a child, adolescent, or young adult with a family history of bipolar disorder
- Depression in an individual with a premorbid hyperthymic temperament
- Brief, frequent, recurrent depressions
- Agitated depression

Epidemiology, Phenomenology, and Course of Bipolar Spectrum Disorders

Bipolar disorder with manic episodes (bipolar I disorder) lies at one of the extremes of the bipolar spectrum and occurs in two percent of the U.S. population (Grant et al., 2005). It is far from being the most common form of bipolar disorder. The universe of bipolar disorders (bipolar I, bipolar II, cyclothymia, and the rest of the bipolar spectrum) has been found to make up as much as 6.4 percent of the U.S. population (Judd & Akiskal, 2003). Pini et al. (2005) conducted a literature search, supplemented by a survey of experts along with selected reanalyses of existing data from epidemiological studies, to determine the prevalence of bipolar disorders in the European Union. They estimated a 6 percent prevalence rate of bipolar spectrum illnesses in Europeans. A report from Swiss researchers indicated a nearly 11 percent prevalence of individuals with soft bipolar disorder in a 20-year prospective community cohort study of young adults (Angst et al., 2003).

The percentage of the population with bipolar illness appears to be increasing and the age of onset decreasing. One factor may be a molecular genetic phenomenon known as trinucleotide repeat expansion. Trinucleotide repeats (TNRs) are parts of DNA that contain the same trinucleotide sequence repeated many times. If the repeat occurs in a gene, the number of trinucleotide repeats will increase and may result in disease. Genes with TNRs have been implicated in the etiology of bipolar disorder (Lange & McInnis, 2002; McInnis et al., 1993).

Other possible factors causing increased prevalence and decreased age of onset include increased exposure to light at night, environmental toxins, increased substance abuse, increased use of antidepressants, decreased omega-3 fatty acid intake, or psychosocial stress on children from the increasing divorce rate. Severe childhood adversity has been associated with earlier onset of bipolar disorder and greater recurrence (Dienes et al., 2006).

One reason for the misdiagnosis of bipolar patients is that they typically spend a great deal more time depressed than they do manic or hypomanic. Bipolar I patients are symptomatic about 45 percent of their lives. They spend about two-thirds of this time in the depressive phase of their illness (Judd et al., 2002). If a clinician is not familiar with the symptoms that suggest bipolar as opposed to unipolar depression or does not probe for a history of hypomania, he or she will arrive at the wrong diagnosis (see Figure 1.1).

Depression at first episode predicts more depressive episodes in the course of the illness (Perlis et al., 2005). Turvey et al. (1999) reported that, in a cohort of bipolar patients, those whose illness began with depression had higher overall morbidity over a 15-year follow up than those with a manic onset. Studies differ on what percentage of patients with bipolar illness have depression as opposed to mania as a first episode, but Roy-Byrne et al. (1985) reported that 60 percent of 71 patients had a depressive first episode. Perugi et al. (2000) found that among 320 bipolar patients, 50 percent had a depressive first episode, 25 percent had a manic first episode, and 25 percent had a mixed first episode.

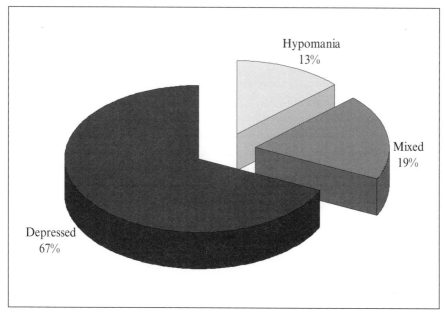

Figure 1.1 *Bipolar I Disorder: Symptoms during Time Ill (146 patients over 12.8 years)*

There have been studies on several other dimensions of bipolar illness, as well. Goodwin and Jamison (1990) note, for example, that research on the course of bipolar illness has shown that, as episodes recur, they tend to occur closer together (cycle length decreases, frequency increases). In addition, they report that initial episodes are often triggered by some well-defined psychosocial or biological stress (work, childbirth), whereas later episodes require less stress. Kraepelin (1921) wrote:

> The kind and duration of the attacks and the intervals by no means remain the same in the individual case but may frequently change, so that the case must be reckoned always to new forms. (p. 139)

Given the variety of expressions of bipolar illness (phenotypes) seen in outpatient practice today and the course-altering influence of the antidepressants so many patients have been exposed to, it would seem even more difficult for a clinician to predict the course of any particular patient's illness. However, patients will often ask about the prognosis for their illness. Perhaps the best and most critical information that can be given is that the illness is recurrent and that, without aggressive treatment, it is likely to adversely affect quality of life and impair functioning. Untreated bipolar illness can also shorten an individual's life span. This is not due solely to suicide. All-cause mortality is twice as high for individuals with bipolar illness as for the general population (Keller, 2004).

According to data by Tohen et al. (2003), 98 percent of patients recovered from their manic episode within 2 to 4 years of first hospitalization, but 57 percent of them switched to a depressive episode or had another manic episode during that period. Patients with mixed episodes tend to make slower recoveries and have shorter time to relapse than pure manic patients (Keller et al., 1993). In a group of bipolar I patients hospitalized with mania, those who had above-median Hamilton-Depression rating scale depression scores (i.e., were in a mixed state) were only half as likely to recover and did so much later than those with lower scores (Chengappa et al., 2005).

Although 98 percent of patients recovered symptomatically from their manic episodes in the Tohen et al (2003) study, only 43 percent achieved functional recovery. Clinicians should be aware that functional recovery very often lags symptomatic recovery for many bipolar patients. Keller et al. (1993) found that, on average, 80 percent of bipolar patients relapse after 5 years. According to O'Connell et al. (1991), predictors of relapse included a depression to mania course, a family history of mania, and nonadherence to medication.

An individual patient's chances for stability can be increased, however, if he or she works closely with a prescriber to find the right combination of medications; maintains stable social and biological rhythms (especially sleep habits); learns how to calmly solve interpersonal problems; and avoids alcohol, drugs, and caffeine. Scott et al. (2006), in a review of published, randomized controlled studies of psychological therapies for bipolar patients, found that adjunctive psychotherapy reduces relapse rates compared to standard psychiatric care. Table 1.5 summarizes key phenomenologic and course features of bipolar I disorder.

TABLE 1.5

Bipolar I Disorder: Phenomenology and Course

- There is a 10-year gap between first symptoms and correct diagnosis (Ghaemi et al., 2000).
- BP I patients spend 45 percent of their lives ill (Judd et al., 2002).
- Well intervals between episodes tend to decrease with time (Goodwin & Jamison, 1990).
- Functional recovery substantially lags symptomatic recovery (Tohen et al., 2003).
- More rapid onset and offset of symptoms than in unipolar depression (Bowden, 1993).
- BP I patients spend considerably more time depressed than manic (Judd et. al., 2002).
- Earlier age of onset for bipolar disorder than for unipolar disorder (Ghaemi et al., 2006).
- About 30 to 40 percent of BP I patients have mixed episodes (Akiskal et al., 2000).

Bipolar II Disorder

Although first described by Dunner in 1976, bipolar II disorder did not become an officially recognized diagnosis until the publication of *DSM-IV* in 1994. The excited phase of bipolar II disorder may be less intense than in bipolar I, but bipolar II illness is quite debilitating, largely because of the depressive phase of the illness. In fact, there is some evidence bipolar II disorder causes more family dysfunction than bipolar I disorder (Coryell et al., 1985).

Akiskal et al. (1995) have found that bipolar II patients have more mood instability between major episodes than bipolar I patients. Patients with bipolar II disorder have a background temperament that is basically cyclothymic. Akiskal and his colleagues believe that this temperamental profile may be the defining characteristic of bipolar II illness rather than the hypomanic episodes emphasized in *DSM-IV-TR*.

Bipolar II patients spend 93 percent of the time they are ill in the depressive phase of their illness, compared to only 2 percent of the time they are ill in the hypomanic phase and 4 percent in mixed phases (Judd et al., 2003b). See Figure 1.2.

In adults, bipolar II disorder is a fairly stable diagnosis. Relatively few adult bipolar II patients go on to develop manic episodes (Coryell et al., 1995). Children with bipolar II, on the other hand, have a more unstable course. About

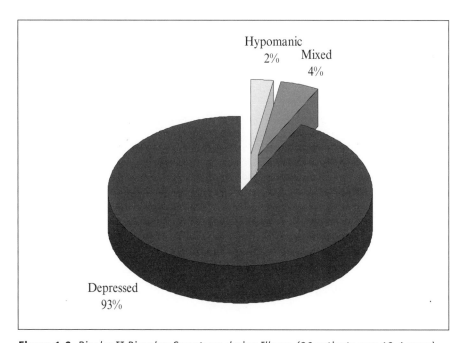

Figure 1.2 *Bipolar II Disorder: Symptoms during Illness (86 patients over 13.4 years)*
Source: Data from Judd et al. (2003b).

20 percent of bipolar II children convert to bipolar I over time (Birmaher et al., 2006).

A clinician may need to look for more than a family history of bipolar illness to validate a suspected diagnosis of bipolar II disorder. While Benazzi (2004) found that bipolar II was the most common diagnosis in family members of bipolar II patients, Joyce et al. (2004) found that only seven percent of bipolar II patients had a family history of bipolar II disorder. Another seven percent had a family history of bipolar I disorder. Forty-two percent, however, had relatives with depression. Family histories that suggest bipolar II disorder and other bipolar spectrum illnesses will be discussed in detail in the next chapter. However, an example of what clinicians might look for is a family history of creativity and achievement. Several studies have found a high rate of creativity among relatives of patients with bipolar II disorder (Coryell et al., 1989; Simeonova et al., 2005). Hypomania can be adaptive, leading to superior functioning and achievement in the arts, politics, sales, business, and the entertainment industry. Table 1.6 lists reported differences between bipolar I and bipolar II disorder.

TABLE 1.6

Reported Differences between Bipolar I (BP I) and Bipolar II (BP II) Disorder

- BP II patients spend much more time depressed than BP I patients (Judd et al., 2003b).[a]

- Higher episode frequency, more rapid-cycling (Ayuso-Gutierrez & Ramos-Brieva, 1982; Baldessarini et al., 2000) in BP II patients.

- Less psychotic features in BP II patients (Vieta et al., 2005).

- BP II patients are less often hospitalized than BP I patients (Vieta et al., 2005).

- BP II patients have more interepisode moodiness (Akiskal et al., 1995).

- Higher rates of divorce, separation, and interpersonal conflicts (Coryell et al., 1985; Rihmer, 2002) in BP II patients.

- BP II patients have shorter duration of episodes (Coryell et al., 1985; Rihmer, 2002).

- Higher rate of anxiety disorders in BP II patients (Judd et al., 2003a).

- Higher rate of attempted and completed suicide in BP II patients (Rhimer & Pestality, 1999).[a]

[a]Contrary data exist.

Cyclothymia

Cyclothymia is a term first used by Karl Ludwig Kahlbaum in 1882 to refer to a mild form of "cyclical insanity" (Howland & Thase, 1993). It is a heterogeneous group of disorders that are typically of early onset, chronic, and without intervening euthymic periods. They are little studied, except by Akiskal (Akiskal, 1996; Akiskal et al., 1977). Estimates of prevalence vary widely and are probably unreliable due, in part, to varied diagnostic criteria, levels of expertise in diagnosing the disorder, and the population studied. Patients with cyclothymia had more relatives with bipolar disorders than controls in a study by Depue et al. (1981). The depressive episodes are generally characterized by hypersomnia (Akiskal et al., 1977). Cyclothymia is probably best viewed as a temperament out of which can grow more severe mood episodes (Akiskal et al., 1979; Kraepelin, 1921, 1921). Because many patients with this temperament go on to develop more pronounced mood episodes, it is a very unstable diagnosis (Akiskal et al., 1979). Dysthymia might be a form of cyclothymia according to Akiskal (1996). He cites as evidence the early age of onset, atypical symptoms, and family histories of bipolar disorder seen in some dysthymic patients.

Mixed States

About 30 to 40 percent of bipolar I patients have mixed episodes (Akiskal et al., 2000; Swann, 1995). Nearly 49 percent of depressed bipolar II patients had three or more hypomanic symptoms (Benazzi, 2000). Mixed episodes are those in which a patient has both depressive and manic symptoms at the same time. Some mixed episodes may be a transition state that occurs as a person switches from depression to mania. Many, however, are discrete episodes. In a systematic retrospective examination of a large sample of bipolar I patients, Perugi et al. (2000) found that 50 percent of patients had an initial episode of illness that was depressive, 25 percent had a manic episode, and 25 percent had a mixed episode.

Akiskal (1992) believes that mixed states are more than just the simultaneous occurrence of symptoms of opposite polarity. He has proposed the novel idea that mixed states occur when a manic episode or a major depressive episode is superimposed on a premorbid temperament of the opposite polarity. For instance, a manic or hypomanic episode that occurs in a person with a depressive temperament or dysthymia produces the mixed state referred to as dysphoric mania or hypomania. McElroy et al. (1992), in a review of the studies on dysphoric mania available at the time, concluded that dysphoric mania may be more severe and more likely to be associated with suicidality, a younger age at onset, a longer duration of illness, higher rates of personal and familial depression, concomitant alcohol or sedative-hypnotic abuse, and poorer outcome than euphoric mania.

Depressive mixed states or agitated depressions, which are very common in outpatient practice, may come about when a depressive episode occurs in an individual who has what is referred to as a hyperthymic temperament. (A non-episodic, habitual way of functioning characterized by extroversion, exuberance, optimism, overconfidence, high energy, and a reduced need for sleep.) Patients with depressive mixed states can be identified by one or more of the following: restlessness, hypersexuality, racing thoughts, and pressured speech. Patients with depressive mixed states usually have fewer episodes of longer duration and more interepisode symptoms than patients with pure mania.

Rapid Cycling

The *DSM-IV-TR* states that rapid cycling occurs in 5 to 15 percent of patients with bipolar disorder. Akiskal et al. (2000) estimated a 20 percent or less rate of rapid cycling in bipolar patients. This is the rate that was found in a study of the first 500 patients enrolled in the Systematic Treatment Enhancement Program for Bipolar Disorder (STEP-BD; Schneck et al., 2004). Coryell (2005) estimated a 16 percent rate. But Kupka et al. (2005), in a 1-year, prospective study of 539 outpatients with bipolar I disorder ($N = 419$), bipolar II disorder ($N = 104$), and bipolar disorder not otherwise specified ($N = 16$), reported a 38 percent rate of rapid cycling. The high rate may be due to the large number of very ill patients in that study.

Papadimitriou et al. (2005) state that patients with rapid cycling usually suffer from bipolar II disorder. It is not clear if rapid cycling is genetically determined. There is no increased rate of rapid cycling in the families of patients with rapid cycling compared to the families of nonrapid cycling. Thus, rapid cycling appears to be a temporary phase in the illness, not a separate entity (Kilzieh & Akiskal, 1999). Elhaj and Calabrese (2005) suggest that early onset rapid cycling might have a genetic component, however. Subclinical hypothyroidism, substance abuse, and disturbances in circadian biological and social rhythms might contribute to rapid cycling, according to Papadimitriou and his colleagues.

The role of thyroid dysfunction in rapid cycling and mixed states is not clear. There are studies that indicate there is a higher rate of thyroid dysfunction in mixed and rapid-cycling patients (e.g., Bauer et al., 1990; Oomen et al., 1996; Zarate et al., 1997), but there are also studies that do not find such a relationship (Joffe et al., 1994; Post et al., 1989). However, there is enough evidence of a relationship to warrant investigation of thyroid hormone status in individual patients with rapid cycling and mixed states.

In the Kupka study, patients with rapid cycling more frequently had a history of childhood physical and/or sexual abuse and drug abuse. The average time spent manic/hypomanic increased as a function of episode frequency, but the average time spent depressed was comparable in patients with one episode and in those with more than one episode.

The *DSM-IV-TR* indicates that 70 to 90 percent of rapid-cycling patients are women. In the STEP-BD study, rapid-cycling patients were indeed more likely to be women, although this gender difference was somewhat more pronounced among bipolar I patients than bipolar II patients. In addition, rapid-cycling bipolar patients experienced onset of their illness at a younger age, were more often depressed at study entry, and had poorer global functioning in the year before study entry than nonrapid-cycling patients.

As cycle frequency increases, the number of adult patients experiencing that frequency of cycling decreases (Goodwin & Jamison, 1990). There has apparently been an increase in cycle frequency since 1960 (Wolpert et al., 1990). This may be due, in part, to increased substance abuse or the increased use of antidepressant medication in bipolar patients.

Women and Bipolar Disorder

The studies on phenomenology of bipolar disorder in women have recently been expertly reviewed by McElroy et al. (2006). Following is a summary of their most clinically relevant findings supplemented by studies reported since the publication of their review.

Women suffer from depressive disorders at about twice the rate of men. The incidence of bipolar I disorder, however, is equal in men and women. The data on sex distribution in bipolar II disorder are contradictory, with some studies showing a preponderance of women and some showing equal distribution of the sexes. No studies indicate a preponderance of males. Data from the first 500 patients in the Systematic Treatment Enhancement Program for Bipolar Disorder (STEP-BD) showed BP II was more common in women (Baldassano et al., 2005). Benazzi (2006a) found 67 percent of 374 bipolar II private practice outpatients were women.

Men more often have a manic or hypomanic onset of their illness, an earlier age of onset, and longer duration of manic episodes than women, whereas women more often have a depressive onset of their illness. Epidemiologic studies have shown that mixed and depressive symptoms are more common in women than men (Grant et al., 2005). Among the first 500 STEP-BD patients, women were not found to have a higher number of lifetime episodes of depression, however. Given the number of epidemiologic studies showing that they do, this result has to be questioned.

Kennedy et al. (2005) investigated gender differences in age at onset and incidence of first-episode mania and bipolar disorder in all adults in a portion of southeast London, England, over a 35-year period. Men had an earlier age of onset of mania. In addition, there was an association between antisocial behavior in childhood and an early onset of bipolar disorder. Grigoroiu-Serbanescu et al. (2005), however, found that the presence of a family history of bipolar disorder had a strong influence on age of onset, at least in females. They investigated the effect of the interaction between gender and family history on age of onset of bipolar disorder in 264 Romanian bipolar I patients. Bipolar women with a family history of bipolar disorder had an earlier age of onset than bipolar women without a family history of bipolar illness. (The authors cited a study done on a German sample that had a similar same finding.) Females without a family history of bipolar disorder had a later onset than males with no family history of bipolar illness.

Studies suggest women have more narrowly defined mixed states (full syndrome mania and full syndrome depression), atypical symptoms (especially overeating and weight gain), and rapid cycling then men. The sex distribution appears more equal for less strictly defined mixed states (mania with a few depression symptoms and depression with a few manic symptoms). Although the *DSM-IV-TR* indicates that 70 to 90 percent of rapid cyclers are women, Kupka et al. (2005), in a 1-year, prospective study of 539 outpatients with bipolar I disorder ($N=419$), bipolar II disorder ($N=104$), and bipolar disorder not otherwise specified ($N=16$) found that the proportion of women with rapid cycling was greater than the proportion of men with rapid cycling only among patients with eight or more episodes per year.

The STEP-BD (Baldassano et al., 2005) and other studies have found that, in general, women with bipolar disorder are saddled with a great deal of comorbidity. Women are more vulnerable to thyroid dysfunction than men and even mild thyroid dysfunction can adversely affect the course of mood disorders (Hendrick et al., 1998). Women are more likely to report a history of sexual abuse, which may be a factor leading to greater comorbidity.

Bipolar men more often abuse substances than bipolar women. Still, bipolar women abuse substances much more often than women in the general population (Frye et al., 2003). Baldassano et al. (2005) also found that men were more likely to have a history of legal problems than women. Friedman et al. (2005) found that among a group of rapid-cycling bipolar disorder patients who were substance abusers, men were more likely to have a criminal history. Both Frye and Friedman note that although women with bipolar disorder are less likely to have a criminal history than their male counterparts (Baldassano et al., 2005), they were more likely to have a criminal history than were women in the general population.

In a nationally representative, community mental health survey of over 36,000 Canadian individuals, female bipolar subjects were significantly more likely than male subjects to be prescribed an antidepressant medication (OR = 1.99, $p =$ .01), even in the absence of higher frequency of recent depressions (Schaffer et al., 2006). This is of some concern since women may be more prone to the cycle-inducing effects of antidepressants (Leibenluft, 1997).

Bipolar disorder symptoms may worsen premenstrually, and the postpartum period is a time of high risk for first onset of mood and psychotic episodes for women in general, but especially so for women who are bipolar. Women with bipolar disorder often relapse to depressive, manic, and mixed episodes in subsequent pregnancies. The presence of mood symptoms during pregnancy is associated with postpartum mood episodes. The rate of postpartum psychosis in women with bipolar disorder was reported in one study to be between 20 and 30 percent. Bipolar women who have a family history of postpartum psychosis are at higher risk of postnatal episodes than bipolar women without such a family history. Antidepressants are not the treatment of choice for all women with postpartum depression, especially if they have a family history of bipolar illness. Sharma (2006) described three women with postpartum depression who were treated with antidepressants. None of the three had a past history of psychiatric illness but in each case there was a family history of bipolar (BP) disorder. Treatment with antidepressants resulted in a mixed episode, cycle acceleration, and a postpartum psychosis. Discontinuation of antidepressants and treatment with mood stabilizers and atypical antipsychotics resulted in remission and sustained improvement.

Women are likely to be at some increased risk for unipolar depression during the perimenopause (Rasgon et al., 2005). The risk for increased mood instability for bipolar women who are perimenopausal or postmenopausal seem less clear. Some studies have shown greater mood instability during these periods for a minority of women with bipolar disorder, especially if they are not on hormone replacement therapy.

References

Akiskal, H. (1992). The mixed states of bipolar I, II, III. *Clinical Neuropsychopharmacology, 15*(Suppl. 1a), 632–633.

Akiskal, H. (1996). The prevalent clinical spectrum of bipolar disorders: Beyond *DSM-IV*. *Journal of Clinical Psychopharmacology, 16*(2 Suppl. 1), 4S–14S.

Akiskal, H. (2005). Searching for behavioral indicators of bipolar II in patients presenting with major depressive episodes: The "red sign," the "rule of three" and other biographic signs of temperamental extravagance, activation and hypomania. *Journal of Affective Disorders, 84*(2–3), 279–290.

Akiskal, H., Akiskal, K., Lancrenon, S., et al. (2006a). Validating the bipolar spectrum in the French National EPIDEP Study: Overview of the phenomenology and relative prevalence of its clinical prototypes. *Journal of Affective Disorders, July 4.* [Epub ahead of print]

Akiskal, H. Bourgeois, M., Angst, J., et al. (2000). Re-evaluating the prevalence of and diagnostic composition within the broad clinical spectrum of bipolar disorders. *Journal of Affective Disorders, 59,* 5–30.

Akiskal, H., Djenderedjian, A., Rosenthal, R., & Khani, M. (1977). Cyclothymic disorder: Validity criteria for inclusion in the bipolar affective group. *American Journal of Psychiatry, 134,* 1227–1233.

Akiskal, H., Khani, M., & Scott-Strauss, A. (1979). Cyclothymic temperamental disorders. *Psychiatric Clinics of North America, 2,* 527–554.

Akiskal, H., Kilzieh, N., Maser, J., et al. (2006b). The distinct temperament profiles of bipolar I, bipolar II and unipolar patients. *Journal of Affective Disorders, 92*(1), 19–33.

Akiskal, H., Maser, J., Zeller, P., et al. (1995). Switching from "unipolar" to bipolar II. An

11-year prospective study of clinical and temperamental predictors in 559 patients. *Archives of General Psychiatry, 52,* 114–123.

Akiskal, H. & Pinto, O. (1999). The evolving bipolar spectrum: Prototypes I, II, III, and IV. *Psychiatric Clinics of North America, 22,* 517–534.

Angst, J., Gamma, A., Sellaro, R., et al. (2002). The validity of atypical depression in the community: Results of the Zurich cohort study. *Journal of Affective Disorders, 72,* 125–138.

Angst, J., Gamma, A., Benazzi, F., & Ajdacic, V. (2003). Toward a re-definition of sub-threshold bipolarity: Epidemiology and proposed criteria for bipolar-II, minor bipolar disorders and hypomania. *Journal of Affective Disorders, 73,* 133–146.

American Psychiatric Association. (2000). *Diagnostic and statistical manual of mental disorders* (4th ed.). Washington, DC: Author.

American Psychiatric Association. (2002). Practice guidelines for the treatment of patients with bipolar disorder [Revision]. *American Journal of Psychiatry, 159*(Suppl. 4), 1–50.

Ayuso-Gutierrez, J., & Ramos-Brieva, J. (1982). The course of manic-depressive illness. A comparative study of bipolar I and bipolar II patients. *Journal of Affective Disorders, 4*(1), 9–14.

Baldassano, C., Marangell, L., & Gyulai, L. (2005). Gender differences in bipolar disorder: Retrospective data from the first 500 STEP-BD participants. *Bipolar Disorders, 7*(5), 465–470.

Baldessarini, R., Tondo, L., Floris, G., et al. (2000). Effects of rapid cycling on response to lithium maintenance treatment in 360 bipolar and II disorder patients. *Journal of Affective Disorders, 61,* 13–22.

Bauer, M., Whybrow, P., & Winokur, A. (1990). Rapid-cycling bipolar affective disorder I. Association with grade I hypothyroidism. *Archives of General Psychiatry, 47*(5), 427–432.

Benazzi, F. (2000). Depressive mixed states: Unipolar and bipolar II. *European Archives of Psychiatry and Clinical Neuroscience, 250,* 249–253.

Benazzi, F. (2001). Sensitivity and specificity of clinical markers for the diagnosis of bipolar II disorder. *Comprehensive Psychiatry, 42*(6), 461–465.

Benazzi, F. (2004). Bipolar II disorder family history using the family history screen: Findings and clinical implications. *Comprehensive Psychiatry, 45*(2), 77–82.

Benazzi, F. (2005). Atypical depression and its relation to bipolar spectrum. In A. Maneros & F. Goodwin (Eds.), *Bipolar disorders: Mixed states, rapid cycling and atypical forms* (pp. 131–156). New York: Cambridge University Press.

Benazzi, F. (2006a). Gender differences in bipolar-II disorder. *European Archives of Psychiatry and Clinical Neurosciences, 256*(2), 67–71.

Benazzi, F. (2006b). Symptoms of depression as possible markers of bipolar II disorder. *Progress in Neuropsychopharmacology and Biological Psychiatry, 30*(3), 471–477.

Benazzi, F., & Rihmer, Z. (2000). Sensitivity and specificity of *DSM-IV* atypical features for bipolar II disorder diagnosis. *Psychiatry Research, 93,* 257–262.

Birmaher, B., Axelson, D., Strober, M., et al. (2006). Clinical course of children and adolescents with bipolar spectrum disorders. *Archives of General Psychiatry, 62*(2), 175–183.

Bowden, C. (1993). The clinical approach to the differential diagnosis of bipolar disorder. *Psychiatric Annals, 23*(2), 57-63

Chaudron, L., & Pies, R. (2003). The relationship between postpartum psychosis and bipolar disorder: A review. *Journal of Clinical Psychiatry, 64*(11), 1284–1292.

Chengappa, K., Hennen, J., Baldessarini, R., et al. (2005). Recovery and functional outcomes following olanzapine treatment for bipolar I mania. *Bipolar Disorders, 7,* 68–76.

Coryell, W. (2005). Rapid cycling bipolar disorder: Clinical characteristics and treatment options. *CNS Drugs, 19*(7), 557–569.

Coryell, W., Endicott, J., Andreasen, N., & Keller, M. (1985). Bipolar I, bipolar II, and nonbipolar major depression among the realties of affectively ill probands. *American Journal of Psychiatry, 142,* 817–821.

Coryell, W., Endicott, J., Keller, M., et al. (1989). Bipolar affective disorder and high achievement: A familial association. *American Journal of Psychiatry, 146*(8), 983–988.

Coryell, W., Endicott, J., Maser, J., et al. (1995). Long-term stability of polarity distinctions in the affective disorders. *American Journal of Psychiatry, 152*(3), 385–390.

Delate, T., Gelenberg, A., Simmons, V., & Motheral, B. (2004). Trends in the use of antidepressants in a national sample of commercially insured pediatric patients, 1998 to 2002. *Psychiatric Services, 55,* 387–391.

Depue, R., Slater, J., Wolfstetter-Kausch, H., et al. (1981). A behavioral paradigm for identifying persons at risk for bipolar depressive disorder: A conceptual framework and five validation studies. *Journal of Abnormal Psychology, 90,* 381–437.

Dienes, K., Hammen, C., Henry, R., et al. (2006). The stress sensitization hypothesis: Understanding the course of bipolar disorder. *Journal of Affective Disorders, 95*(1–3), 43–50.

Elhaj, O., & Calabrese, J. (2005). Rapid-cycling bipolar disorder. In A. Marneros & F. Goodwin (Eds.), *Bipolar disorders: Mixed states, rapid cycling and atypical forms* (pp. 61–87). New York: Cambridge University Press.

Friedman, S., Shelton, M., Elhaj, O., et al. (2005). Gender differences in criminality: Bipolar disorder with co-occurring substance abuse. *Journal of the American Academy of Psychiatry and the Law, 33*(2), 188–195.

Frye, M., Altschuler, L., McElroy, S., et al. (2003).Gender differences in prevalence, risk, and clinical correlates of alcoholism comorbidity in bipolar disorder. *American Journal of Psychiatry, 16,* 883–889.

Ghaemi, S., Boiman, E., & Goodwin, F. (2000). Diagnosing bipolar disorder and the effect of antidepressants: A naturalistic study. *Journal of Clinical Psychiatry, 61,* 804–808.

Ghaemi, S., Saggase, J., & Goodwin, F. (2006). Diagnosis of bipolar depression. In R. El-Mallakh & S. Ghaemi (Eds.), *Bipolar depression: A comprehensive guide* (pp. 3–33). Washington, DC: American Psychiatric Publishing.

Goldberg, A. (1975). The evolution of psychoanalytic concepts of depression. In E. Anthony & T. Benedek (Eds.), *Depression and human existence.* Boston: Little, Brown and Company.

Goldberg, J., Garno, J., Portera, L., et al. (2000). Qualitative differences in manic symptoms during mixed versus pure mania. *Comprehensive Psychiatry, 41,* 237–241.

Goodwin, F., & Jamison, K. (1990). *Manic-depressive illness.* New York: Oxford University Press.

Grant, B., Stinson, F., & Hasin, D. (2005). Prevalence, correlates, and comorbidity of bipolar I disorder and axis I and II disorders: Results from the National Epidemiologic Survey on Alcohol and Related Conditions. *Journal of Clinical Psychiatry, 66*(10), 1205–1215.

Grigoroiu-Serbanescu, M., Nöthen, M., Ohlraun, S., et al. (2005). Family history influences age of onset in bipolar I disorder in females but not in males. *American Journal of Medical Genetics. Part B, Neuropsychiatric Genetics, 133*(1), 6–11.

Haustgen, T. (1995). Historical aspects of bipolar disorders in French psychiatry. *Encephale, 6*, 13–20.

Hendrick, V., Altshuler, L., & Whybrow, P. (1998). Psychoneuroendocrinology of mood disorders: The hypothalamic-pituitary-thyroid axis. *Psychiatric Clinics of North America, 21*(2), 277–292.

Hirschfeld, R., Lewis, L., & Vornik, L. (2003). Perceptions and impact of bipolar disorder: How far have we really come? Results of the National Depressive and Manic-Depressive Association 2000 survey of individuals with bipolar disorder. *Journal of Clinical Psychiatry, 64*, 161–174.

Howland, R., & Thase, M. (1993). A comprehensive review of cyclothymic disorder. *The Journal of Nervous and Mental Diseases, 181*(8), 485–493.

Joffe, R., Young, L., Cooke, R., et al. (1994). The thyroid and mixed affective states. *Acta Psychiatrica Scandanavica, 90*, 131–132.

Joyce, P., Doughty, C., Wells, J., et al. (2004). Affective disorders in the first-degree relatives of bipolar probands: Results from the South Island Bipolar Study. *Comprehensive Psychiatry, 45*(3), 168–174.

Judd, L., Akiskal, H., & Schettler, P. (2002). The long-term natural history of the weekly symptomatic status of bipolar I disorder. *Archives of General Psychiatry, 59*(6), 530–537.

Judd, L., & Akiskal, H. (2003). The prevalence and disability of bipolar spectrum disorders in the US population: Re-analysis of the ECA database taking into account subthreshold cases. *Journal of Affective Disorders, 73*, 123–131.

Judd, L., Akiskal, H., Schettler, P., et al. (2003a). The comparative clinical phenotype and long term longitudinal episode course of bipolar I and II: A clinical spectrum or distinct disorders? *Journal of Affective Disorders, 73*, 19–32.

Judd, L., Akiskal, H., Schettler, P., et al. (2003b). A prospective investigation of the natural history of the long-term weekly symptomatic status of bipolar II disorder. *Archives of General Psychiatry, 60*(3), 261–269.

Keller, M., Lavori, P., Coryell, W., et al. (1993). BP I: A five-year prospective follow-up. *Journal of Nervous and Mental Disease, 181*, 238–245.

Keller, M. (2004). Improving the course of illness and promoting continuation of treatment of bipolar disorder. *Journal of Clinical Psychiatry, 65*(Suppl. 15), 10–14.

Kennedy, N., Boydell, J., Kalidindi S., et al. (2005). Gender differences in incidence and age at onset of mania and bipolar disorder over a 35-year period in Camberwell, England. *American Journal of Psychiatry, 162*(2), 257–262.

Kilzieh, N., & Akiskal, H. (1999). Rapid-cycling bipolar disorder. An overview of research and clinical experience. *Psychiatric Clinics of North America, 22*(3), 585–607.

Koukopoulos, A., & Koukopoulos, A. (1999). Agitated depression as a mixed state and the problem of melancholia. *Psychiatric Clinics of North America, 22*(3), 547–564.

Kraepelin, E. (1921). *Manic-depressive insanity and paranoia.* Salem, NH: Ayer Company

Kupka, R., Luckenbaugh, D., Post, R., et al. (2005). Comparison of rapid-cycling and non-rapid-cycling bipolar disorder based on prospective mood ratings in 539 outpatients. *American Journal of Psychiatry, 162*(7), 1273–1280.

Lange, K., & McInnis, M. (2002). Studies of anticipation in bipolar affective disorder. *CNS Spectrum, 7*(3), 196–202.

Levitt, A., & Boyle, M. (2002). The impact of latitude on the prevalence of seasonal depression. *Canadian Journal of Psychiatry, 47*(4), 361–367.

Liebenluft, E. (1997). Issues in the treatment of women with bipolar illness. *Journal of Clinical Psychiatry, 58,* 5–11.

Lish, J., Dime-Meenan, S., Whybrow, P., Price R., et al. (1994). The National Depressive and Manic-Depressive Association (DMDA) survey of bipolar members. *Journal of Affective Disorders, 31,* 281–294.

Manning, J., Connor, P., & Sahai, A. (1998). The bipolar spectrum: A review of current concepts and implications for the management of depression in primary care. *Archives of Family Medicine, 6,* 63–71.

Marneros, A., & Goodwin, F. (2005). Bipolar disorders beyond major depression and euphoric mania. In A. Marneros & F. Goodwin (Eds.), *Bipolar disorders: Mixed states, rapid cycling and atypical forms* (pp. 1–44). New York: Cambridge University Press.

McElroy, S., Keck, P., Pope, H., et al. (1992). Clinical and research implications of the diagnosis of dysphoric or mixed mania or hypomania. *American Journal of Psychiatry, 149*(12), 1633–1644.

McElroy, S., Arnold, L., & Altshuler, L. (2006). Bipolarity in women: Therapeutic issues. In H. Akiskal & M. Tohen (Eds.), *Bipolar psychopharmacotherapy* (pp. 235–277). West Sussex, England: Wiley.

McInnis, M., McMahon, F., Chase, G., et al. (1993). Anticipation in bipolar affective disorder. *American Journal of Human Genetics, 53*(2), 385–390.

O'Connell, R., Mayo, J., Flatow, L., et al. (1991) Outcome of bipolar disorder on long-term treatment with lithium. *British Journal of Psychiatry, 159,* 123–129.

Oomen, H., Schipperijn, A., & Drexhage, H. (1996). The prevalence of affective disorder and in particular of a rapid cycling of bipolar disorder in patients with abnormal thyroid function tests. *Clinical Endocrinology, 45*(2), 215–223.

Papadimitriou, G., Calabrese, J., Dikeos, D., & Christodoulou, G. (2005). Rapid cycling bipolar disorder: Biology and pathogenesis. *International Journal of Neuropsychopharmacology, 8*(2), 281–292.

Perlis, R., Delbello, M., & Miyahara, S. (2005). Revisiting depressive-prone bipolar disorder: Polarity of initial mood episode and disease course among bipolar I systematic treatment enhancement program for bipolar disorder participants. *Biological Psychiatry, 58*(7), 549–553.

Perugi, G., Micheli, C., Akiskal, H., et al. (2000). Polarity of the first episode, clinical characteristics, and course of manic depressive illness: A systematic retrospective investigation of 320 bipolar I patients. *Comprehensive Psychiatry, 41,* 13–18.

Pichot, P. (2004). Circular insanity, 150 years on. *Bulletin of the Academy of National Medicine, 188*(2), 275–284.

Pini, S., de Queiroz, V., Pagnin, D., et al. (2005). Prevalence and burden of bipolar disorders in European countries. *European Neuropsychopharmacology, 15*(4), 425–434.

Post, R., Rubinow, D., Uhde, T., et al. (1989). Dysphroic mania. Clinical and biological correlates. *Archives of General Psychiatry, 46,* 353–358.

Rasgon, N., Shelton, S., & Halreich, U. (2005). Perimenopausal mental disorders: Epidemiology and phenomenology. *CNS Spectrum, 10*(6), 471–478.

Rhimer, Z., & Pestality, P. (1999). Bipolar II disorder and suicidal behavior. *Psychiatric Clinics of North America, 22*(3), 667–673.

Rihmer, Z. (2002). Bipolar II is bipolar, too. In M. Maj, H. Akiskal, J. Lopez-Ibor, & N. Sartorius (Eds.), *Bipolar disorder* (pp. 87–89). New York: Wiley.

Rosenthal, N., & Wehr, T. (1987). Seasonal affective disorders. *Psychiatric Annals, 17,* 670–674.

Roy-Byrne, P., Post, R., Uhde, T., et al. (1985). The longitudinal course of recurrent affective illness: Life chart data from research patients at the NIMH. *Acta Psychiatrica Scandanavica, 31,* 1–34.

Schaffer, A., Cairney, J., Cheung, A., et al. (2006). Use of treatment services and pharmacotherapy for bipolar disorder in a general population-based mental health survey. *Journal of Clinical Psychiatry, 67*(3), 386–393.

Schneck, C., Miklowitz, D., Calabrese, J., et al. (2004). Phenomenology of rapid-cycling bipolar disorder: Data from the first 500 participants in the Systematic Treatment Enhancement Program. *American Journal of Psychiatry, 161*(10), 1902–1908.

Scott, J., Colom, F., & Vieta, E. (2006). A meta-analysis of relapse rates with adjunctive psychological therapies compared to usual psychiatric treatment for bipolar disorders. *International Journal of Neuropsychopharmacology, June 20,* 1–7. (Epub ahead of print)

Sharma, V. (2006). A cautionary note on the use of antidepressants in postpartum depression. *Bipolar Disorders, 8*(4), 411–414.

Simeonova, D., Chang, K., Strong, C., & Ketter, T. (2005). Creativity in familial bipolar disorder. *Journal of Psychiatric Research, 39*(6), 623–631.

Swann, A. (1995). Mixed or dysphoric manic states: Psychopathology and treatment. *Journal of Clinical Psychiatry, 56*(Suppl. 3), 6–10.

Tohen, M., Zarate, Jr., C., Hennen, J., et al. (2003). The McLean-Harvard First-Episode Mania Study: Prediction of recovery and first recurrence. *American Journal of Psychiatry, 160,* 2099–2107.

Turvey, C., Coryell, W., Arndt, S., et al. (1999). Polarity sequences, depression, and chronicity in bipolar I disorder. *Journal of Nervous and Mental Diseases, 187*(3), 181–187.

Vieta, E., Reinares, M., & Bourgeois, M. (2005). Bipolar I and bipolar II: A dichotomy? In A. Marneros & F. Goodwin (Eds.), *Bipolar disorders: Mixed states, rapid cycling and atypical forms* (pp. 88–108). New York: Cambridge University Press.

Wolpert, E., Goldberg, J., & Harrow, M. (1990). Rapid-cycling in unipolar and bipolar affective disorders. *American Journal of Psychiatry, 147,* 725–728.

Zarate, C., Tohen, M., & Zarate, S. (1997). Thyroid function tests in first-episode bipolar disorder manic and mixed states. *Biological Psychiatry, 42,* 302–304.

Differential Diagnosis and Comorbidity

**THE WILEY
CONCISE GUIDES
TO MENTAL HEALTH**

Bipolar
Disorder

CHAPTER 2

Differentiating Unipolar from Bipolar Depression

Along with changing symptoms which may appear temporarily or may be completely absent, we meet in all forms of manic-depressive insanity a quite definite, narrow group of disorders, though certainly of very varied character and composition. Without any one of them being absolutely characteristic of the malady, still in association they impress a uniform stamp on all the multiform clinical states. If one is conversant with them, one will in the great majority of cases be able to conclude in regard to any one of them that it belongs to the large group of forms of manic-depressive insanity by the peculiarity of the condition. (Kraepelin, 1921)

It is critical for health care professionals working with patients seeking relief from symptoms of depression to become familiar with the markers that help distinguish unipolar from bipolar depression. Untreated or improperly treated bipolar depression is associated with high morbidity and mortality. There tends to be a lengthy delay between the time of onset of first symptoms and the diagnosis of bipolar illness. In a young person, allowing the illness to go unchecked for many years can severely disrupt psychosocial development. Multiple mood episodes may contribute to treatment resistance and increase the risk an individual will develop cognitive impairment in later life. Kessing and Andersen (2004), for instance, showed that having four or more affective episodes in either unipolar or bipolar disorder doubled the risk of dementia in old age. Patients with bipolar illnesses can suffer a number of serious adverse consequences if given antidepressant medication alone, including switch into hypomania, cycle acceleration, and refractory depression (Perugi et al., 2006).

The identification of individuals with bipolar depression may someday be more reliably accomplished through imaging technology or the identification of biochemical markers unique to such patients. For now, however, differentiating individuals with bipolar from unipolar depression can only be done through a recognition of the phenomenological, course, and family history characteristics that suggest bipolar depression (Ghaemi et al., 2006). Nonresponse and a variety of adverse responses to antidepressant treatments can also be used to help identify individuals with bipolar depression. With the exception of a history of manic or hypomanic episodes, the *DSM-IV-TR* does not discuss any clinical characteristics that differentiate bipolar from unipolar depression.

Mental health professionals are today in the same position doctors were in the early to mid 1800s in diagnosing physical illnesses. Diagnostic technologies (with the exception of the stethoscope and ophthalmoscope) did not yet exist. The best diagnosticians were those who had an in-depth knowledge not only of symptoms, but also of the course characteristics of illnesses. The history was critical to making the right diagnosis. So it is with the spectrum of bipolar illnesses.

Based on clinical validating principles described by Akiskal (2002) and Ghaemi et al. (2006), features suggesting the presence of bipolar depression can be grouped into the following categories: phenomenology (signs), clinicians affective response to the patient, phenomenology (symptoms), course and premorbid history, pattern of comorbidity, family history, and response to antidepressant monotherapy. No research data exist indicating that affective response can be used to validate the diagnosis of bipolar disorder. These responses are merely suggestive.

Phenomenology (Signs)

In the initial phone call, Dorothy, age 23, spoke rapidly and in great detail about her problems with depressed mood, lack of self-confidence, and a tendency to be overly self-critical. The therapist found it difficult to tactfully end this initial conversation, but finally managed to set a time to meet with the prospective patient. At the appointed time, the therapist went to the waiting room to greet the patient. Just as he opened the door, she rushed in the outer door to the office, apologized for being late, and explained she had gotten lost. She made several jokes about how lousy she was at following directions. She vigorously shook the therapist's hand and—before she could be escorted to the therapist's office—started talking loudly about her problems.

Once seated in the therapist's office, she told a series of stories in a light-hearted, self-effacing manner illustrating the problems she had had in asserting herself with a series of boyfriends. At times, the therapist found himself chuckling at some of the patient's anecdotes. The therapist noted that, while the patient's narrative was coherent, she tended to jump from one topic to another. She occasionally became tearful but the therapist found it hard to get her to focus on the source of her sadness.

Therapists who work with severely depressed patients know that they typically speak softly and slowly. They often respond slowly to questions. They sometimes have little to say (poverty of content). They will frequently dress in drab or dark colored clothing. Depressed women may wear little or no make-up. The movement of facial muscles may be reduced, and the range of emotions limited.

Patients who complain of depression but who have loud, pressured, excessive, or accelerated speech should raise a clinician's index of suspicion for bipolar disorder (Benazzi & Akiskal, 2005; Goodwin & Jamison, 1990). Pressure of speech occurs in 72 percent of bipolar patients and only 6 percent of unipolar patients, derailment in 56 percent of bipolar patients as opposed to 14 percent of unipolar patients, and distractibility in 31 percent of bipolar patients versus 0 percent of unipolar patients (Goodwin & Jamison, 1990). Pressure of speech is often accompanied by flight of ideas (the patient's thoughts rapidly jump from one topic to another). Patients with signs and symptoms of depression who dress flamboyantly or provocatively might also be suspected of having a bipolar diathesis (Akiskal, 2005).

Clinicians should consider that patients with signs and symptoms of major depression who present with any one of the following three mood states could have a bipolar diathesis.

Euphoric mood: Excessive joking, laughter or pronounced wit and charm. It can be quite surprising when a chatty, pleasant, witty, or engaging patient scores in the severely depressed range on an inventory of depression symptoms.

Dysphoric mood: The presence of intense anger, hostility, sarcasm and psychomotor agitation. Irritable or dysphoric mood is more common than euphoric mood.

Labile mood: Sudden switch from laughter to tears or anger or the reverse. Mood lability has been validated prospectively as a sensitive and specific predictor of bipolar II outcome in major depressives (Perugi & Akiskal, 2002).

The Clinician's Reaction to the Patient

The therapist will typically find him- or herself speaking quietly, softly, and slowly to a unipolar depressed patient. He or she may find him- or herself pausing to allow the patient to think quietly for a moment, cry, or gather his or her thoughts. The therapist will notice that his or her mood will dip somewhat in response to the patient. The interview can be difficult and painful for the patient and a challenge for the therapist. The therapist may feel valued and needed by the patient. If the patient is severely depressed, pessimistic, or brooding and resentful, the therapist may feel uncomfortable or impotent. Some therapists experience boredom, frustration, or annoyance in ongoing therapy sessions if the patient brings up little new material or is persistently pessimistic.

In similar fashion, a clinician will typically find him- or herself having certain characteristic reactions to what have been referred to as the *sunny* and *dark* expressions of bipolar spectrum illnesses (Akiskal et al., 2003). These reactions should be attended to as possible clues to hypomanic or mixed states.

The *sunny* expressions are prototypical euphoric hypomanic or hyperthymic signs: talkativeness, cheerfulness, warmth, exuberance, jocularity, and a knack for telling vivid and engaging stories. On the one hand, the therapist might notice a lifting of his or her mood, a feeling of being energized, amused, and entertained. The clinician may find he or she looks forward to seeing the patient, especially after a long day of helping depressed patients. The patient's enthusiastic mood can be infectious. The clinician will certainly find the patient likable, perhaps even attractive. The therapist might feel that this is someone with whom he or she could have fun with as a friend.

Although the therapist may find him- or herself amused by the patient initially, a feeling of uneasiness and eventually frustration with the patient's chattiness and superficiality may begin to emerge. The therapist may feel as if he or she is functioning as an admiring audience for the patient and so wonder if the patient really needs anything from him or her. Having to talk loudly or interrupt the patient may not be uncommon.

Kraepelin wrote about the experiences clinicians have with these individuals:

> They charm us by their intellectual mobility, their versatility, their wealth of ideas, their ready accessibility . . . their good nature, their cheery, sunny mood. But at the same time they put us in an uncomfortable state of surprise by . . . a capricious temper. Now and then one possibly hears also of periods of causeless depression or anxiety. (p. 129)

The *dark* disposition is marked by extreme sensitivity, irritability, hostility, and impatience. The therapist may still be amused, however, by the patient's sarcastic humor and engaging stories. These stories are often delivered in an animated fashion with vivid descriptions of the presumably wrong-headed attitudes and bumbling behaviors of coworkers, bosses, spouses, relatives, and anyone else that happens to irritate the patient. We may be amused by or briefly admire their brazen ability to confront others with thoughts and feelings the rest of us, with supposedly better judgment, keep to ourselves.

They may also make us feel uneasy, lest we say something to irritate or offend them. The "dark" hypomanic patient may be restless, impatient, and even irritated at times with the therapist's suggestion that he or she reflect on a particular topic. With these patients we may feel on edge, careful about what we say, and even nervous if they have an explosive temper. The therapist may feel unsure of him- or herself, devalued, or as if he or she has to demonstrate a degree of brilliance to impress the patient (sometimes right after having seen a depressed patient with whom he or she felt confident and valued).

Kraepelin described some of these patients this way:

> They are greatly moved by all experiences, frequently in an unpleasant way . . . they are easily offended and hot tempered . . . easily fall into disputes with the people

round them, which they carry on with great passion. In general, the patients are perhaps cheerful . . . but periods are interpolated in which they are irritable and ill-humored, also perhaps sad . . . they shed tears without cause, give expressions to thoughts of suicide. In conversations, the patients are talkative, quick at repartee, pert. (p. 131)

These patients are not really the opposite of those with the sunny disposition. They typically have depression superimposed on a hyperthymic temperament. The *sunny* and *dark* dispositions can mix or rapidly alternate.

Phenomenology (Symptoms)

Peter, age 42, complained to his doctor that he was tired all the time—even after sleeping 12 hours a night. A physical exam and blood work-up revealed no medical problems. The doctor told Peter he was depressed and referred him to a therapist. Peter told the therapist that he had to use all the willpower he could muster to get going in the morning. He was calling in sick a lot. On days when he did not go to work, he would collapse on the couch after getting up and watch TV for most of the day. He didn't feel like doing anything, even though this left him feeling miserable about himself.

Psychotic depression is more common in bipolar than unipolar depression (Dubovsky et al., 2003). An adolescent or young adult with psychotic depression very often goes on to have a bipolar course (Akiskal, 1996). It may not be as easy to recognize psychotic depression as one might expect since patients sometimes conceal their hallucinations and delusions. Clinicians should suspect psychosis in severely depressed patients with marked psychomotor agitation or retardation, pronounced guilt, and suicidal preoccupation (Dubovsky et al., 2003; Schatzberg, 2003), particularly if the patient appears guarded (Ghaemi et al., 2006).

There are two major symptom clusters seen in outpatient settings that should alert the clinician to the possibility of a bipolar depression: mixed depressions (predominantly depressive symptoms and one or more manic or hypomanic features) and depression with what are referred to as atypical symptoms. Mixed manias (predominantly manic symptoms with one or more depressive symptoms mixed in) are probably more common in inpatient settings. Mixed manic states have been the subject of considerable research and clinical attention while depressive mixed states have been relatively neglected until recently.

Kraepelin (1921) delineated several subtypes of manic-depressive illness. The subtypes were based on "three domains of the psychic life" (p. 100): intellect (cognitive processes), emotion, and volition (drive, motivation, or energy). In the pure manic state, all three domains would show changes in the same direction. That is, the patient's mood would be euphoric, their thoughts would be racing, and they would be very active. In pure depression, all three domains show changes in the opposite direction: the patient's mood would be depressed, thoughts would be slowed, and the patient would be lethargic. Mixed states occur when changes in the three domains are in opposite directions. For instance, Kraepelin described the patient whose mood is depressed, but who has flight of ideas. Kraepelin wrote: "We hear from them . . . that they cannot hold fast their thoughts at all, that constantly things come crowding into their head" (pp. 107–108).

Depressive Mixed States

Depression with flight of ideas is one of the more common depressive mixed states seen in outpatient practice today (Benazzi & Akiskal, 2005). Crowding of thoughts sometimes keeps patients awake at night or keeps them from going back to sleep if they wake up. The experience of crowded thoughts appears to be qualitatively different than the rumination some unipolar depressed patients describe. When patients ruminate, they brood about a limited number of painful issues. With crowded thoughts, patients experience a rushing stream of many different, although tangentially related thoughts.

In a study of 379 patients with bipolar II disorder and 271 patients with a major depressive disorder, Benazzi (2006) found that racing or crowded thoughts had roughly a 70 percent positive predictive value for bipolar disorder. The validity of this symptom as a marker of bipolar II disorder was supported by a significant association with bipolar family history. The presence of flight of ideas or the related symptoms of racing or crowded thoughts should alert the clinician to the likelihood the patient has a bipolar disorder. Akiskal et al. (2005) reported that among hypomanic symptoms most likely to intrude on a depressive state are talkativeness, distractibility, and racing thoughts.

Another common feature of mixed depressive states is depression with heightened sexual arousal (Akiskal et al., 2000). Patients may feel a great deal of sexual tension that presses for release. These patients seek frequent sex with their mate or may have multiple affairs. They may masturbate frequently, have an excessive interest in pornography, or go to strip clubs or prostitutes.

A final common feature seen in depressive mixed states is irritability, hostility, and temper outbursts. In a sample of 348 bipolar II patients and 254 unipolar patients, both with symptoms of a major depressive episode, Benazzi and Akiskal (2005) found that irritability was present in 59.7 percent of bipolar II and in 37.4 percent of unipolar patients. Bipolar II patients with irritability were significantly younger and had higher rates of axis I comorbidity and atypical depressive features than bipolar II patients without irritability. Perlis et al. (2004) found that anger attacks occurred in 62 percent of bipolar patients and 26 percent of unipolar patients.

As the reader can see from these studies, irritability and anger attacks do occur in a substantial minority of unipolar patients. Therefore, the presence of irritability and temper outbursts, while more common in bipolar than unipolar patients, do not by themselves validate a diagnosis of bipolar depression. Extreme, severe, prolonged or destructive and assaultive temper outbursts may suggest a bipolar diathesis is more likely, but this is speculative.

Patients with restlessness, tension and agitation have, historically, been considered to have an agitated form of unipolar depression. However, the balance of the clinical evidence now suggests that these patients, with what could be referred to as somatic anxiety are, in fact, in a type of mixed state that is part of the bipolar spectrum (Akiskal et al., 2005; Koukopoulos & Koukopoulos, 1999; Maj et al., 2006). Whether the kind of psychic anxiety (nervousness and worry) seen in so many patients with depressive symptoms reflects a bipolar diathesis remains an open question. Individuals with driven, restless behavior often have a constant sense of time pressure. They may feel tortured by a list of things to do. This has previously been referred to as Type A personality. Although these traits can occur in patients with unipolar illness there are some indications that Type A personality traits are more commonly associated with bipolar illness (Oedegaard et al., 2006).

This inner pressure and sense of urgency can create a great deal of interpersonal tension and be a hidden source of marital problems. These individuals are often irritable, critical, and complaining. They may expect and impatiently demand that their spouses move at the same pace or have the same priorities about what needs to be done as they do. They tend to continually criticize their spouses for not doing things properly and may frequently seem irritated by one thing or another. They typically have little insight into the fact that they have a problem, most often feel quite justified in their irritable complaints, and have a great deal of trouble inhibiting the expression of their irritability. Their perspective is this: If others would only take more responsibility, get more done, or do things properly, then they would not be so cranky. Such patients are often labeled *control freaks* by their spouses.

Atypical Depressions

So-called typical symptoms of depression include middle-of-the-night or early morning awakening, loss of appetite and weight, and lack of mood reactivity. Patients with mild to moderate bipolar depression (the kind most often seen in outpatient practice) often have atypical symptoms: appetite and weight gain, mood reactivity, and especially a tendency to have hypersomnia (oversleeping; Bowden, 1993). Bipolar depression has been dubbed *the great sleep* because some patients can sleep 10 to 20 hours per day or more and still feel fatigued. Benazzi (2006) found that hypersomnia was a symptom with a high predictive value of bipolar II disorder. Since unipolar patients can oversleep, a patient who is currently oversleeping should be asked whether he or she has had periods of decreased need for sleep with increased energy or without fatigue. If that is the case, it is likely that the patient has a bipolar depression. Clinicians should be aware that, when severely depressed, bipolar patients can have middle-of-the-night or early morning awakening (Goodwin & Jamison, 1990.

Akiskal and Benazzi (2005a) found that, in a sample of 254 patients with a major depressive episode and 348 bipolar II patients, those with atypical symptoms had significantly higher rates of bipolar II disorder than patients without atypical symptoms. Atypical features of depression were significantly associated with a number of other markers of bipolarity, including family history of bipolar disorder. A dose-response relationship was found between number of atypical symptoms during a major depressive episode and bipolar family history loading. Bipolar family history was strongly associated with the atypical symptoms of leaden paralysis and hypersomnia. Akiskal concluded that atypical depression is best viewed as a variant of bipolar II disorder and that the presence of atypical symptoms should raise the clinician's index of suspicion for bipolarity.

Perugi et al. (1998) found that atypical features indicate a 63 percent probability of bipolar II disorder and that 72 percent of patients with atypical depression are bipolar II. Benazzi (2001) found that the presence of three symptoms of hypomania and atypical symptoms, alone or in combination, strongly suggests a bipolar II diagnosis.

Course

Early age of onset of depression (childhood to early 20s) predicts a bipolar outcome. Geller et al. (2001) found that 48.6 percent of children diagnosed with

---

By the time he was 13, he could entertain friends with hilarious stories. Other times, he would be serious and brooding. Friends were struck by his similarity to his mother. She was a melancholy woman who accepted adversity as the will of God. . . .

As he grew older, he became obsessed with death and searched with intensity for the meaning of life. He would often sink into a depression that would plague him for days. In his time, it was called *hypochondria,* and throughout his life, friends would talk of his getting *an attack of the hypo.*

Always ambitious, he educated himself and built a career as a gifted lawyer and promising politician. . . . At the age of 31, he met . . . a fiery, impulsive girl who found him refreshing . . . before long they were engaged.

Her family vehemently disapproved of her marrying someone of such low-class origins. Feeling inferior to her, he broke off the engagement. He became so depressed he was in bed for a week. . . . When he finally mustered the strength to return to work, his colleagues were stunned by his emaciated appearance. He plunged back into his work, but continued struggling with bouts of the hypo. In the middle of conversations with friends, he would suddenly slip away into moody introspection. Then, just as suddenly, he would snap out of it and joke and quip.

A story about Abraham Lincoln, in Quinn (1997)

---

depression developed bipolar I or II disorder over a 10-year follow-up. Coryell et al. (1995) followed 381 initially unipolar depressed individuals for 10 years and found that young age of onset of depression predicted a later switch to hypomania or mania. The age of onset for a first episode of unipolar depression is, by contrast, usually from the mid-20s on.

Brief depressive episodes (less than 3 months) are a marker for bipolar illness (Ghaemi et al., 2006). Unipolar major depressive episodes typically have an insidious onset, last 6 months to 1 year, and then gradually fade.

Depressive episodes that come on over days or weeks and then rapidly shut off or switch to a state in which the patient has increased energy and is highly productive are likely bipolar (Bowden, 1993). Strober and Carlson (1982) followed 60 adolescents hospitalized for major depression for 3 to 4 years and found that 80 percent of them with a bipolar outcome had had a rapid onset of depression. In cases of very rapid onset and offset, patients may say their mood changes "as if someone threw a switch."

A substantial number of patients who oversleep, crave carbohydrates, gain weight, and become lethargic in the fall and winter and then become more energetic in the summer (seasonal affective disorder or SAD) may have bipolar illness (Goodwin & Jamison, 1990; Rosenthal & Wehr, 1987).

Postpartum depression may be a marker for bipolar disorder since it is often accompanied by emotional lability and the presence of hypomanic symptoms (Lane et al., 1997). Postnatal hypomania in the absence of symptoms of depression is a bipolar variant, as well (Heron et al., 2005). There is a strong association between postpartum psychosis and bipolar disorder (Chaudron & Pies, 2003). A woman seeking help for depression who has a history of postpartum psychosis should be suspected of having a bipolar disorder.

Premorbid History

Peter, whose symptoms of oversleeping and lack of motivation were described in a previous section, had always been an energetic guy who bounded out of bed after only 5 hours of sleep. He built a successful and lucrative insurance business from scratch and now had 25 employees. He liked to skydive, ride motorcycles, and jet ski. He was known by his friends and business associates as a guy who never let problems get him down. He was outgoing, charming, and could make everyone at a party laugh.

Peter could also be impatient and even nasty with employees who did not perform according to his expectations. Friends and colleagues said he sometimes gave unasked-for advice and came across as a know-it-all. Married and divorced three times, he had been married to his current wife for only 2 years. She threatened to leave him when she found he was having an affair with a secretary at his office.

Prior to the onset of a major depressive episode, some unipolar depressed individuals have had an extended period of normal mood and an absence of symptoms, referred to as *euthymia*. Others, who have had a prior episode of major depression, may not have fully recovered from this episode and are left with less troublesome but still significant residual symptoms such as fatigue or insomnia. A final group of patients may have had chronic, mild symptoms of depression for many years, referred to as *dysthymia*.

Patients with bipolar disorder may also have had periods of euthymia or a history of dysthymia. However, a history of spontaneous periods of increased energy, productivity, overactivity, and less need for sleep, especially those that immediately precede or follow periods of increased need for sleep and lethargy, are diagnostic of bipolar disorder.

Patients troubled by the implications of the label *bipolar disorder* will sometimes say, "I can't be bipolar. I don't have the highs." Clinicians need to keep in mind that most people associate bipolar disorder or manic-depressive illness with the kind of extreme mania seen only in bipolar I disorder and either do not remember episodes of hypomania or do not view them as pathological or worthy of mention. The clinician needs to ask specific questions to uncover hypomania. The questions listed in Table 2.1 can be used to probe for a history of hypomania.

TABLE 2.1

Questions Used to Probe for a History of Hypomania

- Have you had periods when you noticed you felt great on less sleep than you usually need?

- Have you had periods when you were doing and accomplishing a lot more, perhaps by staying up late at night?

- Have you had periods when you get a lot of great ideas or made lots of plans for the future?

- Have you had periods when you felt like being around other people a great deal more?

- During periods when you were very busy and accomplishing a great deal, have others mentioned you were more talkative, commented on your high energy, or said you were more irritable?

- Have you had periods when you have spent money more freely or done impulsive things you later regret?

- Have you had periods when your thoughts seemed to be speeded up or when you found your mind was crowded with many different thoughts?

- Have you had periods when you felt much more self-confident, carefree, or creative?

- Have you ever *crashed* immediately after a period like this and found you suddenly lost interest in things, felt unmotivated, or needed more sleep?

Increases in goal-directed activity and productivity are more reliable markers for hypomania than elated mood. Bipolar disorders met with in outpatient practice may more likely be associated with and identified by behavioral and interpersonal problems rather than mood disturbances (Akiskal, 2005; Akiskal & Benazzi, 2005b). It is often critical for the clinician to ask close family members about periods of increased energy and productivity. Bipolar disorder is underdiagnosed by a factor of two if the family is not interviewed (Goodwin & Jamison, 1990).

Patients and clinicians both wonder how to distinguish periods of happiness from hypomania. Hypomania is characterized by more than just an improvement in mood. Hypomania is marked by changes in a number of areas such as sleep, energy level, risk-taking, and productivity. In addition, the change in mood in hypomania may not be entirely positive. Irritability and irascibility are common. Hypomania is typically spontaneous, whereas positive mood changes are tied to specific positive events. Finally, as Akiskal (1996) points out, hypomania is recurrent, happiness is not.

Clinicians will also want to examine the patient's premorbid adjustment to see if there is a history of what is referred to as *hyperthymia* or *hyperthymic temperament* (Akiskal, 1996). People who have had this relatively stable, persistently *up* temperament (often since adolescence) are typically cheerful, talkative, charming, optimistic, energetic, stimulus seeking, and need relatively little sleep (6 hours a night or less). On the other hand, they may also be boastful, impulsive, obtrusive, and become easily irritated when frustrated. Individuals with this temperament often make highly successful business people, entrepreneurs, salespeople, politicians, and entertainers, according to Akiskal. They sometimes seek help in midlife for problems with depression. Patients with hyperthymic temperament are at high risk for a switch from depression to hypomania when given antidepressants alone (Henry et al., 2001).

Joyce et al. (2004b) found a small sample of bipolar II patients had more borderline, histrionic, and schizotypal personality traits than patients with major depression. Akiskal et al. (1995) has written that bipolar spectrum patients often have borderline personality traits and a tempestuous life course. A patient who presents having had four or more marriages, multiple stormy relationships, or multiple career changes, for example, should be evaluated for bipolar disorder. Smith et al. (2005) found that young adults with bipolar depression exhibit significantly higher levels of borderline personality pathology than those with unipolar depression.

Comorbid Disorders

Patients with bipolar disorder, especially those with mixed depressive features, typically have multiple comorbidities (Benazzi & Akiskal, 2005). Specific patterns of comorbidity can be one tool in helping to identify those patients who might be bipolar (Matza et al., 2005). For instance, the presence of panic attacks, eating

She had a history of epilepsy, alcoholism, and bulimia. She went on spending sprees and fell deeply into debt even though she had won a $1 million contract promoting Fabergé in 1975. Her father described her as an angry woman who constantly lies.

A story about Margaux Hemingway in Quinn (1997)

disorders, and impulse control disorders should raise index of suspicion for bipolar spectrum illness. Patients with intermittent explosive disorder often have a bipolar disorder (McElroy, 1999). Although all of these comorbid conditions can occur in patients with unipolar depression, they are more commonly comorbid with bipolar disorder (MacKinnon et al., 2002; Mangweth et al., 2003). Dilsaver et al. (2006), using structured clinical interviews with 313 Latino adolescents, found that the odds of panic disorder, obsessive-compulsive disorder, and social phobia were 4.4 times, 5.1 times, and 3.3 times higher, respectively, in bipolar individuals compared to those with major depressive disorder.

Alcoholism and drug abuse is also more common in bipolar than unipolar patients (Winokur et al., 1998). Substance abuse in a woman, in particular, should raise the index of suspicion of bipolar disorder. Bipolar men more often abuse substances than women, but bipolar women abuse substances much more often than women in the general population (Frye et al., 2003).

Bipolar spectrum patients can present with or develop over time what may seem to be a bewildering variety of psychopathologic states. Any confusion this creates may be because we expect it to make sense in terms of our current categorical system of diagnosis, which creates the appearance that all these disorders are distinct entities. In fact, at least some of these illnesses share common genetics and pathophysiology.

A number of comorbid medical disorders should also suggest the presence of a bipolar spectrum illness. Rates of bipolar illness are considerably more common in patients with epilepsy and migraines, for instance (Ettinger et al., 2005; Oedegaard & Fasmer, 2005).

Family History

Bipolar disorder is a highly heritable illness. A person seeking help for depression who has a family member with bipolar disease should obviously be evaluated carefully for the presence of a bipolar illness. This is also the case for a patient with a family history of psychotic depression. In a family study of major depression, the prevalence of bipolar illness was nearly six times as high among the relatives of depressed, delusional patients as among the relatives of depressed, nondelusional patients or controls (Weissman et al., 1984).

His grandfather made and lost a lot of money in America and shot himself in the head in a Boston hotel men's room in 1921.

About his father, he said, "You know, I always sensed in my dad a sort of profound sadness."

His father could be caustic with him . . . putting down his ideas as sophomoric while discussing foreign affairs around the dinner table. His father often sent his son, the senator, faxes with advice on what to do about Bosnia and Kosovo. "His father was very tough to please," said his college roommate. "He went over the top . . . he demanded mastery and control over things."

From a story about Senator John Kerry in Wolffe et al. (2004, p. 34)

However, the most common mood disorder seen in family members of someone who is bipolar is depression, not bipolar illness (Goodwin & Jamison, 1990; Joyce et al., 2004a; Perugi et al., 2001). While Benazzi (2004) found that bipolar II was the most common diagnosis in family members of bipolar II patients, Joyce et al. (2004a) found that only 7 percent of bipolar II patients had a family history of bipolar II disorder. Another 7 percent had a family history of bipolar I disorder. Forty-two percent had relatives with depression.

Clinicians therefore need to be alert for the presence of less obvious family markers for bipolar disorder. One marker is the presence of affective illness in multiple relatives over several generations (Strober & Carlson, 1982). There may be a history of family members with antisocial behavior or a number of impulse control problems, such as alcohol abuse, gambling, and intermittent explosive disorder (Akiskal, 2005; McElroy, 1999). A family history of several individuals with hyperthymic temperament or relatives who were entrepreneurs, salespeople, entertainers, or creative in some way should alert the clinician to the possibility of bipolar illness. Several studies have indicated that the relatives of bipolar patients have a greater incidence of creativity, higher achievement, and higher socioeconomic status than controls (Akiskal, 2005; Coryell et al., 1989; Simeonova et al., 2005; Tsuchiya et al., 2004; Verdoux & Bourgeois, 1995).

Roy (1985) reported that bipolar disorder was the most common diagnosis among 137 mood-disordered patients with a family history of suicide. Rihmer (2002) reported that bipolar II patients have a significantly higher number of first-degree relatives who completed suicide than patients with unipolar depression. Tsuchiya et al. (2005) compared 947 subjects with bipolar disorder and 47,350 controls and found that individuals whose mother committed suicide before they were 10 years of age were seven times more likely than controls to develop bipolar disorder.

Response to Antidepressants

Sally, age 19, could be sensitive, emotionally overreactive, and quick to anger at times, but guys she dated and her friends generally forgave her because she was a lot of fun. She was usually outgoing, energetic, and always up for an adventure. During high school, she had several brief periods when her usual enthusiasm for life mysteriously evaporated. For a few weeks at a time she would oversleep and have trouble getting her schoolwork done. Her parents soon learned that if they did not push too hard at these times and gave her a little extra love, she would soon snap out of it. They attributed their daughter's problems to normal teenage moodiness.

Now, during the winter of her sophomore year of college, she developed a more serious depression that did not resolve on its own. She could not get up for morning classes and was sleeping 15 hours a day. She talked to her friends about not wanting to live. Her friends told the resident assistant in their dormitory, who called her parents.

Sally's parents took their daughter home on a medical leave and brought her to a psychiatrist. The psychiatrist advised Sally's parents that she needed to stay home for the rest of the semester and began treatment with Zoloft. After only 3 days on Zoloft, Sally's parents were relieved to see that she was feeling much better. The next day she was getting up after only 6 hours of sleep and saying she was feeling great. "I want to go back to school," she demanded in an angry tone. Her parents had grown accustomed over the years to her occasional irritability. If they stayed calm, she quickly regained her composure and would often apologize. So they were stunned when Sally screamed obscenities at them after being reminded that the doctor thought it would be best for her to stay home for the semester.

Nonresponse and a variety of adverse responses to antidepressant medication can be useful in sorting out bipolar from unipolar depression. A small percentage of bipolar patients may respond well to antidepressants and need to continue taking them to prevent relapse. Others quickly develop problems upon starting antidepressants. Still others appear to do well for a while, and then develop complications later on (see the chapter "The Problem of Bipolar Depression" for details). Following is a description of some common problems bipolar patients may encounter with antidepressants. These problems may occur even if the patient is on a mood stabilizer.

Rapid Switch into Hypomania

Patients with unipolar depression frequently have little response to antidepressant medication within the first week or so. Patients with bipolar depression may respond in as little as 1 to 2 days with dramatic improvement (Post et al., 2001).

This rapid improvement is often followed within a relatively brief period by reemergence of depressive symptoms.

The *DSM-IV-TR* does not consider antidepressant-induced hypomania to be a form of bipolar disorder. But Perugi et al. (2006) report that nearly all patients with antidepressant-induced hypomania develop spontaneous mania or hypomania on prospective follow-up. Chun and Dunner (2004), after a review of the scientific literature, concluded that antidepressant-induced hypomania should be considered a form of bipolar illness.

Induction of or Worsening of Mixed/Dysphoric States

Antidepressants can induce de novo mixed states characterized by irritability, anger, insomnia, and agitation, or they can aggravate existing dysphoric symptoms (Koukopoulos & Koukopoulos, 1999). Mixed states may develop after many years of antidepressant treatment. El-Mallakh and Karripot (2005), for instance, reported that six bipolar depressed patients with a good initial response to antidepressants had a gradual return of depressive symptoms. These symptoms would transiently improve with a dose increase or a change of antidepressants, but ultimately the patients developed a chronic dysphoric, irritable state that resulted in psychosocial dysfunction. Use of mood stabilizers did not appear to help this problem. Discontinuation of antidepressants, however, was associated with gradual improvement in the dysphoria over the following year.

Patients with agitated, mixed bipolar states are at increased risk for suicide (Balazs et al., 2006). Shortly after Prozac was first introduced, there were reports of adult patients who became agitated and suicidal on the drug (Teicher et al., 1990). There has been increasing concern of late that drugs in the Prozac class (called selective serotonin reuptake inhibitors or SSRIs) can cause agitation and suicide in children and adolescents (Jick et al., 2004). In fact, the Food and Drug Administration recently required antidepressant manufacturers to warn that the drugs can cause suicidal thinking in this age group. Part of the problem may be due to the administration of these drugs to children and adults with unrecognized bipolar disorder, which can increase the risk of suicide by inducing or worsening agitated and dysphoric states (Akiskal & Benazzi, 2005c; Akiskal et al., 2005).

Cycle Acceleration

Antidepressants can cause de novo rapid cycling or accelerate cycling between hypomania and depression or between euthymia and depression. Ghaemi et al. (2004) found that cycle acceleration occurred in 25.6 percent of patients with bipolar depression treated with antidepressants, with new rapid cycling occurring in 32.1 percent of patients.

Chronic or Treatment-Resistant Depression

Antidepressants can sometimes cause a patient's illness to go from cycles of hypomania and depression to a chronic course of depression (Goodwin & Jamison,

1990). Bauer and his colleagues (2003) studied a group of 47 bipolar patients taking antidepressants over the course of 3 months and compared them to 33 bipolar patients not taking antidepressants. Those taking the antidepressants were depressed twice as many days as those not taking antidepressants. They stated that the patients on antidepressants "appeared to have a downshift in baseline mood" (p. 31).

Inoue et al. (2006) reported that a long-term follow-up revealed that nearly 25 percent of a small group of antidepressant-refractory depressed patients were bipolar. Patients who have been treated with multiple antidepressant trials, but who remain in a chronically depressed state should be reevaluated for the presence of a bipolar spectrum illness.

Loss of Response to Antidepressants

Development of tolerance to the effects of antidepressants (tachyphylaxis) or what has been referred to as Prozac *poop-out* can occur in unipolar depressed patients. Ghaemi et al. (2004) found, however, that loss of response to antidepressants was 3.4 times as frequent in bipolar as in unipolar depression.

No Response to Multiple Antidepressants

While nonresponse to antidepressants occurs in patients with unipolar depression, it happens more often in patients with bipolar disorder. Ghaemi et al. (2004) found, for example, that among a group of patients treated with antidepressants, 31.6 percent of those with unipolar depression did not respond to an antidepressant whereas 51.3 percent of those with bipolar disorder did not.

Quitkin et al. (2005) found that 66 percent of 171 patients with major depressive disorder eventually achieved remission when they were tried on a second or third antidepressant after failing the first. This is about 20 percent higher than the usual response rate cited in research studies that employ only one antidepressant. Nonresponse to three or more antidepressants should prompt the clinician to reconsider the diagnosis (Ghaemi et al., 2001).

Table 2.2 summarizes the markers for bipolar depression based on work by Akiskal (2002) and Ghaemi et al. (2006). It should be noted that most of these markers, with the exception of a history of hypomania, antidepressant-induced hypomania, and perhaps a family history of bipolar illness, are by themselves not diagnostic of bipolar illness.

Ghaemi and colleagues (2001) have proposed specific criteria for the diagnosis of bipolar spectrum disorders. In the absence of a family history of bipolar disorder or antidepressant-induced hypomania, they suggest that six or more of the following indicates the presence of a bipolar spectrum illness: premorbid hyperthymic personality, more than three major depressive episodes, brief major depressive episodes, atypical symptoms, psychotic depression, onset of depression before the age of 25, postpartum depression, antidepressant tolerance, and lack of response to three or more antidepressants.

Although useful for improving the recognition of bipolar spectrum illnesses,

TABLE 2.2

Clinical Markers Suggesting Bipolar vs. Unipolar Depression

	BPD	UPD
Presentation	euphoric, dysphoric, labile pressured speech, distractible joking, flamboyance	sad, gloomy, flat soft, slowed speech lack of expressiveness
Clinician's reactions	amused, entertained on edge, devalued self-doubting	sad, discouraged bored, annoyed valued, self-assured
Symptoms	atypical mixed states psychosis agitation anger attacks	sometimes atypical middle insomnia congruent symptoms
Premorbid history	hypomania cyclothymia hyperthymia tempestuous	euthymia dysthymia
Family history	bipolar disorder depression loaded, 3 generation psychosis substance abuse hyperthymia achievement, creativity suicide	depression risk aversion
Course	child, teen onset high frequency rapid onset/offset brief depressions SAD PPD, esp. pp psychosis	adult onset lower frequency insidious onset longer depressive episodes
Comorbid disorders	IED substance abuse gambling panic attacks OCD social phobia eating disorders	Less of these
Antidepressant response	rapid hypomania mixed states cycle acceleration long-term tolerance no response to 3+ antidepressants	slow improvement some short-term nonresponse some long-term tolerance

the proposed definition does not help determine appropriate medical or psychosocial treatment. For instance, it is not clear what medication choices might be best for a patient who has only four or five of the nine markers for bipolar disorder. A resolution of this issue will have to await more definitive means of diagnosis.

Inventories for the Diagnosis of BPD

Clinicians often want to know if inventories of manic or hypomanic symptoms can be useful in diagnosing bipolar disorder. I am not aware of any studies comparing the accuracy of trained interviewers to paper-and-pencil questionnaires. My impression is that an informed clinician with experience in identifying patients with bipolar spectrum illnesses would be superior to any of the existing instruments.

However, a number of formal instruments for the diagnosis of bipolar spectrum illnesses have been developed that appear to be valid and reliable screening tools. The two best known are the Mood Disorder Questionnaire (MDQ; Hirschfeld et al., 2000) and the Bipolar Spectrum Diagnostic Scale (BSDS; developed by Ronald Pies). Ghaemi et al. (2005) found that the BSDS was highly sensitive and specific for detecting bipolar spectrum illness.

A Mnemonic for Bipolar Depression

FASTER is a mnemonic aid for identifying features characteristic of bipolar depression:

Flight of ideas: patient feels his or her thoughts are racing.

Atypical symptoms: especially hypersomnia.

Speech: pressured, loud, rapid, excessive, or difficult to interrupt.

Three generation, loaded family history: mood dysregulation, substance abuse, hyperthymic temperament, creativity or achievement, suicide.

Early onset of depression: childhood, adolescence, early twenties.

Rapid onset and offset of depression: onset over days/weeks as opposed to months for unipolar depression.

References

Akiskal, H. (1996). The prevalent clinical spectrum of bipolar: Beyond *DSM-IV. Journal of Clinical Psychopharmacology, 16*(Suppl. 1), 4S–14S.

Akiskal, H. (2002). Classification, diagnosis and boundaries of bipolar disorders: A review. In M. Maj, H. Akiskal, J. Lopez-Ibor, & N. Sartorius (Eds.), *Bipolar disorder* (pp. 1–52). New York: Wiley.

Akiskal, H. (2005). Searching for behavioral indicators of bipolar II in patients presenting with major depressive episodes: The "red sign," the "rule of three" and other biographic signs of temperamental extravagance, activation and hypomania. *Journal of Affective Disorders, 84*(2–3), 279–290.

Akiskal, H., & Benazzi, F. (2005a). Atypical depression: A variant of bipolar II or a bridge between unipolar and bipolar II? *Journal of Affective Disorders, 84*(2–3), 209–217.

Akiskal, H., & Benazzi, F. (2005b). Optimizing the detection of bipolar II disorder in outpatient private practice: Toward a systematization of clinical diagnostic wisdom. *Journal of Clinical Psychiatry, 66*(7), 914–921.

Akiskal, H., & Benazzi, F. (2005c). Psychopathologic correlates of suicidal ideation in major depressive outpatients: Is it all due to unrecognized (bipolar) depressive mixed states? *Psychopathology, 38*(5), 273–280.

Akiskal, H., Maser, J., Zeller, P., et al. (1995). Switching from "unipolar" to bipolar II. An 11-year prospective study of clinical and temperamental predictors in 559 patients. *Archives of General Psychiatry, 52*(2), 114–123.

Akiskal, H., Bourgeois, M., Angst J., et al. (2000). Re-evaluating the prevalence of and diagnostic composition within the broad clinical spectrum of bipolar disorders. *Journal of Affective Disorders, 59*(Suppl. 1), S5–S30.

Akiskal, H., Hantouche, E., & Allilaire, J. (2003). Bipolar II with and without cyclothymic temperament: "Dark" and "sunny" expressions of soft bipolarity? *Journal of Affective Disorders, 73*(1–2), 49–57.

Akiskal, H., Benazzi, F., Perugi, G., & Rihmer, Z. (2005). Agitated "unipolar" depression re-conceptualized as a depressive mixed state: Implications for the antidepressant-suicide controversy. *Journal of Affective Disorders, 85*(3), 245–258.

Balazs, J., Benazzi, F., Rihmer, Z., et al. (2006). The close link between suicide attempts and mixed (bipolar) depression: Implications for suicide prevention. *Journal of Affective Disorders, 91*(2–3), 133–138.

Bauer, M., Rasgon, N., Grof, P., et al. (2003, June 12–14). Mood patterns in patients with bipolar disorder: Influence of antidepressants. Presented at the 5th International Conference on Bipolar Disorder, Pittsburgh, PA. Reported in *Bipolar Disorders, 5*(Suppl. 1), 31.

Benazzi, F. (2001). Sensitivity and specificity of clinical markers for the diagnosis of bipolar II disorder. *Comprehensive Psychiatry, 42*(6), 461–465.

Benazzi, F. (2004). Bipolar II disorder family history using the family history screen: Findings and clinical implications. *Comprehensive Psychiatry, 45*(2), 77–82.

Benazzi, F. (2006). Symptoms of depression as possible markers of bipolar II disorder. *Progress in Neuropsychopharmacology and Biological Psychiatry, 30*(3), 471–477.

Benazzi, F., & Akiskal, H. (2005). Irritable-hostile depression: Further validation as a bipolar depressive mixed state. *Journal of Affective Disorders, 84*(2–3), 197–207.

Bowden, C. (1993). The clinical approach to the differential diagnosis of bipolar disorder. *Psychiatric Annals, 23*(2), 57–63

Chun, B., & Dunner, D. (2004). A review of antidepressant-induced hypomania in major depression: Suggestions for *DSM-V. Bipolar Disorders, 1*(6), 32–42.

Coryell, W., Endicott, J., & Keller, M., et al. (1989). Bipolar affective disorder and high achievement: A familial association. *American Journal of Psychiatry, 146*(8), 983–988.

Coryell, W., Endicott, J., & Maser, J., et al. (1995). Long-term stability of polarity distinctions in the affective disorders. *American Journal of Psychiatry, 152*(3), 385–390.

Chaudron, L., & Pies, R. (2003). The relationship between postpartum psychosis and bipolar disorder: A review. *Journal of Clinical Psychiatry, 64*(11), 1284–1292.

Dilsaver, S., Akiskal, H., Akiskal, K., et al. (2006). Dose-response relationship between number of comorbid anxiety disorders in adolescent bipolar/unipolar disorders, and psychosis, suicidality, substance abuse and familiality. *Journal of Affective Disorders, Aug.* 9. (Epub ahead of print)

Dubovsky, S., Davies, R., & Dubovsky, A. (2003). Mood disorders. In R. Hales & S. Yudofsky (Eds.), *The American psychiatric textbook of clinical psychiatry* (4th ed., pp. 439–542). Washington, DC: American Psychiatric Publishing.

El-Mallakh, R., & Karippot, A. (2005). Antidepressant-associated chronic irritable dysphoria (acid) in bipolar disorder: A case series. *Journal of Affective Disorders, 84*(2–3), 267–272.

Ettinger, A., Reed, M., Goldberg, J., & Hirschfeld, R. (2005). Prevalence of bipolar symptoms in epilepsy vs other chronic health disorders. *Neurology, 65*(4), 535–540.

Frye, M., Altshuler, L., McElroy, S., et al. (2003). Gender differences in prevalence, risk, and clinical correlates of alcoholism comorbidity in bipolar disorder. *American Journal of Psychiatry, 160,* 883–889.

Geller, B., Zimmerman, B., Williams, M., et al. (2001). Bipolar disorder at prospective follow-up of adults who had prepubertal major depressive disorder. *American Journal of Psychiatry, 158,* 125–127.

Ghaemi, N., Miller, C., Berv, D., Klugman, J., et al. (2005). Sensitivity and specificity of a new bipolar spectrum diagnostic scale. *Journal of Affective Disorders, 84*(2–3), 273–277.

Ghaemi, S., Ko, J., & Goodwin, F. (2001). The bipolar spectrum and the antidepressant view of the world. *Journal of Psychiatry Practice, 7,* 287–297.

Ghaemi, S., Rosenquist, K., Ko, J., et al. (2004). Antidepressant treatment in bipolar versus unipolar depression. *American Journal of Psychiatry, 161*(1), 163–165.

Ghaemi, S., Saggase, J., & Goodwin, F. (2006). Diagnosis of bipolar depression. In R. El-Mallakh & S. Ghaemi (Eds.), *Bipolar depression: A comprehensive guide* (pp. 3–33). Washington, DC: American Psychiatric Publishing.

Goodwin, F., & Jamison, K. (1990). *Manic-depressive illness.* New York: Oxford University Press.

Henry, C., Sorbara, F., Lacoste, J., et al. (2001). Antidepressant-induced mania in bipolar patients: Identification of risk factors. *Journal of Clinical Psychiatry, 62*(4), 249–255.

Heron, J., Chaddock, N., & Jones, I. (2005). Postnatal euphoria: Are "the highs" an indicator of bipolarity? *Bipolar Disorders, 7,* 103–110.

Hirschfeld, R., Williams, J., & Spitzer, R. et al. (2000). Development and evaluation of a screening instrument for bipolar spectrum disorder: The Mood Disorder Questionnaire. *American Journal of Psychiatry, 157,* 1873–1875.

Inoue, T., Nakagawa, S., Kitaichi, Y., et al. (2006). *Journal of Affective Disorders, 95*(1), 61–67.

Jick, H., Kaye, J., & Jick, S. (2004). Antidepressants and the risk of suicidal behaviors. *Journal of the American Medical Association, 292*(3), 338–343.

Joyce, P., Doughty, C., Wells, J., et al. (2004a). Affective disorders in the first-degree relatives of bipolar probands: Results from the South Island Bipolar Study. *Comprehensive Psychiatry, 45*(3), 168–174.

Joyce, P., Luty, S., McKenzie, J., et al. (2004b). Bipolar II disorder: Personality and outcome in two clinical samples. *Australian and New Zealand Journal of Psychiatry, 38*(6), 433–438.

Kessing, L., & Andersen, P. (2004). Does the risk of developing dementia increase with the number of episodes in patients with depressive disorder and in patients with bipolar disorder? *Journal of Neurology, Neurosurgery and Psychiatry, 75*(12), 1662–1666.

Koukopoulos, A., & Koukopoulos, A. (1999). Agitated depression as a mixed state and the problem of melancholia. *Psychiatric Clinics of North America, 22*(3), 547–564.

Kraepelin, E. (1921). *Manic-depressive insanity and paranoia.* Salem, MA: Ayer.

Lane, A., Keville, R., Morris, M., et al. (1997). Postnatal depression and elation among mothers and their partners: Prevalence and predictors. *British Journal of Psychiatry, 171,* 550–555.

Maj, M., Pirozzi, R., & Magliano, L. (2006). Agitated "unipolar" major depression: Prevalence, phenomenology, and outcome. *Journal of Clinical Psychiatry, 67*(5), 712–719.

MacKinnon, D., Zandi, P., Cooper, J., et al. (2002). Comorbid bipolar disorder and panic disorder in families with a high prevalence of bipolar disorder. *American Journal of Psychiatry, 159*(1), 30–35.

Mangweth, B., Hudson, J., Pope, H., et al. (2003). Family study of the aggregation of eating disorders and mood disorders. *Psychological Medicine, 33*(7), 1319–1323.

Matza, L., Rajagopalan, K., Thompson, C., & de Lissovoy, G. (2005). Misdiagnosed patients with bipolar disorder: Comorbidities, treatment patterns, and direct treatment costs. *Journal of Clinical Psychiatry, 66*(11), 1432–1440.

McElroy, S. (1999). Recognition and treatment of *DSM-IV* intermittent explosive disorder. *Journal of Clinical Psychiatry, 60*(Suppl. 15), 12–16.

Oedegaard, K., & Fasmer, O. (2005). Is migraine in unipolar depressed patients a bipolar spectrum trait? *Journal of Affective Disorders, 84*(2–3), 233–242.

Oedegaard, K., Neckelmann, D., & Fasmer, O. (2006). Type A behavior differentiates bipolar II from unipolar depressed patients. *Journal of Affective Disorders, 90*(1), 7–13.

Perlis, R., Fraguas, R., Fava, M., et al. (2004). The prevalence and clinical correlates of anger attacks during depressive episodes in bipolar disorder. *Journal of Affective Disorders, 79,* 291–295.

Perugi, G., & Akiskal, H. (2002). The soft bipolar spectrum redefined: Focus on the cyclothymic, anxious-sensitive, impulse-dyscontrol, and binge-eating connection in bipolar II and related conditions. *Psychiatric Clinics of North America, 25*(4), 713–737.

Perugi, G., Akiskal, H., Gemiganani, A., et al. (1998). Episodic course in obsessive-compulsive disorder. *European Archives of Psychiatry and Clinical Neuroscience, 248,* 240–244.

Perugi, G., Akiskal, H., Micheli, C., et al. (2001). Clinical characterization of depressive mixed state in bipolar-I patients: Pisa-San Diego collaboration. *Journal of Affective Disorders, 67,* 105–114.

Perugi, G., Ghaemi, S., & Akiskal, H. (2006). Diagnostic and clinical management approaches to bipolar depression, bipolar II and their co-morbidities. In H. Akiskal & M. Tohen (Eds.), *Bipolar psychopharmacotherapy* (pp. 193–234). West Sussex, England: Wiley.

Post, R., Altshuler, L., Frye, M., et al. (2001). Rate of switch in bipolar patients prospectively treated with second-generation antidepressants as augmentation to mood stabilizers. *Bipolar Disorders, 3*(5), 259–265.

Quinn, B. (1997). *The depression sourcebook* (2nd ed.). Lincolnwood, IL: NTC/Contemporary Publishing.

Quitkin, F., McGrath, P., Stewart, J., et al. (2005). Remission rates with 3 consecutive antidepressant trials: Effectiveness for depressed outpatients. *Journal of Clinical Psychiatry, 66*(6), 670–676.

Regeer, R., Krabbendam, L., deGraaf, R., et al. (2006). A prospective study of the transition rates of subthreshold (hypo)mania and depression in the general population. *Psychological Medicine, 36*(5), 619–627.

Rihmer, Z. (2002). Bipolar II patients are bipolar, too. In M. Maj, H. Akiskal, J. Lopez, & N. Sartorius (Eds.), *Bipolar disorder* (pp. 87–89). New York: Wiley.

Rosenthal, N., & Wehr, T. (1987). Seasonal affective disorders. *Psychiatric Annals, 17,* 670–674.

Roy, A. (1985). Family history of suicide in affective disorder patients. *Journal of Clinical Psychiatry, 46*(8), 317–319.

Schatzberg, A. (2003). New approaches to managing psychotic depression. *Journal of Clinical Psychiatry, 64*(Suppl. 1), 19–23.

Simeonova, D., Chang, K., Strong, C., & Ketter, T. (2005). Creativity in familial bipolar disorder. *Journal of Psychiatric Research, 39*(6), 623–631.

Smith, D., Muir, W., & Blackwood, D. (2005). Borderline personality disorder characteristics in young adults with recurrent mood disorders: A comparison of bipolar and unipolar depression. *Journal of Affective Disorders, 87*(1), 17–23.

Strober, M., & Carlson, G. (1982). Bipolar illness in adolescents with major depression: Clinical, genetic, and psychopharmacologic predictors in a three- to four-year prospective follow-up investigation. *Archives of General Psychiatry, 39*(5), 549–555.

Teicher, M., Glod, C., & Cole, J. (1990). Emergence of intense suicidal preoccupation during fluoxetine treatment. *American Journal of Psychiatry, 147*(2), 207–210.

Tsuchiya, K., Agerbo, E., Byrne, M., & Mortensen, P. (2004). Higher socio-economic status of parents may increase risk for bipolar disorder in the offspring. *Psychological Medicine, 34*(5), 787–793.

Tsuchiya, K., Agerbo, E., & Mortensen, P. (2005). Parental death and bipolar disorder: A robust association was found in early maternal suicide. *Journal of Affective Disorders, 86*(2–3), 151–159.

Verdoux, H., & Bourgeois, M. (1995). Social class in unipolar and bipolar probands and relatives. *Journal of Affective Disorders, 33*(3), 181–187.

Weissman, M., Prusoff, B., & Merikangas, K. (1984). Is delusional depression related to bipolar disorder? *American Journal of Psychiatry, 141*(7), 892–893.

Winokur, G., Turvey, C., Akiskal, H., et al. (1998). Alcoholism and drug abuse in three groups—bipolar I, unipolar and their acquaintances. *Journal of Affective Disorders, 50*(2–3), 81–89.

Wolffe, R., Romano, A., Campo-Flores, A., & Meadows, S. (2004). In search of John Kerry. The keys to his character. *Newsweek*, August 2.

CHAPTER 3

Differentiating Bipolar Illness from Organic Illnesses and Other Psychiatric Disorders

General Principles of Differential Diagnosis

Clinicians are inclined to help patients based on one or two models of therapy in which they have been trained or with which they have become accustomed to working. For instance, a clinician confronted with a depressed patient may think about which medication to administer, dysfunctional cognitive schemas to address, or potentially rewarding behaviors to have the patient engage in. He or she might also address the patient's defenses against the recognition and expression of hostile impulses or have the patient practice interpersonal problem-solving skills. Clinicians, especially those in private practice, also tend to specialize in the treatment of particular kinds of human problems or disorders: marriage and family, depression, or trauma, for instance. There may be a tendency to fit a wide range of human problems into known problem areas with which they feel familiar. These models are both helpful and a hindrance to good patient care. They help organize a clinician's observations and guide interventions. But they also cause the clinician to narrow his or her focus to data that are accounted for by his or her preferred model and to overlook clinical data that may suggest a need for a different intervention.

The mental health professional must be willing to consider a new patient's problems from a number of different perspectives. We have already seen how going from symptoms of depression to diagnosis of depression and treatment with antidepressants does not properly serve the needs of the patient with a bipolar spectrum illness. Other mistakes clinicians must avoid, especially if they

TABLE 3.1

Differential Diagnosis of Bipolar Disorder

- Medical disorders
- Cocaine, methamphetamine, and anabolic steroid use
- Schizophrenia and schizoaffective disorder
- Attention deficit hyperactivity disorder
- Dissociative disorders
- *DSM-IV-TR,* Axis II, Cluster B personality disorders

---

are nonmedically trained, are failing to consider the possibility an organic illness might account, at least in part, for a patient's symptoms, misdiagnosing a bipolar spectrum illness as borderline personality disorder, failing to consider the possibility of substance abuse, or misdiagnosing a patient with a dissociative disorder as bipolar.

Table 3.1 shows the diagnoses a clinician should consider when seeing patients with episodic mood, cognitive, or behavioral symptoms.

Medical Disorders

Clinicians without formal medical training may be the first to see patients whose chief complaints are psychiatric or emotional but who have an underlying medical problem.

Carol, a 45-year-old woman, contacted a therapist saying she needed to talk about some marital problems she was having. There were no other apparent psychosocial stressors. She complained that she had been feeling depressed lately and also fatigued and lethargic. She was not feeling excessively guilty, was able to look forward to and enjoy the company of friends, and, except for a bit of oversleeping, did not have any disturbance of sleep or appetite. She had never had depressive symptoms before and had no family history of depression. She was a social drinker and did not use any illicit drugs. She was on no medications. She had a family history of thyroid disorder but blood work she had had over the years as part of routine physical exams did not reveal any abnormalities of thyroid function. She exercised regularly, was of normal weight, and was a vegetarian. She had no known medical problems.

The therapist reasoned that the mild depressive symptoms could certainly be an adjustment reaction to the marital problems, but some key symptoms typical of depression were missing. The absence of a personal and family history of mood disorder also troubled the therapist.

The therapist asked the patient if she had noticed any unusual physical symptoms other than the fatigue. She thought for a few seconds and then said she had had a weird tingling feeling in her fingertips for the past several months. Subsequent laboratory evaluation revealed a vitamin B-12 deficiency, a not uncommon problem in strict vegetarians who do not take vitamin supplements.

Medical disorders occur in patients with bipolar disorder at rates greater than predicted by chance, although it is not always clear if they are a cause or a consequence of bipolar disorder and its treatment (Krishnan, 2005). Nevertheless, some research exists that suggests medical disorders that contribute to or cause psychiatric symptoms and mental status abnormalities are not rare. Koranyi and Potoczny (1992) reviewed 21 studies conducted over a span of 45 years dealing with physical illnesses in psychiatric patients. About 14 percent of the patients studied suffered from physical illnesses that contributed directly to their psychopathology.

Nonmedically trained clinicians are not expected to diagnose these illnesses. However, they do have an ethical and professional responsibility to consider organic causes for the syndromes they are treating and to refer patients to physicians for further evaluation when organic pathology is suspected. In some states, such as New York, some mental health professionals, licensed clinical social workers, and psychologists, for example, have a legal responsibility to consider the patient's medical condition and make appropriate referrals for medical care.

Mania caused by a medical disorder is referred to as secondary mania. The incidence of medical disorders specifically causing mania varies greatly depending on setting and the age of the patients studied. For instance, only 12 of 14,889 patients presenting at a psychiatric institute had clear organic causes for their mania. The features that distinguished organically caused mania from idiopathic mania were perinatal problems, developmental delays, presence of seizure disorder, and negative family history of bipolar disorder (Cornelius et al., 1994). In contrast, Rundell and Wise (1989) found that 87 percent of 755 patients seen by a consultation-liaison psychiatry service in a general hospital had an organic manic syndrome. The most common causes were steroid medications, HIV infection, and temporal lobe epilepsy.

The list of possible medical causes for manic or hypomanic and depressive symptoms is long. Some organic causes of mania are shown in Table 3.2. Some organic causes of depression are shown in Table 3.3.

In the absence of formal medical training, what can the clinician do to ensure that medical illnesses are not contributing to or causing mania and depression? Familiarizing oneself with all the medical diseases that can cause psychiatric

TABLE 3.2

Some Organic Causes of Mania

Drugs of abuse:

Anabolic steroids

Cocaine

Methamphetamine

Prescription drugs:

Corticosteroids

Ritalin

Interferon

Antibiotics (case reports, especially of clarithromycin and ciprofloxacin: Abouesh et al., 2002; Ortiz-Dominguez et al., 2004)

Neurological:

Head injury with brain trauma

Epilepsy

Temporal lobe epilepsy

Multiple sclerosis

Brain tumor

Infectious:

Neurosyphilis

HIV

Lyme

Metabolic:

Vitamin B-12 deficiency

Addison's

Cushing's

Hyperthyroidism

symptoms by reading medical texts is not practical. Without training, supervised clinical experience, and observation of patients, such book knowledge would likely be of little help.

If the patient has a doctor, therapists might assume they do not need to concern themselves with staying alert for medical mimics of psychiatric disorders. But if the patient has not mentioned psychiatric symptoms to the doctor or the

TABLE 3.3

Some Organic Causes of Depression

Drugs of abuse:

Alcohol withdrawal

Cocaine withdrawal

Methamphetamine withdrawal

Prescription drugs:

Antihypertensives

Anticholesteremics

Oral contraceptives

Neurologic:

Parkinson's

Huntington's

Head injury

Brain tumor

Infectious:

Hepatitis

Mononucleosis

Lyme

Metabolic:

Hypothyroidism

Folate deficiency

---

doctor has not taken the time to assess the patient thoroughly, an underlying medical condition might be missed.

Some clinicians might also leave medical diagnostic issues up to the psychiatrist. There are problems with this solution, as well. Psychiatrists sometimes see patients for only brief periods. They may not take a thorough medical history and will almost certainly not do a physical exam. They can be prone to approaching the patient's complaints with a specific model, as well: Which prescription psychotropic drug or combination of drugs might help this patient?

One answer might be to ask *all* new patients with Axis I psychiatric diagnoses to see their doctor for a physical, medical history, and lab tests. The therapist should give the patient a letter to take to their doctor, which describes the patient's psychiatric signs and symptoms, along with any mental status abnormalities.

However, mental health professionals still need to stay alert for signs and symptoms that suggest medical causes for psychiatric symptoms. Doctors can make mistakes and patients can develop new symptoms while in therapy. Reisch et al. (2005) reported the case of a 22-year-old male patient with a 2-year history of manic and depressive symptoms. He was treated for bipolar disorder for 3 months before being given an MRI of the brain. A 5 mm space-occupying lesion was discovered, which was blocking the flow of cerebrospinal fluid and causing the mania and depression. In the Koranyi and Potoczny (1992) report mentioned earlier, half the psychiatric patients with physical illnesses went undiagnosed in spite of being seen by physicians.

A reasonable and practical solution to this problem has been provided by Taylor (1990). The mental health clinician needs to become familiar with a relatively short list of items that should raise his or her index of suspicion for an organic illness. The clinician must develop an appreciation of what does not fit with the clinical presentation of idiopathic mania and depression. For example, the usual age of onset for a first episode of mania is before the age of 25. Onset after that age and certainly after the age of 35 should lead the clinician to suspect an organic cause (Larson & Richelson, 1988). As one physician put it, mental health professionals cannot become medical diagnosticians but they can become *suspecticians.*

Table 3.4 lists clues to medical mimics. Table 3.5 lists medical tests that physicians and other medical professionals may order to rule out organic illness. Taylor (1990) suggests that the presence of any of the alerting clues should raise the clinician's index of suspicion for an organic illness. The presence of presumptive clues indicates the presence of organic illness.

Cocaine, Methamphetamine, and Anabolic Steroid Use

Acute stimulant use can mimic mania (especially increased psychomotor activity, impulsivity, euphoria, and racing thoughts). Poststimulant withdrawal can closely mimic the kind of anergic depression often seen in bipolar disorder. It is very difficult to distinguish stimulant-induced mania from the acute manic symptoms that occur with bipolar disorder. In trying to differentiate the two it is important to look at the relationship between the use of the drug and the symptoms. Were symptoms present before the start of drug use? Have symptoms continued during periods of abstinence? If not, then a bipolar disorder diagnosis is less likely. Is there a family history of mood symptoms? If so, that would increase the possibility of a bipolar disorder. Gathering information from a spouse or family members will be critical. Urine toxicology screens are obviously a critical tool.

All addictions are *lying diseases.* That is, patients with addictions routinely lie about the quantity and frequency of their drinking and drug use and minimize the consequences of their addiction. Drug abusers will often deny that they are using illicit substances, even when confronted with positive urine screens. Clini-

TABLE 3.4

Clues to Medical Mimics

Alerting clues:

No history of similar symptoms

No readily identifiable cause

Age 55 or older

Coexistence of chronic disease

Drug use

Presumptive clues:

Brain syndrome (disorientation, recent memory impairment, diminished reasoning, sensory)

Head injury

Changes in headache pattern

Visual disturbances, visual hallucinations

Speech deficits

Abnormal body movements

Changes in consciousness

To these might also be added:

No family history of mood disorder

Nonresponse to or worsening on multiple mood-stabilizing medications

New prescription drugs

Any new or unusual physical symptoms

Source: Adapted from Taylor (1990).

---

cians should therefore have a very high index of suspicion for occult alcohol and drug abuse in all patients with manic and depressive symptoms.

There are a few clues that substance abuse may play a role in patients' problems. Caton et al. (2005) studied patients seen in upper Manhattan, New York, emergency departments serving low-income individuals as part of a 3-year longitudinal study aimed at identifying differences in substance-induced psychosis and primary psychotic disorders. The authors found that just a few variables accounted for most of the differences between the groups: Those with substance-induced psychosis more often had a parent with a substance-abuse problem and had visual hallucinations.

Complicating the differential diagnosis of bipolar disorder and cocaine abuse

TABLE 3.5

Tests Used to Identify Organic Illness in Patients with Mood Disorders

Basic:

CBC

Renal and liver function tests

Electrolytes, calcium

Serum ferritin (measure of iron stores)

Fasting blood glucose or HbA1c

Total T3, T4, and TSH (thyroid indices), perhaps free T4 (direct)

Urinalysis

Others sometimes used:

Folate (preferably rbc level)

Methylmalonic acid (sensitive measure of B-12 status)

Sleep study (to rule out sleep apnea)

MRI or CAT (when there are serious m.s. abnormalities)

Estradiol, progesterone, free/total testosterone, DHEA-S

VDRL (venereal disease)

HIV

Lyme's titer

Source: Adapted from Taylor (1990).

---

are two facts: First, in addition to alcohol, stimulants may be a drug of choice for adult bipolar patients (Winokur et al., 1998). Second, a substantial minority of cocaine abusers have autonomous bipolar spectrum traits or disorders. See Chapter 5 for details.

Methamphetamine (MA) is called *meth, crystal,* or *speed* on the street. It is a central nervous system stimulant that is generally injected, smoked, or snorted, although it can be ingested orally. Acute MA use can mimic the manic phase of bipolar illness causing agitation, aggressive behavior, rapid mood swings, auditory hallucinations, and paranoia. In a study of 106 respondents, 34.9 percent had committed violence while under the influence of methamphetamine. Psychiatric symptoms are usually accompanied by tachycardia and hypertension. MA withdrawal can mimic bipolar depression and is characterized by increased sleeping and eating and other depression-related symptoms. The severity of withdrawal symptoms begins to decline within 24 hours of last use. Most withdrawal symptoms abate after a week, although low-grade symptoms can continue for another 2 weeks or so.

Illicit anabolic steroid use has the potential to induce manic or aggressive behavior. Perry et al. (2003) reported that supra-normal testosterone concentrations in weightlifters that used anabolic steroids were associated with increased aggression. In a randomized, placebo-controlled, crossover trial, Pope et al. (2000) administered testosterone for 6 weeks and placebo for 6 weeks (separated by 6 weeks of no treatment) to 56 men aged 20 to 50 years. Testosterone significantly increased measures of mania and aggressiveness in a limited number of individuals. Pope and Katz (1988) had previously reported that 9 of 41 athletes taking anabolic steroids who were assessed with structured interviews had a "full affective syndrome" and that 5 displayed psychosis (p. 487).

Schizophrenia and Schizoaffective Disorder

In the late nineteenth century, Kraepelin believed that there were two different forms of psychosis, which he divided, on the basis of course characteristics and family history, into dementia praecox (schizophrenia) and manic-depressive illness.

The Austrian philosopher Ludwig Wittgenstein noted how our use of language can create pseudoproblems. At least part of the problem in differentiating bipolar disorder from schizophrenia and schizoaffective disorder, as well as from attention-deficit hyperactivity disorder and borderline personality, is due to confusion created by our use of language. The use of different nouns (diagnostic labels) to describe mental illnesses implies that they are distinct disease entities. However, recent research suggests that many of these apparently discrete diseases share at least some common genetics and pathophysiology. Bipolar disorder and schizophrenia may not be not entirely separate disease entities with distinct etiologies (Maier et al., 2006; Potash, 2006). Given this emerging science and the broad efficacy of atypical antipsychotic drugs in treating schizophrenia, mania, and depression, further rumination about diagnostic labels and additional refinements to the diagnostic schema might best be held off until pathophysiologies of the various psychiatric disorders are elucidated.

Nevertheless, thinking regarding the differential diagnosis of these two illnesses has generally gone as follows: Sorting out psychotic bipolar disorder from schizophrenia can be difficult. Clinicians need to keep in mind that psychosis does not mean schizophrenia. Mood-congruent delusions (a manic patient's belief he is Jesus Christ or a depressed patient's conviction her sins will bring the world to an end) may more readily suggest the possible diagnosis of bipolar disorder or psychotic depression, but bipolar patients can have bizarre or mood-incongruent delusions (Winokur et al., 1985). In addition, psychosis does not necessarily imply a diagnosis of schizophrenia or bipolar disorder. Dissociative phenomena can produce psychotic-like symptoms (see the section to follow on dissociative disorders).

The clinician needs to examine the temporal relation of the psychotic and mood symptoms, gather information about the patient from family members, and look to family history to distinguish schizophrenia from bipolar disorder. Manic-depressive illness will generally be diagnosed if psychotic symptoms are confined to periods when the patient is manic or depressed. Schizophrenia will be diagnosed if delusions or hallucinations occur during times when mood symptoms are not present.

The patient's presentation may hold clues to the diagnosis, as well. Schizophrenic patients may be quite withdrawn and emotionally disconnected from the interviewer. The interviewer who has an emotional response to the patient (she is amused, nervous, or taken aback by intrusive behavior) should consider he or she might be dealing with a manic patient. Although a severely manic patient's thinking may be disorganized to some extent, the connection between ideas is generally apparent. The patient's train of thought can be followed. Schizophrenic thinking tends to be illogical and difficult to follow.

From a practical standpoint, the differential diagnostic dilemma is more likely to surface in a psychiatric emergency room or on an inpatient unit than in outpatient private or clinic practice. The most critical differential diagnostic task faced by outpatient clinicians today is sorting out unipolar from bipolar depression.

The clearest example of a pseudoproblem arising from our use of language might be the struggle to differentiate bipolar disorder from schizoaffective disorder, bipolar type. The question of how to define schizoaffective disorder and whether it is a variant of schizophrenia, of mood disorders, or of something entirely different from both has been debated for years. However, the essential features of *DSM-IV-TR* schizoaffective disorder are: (a) the presence of a major depressive episode (with pervasive depressed mood), a manic episode, or a mixed episode, which persists for a substantial portion of the duration of the illness, in a patient who is psychotic (see *DSM-IV-TR* Criterion A for schizophrenia), and (b) 2-week duration of delusions or hallucinations in the absence of prominent mood symptoms.

Lake and Hurwitz (2006), in an article titled "Schizoaffective Disorders Are Psychotic Mood Disorders; There Are No Schizoaffective Disorders," state that the weight of the evidence suggests that "a single disease, a mood disorder, with a broad spectrum of severity, rather than three different disorders [schizoaffective, schizophrenia, and psychotic mood disorders] accounts for the functional psychoses" (p. 255).

Vollmer-Larsen et al. (2006) examined the clinical utility of *DSM-IV-TR* criteria for diagnosing schizoaffective disorder. None of 57 patients previously diagnosed as schizoaffective could be so diagnosed by a strict application of *DSM-IV-TR* criteria. They called for a moratorium on the clinical use of the term schizoaffective disorder. The current thinking is that patients with schizoaffective illness belong to the bipolar spectrum (Nardi et al., 2005) and that all psychoses are all pathophysiologically related.

Adult Attention-Deficit Hyperactivity Disorder (ADHD)

Sorting out attention-deficit hyperactivity disorder (ADHD) from bipolar spectrum illnesses in adults can be difficult for three reasons. First, a number of the symptoms of the two disorders overlap. Distractibility, talkativeness, irritability, and trouble completing tasks occur in both ADHD and bipolar illness. Second, adults with bipolar disorder sometimes have comorbid ADHD or ADHD symptoms. Of the first consecutive 1,000 adults with bipolar disorder enrolled in the National Institute of Mental Health's Systematic Treatment Enhancement Program for Bipolar Disorder (STEP-BD) study, for example, 14.7 percent of male patients and 5.8 percent of female patients with bipolar disorder had lifetime ADHD (Nierenberg et al., 2005). Third, there are some indications ADHD may be an early onset form of bipolar disorder (Geller & Luby, 1997).

The differential diagnosis is important, however, at least in children, since treatments used for ADHD (stimulants and atomoxetine—Strattera) may precipitate mania, hypomania, or mixed states with pronounced irritability or an earlier onset of mania (DelBello et al., 2001; Faedda et al., 2004; Henderson, 2004; Weller et al., 1998). Reichart and Nolen (2004) proposed that greater use of stimulants and antidepressants in the United States than in the Netherlands could explain the higher rates of childhood bipolar disorder diagnosed in the United States.

Although a patient's ADHD symptoms may fluctuate to some degree depending on context and motivational state (Purper-Ouakil et al., 2004), cycling or episodic recurrence of symptoms, especially cycles in productivity, should suggest bipolar disorder. Symptoms of bipolar disorder that do not overlap with ADHD in children and younger adolescents include elation, grandiosity, flight of ideas/racing thoughts, decreased need for sleep, and hypersexuality (Geller et al., 2002). These symptoms might also be useful markers for bipolar disorder in adults who are talkative, agitated, and distractible. Intermittent explosive disorder or rage attacks might also suggest the presence of bipolar disorder (McElroy, 1999). Family history of bipolar disorder can obviously be important, as well, in making the differential diagnosis.

Dissociative Disorders and Symptoms

This is an important but rarely considered differential diagnosis. There is remarkably little written about dissociative disorders and bipolar illness in the medical literature.

As the *DSM-IV-TR* notes, there is considerable controversy concerning the diagnosis of dissociative identity disorder (formerly called multiple personality disorder). Some clinicians have argued that the dissociative disorders are being underdiagnosed while others claim that identification and treatment of the disorders are becoming somewhat of a cult-like phenomenon.

In general, clinicians have been poorly trained to recognize dissociative phenomena and may too often be ready to dismiss dissociative disorders as rare and unlikely to be encountered in outpatient practice. Data suggest this may not be the case. Ross (1991), based on a survey of a large sample of the general population in the city of Winnipeg, Canada, showed that about 10 percent of the adult population had a dissociative disorder of some kind. Ross et al. (1991) found that 3.3 percent of 299 consecutive patients admitted to two 23-bed acute care wards in a teaching hospital over 2 years had multiple personality disorder based on screening with the dissociative experiences scale and a structured interview for dissociative disorders. Saxe et al. (1993) found that 15 percent of 110 patients consecutively admitted to a state psychiatric hospital met criteria for a dissociative disorder. These patients had significantly higher rates of major depression, posttraumatic stress disorder, substance abuse, and borderline personality disorder than did a group of comparison patients.

The incidence of dissociative disorders in outpatient settings may be underestimated, as well. Foote et al. (2006) found that about 10 percent of 231 consecutive admissions to an inner-city, hospital-based outpatient psychiatric clinic had a dissociative disorder. The vast majority had not been previously diagnosed. Sar et al. (2000) reported that 12 percent of 150 consecutive outpatients admitted to the psychiatry clinic of a university hospital in Turkey had a dissociative disorder.

To my knowledge, no data exist on the incidence of dissociative identity disorder in bipolar patients. Bipolar disorder was not mentioned as a comorbidity in patients with dissociative identity disorder in any of the studies cited in this section. Nevertheless, many individuals with bipolar disorder have a history of childhood trauma (Garno et al., 2005; Neria et al., 2005) and childhood trauma has been linked to the development of dissociative disorders. The link between childhood trauma and dissociative disorders has been established primarily on the basis of retrospective patient reports. But Coons (1994) confirmed that child abuse had occurred in eight of nine patients with multiple personality disorder, through a review of child protective services records.

Clinicians need to ask about a history of childhood trauma (particularly if the patient is psychotic), be familiar with symptoms of posttraumatic stress disorder, and be able to screen for dissociative experiences. Dissociative symptoms include amnesia, feeling detached from one's mental processes or body (depersonalization), feelings of unreality (derealization), emotional states or behavior the patient does not remember having or engaging in (fugue), and medical symptoms for which there is no physical basis (somatoform disorders). Screening tools such as the Dissociative Experiences Scale (DES) can help the clinician not familiar with dissociative phenomena identify patients who need additional evaluation.

Clinicians should also be familiar with the intrasession signs and symptoms of dissociation (extreme anxiety, eye-rolling, blinking, shaking, and unresponsiveness). Many patients hospitalized for severe mental disorders such as psychosis may have posttraumatic stress disorder and/or dissociative disorders (Darves-Bornoz et al., 1995). Multiple identities and conversations between identities can be mistaken for psychotic symptoms. A number of studies suggest a link between trauma, dissociation, and psychotic symptoms, including visual, auditory, and tactile hallucinations (Moskowitz et al., 2005; Shevlin et al., 2006).

Symptoms of posttraumatic stress disorder can overlap with those seen in depression and some phases of bipolar illness: Reexperiencing of trauma in a variety of ways can be associated with panic and agitation; avoidance of stimuli associated with the trauma that can lead to withdrawal, flattening of affect and anhedonia, and increased arousal can present as irritability and temper outbursts. Rapid shifts in mood and personality when individuals switch identities could be mistaken for rapid-cycling bipolar illness (Steingard & Frankel, 1985).

It is possible, of course, for a patient to have both bipolar disorder and a dissociative disorder. One possible mechanism for this: Children with irritable and explosive temperaments who later develop bipolar disorder may be difficult to manage, especially for those parents who are themselves irritable or explosive. These parents may be more likely to abuse their explosive children, thereby setting the stage for the development of dissociative disorders.

Clinicians without expertise in working with patients who have dissociative disorders should proceed with great caution in exploring traumatic memories. Unwitting therapists can inadvertently retraumatize and overwhelm patients with dissociative disorders by prematurely exploring these memories. These patients can be vulnerable to re-experiencing early childhood trauma while discussing it with their therapists. Decompensation, self-injurious behavior, and suicidal crises requiring hospitalization can be the result. Pontius and Weiser (2004) report the case of a patient who developed a nonconvulsive, bizarre seizure-like episode apparently kindled by a traumatic memory.

Referring patients with a dissociative disorder to a colleague trained and experienced to deal with such patients may be in order. If such a colleague is not available, supportive counseling, psychoeducation, teaching affect-management skills, and cognitive therapy to reduce the patient's reactions to dissociative triggers might be preferable to exploration of memories. These approaches can provide benefit (Goldstein et al., 2004; Zlotnick et al., 1997) and their use in place of exploration of traumatic memories may decrease the risk of iatrogenic decompensation. In any case, the clinician must carefully titrate the amount of pain these patients must endure in therapy.

Therapists interested in learning how to work with these patients' traumatic memories might want to begin by reading Putnam (1989). Supervision is recommended. Clinicians should keep in mind that unusual temper outbursts and dissociative-like symptoms can be caused by seizures.

DSM-IV-TR Cluster B Personality Disorders (Antisocial, Histrionic, Borderline, and Narcissistic Personality Disorders)

Temperament (the relatively stable, genetically influenced individual differences in type and intensity of emotional reaction), personality (patterned, maladaptive learned styles of coping), and mood disorders are intertwined and influence each other in complex ways that are not fully understood. What is clear is that *DSM-IV-TR* personality disorders cannot always be as clearly separated from mood disorders as the diagnostic manual implies (Akiskal et al., 1983; Akiskal et al., 2006).

Common genetic and biological roots of personality and mood may partially explain why population and clinical studies so often show that bipolar patients frequently meet diagnostic criteria for a personality disorder. For example, Grant et al. (2005), in a population-based study of 43,000 people of whom roughly 860 had bipolar I disorder, found that nearly two-thirds of the bipolar patients met diagnostic criteria for a personality disorder. Perugi et al. (2006) found a high prevalence of cyclothymic temperament in patients with narcissistic, histrionic, and borderline traits. Bipolar patients with mixed manic features are especially likely to be misdiagnosed as personality disordered (Hantouche et al., 2006). Antisocial personality disorder was found to be the most common personality disorder among patients with childhood-onset bipolar disorder (Goldstein & Levitt, 2006). Perhaps this is because the manic or mixed features of early onset bipolar disorder can lead to the development of antisocial behaviors and traits (failure to conform, impulsiveness, irritability and aggressiveness, recklessness, irresponsibility).

The chronic behavioral disturbances, unstable interpersonal relationships, mood instability, and other dramatic features of patients with borderline personality disorder have been considered by psychoanalytic clinicians to be the result of difficulties in self and object constancy derived from problems in the separation-individuation process (Akhtar, 1992). Now, however, some researchers believe these problems may be better explained by viewing them as manifestations of bipolar spectrum illness (Akiskal, 2004; Tyre & Brittlebank, 1993). In 1994, Akiskal estimated that from one-half to two-thirds of patients identified as borderline actually had subthreshold expressions of bipolar disorder. MacKinnon and Pies' (2006) review of the literature showed a substantial number of phenomenological and biological overlaps between patients with borderline personality and patients with extremely rapid cycling bipolar disorder. When carefully interviewed, patients with borderline personality disorder frequently meet diagnostic criteria for multiple axis I disorders including bipolar disorder, panic disorder, social phobia, posttraumatic stress disorder, obsessive-compulsive disorder, and eating disorder (Zimmerman & Mattia, 1999). Benazzi (2006) also found a significant association between bipolar II disorder and borderline personality in terms of affective instability, which included unstable mood, interpersonal relationships, and self-image, as well as chronic emptiness and anger. Akiskal et al. (2000) have suggested that when major depressions are superimposed on cyclothymic temperament, the constellation of symptoms produced can be mistaken for borderline or other personality disorders in the dramatic cluster. Perugi et al. (2003) examined 107 consecutive patients who met criteria for a major depressive episode with atypical features (a robust predictor of bipolar depression) in a semi-structured format for Axis II comorbidity. They found that patients with cyclothymic traits were significantly more likely to meet borderline personality diagnostic criteria than those without cyclothymic traits. They concluded that cyclothymic temperament appeared to underlie the complex pattern of anxiety, mood, and impulse control problems seen in borderline patients.

Further support for the idea that some borderline patients are part of the bipolar spectrum comes from studies that show similar abnormalities in brain function (amygdala hyperreactivity) in the two groups of patients (Blumberg et al., 2005; Donegan et al., 2003). In addition, dimensions of borderline personality have been found to be responsive to mood-stabilizing and antipsychotic medications (Bogenschutz & Nurnberg, 2004; Preston et al., 2004). Pharmacologic interventions may strengthen borderline patients' stress-coping capabilities and decrease sensitivity to loss, thereby ameliorating what was previously thought to be personality pathology (Akiskal, 1996; Perugi & Akiskal, 2002).

Although Benazzi (2000) found a high incidence of borderline personality disorder among 63 consecutive unipolar and 50 bipolar II major depressive episode outpatients interviewed with the Structured Clinical Interviews for *DSM-IV* Axis I/II Disorders, he implied that borderline patients who are not part of the bipolar spectrum exist and that borderline personality disorder and bipolar II illness could be distinguished using *DSM-IV* criteria.

If a patient has phasic, spontaneous changes in productivity and energy, grandiosity, flight of ideas, pressured speech, racing thoughts, and distractibility, the clinician should consider a diagnosis of bipolar disorder in addition to or instead of borderline personality. On the other hand, if the patient has *none* of these signs but does have a profound fear of being abandoned, makes frantic efforts to avoid being alone, and self-mutilates or threatens suicide in response to actual or potential loss, the clinician would likely diagnose borderline personality disorder.

In practice, a patient with pure borderline personality may be rare. That is, a patient who does not have at least *some* of the characteristic features of bipolar disorders might be hard to find. If a patient displays features of both bipolar illness and borderline personality disorder, one can, of course, diagnose both conditions. Spending time trying to decide whether a patient has bipolar illness or borderline personality may not be worth the effort when it comes to making treatment decisions. If the majority of patients have features of both bipolar illness and borderline personality, then it is best to spend one's time trying to determine what combination of pharmacologic and psychotherapeutic treatments are likely to be most helpful.

Some clinicians and researchers have suggested that patients with borderline personality traits may be suffering from complex posttraumatic stress disorder and/or dissociative disorders because of childhood abuse and neglect (Herman, 1997; Van Den Bosch et al., 2003). Watson et al. (2006) found that patients with borderline personality disorder demonstrated levels of dissociation that increased with levels of childhood trauma. Saunders and Arnold (1993) found a highly significant correlation between childhood abuse and the diagnosis of borderline personality disorder.

References

Abouesh, A., Stone, C., & Hobbs, W. (2002). Antimicrobial-induced mania (antibiomania): A review of spontaneous reports. *Journal of Clinical Psychopharmacology, 22*(1), 71–81.

Akhtar, S. (1992). *Broken structures, Severe personality disorders and their treatment.* New York: Jason Aronson.

Akiskal, H. (1996). The prevalent clinical spectrum of bipolar disorders: Beyond *DSM-IV. Journal of Clinical Psychopharmacology, 16*(2 Suppl. 1), 4S–14S.

Akiskal, H. (2004). Demystifying borderline personality: Critique of the concept and unorthodox reflections on its natural kinship with the bipolar spectrum. *Acta Psychiatrica Scandanavica, 110*(6), 401–407.

Akiskal, H., Hirschfeld, R., & Yerevanian, B. (1983). The relationship of personality to affective disorders. *Archives of General Psychiatry, 40*(7), 801–810.

Akiskal, H., Bourgeois, M., Angst J., et al. (2000). Re-evaluating the prevalence of and diagnostic composition within the broad clinical spectrum of bipolar disorders. *Journal of Affective Disorders, 59*(Suppl. 1), S5–S30.

Akiskal, H., Kilzieh, N., Maser, J., et al. (2006). The distinct temperament profiles of bipolar I, bipolar II and unipolar patients. *Journal of Affective Disorders, 92*(1), 19–33.

Albanese, M., Clodfelter, Jr., R., Pardo, T., & Ghaemi, S. (2006). Underdiagnosis of bipolar disorder in men with substance use disorder. *Journal of Psychiatric Practice, 12*(2), 124–127.

Benazzi, F. (2000). Borderline personality disorder and bipolar II disorder in private practice depressed outpatients. *Comprehensive Psychiatry, 41*(2), 106–110.

Benazzi, F. (2006). Borderline personality-bipolar spectrum relationship. *Progress in Neuropsychopharmacology and Biological Psychiatry, 30*(1), 68–74.

Blumberg, H., Donegan, N., Sanislow, C., et al. (2005). Preliminary evidence for medication effects on functional abnormalities in the amygdala and anterior cingulated in bipolar disorder. *Journal of Psychopharmacology, 183*(3), 308–313.

Bogenschutz, M., & Nurnberg, G. (2004). Olanzapine versus placebo in the treatment of borderline personality disorder. *Journal of Clinical Psychiatry, 65*(1), 104–109.

Caton, C., Drake, R., & Hasin, D. (2005). Differences between early-phase primary psychotic disorders with concurrent substance use and substance-induced psychoses. *Archives of General Psychiatry, 62*(2), 137–145.

Coons, P. (1994). Confirmation of childhood abuse in child and adolescent cases of multiple personality disorder and dissociative disorder not otherwise specified. *Journal of Nervous and Mental Disorders, 182*(8), 461–464.

Cornelius, J., Fabrega, H., Mezzich, J., et al. (1994). Characterizing organic mood syndrome, manic type. *Comprehensive Psychiatry, 35*(5), 354–360.

Darves-Bornoz, J., Benhamou-Ayache, P., Degiovanni, A., et al. (1995). Psychological trauma and mental disorders. *Annales Medico-Psychologiques, 153*(1), 77–80.

DelBello M., Soutullo, C., & Hendricks, W. (2001). Prior stimulant treatment in adolescents with bipolar disorder: Association with age at onset. *Bipolar Disorders, 3*(2), 53–57.

Donegan, N., Sanislow, C., Blumberg, H., et al. (2003). Amygdala hyperreactivity in borderline personality disorder: Implications for emotional dysregulation. *Biological Psychiatry, 54*(11), 1284–1293.

Faedda, G. L., Baldessarini R. J., Glovinsky I. P., & Austin, N. B. (2004). Treatment-emergent mania in pediatric bipolar disorder: A retrospective case review. *Journal of Affective Disorders, 82*(1), 149–158.

Foote, B., Smolin, Y., Kaplan, M., et al. (2006). Prevalence of dissociative disorders in psychiatric outpatients. *American Journal of Psychiatry, 163*(4), 623–629.

Garno, J., Goldberg, J., Ramirez, P., & Ritzler, B. (2005). Impact of childhood abuse on the clinical course of bipolar disorder. *British Journal of Psychiatry, 186,* 121–125.

Geller, B., & Luby, J. (1997). Child and adolescent bipolar disorder: A review of the past 10 years. *Journal of the American Academy of Child and Adolescent Psychiatry, 36*(9), 1168–1176.

Geller, B., Zimmerman, B., Williams, M., et al. (2002). *DSM-IV* mania symptoms in a prepubertal and early adolescent bipolar disorder phenotype compared to attention-deficit hyperactive and normal controls. *Journal of Child and Adolescent Psychopharmacology, 12*(1), 11–25.

Goldstein, B., & Levitt, A. (2006). Further evidence for a developmental subtype of bipolar disorder defined by age at onset: Results from the National Epidemiologic Survey on Alcohol and Related Conditions. *American Journal of Psychiatry, 163*(9), 1633–1636.

Goldstein, L., Deale, A., Mitchell-O'Malley, S., et al. (2004). An evaluation of cognitive behavioral therapy as a treatment for dissociative seizures: A pilot study. *Cognitive and Behavioral Neurology, 17*(1), 41–49.

Grant, B., Stinson, F., & Hasin, D. (2005). Prevalence, correlates, and comorbidity of bipolar I disorder and axis I and II disorders: Results from the National Epidemiologic Survey on Alcohol and Related Conditions. *Journal of Clinical Psychiatry, 66*(10), 1205–1215.

Hantouche, E., Akiskal, H., Azorin, J., et al. (2006). Clinical and psychometric characterization of depression in mixed mania: A report from the French National Cohort of 1090 manic patients. *Journal of Affective Disorders, Jan. 18.* (Epub ahead of print)

Henderson, T. (2004). Mania induction associated with atomoxetine. *Journal of Clinical Psychopharmacology, 24*(5), 567–568.

Herman, J. (1997). *Trauma and recovery.* New York: Basic Books

Koranyi, E., & Potoczny, W. (1992). Physical illnesses underlying psychiatric symptoms. *Psychotherapy and Psychosomatics, 58*(3–4), 155–160.

Krishnan, K. (2005). Psychiatric and medical comorbidities of bipolar disorder. *Psychosomatic Medicine, 67*(1), 1–8.

Lake, C., & Hurwitz, N. (2006). Schizoaffective disorders are psychotic mood disorders; there are no schizoaffective disorders. *Psychiatry Research, 143*(2–3), 255–287.

Larson, E., & Richelson, E. (1988). Organic causes of mania. *Mayo Clinic Proceedings, 63*(9), 906–912.

Mackinnon, D., & Pies, R. (2006). Affective instability as rapid cycling: Theoretical and clinical implications for borderline personality and bipolar spectrum disorders. *Bipolar Disorders, 8*(1), 1–14.

Maier, W., Zobel., A., & Wagner, M. (2006). Schizophrenic and bipolar disorder: Differences and overlaps. *Current Opinion in Psychiatry, 19*(2), 165–170.

McElroy, S. (1999). Recognition and treatment of *DSM-IV* intermittent explosive disorder. *Journal of Clinical Psychiatry, 60*(Suppl. 15), 12–16.

Moskowitz, A., Barker-Collo, S., & Ellson, L. (2005). Replication of dissociation-psychosis link in New Zealand students and inmates. *Journal of Nervous and Mental Disorders, 193*(11), 722–727.

Nardi, A., Nascimento, I., Freire, R., et al. (2005). Demographic and clinical features of schizoaffective (schizobipolar) disorder–A 5-year retrospective study. Support for a bipolar spectrum disorder. *Journal of Affective Disorders, 89*(1–3), 201–206.

Neria, Y., Bromet, E., Carlson, G., & Naz, B. (2005). Assaultive trauma and illness course in psychotic bipolar disorder: Findings from the Suffolk county mental health project. *Acta Psychiatrica Scandanavica, 111*(5), 380–383.

Nierenberg, A., Miyahara, S., Spencer, T., et al. (2005). Clinical and diagnostic implications of lifetime attention-deficit/hyperactivity disorder comorbidity in adults with bipolar disorder: Data from the first 1000 STEP-BD participants. *Biological Psychiatry, 57*(11), 1467–1473.

Ortiz-Dominguez, A., Berlanga, C., & Gutierrez-Mora, D. (2004). A case of clarifthromycin-induced manic episode (antibiomania). *International Journal of Neuropsychopharmacology, 7*(1), 99–100.

Perry, P., Kutscher, E., Lund, B., et al. (2003). Measures of aggression and mood changes in male weightlifters with and without androgenic anabolic steroid use. *Journal of Forensic Science, 48*(3), 646–651.

Perugi, G., & Akiskal, H. (2002). The soft bipolar spectrum redefined: Focus on the cyclothymic, anxious-sensitive, impulse-dyscontrol, and binge-eating connection in bipolar II and related conditions. *Psychiatric Clinics of North America, 25*(4), 713–737.

Perugi, G., Ghaemi, S., & Akiskal, H. (2006). Diagnostic and clinical management approaches to bipolar depression, bipolar II and their co-morbidities. In H. Akiskal & M. Tohen (Eds.), *Bipolar psychopharmacotherapy* (pp. 193–234). West Sussex, England: Wiley.

Perugi, G., Toni, C., Travierso, M., & Akiskal, H. (2003). The role of cyclothymia in atypical depression: Toward a data-based reconceptualization of the borderline-bipolar II connection. *Journal of Affective Disorders, 73*(1–2), 87–98.

Pontius, A., & Wieser, H. (2004). Can memories kindle nonconvulsive behavioral seizures in humans? Case report exemplifying the "limbic psychotic trigger reaction." *Epilepsy and Behavior, 5*(5), 775–783.

Pope, Jr., H., & Katz, D. (1988). Affective and psychotic symptoms associated with anabolic steroid use. *American Journal of Psychiatry, 145*(4), 487–490.

Pope, Jr., H., Kouri, E., & Hudson, J. (2000). Effects of supraphysiologic doses of testosterone on mood and aggression in normal men: A randomized controlled trial. *Archives of General Psychiatry, 57*(2), 133–140.

Potash, J. (2006). Carving chaos: Genetics and the classification of mood and psychotic syndromes. *Harvard Review of Psychiatry, 14*(2), 47–63.

Preston, G., Marchant, B., Reimherr, F., et al. (2004). Borderline personality disorder in patients with bipolar disorder and response to lamotrigine. *Journal of Affective Disorders, 79*(1–3), 297–303.

Purper-Ouakil, D., Wohl, M., Michel, G., et al. (2004). Symptom variations in ADHD: Importance of context, development and comorbidity. *Encephale, 30*(6), 533–539.

Putnam, F. (1989). *Diagnosis and treatment of multiple personality disorder.* New York: Guilford.

Reisch, T., Brekenfeld, C., & Barth, A. (2005). A case of hydrocephalus occlusus presenting as bipolar disorder. *Acta Psychiatrica Scandinavica, 112*(2), 159.

Reichart, C., & Nolen, W. (2004). Earlier onset of bipolar disorder in children by antidepressants or stimulants? An hypothesis. *Journal of Affective Disorders, 78*(1), 81–84.

Ross, C. (1991). Epidemiology of multiple personality disorder and dissociation. *Psychiatric Clinics of North America, 14*(3), 503–517.

Ross, C., Andersen, G., Fleisher, W., & Norton, G. (1991). The frequency of multiple personality disorder among psychiatric inpatients. *American Journal of Psychiatry, 148*(12), 1717–1720.

Rundell, J., & Wise, M. (1989). Causes of organic mood disorder. *Journal of Neuropsychiatry and Clinical Neurosciences, 1*(4), 398–400.

Sar, V., Tutkun, H., Alyanak, B., et al. (2000). Frequency of dissociative disorders among psychiatric outpatients in Turkey. *Comprehensive Psychiatry, 41*(3), 216–222.

Saunders, E., & Arnold, F. (1993). A critique of conceptual and treatment approaches to borderline psychopathology in light of findings about childhood abuse. *Psychiatry, 56*(2), 188–203.

Saxe, G., van der Kolk, B., Berkowitz, R., et al. (1993). Dissociative disorders in psychiatric inpatients. *American Journal of Psychiatry, 150*(7), 1037–1042.

Shevlin, M., Dorahy, M., & Adamson, G. (2006). Childhood traumas and hallucinations: An analysis of the National Comorbidity Survey. *Journal of Psychiatric Research, Apr. 24.* (Epub ahead of print)

Steingard, S., & Frankel, F. H. (1985). Dissociation and psychotic symptoms. *American Journal of Psychiatry, 142*(8), 953–955.

Taylor, R. (1990). *Distinguishing psychological from organic disorders: Screening for psychological masquerade.* New York: Springer.

Tyre, S., & Brittlebank, A. (1993). Misdiagnosis of bipolar affective disorder as borderline personality disorder. *Canadian Journal of Psychiatry, 38,* 587–591.

Van Den Bosch, L., Verheul, R., Langeland, W., & Van Den Brink, W. (2003). Trauma, dissociation, and posttraumatic stress disorder in female borderline patients with and without substance abuse problems. *Australian and New Zealand Journal of Psychiatry, 37*(5), 549–555.

Vollmer-Larsen, A., Jacobsen, T. B., Hemmingsen, R., & Parnas, J. (2006). Schizoaffective disorder—The reliability of its clinical diagnostic use. *Acta Psychiatrica Scandinavica, 113*(5), 402–407.

Watson, S., Chilton, R., Fairchild, H., & Whewell, P. (2006). Association between childhood trauma and dissociation among patients with borderline personality disorder. *Australian and New Zealand Journal of Psychiatry, 40*(5), 478–481.

Weller, E., Weller, R., & Dogin, J. (1998). A rose is a rose is a rose. *Journal of Affective Disorders, 51*(2), 189–193.

Winokur, G., Scharfetter, C., & Angst, J. (1985). The diagnostic value in assessing mood congruence in delusions and hallucinations and their relationship to the affective state. *European Archives of Psychiatry and Neurological Sciences, 234*(5), 299–302.

Winokur, G., Turvey, C., Akiskal, H., et al. (1998). Alcoholism and drug abuse in three groups—bipolar I, unipolars and their acquaintances. *Journal of Affective Disorders,* *50*(2–3), 81–89.

Zimmerman, M., & Mattia, J. I. (1999). Axis I diagnostic comorbidity and borderline personality disorder. *Comprehensive Psychiatry, 40*(4), 245–252.

Zlotnick, C., Shea, T. M., & Rosen, K. (1997). An affect-management group for women with posttraumatic stress disorder and histories of childhood sexual abuse. *Journal of Trauma and Stress, 10*(3), 425–436.

CHAPTER 4

Comorbidity: Organic Illnesses, ADHD, Personality, Eating, Anxiety, and Impulse Control Disorders

Several organic and functional psychiatric disorders are more common in patients with bipolar disorder than in the general population (Strakowski et al., 1994). A complete list of medical and psychiatric comorbidity is found in Table 4.1.

Akiskal and Akiskal (2006) note that complex psychiatric comorbidity is the rule rather than the exception in bipolar patients. McElroy et al. (2001) evaluated 288 outpatients with bipolar I or II disorder, using structured diagnostic interviews and clinician-administered and self-rated questionnaires to determine the diagnosis of bipolar disorder and comorbid axis I disorder diagnoses. One hundred eighty-seven (65%) of the patients with bipolar disorder also met *DSM-IV* criteria for at least one comorbid lifetime axis I disorder.

These disorders may not simply coexist as separate entities with bipolar illness (true comorbidity). They may share a common pathophysiology with it. "Current formal psychiatric approaches to nosology," Lara et al. (2006) point out, "are plagued by an unwieldy degree of heterogeneity with insufficient appreciation of the commonalities of emotional, personality, behavioral, and addictive disorders" (p. 67). Many psychiatric disorders, such as bipolar, anxiety, eating, and impulse control disorders, have been found to share a common—usually cyclothymic—temperamental diathesis (Perugi & Akiskal, 2002). Maremmani et al. (2006) note: "It is likely that the affective dysregulation of bipolar disorder extends beyond elation and depression to include, among others, such *negative affective arousal states* as anxiety, panic, irritability, impulsivity and mood lability" (p. 4).

Patients with soft bipolar spectrum illnesses and subclinical temperament dysregulation often seek assistance from social workers, psychologists, marriage counselors, and other professionals for help with their comorbid condition. Clinicians must be sure to look beyond the comorbid conditions, which may be the focus of patients' attention, to the temperamental substrate from which these conditions arise. This approach is particularly important since antidepressant and stimulant medications are so often used to treat these presenting comorbid conditions.

The reader will note that some of the disorders discussed in the differential diagnosis section and elsewhere (ADHD, stimulant abuse, and thyroid disorder) are also prominent comorbid disorders. The discussions on these disorders will not be repeated here. Table 4.1 lists disorders commonly found in patients with bipolar disorder.

TABLE 4.1

Bipolar Disorder Comorbidity

Medical comorbidity:

Obesity, cardiovascular disease, and diabetes

Sleep apnea

Epilepsy

Migraine

Hypo/hyperthyroidism

Psychiatric comorbidity:

Substance abuse, especially alcohol and stimulants (cocaine, methamphetamine)

Attention deficit disorder

Borderline personality traits

Eating disorders, especially bulimia and binge eating

Anxiety disorders

   Panic disorders

   Obsessive-compulsive disorders

   Posttraumatic stress disorder

   Social phobia

Impulse control disorders

   IED

   Gambling

   Kleptomania

   Pathological spending

   Trichotillomania

   Possibly, pyromania

Medical Comorbidity

Medical disorders accompany bipolar disorder at rates greater than predicted by chance (Krishnan, 2005). Data collected on 174 patients from the Pittsburgh Maintenance Therapies in Bipolar Disorder study revealed that patients with a high number of medical comorbidities had longer duration of both lifetime depression and lifetime inpatient depression treatment (Thompson et al., 2006). Increasing severity of the comorbid illnesses predicted slower recovery from depressed and mixed episodes. Nonmedically trained therapists who spend time helping their patients recognize, seek care for, and attend to medical illnesses may, according to the authors, help "decrease the morbidity and mortality related to physical illness . . . enhance psychological well-being and possibly improve the course of bipolar illness" (p. 783).

Obesity, Cardiovascular Disease, and Diabetes

The excess medical illness seen in bipolar patients might be accounted for by true comorbidity or some of it may be secondary to the increased rates of obesity in bipolar patients (Wildes et al., 2006). A very large number of bipolar patients are overweight or obese (McElroy et al., 2004; Simon et al., 2006). In fact, comprehensive reviews of the literature and some clinical studies suggest that the prevalence of obesity in bipolar illness and what is referred to as the metabolic syndrome is even greater than that seen in the general population (Basu et al., 2004; Fagiolini et al., 2005; Keck & McElroy, 2003; Morriss & Mohammed, 2005). A person is said to have the metabolic syndrome when three or more metabolic risk factors are present: high blood pressure, abdominal obesity, high triglyceride levels, high LDL levels, low HDL levels, and high fasting levels of blood sugar.

Cardiovascular disease is the leading cause of death in bipolar patients, and mortality due to cardiovascular disease in bipolar patients is much higher than in the general population (Klumpers et al., 2004). Based on a review of the literature, McIntyre et al. (2005) concluded that diabetes might be as much as three times more common in bipolar patients as in the general population.

Increased rates of obesity in bipolar patients may be due to poor self-care, comorbid binge-eating, or the illness itself: Obese patients, for instance, tend to have more depressive recurrences than nonobese patients and depressed bipolar patients sometimes overeat and frequently oversleep. Elmslie et al. (2001) found that bipolar patients also tend to get less exercise than controls.

Another likely culprit for weight gain in bipolar patients is, of course, treatment with mood stabilizers and antipsychotic drugs. Elmslie et al. (2001) found that drug-induced changes in food preference lead to higher carbohydrate and caloric intake, particularly with sucrose-sweetened beverages. Weight gain is associated with the use of mood stabilizers such as lithium and divalproex (Depakote) and some atypical antipsychotic drugs, especially clozapine (Clozaril) and olanzapine (Zyprexa). These atypicals are also associated with development of the metabolic syndrome (Newcomer, 2004).

The overlap in phenomenology, comorbidity, family history, biological abnormalities, and pharmacologic treatment response seen in mood disorders, obesity, and the metabolic syndrome suggests the possibility the conditions may be related on some level (McElroy et al., 2004; Taylor & MacQueen, 2006).

Obese bipolar patients have a poorer treatment outcome than nonobese patients (Fagiolini et al., 2003). Fagolini and his colleagues state that "preventing and treating obesity in bipolar disorder patients could decrease the morbidity and mortality related to physical illness, enhance psychological well-being, and possibly improve the course of bipolar illness" (p. 112).

Sleep Apnea

Weight gain can contribute to the development of obstructive sleep apnea (partial or complete collapse of the soft tissues of the airway while sleeping). Several studies have found an association between mood disorders and obstructive sleep apnea (Reynolds et al., 1982; Sharafkhaneh et al., 2005). Sleep apnea can lead to depressed mood, cognitive difficulties, and irritability. Strakowski et al. (1991) reported on four patients with mania whose course of illness and treatment were complicated by sleep apnea. Older patients and patients who are overweight, have high blood pressure, snore loudly, or have excessive daytime sleepiness should be suspected of having sleep apnea. The disorder is diagnosed by a sleep study.

Treatment of sleep apnea has been reported to improve the symptoms of depression (Kawahara et al., 2005). Interestingly, treatment of apnea has also been associated with the development of mania and psychosis (Chiner et al., 2001; Hilleret et al., 2001).

Epilepsy

The high rate of co-occurrence of bipolar illness and epilepsy has been noted for thousands of years. Since manic symptoms are more prevalent in epileptic patients than in patients with other medical disorders or in the general population (Ettinger et al., 2005), and a number of antiepileptic drugs are effective in bipolar patients, it is thought the two disorders may share some pathophysiologic mechanisms (Bauer & Pfennig, 2005).

Not only does epilepsy co-occur with bipolar illness, but nonconvulsive forms of epilepsy, primarily the ones with a temporal lobe focus, can mimic the symptoms of psychosis and dissociative disorders. Patients with temporal lobe epilepsy likely outnumber those with convulsive seizures (Goodwin & Jamison, 1990).

Clues that should alert the clinician to the presence of temporal lobe epilepsy are visual and olfactory (as opposed to auditory) hallucinations, catatonia and dreamlike or mystical states, deja vu, memory lapses, and poor or paradoxical response to mood-active drugs (Goodwin & Jamison, 1990).

Migraine Headaches

Mahmood et al. (1999) found that, among 81 patients with bipolar disorder responding to a questionnaire, 25.9 percent reported migraine headaches. This study also found that patients who had early onset bipolar disorder were more likely to have migraine headaches. A Swiss prospective epidemiologic study of 27- and 28-year-olds, using interviews to gather data (Merikangas et al., 1990), showed that migraine patients were 2.9 times more likely than controls to have bipolar disorder. The association between social phobia and migraine was very strong, as well, which is an interesting finding in light of the reported association of bipolar illness and social phobia (Dilsaver & Chen, 2003). A Canadian epidemiologic study showed that persons with bipolar disorder had more than twice the rate of migraine as the general population (McIntyre et al., 2006a).

Fasmer and Oedegaard (2001) and Oedegaard and Fasmer (2005) reported evidence suggesting migraine in depressed patients might represent a bipolar spectrum trait. In the first study, mood disorder patients with comorbid migraine had a higher rate of bipolar II illness than those without migraine.

A study of a random sample of 1,007 young adults from a large health maintenance organization in the Detroit, Michigan, area showed there was a nonsignificant trend toward an increased rate of psychiatric disorders in migraine patients with aura (sensations preceding the onset of migraine), but not in those without aura (Breslau et al., 1991). Oedegaard et al. (2006), in data from a Swiss epidemiologic study, found that migraine with aura was associated with depression and anxiety but migraine without aura was not. This was true only for women, however.

Migraine and bipolar disorder both respond to some anticonvulsant drugs, which suggests possible shared neurochemistry.

Thyroid Disease

Thyroid disease is associated with a number of psychiatric disturbances. Placidi et al. (1998) found higher rates of panic disorder, simple phobia, obsessive-compulsive disorder, major depressive disorder, bipolar disorder, and cyclothymia in 93 hospitalized patients with various thyroid diseases than in the general population. The relationship between hypothyroidism and bipolar illness will be discussed in Chapters 6 and 7.

Thomsen et al. (2005) found that patients hospitalized with hyperthyroidism (thyrotoxicosis) are at greater risk of later readmission with depressive disorder or bipolar disorder than control patients, suggesting that thyrotoxicosis is associated with long-term mood disturbances. Thyrotoxicosis can also mimic mania and psychosis (Brownlie et al., 2000; Regan, 1988).

Psychiatric Comorbidity

Substance Abuse

Bipolar I patients have a lifetime prevalence of alcohol abuse of nearly 60 percent (Grant et al., 2005), compared to a lifetime prevalence of 28.6 percent in the general population (Kessler et al., 2005). High rates of alcohol and drug abuse are not confined to bipolar I patients. Substance abuse is highly prevalent in individuals across the bipolar spectrum including those with hyperthymic, irritable, and cyclothymic temperaments (Maremmani et al., 2006). In fact, Maremmani and colleagues cite evidence suggesting that these temperaments may predispose people, perhaps through increased impulsivity, risk taking, and stimulus seeking, to abuse alcohol and drugs. Substance abuse will be discussed in depth in the next chapter.

Attention-Deficit Hyperactivity Disorder (ADHD)

Attention-deficit hyperactivity disorder (ADHD) and bipolar disorder overlap symptomatically and may be related disorders. Perhaps 15 percent of adults with bipolar illness have comorbid ADHD (Nierenberg et al., 2005), compared to about 8 percent in the general population (Kessler et al., 2005). The current thinking is that patients who have both bipolar disorder and ADHD are best treated first with mood stabilizers. Stimulants can induce mixed hypomanic or manic states. Please refer to Chapter 3 for a full discussion of the relationship between ADHD and bipolar illness.

Personality Disorders

Both population and clinical studies show that bipolar patients often meet diagnostic criteria for a personality disorder. For example, Grant et al. (2005), in a population-based study of 43,000 people, of whom roughly 860 had a bipolar I disorder, found that nearly two-thirds of the bipolar patients met diagnostic criteria for a personality disorder. Garno et al. (2005) found that, among 100 patients with either bipolar I or bipolar II disorder, 30 percent met diagnostic criteria for a *DSM-IV* Cluster B personality disorder (largely borderline and narcissistic types). George et al. (2003) found that 36 percent of 52 bipolar patients met diagnostic criteria for a cluster B personality disorder. Bipolar patients with personality disorders in this study had greater severity of residual mood symptoms. Antisocial personality disorder was found to be most common in bipolar patients with childhood-onset bipolar disorder (Goldstein & Levitt, 2006).

Some patients with bipolar disorder meet diagnostic criteria for borderline personality and many bipolar patients have what are considered borderline personality traits. Narcissistic, histrionic, and borderline traits seem to be related to the presence of a cyclothymic disposition (Perugi et al., 2006). Please refer to Chapter 3 for more details.

Eating Disorders

Results of epidemiological studies indicate that features of subthreshold bipolar disorder often occur together with disordered eating in adolescents (McElroy et al., 2005; Mury et al., 1995). Adult patients with bipolar disorder frequently have eating disorders, especially binge eating and bulimia (Kruger et al., 1996; McElroy et al., 2005). Patients with eating disorders frequently have depression with atypical features (a robust marker for bipolar spectrum illness) and bipolar II disorder with cyclothymic temperament (Hudson et al., 1983b; Perugi et al., 2006; Simpson et al., 1992). Body dysmorphias, especially the perception that one's body is fat and disgusting, are also higher in subjects with atypical depression and are probably common among eating disordered patients.

Atypical features of depression include interpersonal sensitivity and mood reactivity. Individuals with these characteristics may binge when they feel criticized, rejected, or when they become self-loathing. Ramacciotti et al. (2005) studied a sample of 51 outpatients with bipolar I disorder and found that the onset of bipolar disorder generally preceded the onset of an eating disorder, suggesting to them that the disordered eating evolved as an attempt to modulate emotion with food. Eating disorder patients may also have various anxiety disorders, substance abuse, and sometimes kleptomania (Hudson et al., 1983b; Woodside & Staab, 2006).

Relatives with unipolar and bipolar disorder are frequently found in the family history of patients with eating disorders (Hudson et al., 1983a; Mangweth et al., 2003; Winokur et al. 1980). Patients with bipolar illness and those with eating disorders both have increased rates of childhood trauma (Basurte et al., 2004).

Patients with mood disorders and patients with eating disorders have similar responses to some biological tests (Basurte et al., 2004) and there are case reports of concomitant remission of both disorders with anticonvulsants or lithium (Mury et al., 1995). Topiramate (Topamax) is an anticonvulsant drug that can be helpful in patients with bulimia and in some patients with bipolar disorder (Barbee, 2003).

All of these similarities suggest shared pathophysiology between eating disorders and illnesses in the bipolar spectrum. Overall, a review of the literature, "leaves little doubt that bipolar and eating disorders—particularly bulimia nervosa and bipolar II disorder—are related" (p. 107), according to McElroy et al. (2005). Mangweth et al. (2003) concluded that "the familial coaggregation of eating disorders with mood disorders . . . suggests that eating disorders and mood disorders have common familial causal factors" (p. 1319).

Torrent et al. (2004) developed a 10-item Bipolar Eating Disorders Scale (BEDS) modeled on existing eating scales, but modified for bipolar patients, in order to help clinicians evaluate bipolar patients for a variety of eating disorders.

Anxiety Disorders

Anxiety disorders are among the most common comorbid conditions seen in bipolar patients (Grant et al., 2005). Grant and his colleagues reported data from the 2001–2002 United States National Epidemiologic Survey on Alcohol and Related Conditions ($N = 43,093$). They found a lifetime prevalence of anxiety disorder of 56.3 percent in bipolar I patients. This compares to a lifetime prevalence rate in the general population of 28.8 percent (Kessler et al., 2005).

Schaffer et al. (2006) did a study on the lifetime prevalence and illness characteristics of bipolar disorder in a large, representative sample of Canadians and found that nearly 52 percent of bipolar patients reported an anxiety disorder. Boylan et al. (2004), using structured clinical interviews of 138 patients with bipolar disorder, found that 31.8 percent of them had two or more anxiety disorder diagnoses.

A French study by Henry et al. (2003) of 318 bipolar patients consecutively hospitalized in two centers found a correlation between comorbid anxiety disorders and depressive temperament in bipolar patients. Dilsaver and Chen (2003) reported that, in a small sample of bipolar patients, those who had depressive (mixed) but not pure mania exhibited high rates of both interepisode panic disorder and social phobia. These and other clinical studies suggest anxiety disorders may be more common in patients with mixed and softer forms of bipolar disorder (more of whom are women). Since these forms of bipolar illness are not as reliably diagnosed as bipolar I mania, epidemiological studies may underestimate the prevalence of anxiety disorders in patients with bipolar disorder (McIntyre et al., 2006).

Grant et al. (2005) found a lifetime prevalence of 23.7 percent of social phobia in bipolar I patients. In the general population, the rate is about 12 percent (Kessler et al., 2005). Kessler et al. (1999) used data from the United States National Comorbidity Survey and found lifetime social phobia increased the odds of having bipolar disorder by nearly sixfold, whereas it nearly tripled the odds of developing a major depressive episode. Himmelhoch (1998) reported that 18 of 32 social phobic patients administered either the reversible MAOI meclobomide or the irreversible MAOI phenelzine achieved remission. However, 14 of those 18 became hypomanic, disinhibited, and extroverted, suggesting there is a subset of socially phobic patients whose social anxiety reflects depressive inhibition in the midst of bipolar illness.

Chen and Dilsaver (1995) reported that the lifetime rates of obsessive-compulsive disorder were 21 percent in bipolar patients and 12.8 percent in unipolar patients. Angst et al. (2005) reported that obsessive-compulsive disorder was significantly comorbid with bipolar disorder in a Swiss longitudinal study of 591 adults, whereas there was no clear association between obsessive-compulsive disorder and major depressive disorder among this cohort. Pashinian et al. (2006), in an Israeli study, noted that the higher rates of obsessive-compulsive disorder seen in bipolar patients compared to the general population might be due to confounding factors such as greater treatment seeking in bipolar patients. In an attempt to eliminate these factors, they looked only at patients with first hospital admission for bipolar I disorder. They found the rate of obsessive-compulsive disorder in 56 of these patients did not differ significantly from that found in the general population. The authors reported that a substantial number of the patients did have substance use, eating disorders, and anxiety disorders other than obsessive-compulsive disorder. Hasler et al. (2005) looked at the association between specific obsessive-compulsive symptom clusters and other disorders. They found that among 371 patients with obsessive-compulsive disorder symmetry, repeating, counting, and ordering/arranging compulsions were correlated with bipolar disorders and panic disorder/agoraphobia.

Grant et al. (2005) reported a lifetime prevalence of panic with or without agoraphobia of 25.5 percent in bipolar I patients. In the general population, the rate is 4.7 percent (Kessler et al., 2005). Bipolar disorder and panic may share pathophysiology since they aggregate in families (Doughty et al., 2004). Doughty and his colleagues also reported that, in 109 patients with bipolar disorder and their 226 siblings, panic was found more often in those with bipolar disorder than in unipolar disorder. Evidence for a connection between panic and bipolar illness was found, as well, in an earlier study by MacKinnon et al. (2003). Familial panic and the diagnosis of panic disorder in an individual subject were associated with episodes of rapid mood switching. Frank et al. (2002), in a sample of 66 patients with bipolar I disorder who completed a self-report measure of lifetime panic-agoraphobic spectrum symptoms, found that panic spectrum symptoms were associated with greater levels of depression, more suicidal ideation, and a marked (6-month) delay in time to remission with acute treatment.

A significant number of bipolar patients have been abused as children and have comorbid posttraumatic stress disorder. Levitan et al. (1998) asked 8,116 individuals aged 15 to 64 years in a community sample from Ontario about early physical and sexual abuse using a structured interview: A history of physical or sexual abuse in childhood was associated with mania and major depression with atypical features (a robust marker for bipolar depression). Kolodziej et al. (2005) found that, among 90 patients diagnosed with bipolar I or II disorder and substance abuse, 43 (48%) had a lifetime anxiety disorder, with posttraumatic stress disorder occurring most frequently. Brown et al. (2005) reported on 330 veterans with bipolar I or II disorder enrolled in a 3-year prospective study who were assessed with a semistructured interview to determine exposure to childhood physical or sexual abuse. Nearly 50 percent of subjects reported a childhood history of some form of abuse. Childhood abuse was associated with a higher likelihood of current posttraumatic stress disorder and lifetime diagnoses of alcohol use disorders, as well as higher likelihood of at least one suicide attempt. Goldberg and Garno (2005) studied 100 consecutive bipolar patients who were evaluated for childhood physical, sexual, and emotional abuse, traumatic events in adulthood, and lifetime posttraumatic stress disorder. Their findings suggested that about one-third of bipolar patients with severe childhood abuse histories, particularly sexual abuse, manifest comorbid adult posttraumatic stress disorder. Risk for posttraumatic stress disorder rose in step with the number of childhood abuse subtypes present. Adult sexual assault was significantly more likely to be associated with posttraumatic stress disorder if the patient had been sexually abused in childhood. These data on the incidence of childhood abuse and posttraumatic stress disorder in patients with bipolar illness provide additional support for the recommendations made in the last chapter on screening bipolar patients for the presence of dissociative disorders.

Anxiety disorder comorbidity has a substantial adverse impact on patients with bipolar disorder. Bipolar patients with anxiety disorders have been reported to have longer times to remission, higher rates of relapse and rehospitalization, increased suicidality, and poorer response to treatment than bipolar patients without anxiety disorders (McIntyre et al., 2006b).

Impulse Control Disorders

McElroy et al. (1996) proposed that similarities between impulse control problems and bipolar disorder indicate that the two conditions may be related and share some common pathophysiology. McElroy and her colleagues (1998) then reported on 27 subjects examined with structured diagnostic interviews who met *DSM-IV* criteria for a current or past history of intermittent explosive disorder. Twenty-five (93%) of 27 subjects had lifetime *DSM-IV* diagnoses of mood disorders, most characterized by changes in mood and energy level, which suggested a bipolar diathesis. In a later commentary on these same patients, McElroy and colleagues noted that "the association of the explosive episodes in these subjects with manic-like affective symptoms, the high rate of lifetime comorbid bipolar disorder, and the favorable response of explosive episodes to mood-stabilizing drugs suggest that intermittent explosive disorder may be linked to bipolar disorder" (McElroy, 1999, p. 12). Interestingly, McElroy's subjects also displayed high rates of comorbid migraine headaches.

McElroy and her colleagues noted in the 1996 study that there were no studies directly comparing a cohort of impulse control problems with a cohort of mood disorder patients. Subsequently, however, Lejoyeux et al. (2002) found that bipolar disorders were more common among 31 depressed inpatients who met criteria for impulse control disorders compared to a group of depressed patients without impulse-control problems. Bulimia and compulsive buying were also higher in the group of patients with impulse control disorders.

Divalproex (Depakote) is a medication that is effective in treating bipolar disorder and migraine headaches. It has also been found to be effective in children and adolescents with target symptoms of explosive temper who are believed to have bipolar spectrum disorder (Barzman et al., 2005). Intermittent explosive disorder also responds to carbamazepine, another drug effective in the treatment of mania (Campbell et al., 1992; Mattes, 1990).

Evidence suggests that some patients with pathological gambling may have a bipolar diathesis. Kim et al. (2006) reviewed the literature on the frequency of various mood disorders among patients with pathological gambling and the frequency of pathological gambling among patients with mood disorders. In those studies using a structured interview to make diagnoses, a close link between gambling and mood disorders was shown. One fourth of gamblers were found to have bipolar disorder. A study not reviewed by Kim and his colleagues (Zimmerman et al., 2006) examined 1,709 Rhode Island psychiatric outpatients with a structured interview designed to diagnose pathological gambling. The 40 patients with pathological gambling had significantly higher rates of bipolar disorder, social phobia, panic disorder with agoraphobia, alcohol use disorder, and other impulse control disorders than patients without pathological gambling.

A number of other impulse control problems may be found in patients with bipolar illness. There have been case reports of trichotillomania (Berk et al., 2003; Damodaran et al., 1995) and kleptomania (Kmetz et al., 1997; Rocha & Rocha, 1992) occurring in bipolar illness. In these cases, both the bipolar illness and the impulse control problem responded to lithium. Ritchie and Huff (1999) found that 38 percent of 283 arsonists had either schizophrenia or bipolar illness. Shapira et al. (2000) evaluated 20 individuals with problematic Internet use with the Structured Clinical Interview for *DSM-IV.* Fourteen (70.0%) had a lifetime diagnosis of bipolar disorder.

References

Akiskal, H., & Akiskal, K. (2006). Principles of caring for the bipolar patient. In H. Akiskal & M. Tohen (Eds.), *Bipolar psychopharmacotherapy: Caring for the patient* (pp. 367–387). West Sussex, England: Wiley.

Angst, J., Gamma, A., Endrass, J., et al. (2005). Obsessive-compulsive syndromes and disorders: Significance of comorbidity with bipolar and anxiety syndromes. *European Archives of Psychiatry and Clinical Neurosciences, 255*(1), 65–71.

Barbee, J. (2003). Topiramate in the treatment of severe bulimia nervosa with comorbid mood disorders: A case series. *International Journal of Eating Disorders, 33*(4), 468–472.

Barzman, D., McConville, B., Masterson B., et al. (2005). Impulsive aggression with irritability and responsive to divalproex: A pediatric bipolar spectrum disorder phenotype? *Journal of Affective Disorders, 88*(3), 279–285.

Basu, R., Brar, J., Chengappa, K., et al. (2004). The prevalence of the metabolic syndrome in patients with schizoaffective disorder–bipolar subtype. *Bipolar Disorders, 6*(4), 314–318.

Basurte, E., Diaz-Marsa, M., Martin, O., & Carrasco, L. (2004). Traumatic childhood background, impulsiveness and hypothalamus-pituitary-adrenal axis dysfunction in eating disorders. A pilot study. *Actas Españolas de Psiquiatría, 32*(3), 149–152.

Bauer, M., & Pfennig, A. (2005). Epidemiology of bipolar disorders. *Epilepsia, 46*(Suppl. 4), 8–13.

Berk, M., McKenzie, H., & Dodd S. (2003). Trichotillomania: Response to lithium in a person with comorbid bipolar disorder. *Human Psychopharmacology, 18*(7), 576–577.

Boylan, K., Bieling, P., Marriott, M., et al. (2004). Impact of comorbid anxiety disorders on outcome in a cohort of patients with bipolar disorder. *Journal of Clinical Psychiatry, 65*(8), 1106–1113.

Breslau, N., Davis, G., & Andreski, P. (1991), Migraine, psychiatric disorders, and suicide attempts: An epidemiologic study of young adults. *Psychiatry Research, 37*(1), 11–23.

Brown, G., McBride, L., Bauer, M., et al. (2005). Impact of childhood abuse on the course of bipolar disorder: A replication study in U.S. veterans. *Journal of Affective Disorders, 89*(1–3), 57–67.

Brownlie, B., Rae, A., Walshe, J., & Wells, J. (2000). Psychoses associated with thyrotoxicosis—"thyrotoxic psychosis." A report of 18 cases, with statistical analysis of incidence. *European Journal of Endocrinology, 142*(5), 438–444.

Campbell, M., Gonzalez, N., & Silva, R. (1992). The pharmacologic treatment of conduct disorders and rage outbursts. *Psychiatric Clinics of North America, 15*(1), 69–85.

Chen, Y., & Dilsaver, S. (1995). Comorbidity for obsessive-compulsive disorder in bipolar and unipolar disorders. *Psychiatry Research, 59*, 57–64.

Chiner, E., Arrierio, J., Signes-Costa, J., & Marco, J. (2001). Acute psychosis after CPAP treatment in a schizophrenic patient with sleep apnoea-hypopnoea syndrome. *European Respiratory Journal, 17*(2), 313–315.

Damodaran, S., Jayalekshmi, K., & Khanna R. (1995). Trichotillomania: Symptom or syndrome? A need for revision. *Psychopathology, 28*(3), 127–130.

Dilsaver, S., & Chen, Y. (2003). Social phobia, panic disorder and suicidality in subjects with pure and depressive mania. *Journal of Affective Disorders, 77*(2), 173–177.

Doughty, C., Wells, J., Joyce, P., et al. (2004). Bipolar-panic disorder comorbidity within bipolar disorder families: A study of siblings. *Bipolar Disorders, 6*(3), 245–252.

Elmslie, J., Mann, J., Silverstone, J., et al. (2001). Determinants of overweight and obesity in patients with bipolar disorder. *Journal of Clinical Psychiatry, 62*(6), 486–491.

Ettinger, A., Reed, M., Goldberg, J., & Hirschfeld, R. (2005). Prevalence of bipolar symptoms in epilepsy vs. other chronic health disorders. *Neurology, 65*(4), 535–540.

Fagiolini, A., Frank, E., Scott, J., et al. (2005). Metabolic syndrome in bipolar disorder: Findings from the Bipolar Disorder Center for Pennsylvanians. *Bipolar Disorders, 7*(5), 424–430.

Fagiolini, A., Kupfer, D., & Houck, P. (2003). Obesity as a correlate of outcome in patients with bipolar I disorder. *American Journal of Psychiatry, 160*(1), 112–117.

Fasmer, O., & Oedegaard, K. (2001). Clinical characteristics of patients with major affective disorders and comorbid migraine. *World Journal of Biological Psychiatry, 2*(3), 149–155.

Frank, E., Cyranowski, J., Rucci, P., et al. (2002). Clinical significance of lifetime panic spectrum symptoms in the treatment of patients with bipolar I disorder. *Archives of General Psychiatry, 59*(10), 905–911.

Garno, J., Goldberg, J., Ramirez, P., & Ritzler, B. (2005). Bipolar disorder with comorbid cluster B personality disorder features: Impact on suicidality. *Journal of Clinical Psychiatry, 66*(3), 339–345.

George, E., Miklowitz, D., Richards, J., et al. (2003). The comorbidity of bipolar disorder and axis II personality disorders: Prevalence and clinical correlates. *Bipolar Disorders, 5*(2), 115–122.

Goldberg, J., & Garno, J. (2005). Development of posttraumatic stress disorder in adult bipolar patients with histories of severe childhood abuse. *Journal of Psychiatric Research, 39*(6), 595–601.

Goldstein, B., & Levitt, A. (2006). Further evidence for a developmental subtype of bipolar disorder defined by age at onset: Results from the National Epidemiologic Survey on Alcohol and Related Conditions. *American Journal of Psychiatry, 163*(9), 1633–1636.

Goodwin, F., & Jamison, K. (1990). *Manic-depressive illness*. New York: Oxford University Press.

Grant, B., Stinson, F., Hasin, D., et al. (2005). Prevalence, correlates, and comorbidity of bipolar I disorder and axis I and II disorders: Results from the National Epidemiologic Survey on Alcohol and Related Conditions. *Journal of Clinical Psychiatry, 66*(10), 1205–1215.

Hasler, G., LaSalle-Ricci, V., Ronquillo, J., Crawley, S., et al. (2005). Obsessive-compulsive disorder symptom dimensions show specific relationships to psychiatric comorbidity. *Psychiatry Research, 135*(2), 121–132.

Henry, C., Van den Bulke, D., & Bellivier, F. (2003). Anxiety disorders in 318 bipolar patients: Prevalence and impact on illness severity and response to mood stabilizer. *Journal of Clinical Psychiatry, 64*(3), 331–335.

Hilleret, H., Jeunet, E., Osiek, C., et al. (2001). Mania resulting from continuous positive airways pressure in a depressed man with sleep apnea syndrome. *Neuropsychobiology, 43*(3), 221–224.

Himmelhoch, J. (1998). Social anxiety, hypomania and the bipolar spectrum: Data, theory and clinical issues. *Journal of Affective Disorders, 50*(2–3), 203–213.

Hudson, J., Pope, Jr., H., Jonas, J., & Yurgelun-Todd, D. (1983a). Family history study of anorexia nervosa and bulimia. *British Journal of Psychiatry, 142*, 133–138.

Hudson, J., Pope, Jr., H., Jonas, J., & Yurgelun-Todd, D. (1983b). Phenomenologic relationship of eating disorders to major affective disorder. *Psychiatry Research, 9*(4), 345–354.

Kawahara, S., Akashiba, T., Akahoshi, T., & Horie, T. (2005). Nasal CPAP improves the quality of life and lessens the depressive symptoms in patients with obstructive sleep apnea syndrome. *Internal Medicine, 44*(5), 422–427.

Keck, P., & McElroy, S. (2003). Bipolar disorder, obesity, and pharmacotherapy-associated weight gain. *Journal of Clinical Psychiatry, 64*(12), 1426–1435.

Kessler, R., Chiu, W., Demler, O., et al. (2005). Prevalence, severity, and comorbidity of 12-month *DSM-IV* disorders in the National Comorbidity Survey Replication. *Archives of General Psychiatry, 62*(6), 617–627.

Kessler, R., Stang, P., Wittchen, H., et al. (1999). Lifetime co-morbidities between social phobia and mood disorders in the US National Comorbidity Survey. *Psychological Medicine, 29*(3), 555–567.

Kim, S., Grant, J., Eckert, E., et al. (2006). Pathological gambling and mood disorders: Clinical associations and treatment implications. *Journal of Affective Disorders, 92*(1), 109–116.

Klumpers, U., Boom, K., Janssen, F., et al. (2004). Cardiovascular risk factors in outpatients with bipolar disorder. *Pharmacopsychiatry, 37*(5), 211–216.

Kmetz, G. F., McElroy, S. L., & Collins, D. J. (1997). Response of kleptomania and mixed mania to valproate. *American Journal of Psychiatry, 154*(4), 580–581.

Kolodziej, M., Griffin, M., Najavits, L., et al. (2005). Anxiety disorders among patients with co-occurring bipolar and substance use disorders. *Drug and Alcohol Dependence, 80*(2), 251–257.

Krishnan, K. (2005). Psychiatric and medical comorbidities of bipolar disorder. *Psychosomatic Medicine, 67*(1), 1–8.

Kruger, S., Shugar, G., & Cooke, R. (1996). Comorbidity of binge eating disorder and the partial binge eating syndrome with bipolar disorder. *International Journal of Eating Disorders, 19*(1), 45–52.

Lara, D., Pinto, O. Akiskal, K., & Akiskal, H. (2006). Toward an integrative model of the spectrum of mood, behavioral, and personality disorders based on fear and anger traits. *Journal of Affective Disorders, 94*(1-3), 67-87.

Lejoyeux, M., Arbaretaz, M., McLoughlin, M., & Ades, J. (2002). Impulse control disorders and depression. *Journal of Nervous and Mental Disorders, 190*(5), 310–314.

Levitan, R., Parikh, S., Lesage, A., et al. (1998). Major depression in individuals with a history of childhood physical or sexual abuse: Relationship to neurovegetative features, mania, and gender. *American Journal of Psychiatry, 155*(12), 1746–1752.

MacKinnon, D., Zandi, P., & Gershon, E. (2003). Association of rapid mood switching with panic disorder and familial panic risk in familial bipolar disorder. *American Journal of Psychiatry, 160*(9), 1696–1698.

Mahmood, T., Romans, S., & Silverstone, T. (1999). Prevalence of migraine in bipolar disorder. *Journal of Affective Disorders, 52*(1–3), 329–341.

Mangweth, B., Hudson, J., Pope, H., et al. (2003). Family study of the aggregation of eating disorders and mood disorders. *Psychological Medicine, 33*(7), 1319–1323.

Maremmani, I., Perugi., G., Paeini., M., & Akiskal, H. (2006). Toward a unitary perspective on the bipolar spectrum and substance abuse: Opiate addiction as a paradigm. *Journal of Affective Disorders, 93*, 1–12.

Mattes, J. (1990). Comparative effectiveness of carbamazepine and propranolol for rage outbursts. *Journal of Neuropsychiatry and Clinical Neurosciences, 2*(2), 159–164.

McElroy, S. (1999). Recognition and treatment of *DSM-IV* intermittent explosive disorder. *Journal of Clinical Psychiatry, 60*(Suppl. 15), 12–16.

McElroy, S., Altshuler, L., Suppes, T., et al. (2001). Axis I psychiatric comorbidity and its relationship to historical illness variables in 288 patients with bipolar disorder. *American Journal of Psychiatry, 158*(3), 420–426.

McElroy, S., Kotwal, R., Keck, Jr., P., Akiskal, H. (2005). Comorbidity of bipolar and eating disorders: Distinct or related disorders with shared dysregulations? *Journal of Affective Disorders, 86*(2–3), 107–127.

McElroy, S., Kotwal, R., Malhotra, S., et al. (2004). Are mood disorders and obesity related? *Journal of Clinical Psychiatry, 65*(5), 634–651.

McElroy, S., Pope, Jr., H., Keck, Jr., P., et al. (1996). Are impulse-control disorders related to bipolar disorder? *Comprehensive Psychiatry, 37*(4), 229–240.

McElroy, S., Soutullo, C., Beckman, D., et al. (1998). *DSM-IV* intermittent explosive disorder: A report of 27 cases. *Journal of Clinical Psychiatry, 59*(4), 203–210.

McIntyre, R., Konarski, J., Misener, V., & Kennedy, S. (2005). Bipolar disorder and diabetes mellitus: Epidemiology, etiology, and treatment implications. *Annals of Clinical Psychiatry, 17*(2), 83–93.

McIntyre, R., Konarski, J., Wilkins, K., et al. (2006a). The prevalence and impact of migraine headaches in bipolar disorder: Results from the Canadian Community Health Survey. *Headache, 46*(6), 973–982.

McIntyre, R. Soczynska, J., Bottas, A., et al. (2006b). Anxiety disorders and bipolar disorder: A review. *Bipolar Disorders, 8*, 665–676.

Merikangas, K., Angst, J., & Isler, H. (1990). Migraine and psychopathology. Results of the Zurich cohort study of young adults. *Archives of General Psychiatry, 47*(9), 849–853.

Morriss, R., & Mohammed, F. (2005). Metabolism, lifestyle and bipolar affective disorder. *Journal of Psychopharmacology, 19*(Suppl. 6), 94–101.

Mury, M., Verdoux, H., & Bourgeois, M. (1995). Comorbidity of bipolar and eating disorders. Epidemiologic and therapeutic aspects. *Encephale, 21*(5), 545–553.

Newcomer, J. (2004). Abnormalities of glucose metabolism associated with atypical antipsychotic drugs. *Journal of Clinical Psychiatry, 65*(Suppl. 18), 36–46.

Nierenberg, A., Miyahara, S., Spencer, T., et al. (2005).Clinical and diagnostic implications of lifetime attention-deficit/hyperactivity disorder comorbidity in adults with bipolar disorder: Data from the first 1000 STEP-BD participants. *Biological Psychiatry, 57*(11), 1467–1473.

Oedegaard, K., Neckelmann, D., Mykletun, A., et al. (2006). Migraine with and without aura: Association with depression and anxiety disorder in a population-based study. The HUNT study. *Cephalagia, 26*(1), 1–6.

Oedegaard, K., & Fasmer, O. (2005). Is migraine in unipolar depressed patients a bipolar spectrum trait? *Journal of Affective Disorders, 84*(2–3), 233–242.

Pashinian, A., Faragian, S., Levi, A., et al. (2006). Obsessive-compulsive disorder in bipolar disorder patients with first manic episode. *Journal of Affective Disorders, 94*(1–3), 151–156.

Perugi, G., & Akiskal, H. (2002). The soft bipolar spectrum: Focus on the cyclothymic, anxious-sensitive, impulse-dyscontrol, and binge-eating connection in bipolar II and related conditions. *Psychiatric Clinics of North America, 25*(4), 713–737.

Perugi, G., Toni, C., Passino, M., et al. (2006). Bulimia nervosa in atypical depression: The mediating role of cyclothymic temperament. *Journal of Affective Disorders, 92*(1), 91–97.

Placidi, G., Boldrini, N., Patronelli, A., et al. (1988). Prevalence of psychiatric disorders in thyroid diseased patients. *Neuropsychobiology, 38*(4), 222–225.

Ramacciotti, C., Paoli, R., Marcacci, G., et al. (2005). Relationship between bipolar illness and binge-eating disorders. *Psychiatry Research, 135*(2), 165–170.

Regan, W. (1988). Thyrotoxicosis manifested as mania. *South Medical Journal, 81*(11), 1460–1461.

Reynolds, 3rd, C., Coble, P., Spiker, D., et al. (1982). Prevalence of sleep apnea and nocturnal myoclonus in major affective disorders: Clinical and polysomnographic findings. *Journal of Nervous and Mental Disorders, 170*(9), 565–567.

Ritchie, E., & Huff, T. (1999). Psychiatric aspects of arsonists. *Journal of Forensic Sciences, 44*(4), 733–740.

Rocha, F., & Rocha, M. (1992). Kleptomania, mood disorder and lithium. *Arquivos de Neuro-psiquiatria, 50*(4), 543–546.

Schaffer, A., Cairney, J., & Cheung, A. (2006). Community survey of bipolar disorder in Canada: Lifetime prevalence and illness characteristics. *Canadian Journal of Psychiatry, 51*(1), 9–16.

Shapira, N., Goldsmith, T., & Keck, Jr., P. (2000). Psychiatric features of individuals with problematic internet use. *Journal of Affective Disorders, 57*(1–3), 267–272.

Sharafkhaneh, A., Giray, N., Richardson, P., et al. (2005). Association of psychiatric disorders and sleep apnea in a large cohort. *Sleep, 28*(11), 1405–1411.

Simon, G., Von Korff, M., Saunders, K., et al. (2006). Association between obesity and psychiatric disorders in the U.S. adult population. *Archives of General Psychiatry, 63*(7), 824–830.

Simpson, S., al-Mufti, R., Andersen, A., & DePaulo, Jr., J. (1992). Bipolar II affective disorder in eating disorder inpatients. *Journal of Nervous and Mental Disorders, 180*(11), 719–722.

Strakowski, S., Hudson, J., Keck, Jr., P., et al. (1991). Four cases of obstructive sleep apnea associated with treatment-resistant mania. *Journal of Clinical Psychiatry, 52*(4), 156–158.

Strakowski, S. M., MeElroy, S. L., Keck, P. W., Jr., & West, S. A. (1994). The co-occurrence of mania with medical and other psychiatric disorders. *International Journal of Psychiatry in Medicine, 24*(4), 305–328.

Taylor, V., & MacQueen, G. (2006). Associations between bipolar disorder and metabolic syndrome: A review. *Journal of Clinical Psychiatry, 67*(7), 1034–1041.

Thompson, W., Kupfer, D., & Fagiolini, A. (2006). Prevalence and clinical correlates of medical comorbidities in patients with bipolar I disorder: Analysis of acute-phase data from a randomized controlled trial. *Journal of Clinical Psychiatry, 67*(5), 783–778.

Thomsen, A., Kvist, T., Andersen, P., & Kessing, L. (2005). Increased risk of affective disorder following hospitalisation with hyperthyroidism—a register-based study. *European Journal of Endocrinology, 152*(4), 535–543.

Torrent, C., Vieta, E., Crespo, J. A., et al. (2004). Barcelona Bipolar Eating Disorder Scale (BEDS), A self-administered scale for eating disturbances in bipolar patients. *Actas Eespañolas de Psiquiatría, 32*(3), 127–131.

Wildes, J., Marcus, M., & Fagiolini A. (2006). Obesity in patients with bipolar disorder: A biopsychosocial-behavioral model. *Journal of Clinical Psychiatry, 67*(6), 904–915.

Winokur, A., March, V., & Mendels, J. (1980). Primary affective disorder in relatives of patients with anorexia nervosa. *American Journal of Psychiatry, 137*(6), 695–698.

Woodside, B. D., & Staab, R. (2006). Management of psychiatric comorbidity in anorexia nervosa and bulimia nervosa. *CNS Drugs, 20*(8), 655–663.

Zimmerman, M., Chelminski, I., & Young, D. (2006). Prevalence and diagnostic correlates of *DSM-IV* pathological gambling in psychiatric outpatients. *Journal of Gambling Studies, July 1.* (Epub ahead of print)

CHAPTER 5

Comorbidity: Alcohol and Drug Abuse

Prevalence of Alcohol and Drug Abuse in Bipolar Patients

Bipolar disorder is the Axis I disorder with the highest risk for coexisting substance use disorder (Goldstein & Levitt, 2006a; Weiss et al., 2004). Patients with child and adolescent-onset, as compared with adult-onset, bipolar illness have a higher rate of substance abuse disorders (Goldstein & Levitt, 2006b).

Substance abuse is one of the most critical comorbid conditions for the clinician to recognize and manage. Unrecognized and untreated alcohol and drug abuse adversely affect the course, treatment and outcome of bipolar disorder, and increase morbidity and the risk of suicide in patients with dysphoric states (Goldberg et al., 1999; Goodwin & Jamison, 1990; Tondo et al., 1999). These effects may be due to the direct effects of alcohol and drugs or to indirect effects on treatment compliance (Strakowski et al., 2000). Recovery from alcohol and drug abuse can be associated with substantial improvements in functioning and quality of life, even in the absence of full recovery from bipolar disorder (Drake et al., 2004) and recovery from substance abuse has been shown to improve the course of bipolar illness (Weiss et al., 2005).

Alcohol and drug abuse are far more common in bipolar patients than in the general population. Grant et al. (2005), in data derived from the 2001–2002 National Epidemiologic Survey on Alcohol and Related Conditions (NESARC) in 43,093 individuals, found that alcohol abuse and dependence had a 12-month prevalence of 23.6 percent and a lifetime prevalence of 58 percent in bipolar I patients, with about two-thirds of that being dependence. The 12-month prevalence of drug abuse and dependence was reported as 12.9 percent and the lifetime prevalence was 37.5 percent in bipolar I patients in the same study. Comparisons to prevalence rates in the general population are shown in Table 5.1.

TABLE 5.1

Prevalence of *DSM-IV* Alcohol and Drug Problems in the General Population and in Bipolar I Patients (12 month/lifetime)

	General Population	BP I Patients
Alcohol	4.65[a]/18.6[b]	23.6[c]/57.9[c]
Drugs	3.81[a]/10.9[b]	12.9[c]/37.5[c]

Notes: Includes both *DSM-IV*-defined dependence and abuse. Figures shown are in percentages.

[a] Data from Grant et al. (2004).

[b] Data from Kessler et al. (2005).

[c] Data from Grant et al. (2005).

The lifetime prevalence of alcohol abuse and dependence in bipolar I patients in the Grant study is considerably higher than the data from the 1990 Epidemiological Catchment Area Study in which 46 percent of bipolar type I patients had lifetime histories of alcohol abuse or dependence (Regier et al., 1990). Minnai et al. (2006) state that there has been an increase of comorbid substance abuse disorders among first admissions for mood disorder, especially in young males, which parallels the increase in the number of bipolar disorder diagnoses over the past quarter of a century. Preisig et al. (2001) studied 226 people with alcoholism and their family members. There was a far greater association between alcoholism and bipolar disorder (odds ratio = 14.5) than between alcoholism and unipolar depression (OR = 1.7).

Just as there is a significantly higher rate of substance abuse in bipolar patients, there is also an increased rate of bipolar illness in substance abusers (Goodwin & Jamison, 1990). Goodwin and Jamison cite studies by Weiss and Mirin (1986), who found that the rate of mood disorders was higher in cocaine abusers than in other types of drug abusers, and Weiss et al. (1988), who found bipolar illness was more common in cocaine abusers than in opiate addicts.

Schuckit et al. (1997) gathered data from 2,713 alcohol-dependent subjects and 919 controls and found alcoholics had higher rates of independent bipolar disorder than controls. The alcoholic patients also had significantly higher rates of anxiety disorders than controls, with most of the difference being accounted for by panic disorder (4.2% vs. 1.0%) and social phobia (3.2% vs. 1.4%). This is an interesting finding in light of more recent findings regarding the comorbidity of bipolar disorder and social phobia and, in particular, the strong relationship between bipolar II disorder and alcohol abuse comorbidity in patients with social phobia, reported by Perugi et al. (2002).

Skinstad and Swain (2001) looked at a sample of 125 males admitted to one of two substance abuse inpatient facilities in Iowa. They found that polysubstance-dependent individuals were more likely to be diagnosed with anxiety disorder or bipolar disorder than were those who were not polysubstance dependent.

Patients with mixed states and rapid cycling may abuse substances more frequently than those with pure manic episodes, although studies on this topic are not consistent (Brieger, 2005).

Alcohol Abuse and Dependence in Patients with Bipolar Disorder

Alcohol abuse and dependence occur more often than any other form of substance abuse in bipolar patients (Goldstein & Levitt, 2006b). Patients generally increase their use of alcohol when in mixed, hypomanic, or manic states (Goodwin & Jamison, 1990). As in the general population, more men than women with bipolar disorder meet diagnostic criteria for lifetime alcoholism. However in a sample of 267 outpatients, the risk of developing alcoholism compared to the general population was substantially higher for bipolar women than bipolar men (Frye et al., 2003) Yet, alcohol abuse in bipolar women is often overlooked (Goldstein & Levitt, 2006c). Conversely, bipolar disorder is often overlooked in alcoholic men (Goldstein & Levitt, 2006c). Albanese et al. (2006), in a retrospective chart review, found 85 out of 295 men who were admitted to an inpatient substance abuse treatment program had previously undiagnosed bipolar disorder. Fourteen percent had received no mood disorder diagnosis at all and 86 percent of these bipolar men had been misdiagnosed as unipolar.

Individuals with comorbid bipolar disorder and alcoholism, particularly women, often have posttraumatic stress disorder. A large number of women with comorbid bipolar disorder and substance abuse have been sexually abused in childhood (Kolodziej et al., 2005). This finding underscores the importance of clinicians taking a trauma history in patients who have comorbid bipolar disorder and alcohol abuse.

There have been five recent studies that have looked at the clinical features and family history of bipolar patients with and without comorbid alcohol abuse and dependence (AUD). These studies have also examined the differences between bipolar patients whose alcoholism preceded the onset of their bipolar illness (sometimes referred to as primary alcoholism) and those in whom the bipolar illness preceded their alcoholism (secondary alcoholism).

Winokur et al. (1995), in a 5-year study of 70 bipolar patients with alcoholism and 161 without, their relatives, and a comparison group of the relatives' acquaintances, found there were no significant differences between the alcoholic and nonalcoholic bipolar patients in family history of alcoholism or affective disorders. The authors concluded that alcoholism could primarily be a complication of bipolar illness in comorbid patients and not determined by a separate familial diathesis. The authors also compared 30 of the bipolar alcoholic patients whose bipolar disorder began first, before the onset of AUD (BF) with 34 patients whose AUD began first, before the onset of bipolar disorder (AF). The patients with AF had significantly fewer episodes of affective disorder during follow-up and took longer to relapse, suggesting to the authors that their type of bipolar illness was less severe and may have required alcoholism to trigger it. Patients with BF had the lowest rate of recovery after 5 years. Relatives of comorbid patients were more likely to have comorbid alcoholism and bipolar disorder than relatives of bipolar only patients, suggesting that comorbid patients may form a unique group with a familial diathesis.

Feinman and Dunner (1996), in a retrospective chart review of 188 bipolar patients, compared patients with bipolar disorder alone to comorbid patients with BF and comorbid patients with AF. They found, counterintuitively, that a family history of AUD was not most common among comorbid patients with AF but rather among those with BF.

Strakowski et al. (2005) looked at 144 subjects with bipolar disorder and AUD who were followed up for up to 5 years, including 27 subjects with AF and 33 subjects with BF and 83 subjects with bipolar disorder only (no AUD). The AF group had a later age at bipolar onset, symptomatically recovered more rapidly, and spent less time in affective episodes. However, this group had a higher total drug-abuse severity score in the month before admission than the other two groups. The BF group spent more time in mixed episodes, had more rapid cycling, and had more time with symptoms of alcohol abuse during follow-up and was also more likely to exhibit symptomatic recurrences of an alcohol-use disorder after recovery than the AF group.

Goldstein and Levitt (2006a) used the 2001–2002 National Epidemiologic Survey on Alcohol and Related Conditions to identify three groups of individuals with lifetime comorbid bipolar I disorder and AUD: Three hundred eleven AF patients, 113 who had the onset of both disorders in the same year (SY), and 233 BF patients. They then looked at between-group differences. This is the only population-based study to report such differences. BF individuals were most likely to experience prolonged manic episodes. Unexpectedly, but in keeping with the finding by Feinman and Dunner (1996), there was no higher rate of family AUD reported in the AF group versus the other two groups. The prevalence of family history of comorbid depression and AUD was greatest among those patients whose bipolar disorder and AUD began in the same year. As with the Winokur study, this suggests comorbid patients may form a unique group with a familial loading for comorbidity. The researchers also found that AUD preceded the onset of bipolar disorder by 12 years in the AF group and bipolar disorder preceded AUD by 6 years in the BF group. Most individuals got treatment for their primary disorder before onset of the second disorder.

Fossey et al. (2006) reported that the course differences and outcome between AF and BF patients were not valid once variations in the age of onset of bipolar disorder were taken into account. That is, early age of onset of bipolar disorder is the factor linked to fewer days of euthymia, more episodes of mania and depression, and a greater history of suicide attempts, not the order of onset of substance abuse or bipolar illness.

These studies have two clinical implications. First, clinicians treating bipolar or alcoholic patients need to monitor these patients for some time for the development of the other disorder. Second, patients with early onset bipolar disorder and substance abuse or patients with the BF pattern, particularly those with mixed symptoms, may need more aggressive treatment given the severity of their bipolar illness and the frequent relapses they experience.

Stimulant Abuse (Cocaine, Methamphetamine, Ecstasy, Caffeine)

Cocaine is derived from the leaves of the coca plant and can be used in several ways: It can be used intranasally (snorted) in the powder form, smoked in a chemically altered form of the powder known as *freebase* or *crack*, or the powder can be dissolved in water and injected into a vein (IV use). Some users also dissolve heroin along with the cocaine in a mixture called a *speedball*. This dangerous combination can lead to respiratory arrest or seizures. Those who smoke cocaine occasionally mix it with liquid phencyclidine (PCP or angel dust). This is called *spacebasing* and leads to both stimulant and hallucinogenic effects. The use of freebase, crack, and especially the practice of spacebasing can lead to extremely agitated, violent behavior.

The clinician should be aware of several issues that make cocaine abuse different from alcohol abuse. First, cocaine addiction, especially to crack, freebase, and IV cocaine, can occur very rapidly and well ahead of the worst financial, occupational, and marital or family problems caused by its use. This may make it hard for the patient and therapist to realize that the cocaine abuse is very serious. Alcoholism can take years and even decades to develop, with repeated adverse consequences along the way making it easier to diagnose. Second, unlike alcohol, cravings for cocaine are typically very intense after a week or so of abstinence from intranasal use and shortly after the cessation of freebase or crack use. The patient must be told to expect these cravings and must learn tools for handling them ahead of time in order to have the best chance of avoiding relapse.

It takes about 5 minutes to feel the effects from snorting cocaine. The high lasts roughly 20 minutes or so, after which the user may feel depressed and irritable. It takes only 10 seconds or so to feel the effects from smoking freebase or crack. The high is very intense, but lasts, at the most, 5 minutes. The crash is about as abrupt and intense as the high. IV cocaine takes about a half a minute or so to take effect. The high and the crash are just about as intense as with freebase or crack. The high from IV cocaine typically wears off in 10 minutes or less.

The longing for the euphoric high frequently leads cocaine smokers and IV users to go on binges that last hours or days. Snorting cocaine can lead to addiction, as well, just not as rapidly. In all likelihood, fewer powder users become addicted to cocaine than smokers or IV users.

Cocaine abuse can mimic bipolar disorder, but some studies have indicated that a sizable minority of cocaine abusers have autonomous mood disorders, including bipolar disorder (Albanese et al., 2006; Camacho & Akiskal, 2005; Rosenblum et al., 1999). In the Albanese et al. (2006) study cited in the section on alcohol abuse, 38 percent of the 42 bipolar patients admitted to an in-patient substance abuse treatment program had abused cocaine. It is important for substance abuse treatment professionals to keep this in mind. Just as substance abuse tends to be underdiagnosed by mental health professionals, psychiatric disorders tend to be overlooked by clinicians who treat substance abusers.

There is some evidence that bipolar patients prefer stimulant drugs over other classes of drugs such as opiates (Winokur et al., 1998). Camacho and Akiskal (2005) discussed a possible explanation for this. They proposed that bipolar patients and stimulant abusers may be part of the same spectrum of illness. The authors reported that many of the stimulant-abusing bipolar patients they had studied had premorbid cyclothymic and hyperthymic traits, a family history of bipolar disorder, and subthreshold bipolar signs and symptoms during long periods of sobriety. Other researchers have reported on this phenomenon in the past. Lemere and Smith (1990) noted that 13 percent of 292 private patients treated for cocaine abuse had hypomanic "personality" traits. "This subgroup," they wrote, "had been reasonably well adjusted, fun-loving and action oriented extroverts before their addiction. The rush and lifestyle of cocaine fit the imperatives of their personality" (p. 575). Weiss et al. (1988) found cyclothymia in 11.4 percent of 149 hospitalized cocaine abusers compared to cyclothymia in only 2.7 percent of 293 other drug abusers.

Bipolar patients most often abuse cocaine in the manic phase of their illness. They probably do so for several reasons: one may be that judgment deteriorates and impulsive risk-taking increases during the manic phase. Camacho and Akiskal (2005) point out another possible reason: "to control or maintain a subthreshold rewarding mood condition" (p. 217), that is, to enhance and prolong hypomanic states and ward off depression. Stimulants, of course, as effective as they may be in controlling mood in the short run, will destabilize the long-term course of the illness.

A significant number of cocaine-abusing patients, especially women, have experienced traumatic life events and have posttraumatic stress disorder (PTSD). Najavits et al. (2003) reported that nearly 11 percent of 558 cocaine-abusing patients (75% of whom were male) met criteria for PTSD. Three times as many women as men had PTSD. Irritability was a prominent symptom of these patients' PTSD.

Methamphetamine (MA), a powerful and powerfully addicting central nervous system stimulant that can mimic the manic phase of bipolar illness, is called *meth* or *speed* on the street. It can produce euphoria and increased energy, confidence, and libido but also cause psychosis. Some individuals develop psychosis rather easily, while others can use MA for long periods and not become psychotic. Premorbid schizoid/schizotypal personality may predispose MA users to develop psychosis (Chen et al., 2003). Chen et al. (2005) found that the relatives of MA users with a lifetime diagnosis of MA psychosis had a significantly higher risk for schizophrenia than the relatives of patients who never became psychotic. Methamphetamine can also cause hostile, aggressive, and violent behavior. In a study of 106 individuals drawn from an unspecified population, Sommers et al. (2006), found that 34.9 percent had committed violence while under the influence of MA. Booth et al. (2006) reported that MA users in his sample (706 recent, not-in-treatment, adult cocaine and MA users living in rural Ohio, Arkansas, and Kentucky) were more likely to have been arrested compared with cocaine-only users.

Methamphetamine withdrawal can mimic bipolar depression and is characterized by increased sleeping and eating, anhedonia, irritability, and poor concentration (McGregor et al., 2005; Newton et al., 2004). The severity of withdrawal symptoms begins to decline within 24 hours of last use. Most withdrawal symptoms abate after a week, although low-grade symptoms can continue for another 2 weeks or so (McGregor et al., 2005).

Methamphetamine is chemically related to amphetamine, but its effects on the central nervous system are greater. It is generally smoked, injected, or snorted. Methamphetamine hydrochloride, in clear chunky crystals, is the form that is smoked. It is referred to as *ice* or *crystal*. As with cocaine, when smoked or injected, MA produces an immediate, powerful, and extremely pleasurable high. The effect may last only a few minutes. Methamphetamine is more addictive when smoked or injected than when snorted. Methamphetamine can also be ingested orally in a method called *parachuting* or *body-stuffing*. The user places the MA in a plastic bag, pokes holes in the bag, and then swallows it. Many MA users use a wide variety of other drugs, including crack cocaine, before starting use of MA (Booth et al., 2006; Brecht et al., 2006). The combined MA/cocaine users in the Booth study reported significantly greater use of alcohol and other drugs, including marijuana and nonprescribed opiates and tranquilizers, and reported significantly higher psychological distress.

Methamphetamine abuse, once isolated to urban areas on the West Coast, has spread into rural areas of the Midwest and the southern United States. It is a growing national problem. An estimated 12.3 million Americans (5.2% of the U.S. population) have tried MA at some time in their lives (www.samhsa.gov). In 2004, 6.2 percent of high school seniors had reported lifetime use of MA (www.drugabuse.gov). Use of MA may be considerably higher in urban gay and bisexual men (Shoptaw, 2006), and is much higher among youth in treatment for substance abuse than in the general population. In a sample of 782 such individuals, roughly 30 percent had used MA (Hopfer et al., 2006). No data on the incidence of MA abuse in bipolar patients or psychiatric patients could be located although

Shoptaw et al. (2003) reported that 82 of 155 methamphetamine-dependent, gay and bisexual men at an outpatient drug abuse treatment program met criteria for lifetime depressive disorders.

Ecstasy is a chemical derivative of MA, first synthesized by the German pharmaceutical company Merck in 1912 that has both stimulant and psychedelic properties. Past-year use in 2004 was estimated at 3.1 percent of the population (www.samhsa.gov). Sexual arousal/increased sensual awareness, confused thought, visual effects/changes in visual perception, sleeplessness, and decreased appetite were reported across five or more investigations of subjective effects of the drug (Baylen & Rosenberg, 2006).

Using data from the 2001 National Survey on Drug Use and Health, Martins et al. (2006) discovered that recent-onset ecstasy use was significantly more likely to occur among adolescents and adults (18–34 years old) who engaged in nonviolent deviant behaviors such as selling illegal drugs and stealing. Adults who had past-year symptoms of depression and panic were twice as likely to be recent-onset ecstasy users as compared with those without such past-year symptoms.

Caffeine has been reported to cause mania in vulnerable individuals (Machado-Vieira et al., 2001; Ogawa & Ueki, 2003). Experts have recommended that bipolar patients strictly avoid caffeine (Akiskal & Akiskal, 2006).

Marijuana

The prevalence of 12-month and lifetime *DSM-IV* cannabis abuse in the general population has been reported to be 1.1 and 7.2 percent, respectively. The corresponding rates of cannabis dependence have been reported as 0.3 and 1.3 percent (Stinson et al., 2006). Data on the prevalence of marijuana abuse and dependence in bipolar patients could not be located, but researchers seem to agree that it is common and higher than that found in the general population (Henquet et al., 2006). Salloum et al. (2005a) reported that among 52 bipolar alcoholics treated with divalproex, 48 percent reported marijuana abuse. Those with co-occurring marijuana abuse had more severe alcohol and other drug use and were significantly more likely to present in the manic phase.

In low doses, the psychoactive cannabinoid compound in marijuana, delta-9-tetrahydrocannabinol (THC or cannabis), produces sedation and a feeling of well-being that many agitated bipolar patients find medicinal. There is evidence to suggest that the potency of marijuana products (the THC content) has increased over at least the last decade (Compton et al., 2004).

The brain has an endogenous cannabinoid system (Mackie & Stella, 2006). Some cannabinoid receptors are located in the amygdala, a part of the limbic system of the brain responsible for emotion and motivation (Mackie, 2005). Gruber et al. (1996), based on a review of the literature and a case series of five individuals, believed there was clear evidence that cannabis had an antidepressant effect. Grinspoon and Bakalar (1998) reported several patients with bipolar illness who found cannabis had mood-stabilizing and antidepressant properties. Ashton et al. (2005), based on patient reports and a review of the literature, proposed that synthetic cannabinoids might have therapeutic potential in patients with bipolar illness and advocated controlled trials of the compounds in these patients. Many studies on cannabinoids have suggested that they may provide protection against several neurodegenerative disorders (Bahr et al., 2006).

Unfortunately, frequent marijuana use can lead to lethargy, lack of motivation, and cognitive impairments including problems in memory, attention, concentration, and mental efficiency. Marijuana is not a performance-enhancing drug. This can obviously be a major problem for young patients with bipolar depression, who are typically quite lethargic and unmotivated, as well as cognitively impaired from their bipolar illness. The combined effects of bipolar illness and marijuana use can derail a youngster's psychosocial development and academic success, and interfere with the formulation and implementation of life goals. Hall (2006), based on a search of the literature for large-scale longitudinal studies of representative samples of adolescents and young adults conducted in developed societies over the past 20 years, reported consistent evidence that cannabis dependence in young people predicts increased risks of underperforming in school. Strakowski et al. (2007) reported that cannabis use was associated with more time in affective episodes and with rapid cycling in 144 bipolar patients followed over 5 years.

High doses of cannabis can have hallucinogenic effects and lead to severe anxiety and paranoia. Even modest doses of cannabis may contribute to the development of psychotic symptoms in vulnerable individuals (Henquet et al., 2005; Rottanburg et al., 1982; van Os et al., 2002). More specifically, Henquet et al. (2006), in a longitudinal, population-based study of 4,815 individuals aged 18 to 64 years in the Netherlands, found that the use of cannabis nearly tripled the risk for developing manic symptoms during 1- and 3-year follow-up. Triggering of full-blown bipolar disorder may be more likely in those individuals with childhood signs of cyclothymic, hyperthymic, or depressive temperament.

Contrary to popular opinion, chronic use can lead to a dependence syndrome characterized by tolerance and symptoms of withdrawal (agitation, irritability, and sleep disturbance; Nocon et al., 2006).

Prescription Drug Abuse

Prescription drug abuse is pervasive and highly comorbid with other psychiatric disorders, yet often receives little clinical attention (Huang et al., 2006). Stimulant misuse in the United States (particularly among youth) involves prescription drugs more often than methamphetamine (Kroutil et al., 2006). Using data derived from the National Epidemiologic Survey on Alcohol and Related Conditions, Huang and his colleagues determined that lifetime prevalences of nonprescribed use of sedatives, tranquilizers, opioids, and amphetamines were

4.1, 3.4, 4.7, and 4.7 percent, respectively. Rates of abuse and/or dependence on these substances were 1.1, 1.0, 1.4, and 2.0 percent, respectively.

Eighty-seven percent of 143 ecstasy users in Miami (50% of the sample was Hispanic), recruited through nightclub and college campus outreach and through respondent referrals, abused prescription drugs (Kurtz et al., 2005). Alprazolam (Xanax) was abused by 57 percent of these individuals, oxycodone (Percodan) by 36 percent, hydrocodone (Norco) by 32 percent, and diazepam (Valium) by 30 percent. Prescription drug abusers were more likely to report polydrug use, drug treatment histories, risky drug use behaviors, and symptoms of depression.

Benzodiazepine drugs such as Xanax or Ativan have a high abuse potential. Therapists working with alcohol and drug-abusing bipolar patients, particularly young patients, need to ask these patients about their use of prescription amphetamines, narcotics, and benzodiazepines. Benzodiazepines are frequently, and mistakenly, prescribed to bipolar patients with substance use disorders (Brunette et al., 2003).

Identifying Alcohol-Abusing Patients in Mental Health Practice Settings

Most therapists have not been trained to detect alcohol abuse in their patients and many prefer not to deal with individuals who have substance abuse problems. However, given the frequency with which bipolar patients abuse alcohol, clinicians interested in working with bipolar patients must have at least a basic understanding of how to identify and manage patients who abuse alcohol. (In similar fashion, given the frequency with which alcohol and drug abusers have autonomous bipolar spectrum illnesses, it is imperative that substance abuse treatment professionals learn how to detect these disorders in their patients. Unrecognized and untreated bipolar disorders increase the likelihood of relapse.)

Clinicians understand that individuals seeking mental health services are not likely to spontaneously discuss their use of alcohol and drugs, yet they struggle with how to approach the issue with their patients and how to best sort out social drinking from problem drinking. Many clinicians seem to believe that asking the patient about the quantity and frequency of their alcohol use is the way to proceed. Indeed, several articles in the literature recommend asking one, two, or three specific questions about quantity and frequency in order to identify heavy, at-risk drinkers (Brown et al., 1997; Gordon et al., 2001; Williams & Vinson, 2001). While such questions may be appropriate at some point in an evaluation, there are a number of problems with this approach.

First, while frequent, heavy drinking or repeated drunkenness are risk factors for developing alcohol abuse, they do not in themselves constitute alcohol abuse. Winston Churchill drank a tremendous amount yet the Churchill Center states that "no colleague who can be taken seriously ever reports seeing Churchill the worse for drink" (www.winstonchurchill.org). Thus Churchill's famous quip, "I have taken more out of alcohol than alcohol has taken out of me." Conversely, even so-called safe or normal levels of drinking (1 to 2 drinks per day) can be associated with problem drinking (Buchsbaum et al., 1995). This is especially the case with patients suffering from bipolar disorder, whose illness may be adversely affected by even modest levels of alcohol intake (Goldstein, Diamantouros, et al., 2006).

Second, problem drinkers will either lie about the amount they drink or substantially underestimate it. All addictions are lying diseases. That is, it is normal for patients with addictions to lie about the quantity and frequency of their drinking and drug use in order to hide their addiction and the problems associated with it. A clinician should always probe for occult alcohol and drug abuse in any patient with bipolar disorder,

Third, questions about quantity and frequency may not be the best questions with which to start an evaluation. There is some evidence that starting an evaluation with these questions makes it less likely the patient will acknowledge problems associated with his or her drinking (Steinweg & Worth, 1993). Such questions tend to immediately put the patient on the defensive.

Fourth, many people with problem drinking share the misconception with clinicians that alcoholism is defined by quantity and frequency of drinking. They focus on the fact they do not drink often or much or that they can go for days at a time without drinking to convince themselves and others they do not have a problem with alcohol. Focusing on questions of quantity and frequency only tends to cement these misconceptions.

Most important, focusing on quantity and frequency provides no starting point for effective intervention. It does not help increase the patient's motivation to stop drinking. What motivates people to change drinking habits is an awareness of the pain it is causing them and the people they care about.

Clinicians will have an easier time determining whether a patient has a problem with alcohol if they avoid the categorical approach to diagnosis, that is, if they avoid trying to decide whether someone is or is not alcoholic (Saha et al., 2006). Problems caused by the use of alcohol lie on a continuum from none at one end to catastrophic (loss of a marriage, a job, a license, or a liver) at the other. A clinician will not need a great deal of expertise in deciding how to classify someone at either end of the continuum. "The exact point at which minimal alcohol abuse (for example, being arrested once for drunken driving)," writes Vaillant (1995), "merits the label of alcoholism (a pattern of maladaptive alcohol use that malignantly leads to multiple alcohol-related problems) will always be as uncertain as where in the spectrum yellow becomes green" (p. 377).

When working with patients in outpatient mental health treatment settings, clinicians will see many patients whose use of alcohol has not grossly impaired their functioning. In addition, many patients will not have *entirely* lost control of their ability to regulate their alcohol intake. Nevertheless, their use of alcohol can be labeled problematic if they continue to drink in spite of repeated (if only intermittent) problems caused by their drinking. Following is an example of an individual with this type of problem drinking.

John is a 44-year-old, married, father of three children who has worked for 12 years as an accountant. He works 5 or 6 days a week, has been married for many years, has a number of friends, and has been involved, at times, in local political campaigns and charity work.

One night after work, he had four drinks before and with dinner. He got irritated with his wife when she started a discussion about money, lost his temper, and called her a degrading name. She said, as she had several times before during their marriage, that he ought to think about not drinking so much. He complained that if she just quit bugging him about money all the time, he wouldn't get so nasty and maybe would not drink so much. But, he apologized the next morning for his crude insult and decided he would cut back on the amount he drank. He was successful at this for a number of months. His wife was pleased that her husband seemed to have come to his senses.

Then, one night at an office party, he decided it was okay, on this one special occasion, to have more than two drinks. He ended up embarrassing himself and his wife by flirting openly with a female coworker. His wife was surprised, angered, and discouraged that her husband's drinking had once again caused a problem. When she complained she was getting tired of these problems, John got angry. He scowled and said that she was just overly sensitive because her father was an alcoholic. After all, he argued, hadn't he gone for many months without having any problems? The next morning, however, he apologized and said he would stop drinking to prove he did not have a problem.

John kept his word for about 5 months without much trouble at all. He found that he missed having a drink at times but that he did not crave it in any way. He felt reassured that he could go for so long without a drink and believed he had learned his lesson. He was tired of being the only one drinking soda at business affairs and social events, so he started having an occasional drink with business dinners. His wife, although somewhat nervous, felt reassured that her husband could not possibly have a drinking problem if he had gone so long without drinking. Maybe she had been too sensitive after all. Besides, she missed the fun they had had in the past sharing a bottle of wine over dinner.

For a few months, John drank infrequently, moderately, and without incident. But, over time, his wife noticed that his drinking was returning to the kind of pattern that had led to problems in the past. She pointed this out to him one night after he had had a few drinks at home and he again got irritated. But he managed to calm himself, said that he did not want to do anything to hurt her, and reassured her he had things under control. Work had been a bit stressful lately and he found a few drinks with dinner relaxed him. She made a sarcastic remark about him being so relaxed lately that he had started falling asleep in front of the TV after having drinks.

A few months later, John got arrested for a DUI.

Clearly, the fact that John does not drink often or much and is able to go for long periods without drinking is not critical to determining the presence of a drinking problem. In fact, many people with addictions can "go on the wagon" for periods of time with little difficulty. "Stopping smoking is so easy," Mark Twain said, "I did it 20 times." John can be classified as an alcohol abuser primarily because he is unable to *consistently* control his drinking and because he continues drinking even though doing so has *repeatedly* lead to a variety of problems (Vaillant, 1995). Table 5.2 lists the defining characteristics of alcohol and drug abuse.

The more difficulty the person has exercising control, the more problems associated with drinking (the more numerous and frequent and serious they are) and the more focused on drinking they have become, the more serious the drinking problem. Most problems caused by alcohol abuse will be sins of commission: becoming nasty, saying or doing embarrassing things, driving while intoxicated. Other problems may be relatively unobtrusive but still problematic: becoming withdrawn, depressed, emotionally unavailable, or falling asleep after drinking.

TABLE 5.2

Alcohol and Drug Abuse: Defining Characteristics

- Difficulty *consistently* controlling use of alcohol or drugs
- *Repeated* adverse consequences associated with use
- *Continued* use despite repeated adverse consequences
- A narrowing of interests and increasing focus on alcohol or drugs

Some patients with bipolar disorder, who drink very infrequently, can surprise family and clinicians alike with episodes of very heavy drinking that generally do not lead to any problems. Lejoyeux (2005), in discussing the many and varied presentations of bipolar illness, wrote: "rarely, the mask of a bipolar illness is translated into behaviors such as intermittent alcohol abuse. The consummation of alcohol is sudden and paroxysmal. It is a type of dipsomania" (p. 507). *Most* of these episodes of drunkenness, although they may be unwise and unhealthy, do not constitute alcohol abuse if they are not associated with repeated adverse consequences. They may be an expression of the waxing and waning of impulse control problems and the need for sensation-seeking characteristic of bipolar disorder.

The simplest way to begin checking for the presence of problems associated with alcohol use in adults is to ask the patient the four CAGE (Buchsbaum et al., 1991), four RAPS (Cheripitel, 2002), or two TICS (Brown et al., 1997) questions. TICS stands for Two-Item Conjoint Screen. Each letter of the CAGE and RAPS tests represents a question to ask a patient to help determine if he or she has a drinking problem. None of the questions in the CAGE or TICS are about quantity or frequency of alcohol use. Only one question in the RAPS is an indirect measure of heavy drinking. Many of the questions in these screening tools provide a basis for the clinician to discuss problems caused by drinking (Aertgeerts et al., 2002).

CAGE stands for the following: attempts the individual makes to **C**ut down or quit drinking; **A**nnoyance with others about the comments they make about the individual's drinking (or behavior while consuming alcohol); **G**uilt or regret over things said or done while drinking; and **E**ye opener—having a drink first thing in the morning to deal with withdrawal symptoms. One "yes" answer suggests the individual may have a drinking problem. Two or more "yes" answers indicate the individual has a drinking problem. Although no research on the use of the CAGE in a bipolar population could be located, a study on its use in schizophrenic patients indicated it could be reliably used to diagnose alcohol use disorders in this population (Dervaux et al., 2006).

RAPS questions are as follows: Have you felt guilty after drinking (**R**emorse)? Have you not remembered things you said or did after drinking (**A**mnesia)? Have you failed to do what was normally expected after drinking (**P**erform)? Have you had a morning drink (**S**tarter)? Sensitivity for alcohol dependence and alcohol abuse have been reported as 93 percent and 55 percent, respectively, with one positive answer to RAPS questions (Cherpitel, 2002). Data from a 2003 study suggest the RAPS performs well for identifying alcohol dependence and alcohol abuse in African-American and Hispanic individuals seen in inner-city hospital emergency rooms (Cherpitel & Barzagan, 2003).

The two TICS questions are: In the last year, have you ever drunk or used drugs more than you meant to? Have you felt you wanted or needed to cut down on your drinking or drug use in the last year? The TICS detected current substance use disorders with nearly 80 percent sensitivity (Brown et al., 1997).

One "yes" answer to the CAGE has been found to have an 80 to 85 percent sensitivity in identifying alcohol abusers (Aertgeerts et al., 2002; Bush et al., 1987). However, its sensitivity has often been reported as considerably lower when compared to other instruments such as the RAPS (Cherpitel, 2002) or the Alcohol Use Disorders Identification Test (AUDIT), a 10-question screening tool that includes questions about quantity and frequency of use in addition to questions about drinking-related problems and behaviors (Bradley et al., 1998).

These discrepancies may be due, in part, to testing of the instruments on different populations and in different settings or because of differences in administration of the test. Steinweg and Worth (1993), for instance, reported that the CAGE correctly identified only 32 percent of alcoholics when it was given after questions about quantity and frequency of alcohol use compared to a 95 percent accuracy rate with two yes answers when it was introduced "by a simple open-ended question" (p. 520). As a practical matter, clinicians need not concern themselves with which instrument is the best since, as part of a comprehensive evaluation, they will likely ask all the questions on the tests and more. The results of a single screening test should never be relied upon to make a diagnosis of alcohol abuse.

Another instrument clinicians can consider using is the Substance Abuse Subtle Screening Inventory (SASSI; Lazowski et al., 1998). The SASSI consists of 67 true-false questions and a number of additional "face-valid" questions related to alcohol and drug use. It takes 15 minutes to half an hour to complete. The advantages of the test are that it is highly accurate in identifying both alcohol and drug *dependence*, it measures how open the respondent is being, and whether defensiveness is related to attempts to conceal substance abuse or not. The disadvantage of the test is that it is not particularly useful in identifying patients with alcohol or drug *abuse*. Elevations on some of the scales, however, can signal the possibility of such a problem.

Physicians should know that measures of single, traditional biological markers for heavy alcohol consumption, including the mean corpuscular volume, gamma-glutamyl transpeptidase value, and liver transaminase levels, have been found to be very insensitive markers for alcohol abuse compared to a single positive answer on the CAGE (Bush et al., 1987). A relatively new biological marker, carbohydrate-deficient transferrin (CDT), when used alone and certainly in combination with gamma-glutamyltransferase (GGT), may be superior to traditional, single markers at identifying heavy drinking, at least in young adults. It may also offer a reasonable degree of sensitivity in detecting current alcohol abuse (Hietala et al., 2006; Hock et al., 2005; Yersin et al., 1995). The CAGE likely has greater sensitivity to alcohol abuse than the CDT alone (Zeirau et al., 2005). Physicians should consider using the combination of GGT and CDT as a supplement to screening tools and clinician interviews rather than as substitutes for them. Doing so will increase the chances of accurately diagnosing alcohol abuse and allow the physician to more easily transition into a discussion of the problems alcohol use is causing (Aertgeerts et al., 2002; Berner et al., 2006).

Table 5.3 lists questions clinicians can consider asking when evaluating patients for alcohol abuse. Some questions could arguably be placed in other categories.

The clinician should pay attention not only to the patient's answers to questions, but to the patient's style of answering questions, as well. Does he or she give quick, straightforward answers to questions or does he or she become irritated, defensive, or evasive? The latter suggests he or she may have an alcohol problem.

Experts usually advise seeking information about a person's drinking from a spouse or family member to help circumvent the patient's tendency to minimize or lie about his or her use and its consequences. Interestingly, however, Weiss et al. (2000), collected collateral information on 132 occasions for 32 bipolar substance-abusing patients and found a 75 percent level of agreement between collateral reports and self-report and urine screen data. In only three instances did collateral informants report substance use for patients who denied use and who had negative urine screens for drugs of abuse. Although several explanations for these findings are possible, the results would seem to suggest that "obtaining collateral informant data when studying this population may be of limited value" (p. 369).

TABLE 5.3

Questions to Detect Alcohol Abuse

A. Questions related to problems with control of intake:

Have you ever drunk and driven with your kids in the car?

Do you sometimes drink when you feel upset, disappointed, pressured, or angry with a spouse or boss?

Can you usually find good reasons for drinking heavily?

How often have you had more to drink than you intended to?

Have you ever decided to drink only on weekends or special occasions or have you ever switched from distilled spirits to beer?

How often have you noticed that you would like to continue drinking when friends say they are ready to quit for the night?

Have you ever quit or cut down on your drinking or thought about doing so?

If so, have you later started drinking again?

B. Questions related to adverse consequences and continued use:

Have you ever felt guilty about your drinking?

Have you ever said or done anything when you were drinking that you later regretted?

Have others ever annoyed you with comments about your drinking?

Has anyone ever complained you got nasty, annoying, embarrassing, or withdrawn while drinking?

Have you ever been late to work or missed work because of your drinking?

How often have you gone to work with a hangover?

Have you ever passed out or fallen asleep when with your family or friends?

Have you ever not come home to your husband/wife or family when expected while drinking?

Have you ever failed to get up in the morning to be with friends, spouse, or your children because you had been drinking the night before?

Do you have medical problems that are affected by drinking (hypertension, gastritis, ulcers, elevated liver enzymes)?

Have you ever been arrested, ticketed, or questioned by the police for alcohol-related behavior (not just DWI, but drunk and disorderly, disorderly conduct, harassment, public intoxication, public urination, domestic violence)?

Have you ever had an accident, a personal injury, or required emergency medical attention for any drinking-related injury?

TABLE 5.3 (*continued*)

C. Questions related to preoccupation and a narrowing of interests:

Do you sometimes have drinks before a party to get a head start?

Have you ever tried to have drinks without others knowing about it?

Have you ever hidden a supply of alcohol?

Have you looked forward to drinking?

Do most of the patient's recreational activities center on alcohol use?

Have you ever avoided family members or others when you are drinking?

Have there been occasions when you have been uncomfortable that alcohol was not available?

Have you been in a hurry to get that first drink?

Have you skipped meals when drinking?

D. Questions related to tolerance and withdrawal:

Have you noticed you need to drink more than before to get the same effect?

How often have you had the shakes after a night of drinking?

Have often have you taken a little drink in the morning to calm your nerves?

How many times have you had trouble remembering things after a night of drinking?

E. Factors associated with alcohol abuse:

Is there a family history of relatives getting nasty, embarrassing, or uncomfortable to be around because of drinking? (Vaillant, 1995)

Was the patient aggressive as a child or adolescent or did he or she have significant behavior problems? (Brook et al., 1996; Vaillant, 1995)

Did the patient have a low level of response to alcohol as a youth? (Hinckers et al., 2006; Schuckit, 1994; Schuckit et al., 2006)

Does the patient have any of the following temperamental traits: impulsiveness (Liraud & Verdoux, 2000), sensation or novelty seeking (Basiaux et al., 2001), readiness to irritability, aggressiveness, insistence on having one's own way (Giancola, 2002a, 2002b, 2004)?

Does the patient spend time with other heavy or problem drinkers?

Management of Patients with Substance Abuse

Mental health professionals often have an aversion to working with substance-abusing patients. Most have not been trained in substance-abuse counseling, generally feel ill equipped to deal with substance abusers, and believe working with them is frustrating and unrewarding. The work is frustrating, however, only if a clinician expects or insists that a patient immediately give up use of alcohol

TABLE 5.4

Stages of Change

- Precontemplation
- Contemplation
- Preparation
- Action
- Maintenance

or drugs when it becomes obvious to the clinician that the use is problematic. No treatment program and no amount of forceful breaching of a patient's denial has the power to get a patient to commit to abstinence at any one point in time (Vaillant, 1995).

People are obviously not willing or easily able to change bad habits just because they know they should or someone else tells them they should. It is no different with habitual and destructive use of alcohol and drugs. Changing a bad habit is a process, not an event and it can take years to accomplish. Prochaska et al. (1994) have found that individuals go through a process of change when attempting to alter habits. Table 5.4 shows a list of the stages of change people go through in altering any undesirable habit.

Precontemplation is the stage in which a person who abuses alcohol or drugs sees no reason for and has no desire to stop drinking or using drugs. In fact, continued use is associated in his or her mind with more pluses than minuses. Pleasure outweighs pain. Alternatively, perhaps the pain the alcohol or drug use is causing is kept out of conscious awareness or is minimized.

Contemplation is the stage in which someone who abuses alcohol becomes aware, for a time, of the problems his or her drinking has caused. He or she may think about cutting down on or limiting his or her drinking in some way. However, like John, these individuals are not fully convinced of the need to stop drinking nor do they wholeheartedly want to stop drinking. They are not fully aware of or perhaps will not let themselves be fully aware of how their use of alcohol has lead to a pattern of problems. Perhaps memories of each bad incident that occurred as a result of drinking are kept apart, dissociated into compartments that are not linked up with each other. Sometimes the destructive impact of alcohol use is minimized ("What I said wasn't that horrible") or rationalized ("My wife was really being hard on me and deserved a bit of what she got"). Sometimes the memory of the pain, regret, or embarrassment of what was said or done while drinking simply fades. Alcoholics Anonymous members refer to people in these stages of change as "sincerely deluded."

Alcoholics in the contemplation stage are conflicted, at war with themselves about the extent of the problem and what needs to be done. It is at this stage that patients will often attempt to draw spouses or therapists into arguments about their drinking. It is easier to argue with someone else and get him or her to play the role of the critic than it is to argue with your own internal critic.

Table 5.5 lists beliefs and attitudes of patients in the precontemplation and contemplation stages of change.

The other stages of change are *preparation,* in which the patient makes a decision to stop using alcohol and drugs and gets ready to take steps to change; *action,*

TABLE 5.5

Beliefs of Patients in Precontemplation and Contemplation Stages of Change

Patients believe drinking is not a problem because they:

- don't drink a lot or often
- don't crave a drink
- can go for periods of time without drinking
- can drink moderately at times without adverse consequences
- minimize the extent or importance of problems associated with drinking
- believe they drink because of problems, not that drinking causes problems
- do not see that drinking-related problems are becoming repetitive
- believe drinking and drug use are associated with more pros than cons
- are frightened about giving up drinking or pessimistic about their ability to do so
- have no commitment to or perceived need for abstinence or 12-step meetings

in which the person actually takes steps, such as going to Alcoholics Anonymous meetings, to achieve change; and *maintenance,* in which the patient takes steps to prevent relapse.

These stages of change could be compressed into three smaller ones: (a) Whether to quit, (b) How to quit, (c) How to stay sober. Many patients who seek help from mental health professionals for relationship, emotional, or psychiatric problems who also have some degree of alcohol or drug abuse are in the "Whether to quit" stage.

It makes no sense to expect these patients to acknowledge they are addicts, commit to abstinence, and join a 12-step program—a program designed to teach people how to quit and stay sober. Patients cannot be forced to skip past the contemplation and preparation stages of change. Therapists who try to do so will get frustrated and alienate their patients. A mental health clinician does not need to and should not attempt to provide substance abuse treatment (how to quit and how to stay sober) when patients do not believe they need to quit. Contrary to what managed care companies insist upon, individual therapy is *exactly* where alcohol and drug abusers belong if they are in the "Whether to quit" stage, provided, that is, that therapists do not ignore the substance abuse or think that it will go away if they help resolve psychopathology.

How then does a therapist work with a patient who is in the contemplation stage? "We shall sooner have the fowl," said Abraham Lincoln, "by hatching the egg than by smashing it." So, rather than using confrontation to get the alcoholic or addict to change, therapists need to work on the simpler and less frustrating

TABLE 5.6

Major Principles of Motivational Interviewing

Expressing empathy: Demonstrating understanding of the patient's perspective through reflective listening.

Developing discrepancy: Helping patients become aware of how their use of alcohol and drugs is getting in the way of achieving life goals.

Avoiding argumentation: Not pushing the patient to accept your perspective.

Rolling with resistance: Meeting patients' disagreement, minimization, or denial of problems with reflection and other techniques to avoid argumentation.

Supporting self-efficacy: Acknowledging that the patient decides whether and what changes will be made.

Source: From Miller and Rollnick (2002).

process of helping patients move from precontemplation or contemplation to later stages of change.

For a comprehensive review of one way this might be accomplished, the reader is referred to Miller and Rollnick's (2002) work titled *Motivational Interviewing: Preparing People to Change.* Their approach is to gradually help patients realize and express their concerns about the problems alcohol and drug use are causing and how such use is getting in the way of achieving their goals. Motivation to change addictive behavior will begin to develop when the substance abuser realizes that change will serve his or her self-interest. Table 5.6 lists Miller and Rollnick's main principles for conducting motivational interviewing:

Vaillant (2003) reported the results of a 60-year prospective study on the course of alcoholism in a group of socially disadvantaged men from inner-city Boston and a group of Harvard University graduates. He drew a number of conclusions about how to help alcoholic individuals from this research and from the deep wisdom that comes from a lifetime of professional experience with patients. He advocates a similar, although perhaps somewhat more direct, approach to that of Miller and Rollnick. Following are some of his suggestions for "would-be helpers" (Vaillant, 1995).

> The task is to convince the patient not that he or she is alcoholic, but that he or she is a decent person who has an insidious disease, a disease that is a primary *cause* of distress. Patients need to be Socratically taught that alcohol is foe, not friend. . . (p. 365)
> . . . the [would-be helper needs] continuously to review with the patient the objective evidence [of the variety of adverse consequences that are associated with his alcohol abuse] in order to remind the patient that his use of alcohol is putting him out of and not in control. The patient's anger at such confrontations should be construed as a manifestation of anxiety or cognitive dissonance, not lack of gratitude or motivation. (pp. 366–367)

Only when the doctor, family, and patient are all agreed that the patient has an illness that requires treatment can . . . treatment begin. (p. 367)

When a would-be helper acknowledges that recovery from alcoholism is the patient's own responsibility and that he is as powerless over another's alcoholism as he is over another's measles, the helper does not render himself useless. (p. 373)

If clinicians are able to get patients to the point where they are motivated to stop their drinking, some may do so on their own. Vaillant (1995) points out that not all alcoholics require professional help. In fact, most people stop on their own or with the help of 12-step or specialized "double-trouble" meetings. Double-trouble meetings are 12-step meetings set up by and for substance abusers with psychiatric disorders. Some alcoholics will require intensive outpatient or inpatient treatment in special dual-diagnosis programs. Many patients may need the therapist's help in getting to the stage where they are ready to accept help—just as they needed help in acknowledging the need to stop drinking.

Clinicians must realize that patients do not move steadily forward through the stages of change. They often enter the preparation and action stages only to fall back into the contemplation stage, once again wondering if they really need to quit for good or trying to engage in controlled use of alcohol. Multiple relapses are the rule. Good outcomes are still possible even after many slips and falls.

This is important information for the therapist to convey to patients who relapse. It may help head off what is referred to as the abstinence violation effect (Marlatt & Gordon, 1985), a process wherein a patient erroneously attributes relapse to immutable personal characteristics (e.g., weakness of character) and ends up feeling so ashamed and demoralized that he or she drinks or uses even more. The therapist needs to help the patient devise a less malignant explanation: the patient was doing certain things that were best to avoid (e.g., hanging around others who drink or use drugs) or was not doing things that were critical to do when trying to stay sober (calling someone rather than trying to tough out an urge to use). The relapse then becomes an opportunity for learning about things that are not in the least immutable but that are, in fact, quite controllable. This can go a long way toward reducing guilt and shame and reversing demoralization.

Finally, clinicians should know that there are some patients, generally young ones with relatively few alcohol-related problems, who are able to return to controlled, social drinking after realizing their drinking was becoming a problem. It is not a frequent outcome in the natural history of alcoholism, but it does occur, at least in nonpsychiatrically disordered patients (Vaillant, 2003). The more severe and pervasive the alcoholism, the less likely this outcome is, however. It is not clear if controlled drinking is possible for bipolar patients who have abused alcohol. It may not be wise, in any case. Bipolar disorder involves a dysregulation and destabilization of aspects of the central nervous system. Alcohol can be a destabilizing influence, even in limited quantities (Goldstein et al., 2006a).

Mental health clinicians, who often view alcohol and drug abuse as patients' attempts to "self-medicate" dysphoric mood states, must be careful not to think that drug abuse will resolve if the patient's dysphoria is treated and resolved. Regardless of why alcohol or drug abuse begins, it often taken on a life of its own. In bipolar patients with comorbid substance abuse and bipolar illness, substance abuse will very often need specific treatment.

About Cocaine Users

The diagnosis and need for treatment for cocaine abuse depend on the extent to which the patient's life has become centered on cocaine use, the extent to which he or she has lost control of his or her use, and continues to use it in spite of a variety of negative consequences. The therapist's role with bipolar patients who abuse or are addicted to cocaine is the same as with those bipolar patients who have drinking problems. The therapist cannot and should not try to treat cocaine addiction if patients are in the "whether to quit" stage. The therapist's task is to simply raise the patient's awareness of the problem to help move him or her along to the next stage of change.

Many patients who want to stop using cocaine would like to continue drinking or smoking marijuana. They often feel that if alcohol and marijuana have not led to problems, then there is no need to stop using them. This is a mistake, especially for patients with bipolar disorder since any alcohol or drug use is likely to be destabilizing. Moreover, the belief that alcohol and marijuana have not caused problems is often not true. Patients addicted to cocaine frequently forget or minimize the problems associated with their use. More important, even if drinking and smoking marijuana have not led to problems themselves, their use threatens sobriety. Drinking and smoking marijuana can trigger an urge for cocaine. They impair judgment and impulse control and increase the likelihood the recovering person will be exposed to other triggers for the use of cocaine. Finally, alcohol and marijuana use jeopardize not only short-term abstinence from cocaine but also long-term personal growth and recovery. The person recovering from alcohol or drug use needs to develop inner resources for handling life's adversities, learn to turn to others for comfort, and come up with new ways of having fun. Alcohol and drug use stymie this growth.

About Marijuana Users

Clinical experience and research evidence suggest marijuana abuse and dependence in youth are difficult to treat in outpatient settings (Denis et al., 2006). They are more difficult to treat, in fact, than alcohol and stimulant abuse. One reason is that the disinhibiting effects of alcohol and stimulants often cause people to do things that bring them and the people they care about a lot of pain. The problems marijuana causes are insidious and less easily recognized. Second, as previously noted, young, agitated bipolar patients find the sedative properties of marijuana useful.

Clinicians may find it helpful to have bipolar patients verbalize concern about their lethargy, lack of motivation, and aimlessness. They can then be asked about their understanding of the effects of cannibis on motivation and desire. If the young person can be brought to an understanding that cannabis is not used by go-getters and rocket scientists as a performance or cognitive enhancing drug, he or she may be willing to consider curtailing his or her use. The key point is to get the patient interested in the idea that marijuana, by quietly robbing them of their intellectual abilities and their motivation, is getting in the way of achieving goals. They can also be warned about the risk of induction of mania and psychosis.

Readers interested in learning more about how to help marijuana-abusing youth can look into the work done by Dennis et al. (2004) as part of the Cannabis Youth Treatment (CYT) Study. The manuals for this study can be downloaded free of charge from the Substance Abuse and Mental Health Services Administration at www.samhsa.gov.

For a comprehensive review of the full range of options for treating patients who abuse substances, including those with psychiatric disorders, the reader is referred to Lessa and Scanlon (2006). Clinicians will also find Washton and Zweben's (2006) book useful. It describes how psychotherapists without specialized training in addictions can help alcohol and drug abusing patients.

Psychotropic Drugs for the Treatment of Substance Abuse in Patients with Bipolar Illness

A number of psychotropic agents have been investigated as treatments for substance abuse in both nonpsychiatric as well as psychiatric populations. However, relatively few psychopharmacologic trials for the treatment of substance abuse in bipolar patients have been conducted. The anticonvulsant, mood stabilizing drugs lamotrigine (Rubio et al., 2006; Brown et al., 2006), and divalproex (Brady et al., 1995; Salloum et al., 2006), and the atypical antipsychotic quetiapine (Brown et al., 2002) are among the drugs that have been used in open studies to treat bipolar patients with alcohol or cocaine abuse. Results have been modestly positive in terms of reductions in craving and quantity and frequency of use. There are some indications the anticonvulsant drug gabapentin may be helpful in alcohol-abusing bipolar patients (Perugi et al., 2002). Gabapentin has been used, without beneficial effect, to treat smokable cocaine in several studies (e.g., Hart et al., 2006). Other studies have reported modest decreases in cocaine use and increased abstinence time, presumably with intranasal users of cocaine (e.g., Raby & Coomaraswamy, 2004). Geller et al. (1998) conducted a randomized, double-blind, placebo-controlled trial of lithium in adolescents with mostly alcohol and marijuana abuse. They reported decreased numbers of positive urine screens for marijuana.

In the best-designed study to date, Salloum et al. (2005b) did a 24-week, double-blind, placebo-controlled, randomized, parallel-group trial of divalproex in 59 patients with diagnoses of bipolar I disorder and alcohol dependence. In the patients with the best medication compliance, the divalproex-treated patients had significantly fewer drinks per heavy drinking day and fewer drinks per drinking day. Higher blood levels of valproate significantly correlated with improved alcohol use outcomes.

Although the results of this methodologically sound study were statistically significant, divalproex may remain of limited clinical significance in treating alcoholism in bipolar patients. The main problem lies in the investigators' choice of quantity and frequency measures and reduction in craving as measures of improvement. Quantity and frequency of alcohol use bear only a modest relationship at best to the interpersonal and social morbidity of alcohol abuse. There is no significant impact on the family of an alcoholic when he or she reduces the number of heavy drinking days if he or she verbally abuses them whenever he or she drinks. Even if he or she verbally abused them only when he or she drank heavily, would it matter much if this decreased from 18.4 days to 11.3 days (placebo group compared to divalproex group) over a given period of time? One could not reasonably argue that he or she is on the road to recovery. Vaillant (1995) first made this same argument in reference to the reports of antidepressants being effective in reducing alcohol use in depressed alcoholics.

This is not to say that divalproex and other drugs are without merit in substance-abusing patients with bipolar disorder. Stability of mood, improved judgment, and better impulse control may help prevent relapse in a recovering addict. However, alleviation of dysphoric mood states, decreases in craving, and blunting of withdrawal effects through the use of current psychotropic drugs are unlikely, in themselves, to get a patient sober. This should not be a surprise since people do not use drugs primarily to self-medicate emotional pain or to ward off unpleasant withdrawal effects. A major reason why humankind has eagerly experimented with drugs for thousand of years is that, in spite of the long-term pain they cause, they are extremely pleasurable and rewarding in the short run (akin to and in many cases exceeding the pleasure derived from sex and food). In addition, their use becomes habitual, even in the absence of reward. Alcohol and drug use can take on lives of their own. The psychotropic drugs we use to treat psychiatric problems do not reduce reward. Even drugs that do reduce reward, like naltrexone (ReVia), an FDA approved pharmacologic treatment for alcoholism (see Brown, Beard, et al., 2006, for information on the use of naltrexone specifically in bipolar alcoholics), do not ensure remission, or guarantee recovery. Our current psychotherapeutic drugs will not be replacing conventional psychosocial approaches to addictions in the near future.

References

Aertgeerts, B., Buntinx, F., Ansoms, S., & Fevery, J. (2002). Questionnaires are better than laboratory tests to screen for current alcohol abuse or dependence in a male inpatient population. *Acta Clinica Belgica, 57*(5), 241–249.

Akiskal, H., & Akiskal, K. (2006). Principles of caring for bipolar patients. In H. Akiskal &

M. Tohen (Eds.), *Bipolar psychopharmacotherapy* (pp. 367–387). West Sussex, England: Wiley.

Albanese, M., Clodfelter, R., Jr., Pardo, T., & Ghaemi, S. N. (2006). Underdiagnosis of bipolar disorder in men with substance use disorder. *Journal of Psychiatric Practice, 12*(2), 124–127.

Ashton, C., Moore, P., Gallagher, P., & Young, A. (2005). Cannabinoids in bipolar affective disorder: A review and discussion of their therapeutic potential. *Journal of Psychopharmacology, 19*(3), 293–300.

Bahr, B., Karanian, D., Makanji, S., & Makriyannis, A. (2006). Targeting the endocannabinoid system in treating brain disorders. *Expert Opinion on Investigational Drugs, 15*(4), 351–365.

Basiaux, P., le Bon, O., Dramaix, M., et al. (2001). Temperament and Character Inventory (TCI) personality profile and sub-typing in alcoholic patients: A controlled study. *Alcohol and Alcoholism, 36*(6), 584–587.

Baylen, C., & Rosenberg, H. (2006). A review of the acute subjective effects of MDMA/ecstasy. *Addiction, 101*(7), 933–947.

Berner, M., Bentele, M., Kriston, L., et al. (2006). DOVER and QUVER-new marker combinations to detect and monitor at-risk drinking. *Alcoholism: Clinical and Experimental Research, 30*(8), 1372–1380.

Booth, B., Leukefeld, C., Falck, R., et al. (2006). Correlates of rural methamphetamine and cocaine users: Results from a multistate community study. *Journal of Studies on Alcohol, 67*(4), 493–501.

Bradley, K., Bush, K., McDonell, M., et al. (1998). Screening for problem drinking: Comparison of CAGE and AUDIT Ambulatory Care Quality Improvement Project (ACQUIP). Alcohol Use Disorders Identification Test. *Journal of General Internal Medicine, 13*(6), 379–388.

Brady, K., Sonne, S., Anton, R., & Ballenger, J. (1995). Valproate in the treatment of acute bipolar affective episodes complicated by substance abuse: A pilot study. *Journal of Clinical Psychiatry, 56*(3), 118–121.

Brecht, M., Greenwell, L., & Anglin, M. (2006). Substance use pathways to methamphetamine use among treated users. *Addictive Behavior, 32*(1), 24–38.

Brieger, P. (2005) Comorbidity in mixed states and rapid-cycling forms of bipolar disorder. In A. Marneros & F. Goodwin (Eds.), *Bipolar disorders: Mixed states, rapid cycling and atypical forms* (pp. 263–276). New York: Cambridge University Press.

Brook, J., Whiteman, M., Finch, S., & Cohen, P. (1996). Young adult drug use and delinquency: Childhood antecedents and adolescent mediators. *Journal of the American Academy of Child and Adolescent Psychiatry, 35*(12), 1584–1592.

Brown, E., Beard, L., Dobbs, L., & Rush, A. (2006). Naltrexone in patients with bipolar disorder and alcohol dependence. *Depression and Anxiety, 23*(8), 492–495.

Brown, E., Nejtek, V., Perantie, D. & Bobadilla, L. (2002). Quetiapine in bipolar disorder and cocaine dependence. *Bipolar Disorders, 4*(6), 406–411.

Brown, E., Perantie, D., Dhanani, N., et al. (2006). Lamotrigine for bipolar disorder and comorbid cocaine dependence: A replication and extension study. *Journal of Affective Disorders, 93*(1–3), 219–222.

Brown, R., Leonard, T., Saunders, L., & Papasouliotis, O. (1997). A two-item screening test for alcohol and other drug problems. *Journal of Family Practice, 44*(2), 151–160.

Brunette, M., Noordsy, D., Xie, H., & Drake, R. (2003). Benzodiazepine use and abuse among patients with severe mental illness and co-occurring substance use disorders. *Psychiatric Services, 54*(10), 1395–1401.

Buchsbaum, D., Buchanan, R., Centor, R., et al. (1991). Screening for alcohol abuse using CAGE scores and likelihood ratios. *Annals of Internal Medicine, 115*(10), 774–777.

Buchsbaum, D. G., Welsh, J., Buchanan, R. G., & Elswick, R. K., Jr. (1995). Screening for drinking problems by patient self-report. Even "safe" levels may indicate a problem. *Archives of Internal Medicine, 155*(1), 104–108.

Bush, B., Shaw, S., Cleary, P., Delbanco, T. L., & Aronson, M. D. (1987). Screening for alcohol abuse using the CAGE questionnaire. *American Journal of Medicine, 82*(2), 231–235.

Camacho, A., & Akiskal, H. S. (2005). Proposal for a bipolar-stimulant spectrum: Temperament, diagnostic validation and therapeutic outcomes with mood stabilizers. *Journal of Affective Disorders, 85*(1–2), 217–230.

Chen, C., Lin, S., & Sham, P. (2005). Morbid risk for psychiatric disorder among the relatives of methamphetamine users with and without psychosis. *American Journal of Medical Genetics. Part B, Neuropsychiatric Genetics, 136*(1), 87–91.

Chen, C. K., Lin, S. K., Sham, P. C., Ball, D., Loh, E. W., Hsiao, C. C., et al. (2003). Premorbid characteristics and co-morbidity of methamphetamine users with and without psychosis. *Psychological Medicine, 33*(8), 1407–1414.

Cherpitel, C. J. (2002). Screening for alcohol problems in the U.S. general population: Comparison of the CAGE, RAPS4, and RAPS4-QF by gender, ethnicity, and service utilization. Rapid Alcohol Problems Screen. *Alcoholism: Clinical and Experimental Research, 26*(11), 1686–1691.

Cherpitel, C. J., & Borges, G. (2000). Screening instruments for alcohol problems: A comparison of cut points between Mexican American and Mexican patients in the emergency room. *Substance Use and Misuse, 35*(10), 1419–1430.

Compton, W. M., Grant, B. F., Colliver, J. D., Glantz, M. D., & Stinson, F. S. (2004). Prevalence of marijuana use disorders in the United States: 1991–1992 and 2001–2002. *Journal of the American Medical Association, 291*(17), 2114–2121.

Denis, C., Lavie, E., Fatseas, M., & Auriacombe, M. (2006). Psychotherapeutic interventions for cannabis abuse and/or dependence in outpatient settings. *Cochrane Database of Systematic Reviews, 3*, CD005336.

Dennis, M., Godley, S. H., Diamond, G., Tims, F. M., Babor, T., Donaldson, J., et al. (2004). The Cannabis Youth Treatment (CYT) Study: Main findings from two randomized trials. *Journal of Substance Abuse Treatment, 27*(3), 197–213.

Dervaux, A., Bayle, F. J., Laqueille, X., Bourdel, M. C., Leborgne, M., Olie, J. P., et al. (2006). Validity of the CAGE questionnaire in schizophrenic patients with alcohol abuse and dependence. *Schizophrenia Research, 81*(2–3), 151–155.

Drake, R. E., Xie, H., McHugo, G. J., & Shumway, M. (2004). Three-year outcomes of long-term patients with co-occurring bipolar and substance use disorders. *Biological Psychiatry, 56*(10), 749–756.

Feinman, D., & Dunner, J. (1996). The effects of alcohol and substance abuse on the course of bipolar affective illness. *Journal of Affective Disorders, 37*43–49.

Fossey, M. D., Otto, M. W., Yates, W. R., Wisniewski, S. R., Gyulai, L., Allen, M. H., et al. (2006). Validity of the distinction between primary and secondary substance use disorder in patients with bipolar disorder: Data from the first 1000 STEP-BD participants. *American Journal on Addictions, 15*(2), 138–143.

Frye, M., Altschuler, L., McElroy, S., et al. (2003). Gender differences in prevalence, risk, and clinical correlates of alcoholism comorbidity in bipolar disorder. *American Journal of Psychiatry, 160,* 883–889

Geller, B., Cooper, T. B., Sun, K., Zimerman, B., Frazier, J., Williams, M., et al. (1998). Double-blind and placebo-controlled study of lithium for adolescent bipolar disorders with secondary substance dependency. *Journal of the American Academy of Child and Adolescent Psychiatry, 37*(2), 171–178.

Gettig, J. P., Grady, S. E., & Nowosadzka, I. (2006). Methamphetamine: Putting the brakes on speed. *Journal of School Nursing, 22*(2), 66–73.

Giancola, P. R. (2002a). Alcohol-related aggression in men and women: The influence of dispositional aggressivity. *Journal of Studies on Alcohol, 63*(6), 696–708.

Giancola, P. R. (2002b). Irritability, acute alcohol consumption and aggressive behavior in men and women. *Drug and Alcohol Dependence, 68*(3), 263–274.

Giancola, P. R. (2004). Difficult temperament, acute alcohol intoxication, and aggressive behavior. *Drug and Alcohol Dependence, 74*(2), 135–145.

Goldberg, J. F., Garno, J. L., Leon, A. C., Kocsis, J. H., & Portera, L. (1999). A history of substance abuse complicates remission from acute mania in bipolar disorder. *Journal of Clinical Psychiatry, 60*(11), 733–740.

Goldstein, B. I., Diamantouros, A., Schaffer, A., & Naranjo, C. A. (2006). Pharmacotherapy of alcoholism in patients with co-morbid psychiatric disorders. *Drugs, 66*(9), 1229–1237.

Goldstein, B. I., & Levitt, A. J. (2006a). Factors associated with temporal priority in comorbid bipolar I disorder and alcohol use disorders: Results from the national epidemiologic survey on alcohol and related conditions. *Journal of Clinical Psychiatry, 67*(4), 643–649.

Goldstein, B. I., & Levitt, A. J. (2006b). Further evidence for a developmental subtype of bipolar disorder defined by age at onset: Results from the national epidemiologic survey on alcohol and related conditions. *American Journal of Psychiatry, 163*(9), 1633–1636

Goldstein, B. I., & Levitt, A. J. (2006c). A gender-focused perspective on health service utilization in comorbid bipolar I disorder and alcohol use disorders: Results from the national epidemiologic survey on alcohol and related conditions. *Journal of Clinical Psychiatry, 67*(6), 925–932.

Goldstein, B. I., Velyvis, V. P., & Parikh, S. V. (2006). The association between moderate alcohol use and illness severity in bipolar disorder: A preliminary report. *Journal of Clinical Psychiatry, 67*(1), 102–106.

Goodwin, F., & Jamison, K. (1990). *Manic-depressive illness.* New York: Oxford University Press.

Gordon, A. J., Maisto, S. A., McNeil, M., Kraemer, K. L., Conigliaro, R. L., Kelley, M. E., et al. (2001). Three questions can detect hazardous drinkers. *Journal of Family Practice, 50*(4), 313–320.

Grant, B., Stinson, F., Hasin, D., et al. (2005). Prevalence, correlates, and comorbidity of bipolar I disorder and axis I and II disorders: Results from the National Epidemiologic Survey on Alcohol and Related Conditions. *Journal of Clinical Psychiatry, 66*(10), 1205–1215.

Grant, B. F., Dawson, D. A., Stinson, F. S., Chou, S. P., Dufour, M. C., & Pickering, R. P. (2004). The 12-month prevalence and trends in *DSM-IV* alcohol abuse and dependence: United States, 1991–1992 and 2001–2002. *Drug and Alcohol Dependence, 74*(3), 223–234.

Grinspoon, L., & Bakalar, J. B. (1998). The use of cannabis as a mood stabilizer in bipolar disorder: Anecdotal evidence and the need for clinical research. *Journal of Psychoactive Drugs, 30*(2), 171–177.

Gruber, A. J., Pope, H. G., Jr., & Brown, M. E. (1996). Do patients use marijuana as an antidepressant? *Depression, 4*(2), 77–80.

Hall, W. D. (2006). Cannabis use and the mental health of young people. *Australian and New Zealand Journal of Psychiatry, 40*(2), 105–113.

Hart, C. L., Haney, M., Collins, E. D., Rubin, E., & Foltin, R. W. (2006). Smoked cocaine self-administration by humans is not reduced by large gabapentin maintenance doses. *Drug and Alcohol Dependence, 86*(2-3), 71-75.

Henquet, C., Krabbendam, L., de Graaf, R., ten Have, M., & van Os, J. (2006). Cannabis use and expression of mania in the general population. *Journal of Affective Disorders, 95*(1–3), 103–110.

Henquet, C., Krabbendam, L., Spauwen, J., Kaplan, C., Lieb, R., Wittchen, H. U., et al. (2005). Prospective cohort study of cannabis use, predisposition for psychosis, and psychotic symptoms in young people. *British Medical Journal, 330*(7481), 11.

Hietala, J., Koivisto, H., Anttila, P., & Niemela, O. (2006). Comparison of the combined marker GGT-CDT and the conventional laboratory markers of alcohol abuse in heavy drinkers, moderate drinkers and abstainers. *Alcohol and Alcoholism, 41*(5), 528–533.

Hinckers, A. S., Laucht, M., Schmidt, M. H., Mann, K. F., Schumann, G., Schuckit, M. A., et al. (2006). Low level of response to alcohol as associated with serotonin transporter genotype and high alcohol intake in adolescents. *Biological Psychiatry, 60*(3), 282–287.

Hock, B., Schwarz, M., Domke, I., Grunert, V. P., Wuertemberger, M., Schiemann, U., et al. (2005). Validity of carbohydrate-deficient transferrin (%CDT), gamma-glutamyltransferase (gamma-GT) and mean corpuscular erythrocyte volume (MCV) as biomarkers for chronic alcohol abuse: A study in patients with alcohol dependence and liver disorders of non-alcoholic and alcoholic origin. *Addiction, 100*(10), 1477–1486.

Hopfer, C., Mendelson, B., Van Leeuwen, J. M., Kelly, S., & Hooks, S. (2006). Club drug use among youths in treatment for substance abuse. *American Journal on Addictions, 15*(1), 94–99.

Huang, B., Dawson, D. A., Stinson, F. S., Hasin, D. S., Ruan, W. J., Saha, T. D., et al. (2006). Prevalence, correlates, and comorbidity of nonmedical prescription drug use and drug use disorders in the United States: Results of the National Epidemiologic Survey on Alcohol and Related Conditions. *Journal of Clinical Psychiatry, 67*(7), 1062–1073.

Kessler, R., Berglund, P., Demler, O., et al. (2005). Lifetime prevalence and age-of-onset distributions of DSM-IV disorders in the National Comorbidity Survey Replication. *Archives of General Psychiatry, 62*(6), 593–602.

Kolodziej, M. E., Griffin, M. L., Najavits, L. M., Otto, M. W., Greenfield, S. F., & Weiss, R. D. (2005). Anxiety disorders among patients with co-occurring bipolar and sub-stance use disorders. *Drug and Alcohol Dependence, 80*(2), 251–257.

Kroutil, L. A., Van Brunt, D. L., Herman-Stahl, M. A., Heller, D. C., Bray, R. M., & Penne, M. A. (2006). Nonmedical use of prescription stimulants in the United States. *Drug and Alcohol Dependence, 84*(2), 135–143.

Kurtz, S. P., Inciardi, J. A., Surratt, H. L., & Cottler, L. (2005). Prescription drug abuse among ecstasy users in Miami. *Journal of Addictive Diseases, 24*(4), 1–16.

Lazowski, L. E., Miller, F. G., Boye, M. W., & Miller, G. A. (1998). Efficacy of the Substance Abuse Subtle Screening Inventory-3 (SASSI-3) in identifying substance dependence disorders in clinical settings. *Journal of Personality Assessment, 71*(1), 114–128.

Lejoyeux, M. (2005). Clinical masks of bipolar disorders. *La Revue du Praticien, 55*(5), 507–512.

Lemere, F., & Smith, J. (1990). Hypomanic personality trait in cocaine addtiction. *British Journal of Addiction, 85*(4), 575–576.

Lessa, N., & Scanlon, W. (2006). *Wiley concise guides to mental health: Substance use disorders.* New York: Wiley.

Liraud, F., & Verdoux, H. (2000). Which temperamental characteristics are associated with substance use in subjects with psychotic and mood disorders? *Psychiatry Research, 93*(1), 63–72.

Machado-Vieira, R., Viale, C. I., & Kapczinski, F. (2001). Mania associated with an energy drink: The possible role of caffeine, taurine, and inositol. *Canadian Journal of Psychiatry, 46*(5), 454–455.

Mackie, K. (2005). Distribution of cannabinoid receptors in the central and peripheral nervous system. *Handbook of Experimental Pharmacology*, (168), 299–325.

Mackie, K., & Stella, N. (2006). Cannabinoid receptors and endocannabinoids: Evidence for new players. *AAPS Journal, 8*(2), E298–306.

Marlatt, G., & Gordon, J. (Eds.). (1985). *Relapse prevention: Maintenance strategies in the treatment of addictive behaviors.* New York: Guilford

Martins, S. S., Mazzotti, G., & Chilcoat, H. D. (2006). Recent-onset ecstasy use: Association with deviant behaviors and psychiatric comorbidity. *Experimental and Clinical Psychopharmacology, 14*(3), 275–286.

McGregor, C., Srisurapanont, M., Jittiwutikarn, J., Laobhripatr, S., Wongtan, T., & White, J. M. (2005). The nature, time course and severity of methamphetamine withdrawal. *Addiction, 100*(9), 1320–1329.

Miller, W., & Rollnick, S. (2002). *Motivational interviewing: Preparing people for change* (2nd ed.). New York: Guilford.

Minnai, G., Tondo, L., Salis, P., et al. (2006). Secular trends in first hospitalizations for major mood disorders with comorbid substance use. *International Journal of Neuropsychopharmacology, 9*(3), 319–326.

Najavits, L., Runkel, R., Neuner, C., et al. (2003). Rates and symptoms of PTSD among cocaine-dependent patients. *Journal of Studies on Alcohol, 64*(5), 601–606.

Newton, T. F., Kalechstein, A. D., Duran, S., Vansluis, N., & Ling, W. (2004). Methamphetamine abstinence syndrome: Preliminary findings. *American Journal on Addiction, 13*(3), 248–255.

Nocon, A., Wittchen, H., Pfister, H., et al. (2006). Dependence symptoms in young cannabis users? A prospective epidemiological study. *Journal of Psychiatric Research, 40*(5), 394–403.

Ogawa, N., & Ueki, H. (2003). Secondary mania caused by caffeine. *General Hospital Psychiatry, 25*(2), 138–139.

Perugi, G., Frare, F., Madaro, D., Maremmani, I., & Akiskal, H. S. (2002). Alcohol abuse in social phobic patients: Is there a bipolar connection? *Journal of Affective Disorders,* *68*(1), 33–39.

Preisig, M., Fenton, B., Stevens, D., & Merikangas, K. (2001). Familial relationship between mood disorders and alcoholism. *Comprehensive Psychiatry, 42*(2), 87–95.

Prochaska, J., Norcross, J., & DiClemente, C. (1994). *Changing for good.* New York: William Morrow and Company.

Raby, W. N., & Coomaraswamy, S. (2004). Gabapentin reduces cocaine use among addicts from a community clinic sample. *Journal of Clinical Psychiatry, 65*(1), 84–86.

Reiger, D., Farmer, M., Rae, D., et al. (1990). Comorbidity of mental disorders with alcohol and other drug abuse. Results from the Epidemiologic Catchment Area (ECA) Study. *Journal of the American Medical Association, 264*(19), 2511–2518.

Rosenblum, A., Fallon, B., Magura, S., Handelsman, L., Foote, J., & Bernstein, D. (1999). The autonomy of mood disorders among cocaine-using methadone patients. *American Journal on Drug and Alcohol Abuse, 25*(1), 67–80.

Rottanburg, D., Robins, A., Ben-Arie, O., et al. (1982). Cannabis-associated psychosis with hypomanic features. *Lancet, 2*(8312), 1364–1366.

Rubio, G., Lopez-Munoz, F., & Alamo, C. (2006). Effects of lamotrigine in patients with bipolar disorder and alcohol dependence. *Bipolar Disorders, 8*(3), 289–293.

Saha, T. D., Chou, S. P., & Grant, B. F. (2006). Toward an alcohol use disorder continuum using item response theory: Results from the National Epidemiologic Survey on Alcohol and Related Conditions. *Psychological Medicine, 36*(7), 931–941.

Salloum, I. M., Cornelius, J. R., Daley, D. C., Kirisci, L., Himmelhoch, J. M., & Thase, M. E. (2005). Efficacy of valproate maintenance in patients with bipolar disorder and alcoholism: A double-blind placebo-controlled study. *Archives of General Psychiatry, 62*(1), 37–45.

Salloum, I. M., Cornelius, J. R., Douaihy, A., Kirisci, L., Daley, D. C., & Kelly, T. M. (2005). Patient characteristics and treatment implications of marijuana abuse among bipolar alcoholics: Results from a double blind, placebo-controlled study. *Addictive Behaviors, 30*(9), 1702–1708.

Salloum, I., Douaihy, A., Cornelius, J., et al. (2007). Divalproex utility in bipolar disorder with co-occurring cocaine dependence: A pilot study. *Addictive Behaviors, 32*(2), 410–415.

Schuckit, M. (1994). Low level of response to alcohol as a predictor of future alcoholism. *American Journal of Psychiatry, 151*(2), 184–189.

Schuckit, M., Smith, T., Pierson, J., Danko, G., & Beltran, I. A. (2006). Relationships among the level of response to alcohol and the number of alcoholic relatives in predicting alcohol-related outcomes. *Alcoholism: Clinical and Experimental Research, 30*(8), 1308–1314.

Schuckit, M. A., Tipp, J. E., Bucholz, K. K., Nurnberger, J. I., Jr., Hesselbrock, V. M., Crowe, R. R., et al. (1997). The life-time rates of three major mood disorders and four major anxiety disorders in alcoholics and controls. *Addiction, 92*(10), 1289–1304.

Shoptaw, S. (2006). Methamphetamine use in urban gay and bisexual populations. *Top HIV Medicine, 14*(2), 84–87.

Shoptaw, S., Peck, J., Reback, C. J., & Rotheram-Fuller, E. (2003). Psychiatric and substance dependence comorbidities, sexually transmitted diseases, and risk behaviors among methamphetamine-dependent gay and bisexual men seeking outpatient drug abuse treatment. *Journal of Psychoactive Drugs, 35*(Suppl. 1), 161–168.

Skinstad, A. H., & Swain, A. (2001). Comorbidity in a clinical sample of substance abusers. *American Journal of Drug and Alcohol Abuse, 27*(1), 45–64.

Sommers, I., Baskin, D., & Baskin-Sommers, A. (2006). Methamphetamine use among young adults: Health and social consequences. *Addictive Behaviors, 31*(8), 1469–1476.

Steinweg, D. L., & Worth, H. (1993). Alcoholism: The keys to the CAGE. *American Journal of Medicine, 94*(5), 520–523.

Stinson, F. S., Ruan, W. J., Pickering, R., & Grant, B. F. (2006). Cannabis use disorders in the USA: Prevalence, correlates and co-morbidity. *Psychological Medicine, 36*(10), 1447–1460.

Strakowski, S., DelBello, M., Fleck, D., et al. (2005). Effects of co-occurring alcohol abuse on the course of bipolar disorder following a first hospitalization for mania. *Archives of General Psychiatry, 62*(8), 851–858.

Strakowski, S., DelBello, M., Fleck, D., et al. (2007). Effects of co-occurring cannabis use disorders on the course of bipolar disorder after a first hospitalization for mania. *Archives of General Psychiatry, 64*(1), 57-64.

Strakowski, S. M., DelBello, M. P., Fleck, D. E., & Arndt, S. (2000). The impact of substance abuse on the course of bipolar disorder. *Biological Psychiatry, 48*(6), 477–485.

Tondo, L., Baldessarini, R. J., Hennen, J., Minnai, G. P., Salis, P., Scamonatti, L., et al. (1999). Suicide attempts in major affective disorder patients with comorbid substance use disorders. *Journal of Clinical Psychiatry, 60* (Suppl. 2), 63–69, 75–66, 113–116.

Vaillant, G. (1995). *The natural history of alcoholism revisited.* Cambridge, MA: Harvard University Press.

Vaillant, G. E. (2003). A 60-year follow-up of alcoholic men. *Addiction, 98*(8), 1043–1051.

van Os, J., Bak, M., Hanssen, M., Bijl, R. V., de Graaf, R., & Verdoux, H. (2002). Cannabis use and psychosis: A longitudinal population-based study. *American Journal of Epidemiology, 156*(4), 319–327.

Washton, A., & Zweben, J. *Treating alcohol and drug problems in psychotherapy practice.* New York: Guilford.

Weiss, R. D., Kolodziej, M., Griffin, M. L., Najavits, L. M., Jacobson, L. M., & Greenfield, S. F. (2004). Substance use and perceived symptom improvement among patients with bipolar disorder and substance dependence. *Journal of Affective Disorders, 79*(1–3), 279–283.

Weiss, R. D., & Mirin, S. M. (1986). Subtypes of cocaine abusers. *The Psychiatric Clinics of North America, 9*(3), 491–501.

Weiss, R. D., Mirin, S. M., Griffin, M. L., & Michael, J. L. (1988). Psychopathology in cocaine abusers. Changing trends. *Journal of Nervous and Mental Disease, 176*(12), 719–725.

Weiss, R. D., Ostacher, M. J., Otto, M. W., Calabrese, J. R., Fossey, M., Wisniewski, S. R., et al. (2005). Does recovery from substance use disorder matter in patients with bipolar disorder? *Journal of Clinical Psychiatry, 66*(6), 730–735; quiz 808–739.

Williams, R., & Vinson, D. C. (2001). Validation of a single screening question for problem drinking. *Journal of Family Practice, 50*(4), 307–312.

Winokur, G., Coryell, W., Akiskal, H., et al. (1995). Alcoholism and manic-depressive (bipolar) illness: Familial illness, course of illness and the primary-secondary distinction. *American Journal of Psychiatry, 152,* 365–372.

Winokur, G., Turvey, C., Akiskal, H., Coryell, W., Solomon, D., Leon, A., et al. (1998). Alcoholism and drug abuse in three groups—bipolar I, unipolars and their acquaintances. *Journal of Affective Disorders, 50*(2–3), 81–89.

Yersin, B., Nicolet, J. F., Dercrey, H., Burnier, M., van Melle, G., & Pecoud, A. (1995). Screening for excessive alcohol drinking. Comparative value of carbohydrate-deficient transferrin, gamma-glutamyltransferase, and mean corpuscular volume. *Archives of Internal Medicine, 155*(17), 1907–1911.

Zierau, F., Hardt, F., Henriksen, J., et al. (2005). Validation of a self-administered modified CAGE test (CAGE-C) in a somatic hospital ward: Comparison with biochemical markers. *Scandinavian Journal of Clinical Laboratory Investigation, 65*(7), 615–622.

Treatment

THE WILEY
CONCISE GUIDES
TO MENTAL HEALTH

Bipolar
Disorder

CHAPTER 6

Pharmacologic Treatment of Mania and Hypomania

In 1948, an Australian psychiatrist was looking for toxic substances in urine he thought might cause mental illness. He suspected one of the substances might be urea. So he gave guinea pigs lithium urate, the only soluble form of urea available. He was struck by the calming effects the substance had on the jittery rodents. It occurred to him that the compound might prove helpful to some of the agitated patients at the mental asylum where he was an administrator. He took some himself to check on its safety and then administered it to 10 "excited psychotic" patients. All 10 responded. A year later, Dr. John Cade ushered in the era of psychopharmacology when he published his paper on lithium—the first report of a medication effective in the treatment of a mental illness (Cade, 1949).

Lithium is a naturally occurring element in the same chemical family as sodium. It gained widespread use in Europe in the mid-1950s and 1960s, primarily because of the work of Schou et al. (1954). In the United States, lithium was not used extensively in manic patients until the mid to late 1960s, due in part to the use of lithium chloride as a salt substitute, which led to the deaths of some unfortunate diners. American psychiatrists preferred the antipsychotic drug chlorpromazine (Thorazine) for manic patients. Lithium was FDA-approved for the acute treatment of mania in 1970. It and chlorpromazine would remain the only drugs labeled for the illness until 1995, when the anticonvulsant drug divalproex (Depakote) was approved for the treatment of mania (the drug was approved for use in patients with epilepsy in the United States in 1983). The other drugs now FDA labeled for mania or bipolar depression have all been approved just since the year 2000. Pharmacotherapy for bipolar disorder is clearly still in its infancy.

About Drug Treatment Studies

When considering the results of drug treatment studies, the clinician should be aware of several issues. First, the clinician should know who the manufacturer of the drug is and who funded the study. The majority of drug trials are funded by drug manufacturers (Elias, 2006). For some drugs, such as olanzapine (Zyprexa), virtually all the studies have been funded by the manufacturer. Drugs studies funded by the manufacturer often have more favorable results than those funded by the manufacturer of a competing drug (Elias, 2006). Elias determined that 78 percent of drug studies published in four leading psychiatric journals funded by drugs' manufacturers were positive while only 28 percent of those funded by competitors were positive. In a study of olanzapine for the treatment of acute mania funded by the manufacturer, for instance, the drug was found to be superior to divalproex (Depakote; Tohen et al., 2003). But in a study sponsored by Abbott (the manufacturer of divalproex), the drugs were found to be equally effective and divalproex-treated patients were reported to have fewer side effects (Zajecka et al., 2002).

There is also the problem of publication bias. Trials with positive results are the ones that get published. Manufacturers do not like to announce negative or inconclusive studies and journals may be reluctant to publish them. For instance, lamotrigine (Lamictal) is being widely used for the acute treatment of bipolar depression, but the manufacturer has a number of studies on file indicating it has no advantage over placebo for this condition (visit www.gsk.com). The pharmaceutical industry has set up a web site (www.clinicalstudyresults.org) for the publication of all studies, including negative ones, but drug manufacturers are not required to post negative studies on the site.

Finally, it is also important to know something about the quality of the research methodology. The gold standard is the randomized, double-blind, placebo-controlled, prospective study with an adequate number of patients. Randomized means the patients being studied are randomly assigned to the various treatments. Randomization reduces the chances that characteristics many patients may have in common could account for particular results. Double-blind studies are those in which neither the patient nor the investigator know whether the patient is getting an active drug. Double-blind studies minimize the possibility that patients and investigators will find the results for which they are hoping. The number of patients who respond to placebo or inactive pills is high and sometimes quite close to the number of patients responding to an active drug. Without a placebo control, it would be impossible to know if the improvement seen with a drug was actually due to the drug. Studies that follow patients forward from the time of drug administration are called prospective. Investigators who look back at data already collected run the risk of positing a causal relationship between a drug and a result that may have been caused by something other than the drug. Data should be analyzed to account for confounding variables that may have produced the expected result. The first or primary analysis is the most reliable. Secondary analyses have a higher chance of positive results (Ghaemi, personal communication). When looking at results, the effect size of the drug compared to placebo should be considered. Small effect sizes may be statistically significant, especially if the patient sample is quite large, but not be clinically meaningful. Clinicians without specialized training in methods of research and data analysis who are interested in learning how to critically review psychosocial or drug treatment studies should consult Riegelman (2005).

Lithium

Treatment of Acute Mania

The efficacy of lithium in acute mania has been demonstrated repeatedly over the last 50 years (e.g., Bowden et al., 1994; Schou et al., 1954). Lithium works especially well in euphoric, nonrapid-cycling manic patients with a family history of bipolar illness and when a manic episode is the first expression of bipolar illness. A manic episode followed by depression and then a well interval is referred to as the MDI pattern of bipolar illness. About 70 percent of bipolar patients with the MDI pattern respond favorably to lithium (American Psychiatric Association, 2002).

Lithium has fared less well (about a 30 percent response rate) when depression occurs first in the course of the illness (the DMI pattern). This may be due, in part, to the use of tricyclic antidepressants for the initial depressive episode, which can induce manias that are resistant to lithium treatment (Goodwin & Jamison, 1990).

Lithium may also perform less well in patients with depressive symptoms mixed with mania (Swann et al., 1997), when there is no family history of bipolar illness, when the patient has already had many episodes of illness, and when there is a history of substance abuse (Frye & Altshuler, 1997). For some time, lithium has also been thought to be less effective than anticonvulsants in rapid-cycling patients. But Tondo et al. (2003) reported that an analysis of studies identified by a literature search revealed no evidence of superiority for any treatment in these patients. Calabrese et al. (2005), in a 20-month, double-blind, parallel-group comparison of hypomanic/manic patients also found that divalproex was not superior to lithium in preventing relapse to either hypomania/mania or depression in rapid cyclers. Koukopoulos et al. (1983) found lithium worked quite well in rapid-cycling patients never exposed to tricyclic antidepressants.

Lithium is most effective in the earlier, less severe stages of the development of mania. It can take 2 to 4 weeks to calm moderate mania. Lithium usually will not be prescribed if the patient has kidney problems, has had a recent heart attack, is in the first trimester of pregnancy, or is breast-feeding. In patients in the second or third trimester of pregnancy, or those with Parkinson's disease, epilepsy, or thyroid disorders, it will generally be used only under close medical supervision. Table 6.1 lists the available lithium preparations.

TABLE 6.1

Lithium Preparations

Lithium carbonate, 150 mg and 300 mg tablets or capsules

Eskalith CR (controlled release), 450 mg tablets

Lithobid, 300mg tablets, a controlled-release form of lithium

Lithium ER (extended release), 450 mg tablets, generic

Liquid lithium citrate, 5 ml (about a teaspoon) equals 300 mg of lithium carbonate

Dosing in Acute Mania

Initial dosing patterns vary widely depending on the patient's psychiatric and medical status. For healthy, acutely manic adolescent and adult patients (primarily in inpatient settings), 300 milligrams of lithium may be given three times a day to start. When acutely manic, patients may require larger doses of lithium than they do when they are euthymic or when depressed.

Taking the entire dose once a day is acceptable and may help improve compliance. Taking it at bedtime will make the drug more tolerable since the patient will not be aware of acute side effects. It may also lessen thirst and the need to drink large quantities or fluids (polydipsia). Excessive urination (polyuria) may also be lessened.

Pretreatment blood work and periodic checks after starting lithium are necessary to ensure lithium levels are in the therapeutic range (generally 0.8 to 1.2 mEq/L), to monitor kidney function (lithium is excreted by the kidneys), and thyroid hormone levels (lithium can suppress thyroid functioning). Levels should be measured 8 to 12 hours after the last dose. Lithium toxicity can occur at doses close to therapeutic levels (generally above 1.5 mEq/L). Strenuous exercise, hot weather, and diarrhea or vomiting from lithium itself, antibiotics, or illness can raise blood levels of lithium and cause toxicity.

Traditionally, doctors have sent patients to labs to have their blood drawn and tested to check lithium levels. Results generally would not be available for at least a few days. Testing devices that require only a simple finger stick, rather than a blood draw from a vein, are now available for doctors to use in their offices. Results are available in minutes.

Patients who will not be compliant may not be the best candidates for lithium treatment due to the rebound worsening of symptoms and increased suicide risk with abrupt discontinuation.

Side Effects and Their Management

Although there is a great deal of variation in sensitivity to side effects, the incidence of side effects increases with increasing blood levels. Tremor can be treated with beta-blocking drugs such as propranolol (Inderal). Weight gain should be managed early on. Having protein and fat in the morning along with control of simple carbohydrate intake can be key. Many of these patients have a personal and family history of problems in blood glucose regulation. Obviously, exercise can be helpful. The addition of topiramate or zonisamide—anticonvulsant drugs that cause weight loss—can also be tried, although the patient may then have to deal with a new set of side effects from these medications.

Cognitive dulling may be helped by thyroid supplementation (Tremont & Stern, 1997), dosage reduction, switching to an anticonvulsant drug, and possibly by folate supplementation. Folinic acid or L-5-methyltetrahydrofolate (Metafolin) are preferred forms of folate. Some individuals have a genetically-based enzyme deficiency that impairs or does not permit the conversion of folic acid to usuable forms of folate. This is discussed in more detail in Chapter 7.

Folate supplementation for lithium-treated patients may be wise for other reasons: Hasanah et al. (1997) found that red-cell folate levels (but *not* serum folate levels) were significantly lower in patients with mania. Coppen and Abou-Saleh (1982) reported that patients on lithium with lower plasma folate concentration had higher affective morbidity. Coppen et al. (1986) reported that lithium prophylaxis is enhanced by folate supplementation.

Excessive thirst and urination can become so severe with lithium that patients have difficulty sleeping through the night. This problem is called *lithium-induced nephrogenic diabetes insipidus.* The problem can be managed by using controlled-release forms of lithium, reduction of dose, addition of a specific kind of diuretic, or substituting divalproex (Depakote) for some or all of the lithium.

The controlled-release forms of lithium produce lower peak serum lithium levels and reduce the variability in levels seen with immediate-release lithium carbonate. The controlled-release forms are generally better tolerated than the immediate-release forms. They may especially reduce the stomach upset associated with immediate-release lithium carbonate.

Therapists should be aware of the signs that lithium may be suppressing thyroid function: fatigue, lethargy, and cognitive dysfunction, which can sometimes be mistaken for a relapse to depression. Treatment with thyroid supplements may be indicated. Thyroid supplements can also be useful if the patient is, in fact, depressed or rapid cycling. Although unusual, long-term lithium treatment has been found to be associated with hyperthyroidism (thyrotoxicosis; Barclay et al., 1994).

Nonmedically trained therapists, who these days see their patients far more frequently and for longer periods of time than do psychiatrists, need to be aware of the signs a patient may be becoming lithium toxic. Some patients may develop toxicity at lower blood levels than expected and at relatively modest doses. Cognitive impairment is a common first sign of excess lithium. Table 6.2 lists the major side effects of lithium and Table 6.3 lists the signs and symptoms of lithium toxicity.

Lithium interacts with a number of other drugs, including over-the-counter

TABLE 6.2

Major Lithium Side Effects

- Tremor
- Weight gain
- Cognitive dulling
- Excessive thirst and urination

pain relievers. Table 6.4 lists significant drug interactions. (*Note: Table 6.4 is not a complete list. Patients should consult their physicians or pharmacists before taking any other drugs, including over-the-counter medications, with lithium.*)

Maintenance Treatment

Lithium has repeatedly been found effective in preventing relapse to both mania and depression, although it appears to be more effective against manic relapse (Young & Newham, 2006). It was FDA approved in 1974 for the maintenance treatment of bipolar illness and remained the only drug with that indication until lamotrigine (Lamictal) was approved in 2003. Bowden et al. (2005a) found that lithium, although effective in the acute treatment of euphoric manic patients, was relatively less efficacious than divalproex in the maintenance treatment of these patients.

The ideal blood level for maintenance has been a topic of some debate. Gelenberg et al. (1989) found that patients maintained at 0.8 to 1.2 mEq/L had lower relapse rates than those whose blood levels were maintained at 0.4 to 0.6 mEq/L. But patients also have more side effects at the higher level, which leads to greater noncompliance. The researchers did not look at the relapse rate for blood levels between 0.6 and 0.8 mEq/L, where side effects are minimal.

Himmelhoch (1994) has stated that commonly accepted maintenance levels in the United States are too high, especially for patients who are in the depressed

TABLE 6.3

Signs and Symptoms of Lithium Toxicity

- Difficulty concentrating
- Weakness
- Nausea
- Drowsiness
- Lack of coordination
- Vomiting
- Slurred speech
- Blurry vision
- Impaired consciousness
- At blood levels above 2.0 mEq/L: seizures and acute renal failure

TABLE 6.4

Drugs that Interact with Lithium

- Thiazide diuretics, such as hydrochlorothiazide, can increase lithium levels.

- Nonsteroidal anti-inflammatories (NSAIDs): aspirin, ibuprofen, naproxen. These can increase lithium levels. Tylenol is not an NSAID.

- Some antibiotics (Erythromycin) may increase lithium levels or cause diarrhea, which can increase lithium levels.

- Digitalis and high levels of lithium may cause heart arrhythmias.

- Bronchodilators: aminophylline, theophylline. Anticonvulsants and lithium combinations can have complex interactions.

Source: Goodwin and Jamison (1990).

---

phase of the illness. Goodwin and Jamison (1990) recommend reducing the dose of lithium for maintenance to the point where side effects almost disappear or until a blood level of 0.6 to 0.7 mEq/L is reached. Akiskal (1999) recommends levels between 0.3 and 0.8 mEq/L. Schou and Grof (2006) note that European doctors generally keep the maintenance blood level between 0.4 and 0.8 mEq/L.

Patients are often anxious to discontinue lithium because of side effects, because they feel better and believe they no longer need treatment, or because the idea of needing a drug for life is narcissistically wounding. They need to know that there is a high probability of relapse to mania and an increased risk of suicide if they choose to discontinue the drug (Baldessarrini et al. 1999; Suppes et al., 1991). A slow discontinuation of the drug (2 to 4 weeks as opposed to 1 day to 2 weeks) can reduce the risk of immediate relapse (Baldesarinni et al., 1996; Faedda et al., 1993). But even patients who have been stable for many years on lithium and who discontinue the drug gradually may run a high risk of relapse within a year of stopping it (Yazici et al., 2004).

According to studies by Post et al. (1992) and Maj et al. (1995), patients who stop lithium may not respond to it, or respond to it as well, if they decide to restart it. Tondo et al. (1997) and Coryell et al. (1998), on the other hand, found no evidence that lithium was not as effective after restarting it. Ghaemi (personal communication) states that Post's data indicates a lack of response after lithium rechallenge in only 5 to 10 percent of patients.

Lithium: Still Important after All These Years

Lithium may seem like yesterday's technology, but as the information in Table 6.5 shows, it still has a vital role to play in the treatment of patients with bipolar disorder.

TABLE 6.5

Lithium: Still Important

- Lower doses of lithium (450–900 mg/day) and lower blood levels (.6 to .8 mEq/L) may work well and with minimal side effects in patients with bipolar depression and for maintenance treatment (Himmelhoch, 1994).

- Antidepressant response may be rapid (overnight to a couple of weeks) when lithium is given to a patient who is not fully responding to an antidepressant (Himmelhoch, 1994).

- Lithium may be the most effective mood stabilizer for preventing switch to mania when antidepressants are used for bipolar depression (Henry & Demotes-Mainard, 2003).

- Lithium dramatically reduces suicide risk (Ernst & Goldberg, 2004).

- Lithium reduces excess mortality from all medical causes (Cipriani et al., 2005).

- Lithium reverses illness-related atrophy of selected areas of gray matter in responders (Moore et al., 2000).

Divalproex (Depakote) (Manufactured by Abbott)

Unlike virtually all other drugs used in psychiatry, the chemical structure of valproic acid is devoid of rings. It is a synthetic fatty acid, with a linear molecular structure similar to naturally occurring fatty acids. According to Harris et al. (2003), the Germans synthesized valproic acid while attempting to develop substitutes for butter. Apparently, it did not taste very good on corn-on-the-cob, but it was later found to be a useful diluting agent for other drugs, including potential antiepileptic compounds.

In 1963, a French researcher named George Carraz was testing the anticonvulsant activity of a compound that was dissolved in valproic acid. Different doses of the compound did not correlate with anticonvulsant activity, but the mixture nevertheless had antiseizure properties. He then realized the valproic acid itself was an anticonvulsant. Carraz synthesized two related compounds, valproate and valpromide. He then contacted Sergio Borselli, a trainee he knew at a psychiatric hospital in Bassens, France. The hospital had a substantial number of epileptic patients on which to test out the new drugs. Borselli and his supervisor, Pierre Lambert, noticed that, in addition to its antiepileptic properties, valpromide had positive psychotherapeutic effects as well. It alleviated depression, sleep disturbances, and decreased aggression and self-harm.

There are several forms of this compound available in the United States: Valproic acid (Depakene), sodium valproate (Depakene syrup), and divalproex sodium (Depakote), an enteric-coated formulation that contains equal amounts of valproic acid and sodium valproate (see Table 6.6). The divalproex formula is less likely to cause gastrointestinal distress than the other formulas. Divalproex is the formula that received FDA approval for the treatment of epilepsy in 1983 and mania in 1995. It is the form of the drug most often used to treat bipolar illness. It was the first new drug in 22 years to be FDA-approved for acute mania (following chlorpromazine [Thorazine] in 1973).

Divalproex is more effective than lithium in a wider variety of bipolar patients. It works for patients with euphoric mania but also for those with mixed (mania with depressive symptoms), irritable, or dysphoric presentations (Bowden, 1995; Swann et al., 2002). Divalproex may be more effective than lithium in patients who have had many episodes of depression and mania (Swann et al., 1999). However, Ghaemi (personal communication) questions the validity of this finding in light of the Tondo et al. (2003) and Calabrese et al. (2005) studies showing a lack of benefit of divalproex over lithium in rapid-cycling patients.

Divalproex has replaced lithium as the first-line drug used for acute mania for three reasons: its wider spectrum of efficacy, its generally superior tolerability, and because Abbott has vigorously promoted it (no one sends out drug reps to promote the use of lithium).

Divalproex will generally not be prescribed to patients with liver disease or significant liver dysfunction.

Treatment of Acute Mania

Several studies have found divalproex to be more effective than a placebo in acute mania (e.g., Bowden et al., 1994). As with lithium, periodic monitoring of blood levels of the drug, along with liver function (divalproex is metabolized by the liver) and platelet count are required for safety and efficacy. Blood levels should be measured about 12 hours after the last dose and are kept in the 50 to 125 mcg/ml range. Bowden and Singh (2006) cite a study by Keck showing significant differences between valproate and placebo when the divalproex level is kept between 75 and 99 mcg/ml. According to Allen et al. (2006), the best response in acute mania occurs at blood levels above 94 mcg/ml. However, there is probably a great deal of individual variability in effective blood levels of the drug.

Dosing

The starting dose of immediate-release divalproex is generally 250 mg, three times per day. It can also be given all at once at bedtime. Final dosage is generally 750 mg to 3000 mg with many bipolar patients having adequate blood levels and good therapeutic response on 1000 mg to 1500 mg per

TABLE 6.6

Divalproex Preparations

Depakote, enteric-coated tablets: 125 mg, 250 mg, 500 mg

Depakote sprinkle, capsules: 125 mg. Swallowed or opened/sprinkled on food

Depakote ER, enteric-coated extended-release tablets: 250 mg, 500 mg

day. At these dosages and below, many patients have minimal side effects and can expect improvement within 2 weeks given an adequate blood level.

Dosages of Depakote ER (extended release) need to be up to 25 percent higher than dosages of immediate-release Depakote. Thus, a patient taking 1000 mg of Depakote would need to take 1250 mg of Depakote ER to get an equivalent blood level.

Divalproex has also been used in so-called loading doses (large doses) in acutely and severely manic patients in an effort to bring symptoms under rapid control (Hirschfeld et al., 1999).

Side Effects

Except for weight gain and menstrual irregularities, any side effects generally ease with continued treatment. There is generally less of the cognitive dulling seen with lithium. Gastrointestinal distress can be reduced by taking divalproex with food or by using the extended-release form. Increase in appetite and weight gain may be somewhat less with the extended-release form, as well.

Weight gain with divalproex may be more than the weight gain associated with lithium. The problem should be managed early on. Having protein and fat in the morning along with control of simple carbohydrate intake can be key. Exercise obviously can be helpful. The addition of topiramate (Topamax) or zonisamide (Zonegran)—anticonvulsant drugs that cause weight loss—can also be useful.

Hair loss can occur when people take enough divalproex to start gaining weight (around 1000 mg). Hair loss may be helped by taking zinc and selenium supplements.

As a consequence of either weight gain or increased levels of testosterone, long-term use of divalproex in some women may result in menstrual irregularities, abnormal hair growth, acne, male-pattern baldness, or ovarian cysts (McElroy et al., 2006).

TABLE 6.7

Major Side Effects of Divalproex

- Nausea
- Abdominal cramps
- Sedation
- Tremor
- Transient hair loss
- Increased appetite and weight gain
- Oligomenorrhea (irregular or infrequent menstruation) and hyperandrogenism (abnormal growth of hair, acne, male-pattern baldness) in perhaps 10 percent of women (Joffe et al., 2006)

TABLE 6.8

Rare but Dangerous Side Effects of Divalproex

- Sudden, fatal liver failure (hepatotoxicity), most often in children under 2 taking multiple anticonvulsants. Possible warning signs: vomiting, weakness, yellow eyes or skin, swelling, easy bruising
- Inflammation of the pancreas (pancreatitis) which can be fatal. Possible warning signs: abdominal pain, vomiting, loss of appetite.

Table 6.7 lists the major side effects of divalproex; Table 6.8 lists two rare but dangerous side effects; and Table 6.9 lists the signs of divalproex overdose. Table 6.10 lists divalproex's major drug interactions. (*Note: Table 6.10 is not a complete list. Patients should be advised to consult their physicians or pharmacists before taking other drugs, including over-the-counter medications, with divalproex.*)

TABLE 6.9

Signs of Divalproex Overdose

- Severe dizziness
- Severe drowsiness
- Severe tremor
- Irregular or slowed breathing

Maintenance Treatment

Divalproex is not FDA-approved for the maintenance treatment of bipolar disorder, but it is frequently used for and is most likely effective for that stage of treatment. Bowden et al. (2000) found that, in a secondary analysis, it was more effective than placebo and lithium for maintenance in those who initially responded to divalproex before entering the study. Another secondary analysis found that it was effective in the prevention of depressive (but not manic) relapse (Gyulai et al., 2003). These secondary analyses are not definitive, however. Bowden et al. (2005a) found that divalproex, although more effective than lithium in acute treatment of dysphoric mania, did not provide greater prophylactic benefit than lithium in the maintenance treatment of these patients.

TABLE 6.10

Drugs that Interact with Divalproex

- The combination of aspirin and divalproex may increase the risk of bleeding.
- Divalproex may increase the risk of bleeding if taken with warfarin (Coumadin).
- Carbamazepine (Tegretol) can lower blood levels of divalproex.
- Divalproex decreases the clearance of lamotrigine (Lamictal) and increases blood levels of lamotrigine. Using divalproex and lamotrigine together increases the risk of serious rash.

Valnoctamide is a chemical relative of divalproex that apparently has less risk of causing birth defects. It is possible that valnoctamide is antimanic. The drug is being tested in an NIMH-funded trial (visit www .clinicaltrials.gov). If it has efficacy in the treatment of mania, it may be a useful substitute for women of reproductive age with bipolar disorder.

Carbamazepine (Tegretol) (Manufactured by Novartis)

Chemist Walter Schindler synthesized carbamazepine in 1957. Carbamazepine was marketed as a drug for epilepsy and then as a treatment for a type of facial nerve pain (trigeminal neuralgia). It has been used as an anticonvulsant in the United Kingdom since 1965, but was not approved in the United States for that purpose until 1974.

The Japanese, in the early 1970s, were the first to report on the effectiveness of carbamazepine in bipolar disorder. It was also found to be effective in young men with temper outbursts. These men reported they could, for the first time, stop and think about their anger before acting on it (Harris, 2003). But it was not used extensively in the United States until Ballenger and Post (1980) published the results of a double-blind trial showing the effectiveness of carbamazepine in acute manic-depressive illness.

Treatment of Acute Mania

Definitive evidence (based on well-powered, double-blind, placebo-controlled studies) of carbamazepine's effectiveness in acute mania was lacking until 2004. Two trials by Weisler et al. (2004, 2005) provided the evidence that carbamazepine, in an extended-release formulation (Equetro), was an effective antimanic agent. It was FDA approved for treatment of acute mania in 2004. Carbamazepine is used less often in the treatment of acutely manic patients than divalproex. One of the main reasons is that divalproex has far fewer drug interactions than carbamazepine.

Carbamazepine does have advantages, however. It does not cause significant weight gain, it probably works in better in dysphoric, paranoid, and explosive patients than lithium (Perugi et al., 2006), and it is thought it may have a slightly faster onset of action than lithium (Small et al., 1996).

As with lithium and divalproex, blood levels of carbamazepine are required to ensure safety and efficacy. It is critical to check platelet, red, and white cell counts. Carbamazepine is not administered to patients with a history of impaired bone marrow functioning or a condition known as acute intermittent porphyria. Table 6.11 lists the preparations of carbamazepine that are available.

Dosing

Carbamazepine induces liver enzymes that speed its own metabolism. Thus, blood levels tend to drop with time when dosage is held constant. Serum levels

TABLE 6.11

Carbamazepine Preparations

Tegretol, 200 mg tablets

Tegretol, 100 mg chewable tablets

Tegretol, suspension 100 mg/5ml (approximately 1 teaspoon)

Tegretol XR (extended release), 100, 200, 400 mg tablets

Carbatrol, 200, 300 mg extended-release capsules

Equetro, 100, 200, and 300 mg extended-release capsules

of the drug should be in the 6 to 8 mg/L range. Blood levels should be measured 12 hours after the last dose. Dosing for Tegretol XR and Equetro are typically as follows: At first, 200 mg taken two times a day. The final dose is usually not more than 1,600 mg a day.

Side Effects

Initial side effects from carbamazepine can be unpleasant but are usually transient. The major serious, but rare, side effect with carbamazepine is the suppression of bone marrow function and a lowering of white blood cell counts (agranulocytosis). Table 6.12 lists common side effects from carbamazepine, Table 6.13 lists the rare, but dangerous side effects of the drug, and Table 6.14 lists signs of carbamazepine overdose. Table 6.15 shows the drugs with which carbamazepine interacts. (*Note: Table 6.15 is not a complete list.* Patients should be advised to consult their physicians or pharmacists before taking other drugs, including over-the-counter medications, with carbamazepine. Patients should be cautioned about the interaction with grapefruit juice.)

TABLE 6.12

Common Carbamazepine Side Effects

- Dizziness
- Drowsiness
- Unsteadiness
- Nausea
- Vomiting

TABLE 6.13

Rare but Dangerous Side Effects of Carbamazepine

- Skin rash
- Suppression of red and white blood cell production. Warning signs: fever, sore throat, rash, sores in the mouth, easy bruising
- Liver failure

Maintenance

Good data on carbamazepine's effectiveness in preventing new episodes of mania are lacking. Denicoff et al. (1997) compared carbamazepine to lithium in 52 bipolar outpatients in a double-blind design. In the first year patients were treated with lithium or carbamazepine, in the second year they were crossed over to the

TABLE 6.14

Signs and Symptoms of Carbamazepine Overdose

- Irregular breathing
- Restlessness
- Muscular twitching
- Impairment of consciousness
- Convulsions, especially in small children
- Nausea and vomiting

TABLE 6.15

Foods and Drugs that Interact with Carbamazepine

- Grapefruit and grapefruit juice may interact with carbamazepine.
- Carbamazepine accelerates the metabolism of oral contraceptives, rendering them ineffective.
- Carbamazepine decreases the effectiveness of theophylline.
- Carbamazepine decreases the effectiveness of warfarin.
- Carbamazepine decreases blood levels of a number of antidepressants.
- Cimetidine and erythromycin raise carbamazepine levels.

opposite drug, and in the third year they received a combination of lithium and carbamazepine. A large number of patients dropped out of treatment with either agent because of lack of efficacy or side effects. About a third of the patients had marked or moderate improvement on either agent with considerably more having better response to the combination. Because of the small number of patients left in the study, however, the difference in combination treatment did not reach statistical significance. Patients on lithium had a lower rate of relapse to mania than did patients on carbamazepine. Patients with rapid cycling did not do well on monotherapy but did do significantly better on combination treatment.

Kleindienst and Greil (2000) conducted a randomized clinical trial over 2.5 years of lithium versus carbamazepine in 171 bipolar patients. They found that, overall, in bipolar I patients ($N = 114$) lithium was superior to carbamazapine. Carbamazepine was equivalent to lithium in patients with bipolar II disorder or bipolar disorder not otherwise specified ($N = 57$). Classic bipolar I patients (euphoric mania, no mood-incongruent delusions, and no comorbidity; $N = 67$) had a significantly lower hospitalization rate on lithium than on carbamazepine prophylaxis (26 vs. 62%). For the nonclassical group ($N = 104$), a tendency in favor of carbamazepine was found. Patients were generally more satisfied with carbamazepine than lithium.

Hartong et al. (2003), arguing that previous studies on lithium versus carbamazepine were biased, treated 94 remitted patients with at least two episodes of bipolar disorder during the prior 3 years with either carbamazepine or lithium. Patients were randomly assigned to one of these medications in double-blind fashion, either at entry into the study or during the acute index episode previous to entry into the study. They followed the patients for 2 years and found lithium was better than carbamazepine in maintenance treatment.

Overall, the data suggest that carbamazepine should not be expected to provide adequate protection against relapse when used as monotherapy. Combination therapy with lithium is probably best, at least in patients with classic bipolar I disorder. Patients with nonclassical forms of bipolar disorder, however, are much more commonly encountered in outpatient practice. Some evidence suggests they may do well on long-term carbamazepine.

Oxcarbazepine (Trileptil) (Manufactured by Novartis)

This chemical derivative of carbamazepine was FDA approved in 2000 as an add-on drug for seizures. It is structurally similar to carbamazepine but unlike carbamazepine it does not have the potential to suppress bone marrow function. It does not induce its own metabolism, so it is easier to get the patient on a stable dose than it is with carbamazepine. It has fewer side effects than carbamazepine and fewer drug interactions.

Several noncontrolled studies, starting as far back as the 1980s, have provided some evidence that oxcarbazepine is effective in bipolar disorder in general and acute mania in particular. Recent studies on the drug's effectiveness are as follows: Bellino et al. (2005) conducted a study of oxcarbazepine in 17 borderline patients. Four patients did not complete the study because of noncompliance. The 13 patients who completed the study had a statistically significant response on a number of measures including the Hamilton Rating Scales for Depression and the Borderline Personality Disorder Severity Index. Pratoomsri et al. (2005) did an open-label add-on study of oxcarbazepine in 12 patients with bipolar I disorder, two patients with bipolar II disorder, and one with schizoaffective disorder in various mood states. Three patients stopped the medication because of side effects but 9 of 12 were much or very much improved after 1 month on the drug. Raja and Azzoni (2003) compared 27 inpatients with mood or schizoaffective disorders on oxcarbazepine to 27 matched patients on valproate and found similar efficacy on a number of measures. Hummel et al. (2002), in a study with an on-off-on design, showed oxcarbazepine was effective in mild to moderate (but not severe) mania. In a retrospective chart review study, Ghaemi et al. (2002) found that oxcarbazepine appeared effective in about one-half of patients with bipolar disorder and was well tolerated. Reinstein (2001) found that 21 patients first stabilized on valproate and then switched to oxcarbazepine were as stable over 10 weeks as 21 patients continued on valproate.

Controlled trials are needed to verify the efficacy suggested by these open studies. There are no data on the use of oxcarbazepine for maintenance therapy of bipolar disorder.

Licarbazepine is a metabolite of oxcarbazepine under investigation in several NIMH-funded studies (visit www.clinicaltrials.gov) for the treatment of mania when used in combination with lithium or divalproex (visit www.clinicaltrials .gov).

Other Anticonvulsants

The fact that Depakote and Tegretol, both anticonvulsants, are effective in treating mania has naturally led investigators to examine the efficacy of other anticonvulsant drugs. To date, none seem destined to become widely used. Some simply may not work, and others have particularly problematic side effects or have been associated with mood worsening. Some of these drugs, however, have only been tested on patients who have not responded to or who have not responded well to other medications. The possibility exists that the response rate to some of the following agents might be higher if they were used as a first-line treatment. Some may prove to be quite useful in individual patients.

Lamotrigine (Lamictal) (Manufactured by Glaxo)

This drug has gotten the most attention for its role in the acute treatment of bipolar depression, even though it is not FDA labeled for that condition. It is FDA labeled for the maintenance treatment of bipolar disorder because it has been shown to delay relapse in these patients. It is more effective in delaying relapse to depressive than manic episodes (Goodwin et al., 2004). A full discussion of lamotrigine can be found in the next chapter on the treatment of bipolar depression.

Phenytoin (Dilantin)

First synthesized by a German physician in 1908, phenytoin was FDA approved for seizures in 1953. Jack Dreyfus, founder of the Dreyfus Fund, became an advocate for the drug after it was prescribed to him for anxiety and depression. Dreyfus wrote the book *A Remarkable Medicine Has Been Overlooked* and pumped millions of dollars of his own money into an effort to get phenytoin evaluated for alternative uses. The effort has not resulted in widespread use of phenytoin for the treatment of mood disorders.

A group of researchers in Israel have conducted two controlled trials of phenytoin in bipolar disorder. The first was a 5-week double-blind trial of phenytoin and haloperidol versus placebo and haldol in 39 bipolar manic and schizoaffective manic patients (Mishory et al., 2000). Bipolar manic patients taking phenytoin were significantly more improved than patients on placebo. The schizoaffective group did not show improvement. Mishory et al. (2003) then looked at the prophylactic effect of add-on phenytoin in 23 bipolar patients in a placebo-controlled, double-blind cross-over study. These patients were stable at the time of the study but had had at least one mood episode per year in the previous 2 years despite prophylactic treatment with other medications. Nine patients on placebo relapsed but only three on phenytoin had a new mood episode. This was statistically significant, but the study is limited by the small number of patients.

Primidone (Mysoline)

Primidone was first introduced in 1954 as an antiseizure drug. Hayes (1993) was the first to take a look at primidone as a possible mood stabilizer. He studied its effects on 27 seizure-free, affectively ill patients who failed other medications including lithium and divalproex. Nine (33%) of the patients had a sustained positive therapeutic effect to primidone.

Schaffer and Schaffer (1999) treated 26 patients with refractory bipolar disorder with add-on primidone. Eight patients responded, five were considered partial or temporary responders, and 13 were considered treatment failures. The authors noted that although the response rate might be considered low, it was impressive given that the patients had proven refractory to a number of other treatments.

Gabapentin (Neurontin) (Manufactured by Warner-Lambert, now a subsidiary of Pfizer)

Gabapentin was FDA approved in 1993 as an add-on treatment for certain types of seizures and post-herpes infection nerve pain (postherpetic neuralgia). The drug is well tolerated (it is not metabolized but excreted unchanged by the kidneys) and has very few drug interactions, so there had been hopes that it might prove to be a benign, rapid-acting antimanic intervention. Off-label use of gabapentin, including for the treatment of bipolar disorder, grew considerably in the late 1990s and early 2000s, based in part on modest results found in open-label studies (e.g., Ghaemi & Goodwin, 2001) and aggressive marketing of the drug by the manufacturer (originally Parke-Davis, a subsidiary of Warner-Lambert).

Reports began to surface in the media that Warner-Lambert had illegally exaggerated the safety and efficacy of the drug in order to promote its use for patients with bipolar disorder and a number of other conditions. In 2004, Warner-Lambert pleaded guilty to two felonies and paid $430 million in penalties to settle a federal suit charging it fraudulently promoted the drug. Pfizer, who acquired Warner-Lambert in 2000, said the illegal practices took place before it acquired Warner-Lambert (Tansey, 2004).

Indeed, controlled trials have not shown gabapentin to be effective in acute mania (Frye et al., 2000; Guille, 1999; Pande et al., 2000). Vieta et al. (2006) conducted a randomized, 1-year, add-on prophylactic trial of gabapentin in 13 euthymic bipolar I and II patients versus 12 taking placebo. The gabapentin group did somewhat better than the placebo group as measured by the Clinical Global Impressions Scale for Bipolar Illness, Modified. There were no new manic symptoms in the gabapentin group, but there were none in the placebo group either.

As a practical matter, it is doubtful gabapentin will ever be used alone as a treatment for mania when other, clearly effective treatments exist. However, it may well have a role to play as an add-on therapy for some bipolar patients. Clinical experience and some clinical studies (e.g., Carta et al., 2003; Perugi et al., 2002) suggest gabapentin is useful in bipolar patients with comorbid anxiety, panic, and social phobia, and perhaps as a sleep aide.

Side effects include appetite and weight gain, sleepiness, fatigue, problems with coordination, dizziness, and gastrointestinal upset.

Topiramate (Topamax) (Manufactured by Ortho-McNeil)

Topiramate was FDA approved for the treatment of certain seizure disorders in 1999. It is one of only a few psychotropic drugs that cause weight loss. Several noncontrolled trials (e.g., Chengappa et al., 2001; Vieta et al., 2002) indicated that topiramate might be a useful treatment for mania.

But Kushner et al. (2006) recently reported that topiramate showed no effect in acute mania or mixed states in four controlled trials. Despite Kushner's findings, other data suggest topiramate may still be useful in some patients. Loew et al. (2006), for example, found topiramate to be helpful for women meeting diagnostic criteria for borderline personality in a double-blind, placebo-controlled study.

Because of its ability to reduce weight, topiramate can be useful in bipolar patients who are overweight or who may have gained weight as a result of using other psychotropic drugs (Elmslie et al., 2000). For the same reason, it may also be helpful in patients who binge eat or who are bulimic (McElroy et al., 2004b; Nickel et al., 2005).

There can be problems with tolerability. Topiramate can cause significant cognitive dysfunction (leading some clinicians to dub the medication *Dope-amax*). Sleepiness, dizziness, tingling sensations on the skin (paresthesia), and impaired coordination can occur but often decrease with time. Nearsightedness, glaucoma, and kidney stones are potential problems, as well.

Levetiracetam (Keppra) (Manufactured by UCB)

Levetiracetam was FDA approved as an adjunctive treatment for certain types of seizure disorders in 1999. No controlled data exist on this drug for the treatment of mania. Two case reports and several open studies have been published.

Kaufman (2004) reported on one rapid-cycling patient who responded to levetiracetam acutely and remained well for 1 year. This patient had failed 15 other medication trials (either individually or in combination). Bräunig and Kruger

(2003) reported that two patients with rapid-cycling bipolar disorder who had levetiracetam added to conventional treatments improved.

Open studies include Post et al. (2005). Post and colleagues used levetiracetam with 34 bipolar patients who had various symptoms including mania ($N = 7$) and cycling ($N = 14$) despite ongoing treatment with mood stabilizers. The majority of patients with manic symptoms at baseline (seven manic, nine cycling) showed improvement in the Young Mania Rating Scale (YMRS) in the first 2 weeks. Seven of these 16 patients met the criterion for response and remission at last observation, but 4 showed intervening periods of moderate to marked exacerbation. Simon et al. (2004) found open-label levetiracetam to be helpful in 20 adult outpatients who had a primary diagnosis of Social Anxiety Disorder (some of whom had comorbid depression). Finally, Grunze et al. (2003) reported on the use of levetiracetam as an add-on to haloperidol in 10 bipolar I acutely manic patients. He found the drug was effective in reducing YMRS scores 50 percent (considered a response to the drug) in seven of ten patients by day 28.

Common side effects with levetiracetam include dizziness, sleepiness, and feelings of weakness (asthenia). Levetiracetam does not cause weight gain, however.

Zonisamide (Zonegran) (Manufactured by Elan)

Zonisamide was FDA approved as an adjunctive treatment for certain kinds of seizure disorders in 1999. It was developed in Japan and a group of Japanese researchers were the first to report on its effects in mania.

No controlled data exist on the use of zonisamide in the treatment of acute mania. McElroy et al. (2005) evaluated the effects of open-label, adjunctive zonisamide in a group of 62 bipolar patients with various symptoms including mania in a prospective 8-week acute trial followed by a 48-week continuation trial. Thirty-four patients with manic symptoms at the start of the study showed significant reductions in mania in the acute phase. Nineteen of these patients went on to the continuation phase and maintained their improvement. However, 20 of the original 62 patients discontinued zonisamide for worsening mood symptoms. McElroy et al. (2004a) reported that zonisamide was effective in reducing binge-eating frequency in 8 of 15 outpatients with binge-eating disorder during an open-label, prospective trial. One subject discontinued because of lack of response, two for lack of adherence, and four for side effects. Kanba et al. (1994) reported that 12 of 15 patients in this open study showed more than moderate global improvement on zonisamide and five of these responders "showed remarkable global improvement" (p. 707). None of the 15 patients had to be taken off the medication because of side effects.

Zonisamide is one of only a few psychotropic drugs that causes significant weight loss. Although it may be useful in treating bipolar disorder, it appears from open studies that it may carry a significant side-effect burden. Since it is a sulfa drug, those with sulfa allergy should not use it. Common side effects include kidney stones, dizziness, lack of coordination, confusion, and sleepiness.

Tiagabine (Gabitril) (Manufactured by Cephalon)

Tiagabine was FDA approved in 1997 as an adjunctive treatment for certain types of seizure disorders. No controlled data exist on the use of tiagabine in the treatment of acute mania.

Kaufman (1998) reported that adjunctive low-dose tiagabine was helpful in three patients—two with bipolar disorder and one with schizoaffective disorder, bipolar type. He found the drug had no adverse effects. Grunze et al. (1999), on the other hand, reported tiagabine provoked a seizure in one of eight acutely manic bipolar I inpatients and nausea and vomiting in another. None of the eight (two with tiagabine monotherapy and six with the drug as an add-on to other mood stabilizers) had significant improvement in their mania after 2 weeks on the drug. They suspected that the side effects may have been caused by rapid dose escalation.

Schaffer and Schaffer (1999) treated 22 adult outpatients with bipolar disorder considered unsatisfactory responders to standard medications in an open fashion with adjunctive low-dose tiagabine. After 6 months, 8 of the 22 patients were judged to be responders. The 14 nonresponders had to discontinue tiagabine because of side effects, including one who had seizures.

Finally, Suppes et al. (2002) found that only 3 of 13 treatment refractory patients in an open-label tiagabine add-on study showed much or very much improvement. Ten had no improvement or had a worsening of symptoms. Two of these ten may have had seizures.

There have been numerous other reports of new onset seizures and prolonged or continuous seizures (status epilepticus), most often when the drug was used off-label for psychiatric purposes in nonepileptic patients. As a result, in 2005, the FDA asked that a bolded warning be added to the labeling for tiagabine so prescribers would be aware of this risk. The drug's manufacturer also agreed to a plan to discourage health care professionals and patients from such off-label use.

Tiagabine may be useful for some manic patients when used at low doses as an add-on therapy; but given the problems with seizures, it seems unlikely tiagabine will be tested in controlled trials. Common side effects include sleepiness, confusion, dizziness, and lack of coordination.

Typical Antipsychotics

The antipsychotic drug chlorpromazine (Thorazine)—discovered in 1952 and originally developed for use in the field of anesthesia—was a standard treatment for acute mania in the United States for many years. It was formally approved for that purpose by the FDA in 1973. The antipsychotic haloperidol (Haldol) was invented by the Belgian chemist Paul Janssen (founder of Janssen Pharmaceuticals) and became available in 1958. It soon became widely used in the treatment of the violent, agitated behavior and psychotic thinking of acutely ill schizophrenic and manic patients. A comprehensive review of haloperidol studies indicates it is effective in mania and equal in overall efficacy to olanzapine or risperidone, although it causes less weight gain than olanzapine (Cipriani et al., 2006). It rapidly calms manic patients yet causes little of the sedation so characteristic of chlorpromazine. There are at least a dozen other typical antipsychotic drugs available in the United States.

The antipsychotic properties of these and other drugs in this class are due to their ability to block (antagonize) activity of the neurotransmitter dopamine along neural pathways responsible for emotional responses. But, these drugs also block the activity of dopamine along neural pathways that control movement. As a result, they produce a number of movement disorders known collectively as extrapyramidal symptoms, or EPS. Extrapyramidal symptoms include restlessness (akathisia); muscular spasms, typically of the neck, tongue, and jaw (dystonia); muscle stiffness; tremor; and shuffling gait (Parkinsonism).

When typical antipsychotics are used to treat mania, there is some evidence that continuation of these agents after remission of mania results in *shorter* time to depressive relapse and *more* depressive symptoms (Zarate & Tohen, 2004). Bipolar patients may be more prone to EPS on typical antipsychotics than schizophrenic patients (Nasrallah et al., 1988).

Atypical Antipsychotics

The controlled trials that have demonstrated the efficacy of individual atypical antipsychotics in patients with mania have been thoroughly reviewed by Vieta and Goikolea (2005) and Dunner (2005). Following is general information on this class of drugs followed by specific information on each drug's common side effects and dose range.

Except perhaps in emergency rooms, the older antipsychotics such as halo-peridol (Haldol) have been largely replaced by second-generation atypical antipsychotics for the treatment of mania. This is due primarily to their generally more favorable side-effect profiles (especially the lower risk of EPS) and not to any unique effectiveness. However, atypical antipsychotics are far being from benign compounds. Some of them can cause substantial weight gain, for instance, thereby increasing the risk of Type II diabetes and cardiovascular disease.

Atypical antipsychotics were designed to treat schizophrenia. In the early 1990s, shortly after the introduction of the first atypical antipsychotic drug clo-zapine (Clozaril) in the United States, researchers reported the drug appeared useful in schizoaffective and psychotically depressed patients (e.g., McElroy et al., 1991). It was soon discovered in clinical trials for the other atypicals that not only psychotic symptoms were relieved but that schizophrenic patients' mood symptoms improved, as well (Keck & McElroy, 2006). All the atypicals, with the exception of Clozaril, have received FDA approval for the treatment of mania.

On the whole, all are equally effective (Perlis et al., 2006; Vieta & Goikolea, 2005).

Because of their effects on many neurotransmitter pathways, not just dopamine, atypical antipsychotics treat a broader spectrum of symptoms than the older, typical antipsychotics. They all diminish manic symptoms, agitation, and aggression, and can be helpful in treatment-resistant patients (particularly mixed manic and rapid-cycling patients; Ertugrul & Meltzer, 2003). Chengappa et al. (2004) have suggested, as well, that they may have mood-stabilizing properties. This has not been convincingly demonstrated, however. Malhi et al. (2005) believe that "based on the evidence thus far it is perhaps premature to describe the atypical antipsychotics as mood stabilizers. Individual agents may eventually be able to claim this label [but] much further research is needed, especially with respect to maintenance and relapse prevention" (p. 29). Ghaemi (personal communication) does not believe atypicals have substantial mood-stabilizing properties when used alone. Olanzapine and aripiprazole have been FDA approved for maintenance treatment of bipolar disorder, however.

Problems Associated with Many of the Atypical Antipsychotics

Induction of Hypomania

Although atypicals have the same rate of inducing hypomania as placebo in randomized, controlled trials (Ghaemi, personal communication), there have been numerous case reports of atypical antipsychotics causing hypomania. Rachid et al. (2004) did a MEDLINE search from 1999 to 2003 for case reports of hypomania associated with the use of atypical antipsychotics. He found five such reports for olanzapine (Zyprexa), six for risperidone (Risperdal), five for quetiapine (Seroquel), and 11 for ziprasidone (Geodon). If, in fact, these drugs can cause hypomania, it may be because of their effects on serotonin neurotransmission.

EPS and Tardive Dyskinesia

Atypical antipsychotics, as a class, may have less risk of producing EPS than the older, typical antipsychotics. Reduced risk of EPS and the effects on multiple neurotransmitter pathways are why the drugs are called atypical. The reduced risk of EPS may be especially important for bipolar patients, who have been reported to be more prone to EPS than schizophrenic patients, at least on typical antipsychotics (e.g., Nasrallah et al., 1988).

Unfortunately, the risk of EPS with some of the atypicals may be higher in clinical practice than research studies suggest. Rates of EPS are reported to be in the range of 5 to 15 percent in clinical trials. But Ghaemi et al. (2006) found that more than 50 percent of a sample of bipolar patients treated in a clinical setting with a variety of atypical antipsychotics experienced EPS. In a multiple regression analysis that adjusted for confounding variables, they found that akathisia was less common in quetiapine and olanzapine than in risperidone, ziprasidone, and aripiprazole. An earlier study (Guille et al., 2000) found a 28.6 percent rate of EPS in patients treated with risperidone, olanzapine, or clozapine.

EPS can be treated with anticholinergic or antiparkisonian drugs such as benztropine (Cogentin) or trihexyphenidyl (Artane). Many clinicians used to routinely give these drugs to any patient starting typical antipsychotics. They are generally given to patients taking atypical antipsychotics only if the patient develops EPS. Patients can develop cognitive impairment taking these drugs and a few may also develop anticholinergic deliria with fleeting visual hallucinations.

Five patients with various diagnoses including bipolar disorder who developed akathisia on olanzapine (Zyprexa) or risperidone (Risperdal) had their akathisia successfully treated with the antidepressant mirtazapine (Remeron; Ranjan et al., 2006). The mirtazapine also helped treat depressive symptoms in some of the patients. Caution is advised in using this intervention, however. Although antidepressants can be effective in the acute treatment of patients with bipolar depression, there are also a number of significant risks associated with the use of antidepressants in this population (refer to Chapter 7).

Antipsychotic drugs can lead to involuntary, irregular movements of the tongue, the face, and other parts of the body, known as tardive dyskinesia. It is not possible to predict which patients will get tardive dyskinesia. The severity of tardive dyskinesia can range from mild (minor restlessness of the tongue or fingers) to disfiguring. Tardive dyskinesia has traditionally been considered a side effect that emerges only with prolonged treatment. While prolonged treatment increases the risk of tardive dyskinesia, it can emerge early in treatment, as well (Ghaemi et al., 2006; Shirzadi & Ghaemi, 2006).

There is no generally accepted treatment for tardive dyskinesia. Vitamin E, the essential fatty acid EPA, and melatonin have been reported to help some patients. Clozapine and quetiapine have also been reported to help patients who developed tardive dyskinesia on other antipsychotic drugs. Tardive dyskinesia can be irreversible in some patients.

The Metabolic Syndrome

A person is said to have the metabolic syndrome when they have three or more of the following: high blood pressure, abdominal obesity, high triglyceride levels, high LDL levels, low HDL levels, and high fasting levels of blood sugar (Newcomer, 2004). The atypical antipsychotics clozapine (Clozaril), olanzapine (Zyprexa), quetiapine (Seroquel), and risperidone (Risperdal) can contribute to the development of one or more of these metabolic abnormalities and the metabolic syndrome (Abilify generally has minimal and Geodon little to no impact on metabolic parameters in adults). The mean 1-year weight gain with many of the atypicals, for instance, can be substantial, as shown in Figure 6.1. People with the metabolic syndrome are at increased risk for developing cardiovascular disease and other serious medical disorders such as Type II diabetes.

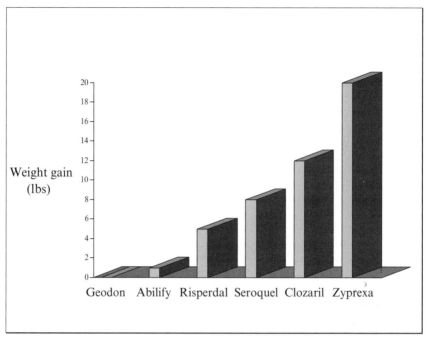

Figure 6.1 *Mean 1-Year Weight Gain with Atypical Antipsychotics*
Source: Data from Meyer (2004).

Bipolar patients tend to be overweight to begin with (Elmslie et al., 2000; Simon et al., 2006) and circulatory disorders are the leading cause of natural death in these patients (Angst et al., 2002; Tsai et al., 2005). Diabetes appears to be more common in bipolar patients than people in the general population, as well (McIntyre et al., 2005; Waxmonsky et al., 2005).

The impact atypical antipsychotics can have on bipolar patients' overall health is clearly something clinicians should attend to and manage. Clinicians from a number of disciplines have come together to address this problem (ADA et al., 2004). Narasimhan et al. (2005), for instance, suggested guidelines shown in Table 6.16.

The Neuroleptic Malignant Syndrome

A potentially life-threatening symptom complex, Neuroleptic Malignant Syndrome (NMS), is associated with the use of both older antipsychotic drugs and the second-generation atypical antipsychotics. Manifestations of NMS are fever, muscle rigidity, confusion, irregular pulse or blood pressure, rapid heart beat, shortness of breath, and cardiac arrhythmias. Most cases of NMS develop over the course of 1 to 3 days within the first month of treatment with antipsychotics. Neuroleptic Malignant Syndrome is a medical emergency. The reported incidence in the typical antipsychotic drugs is 0.02 percent to 2.44 percent (Ananth

TABLE 6.16

Preventing and Managing Weight Gain in Patients Using Atypical Antipsychotics

- Identify patients at high risk of weight gain (family history of obesity, sedentary lifestyle).
- Avoid use of olanzapine in high-risk group.
- Get family and personal history of metabolic or heart disease.
- Get baseline weight, abdominal girth, blood pressure, fasting blood glucose, and lipid profiles and monitor or have these assessed periodically.
- Refer patients to programs that help patients make lifestyle changes.
- Switch patients who gain 5 lbs or more in 1 month or more than 11 lbs in any time frame to ziprasidone or aripiprazole.
- Encourage healthful diet and exercise.
- Consider adding topiramate (Topamax) or zonisamide (Zonegran).

Source: Narasimhan et al. (2005).

et al., 2004). Ananth found 68 reported cases of NMS in the literature: 21 for clozapine (Clozaril), 23 for risperidone (Risperdal), 23 for olanzaping (Zyprexa), and 19 for quetiapine (Seroquel).

Specific Atypicals

Clozapine (Clozaril) (Manufactured by Novartis)

Clozapine was developed in 1961, and first used in Europe. In 1975, it became apparent that clozapine could cause a dangerous reduction in white blood cell (agranulocytosis). Some clozapine-treated patients died as a result of this side effect, so the manufacturer took the drug off the market. When later studies showed clozapine worked for some patients when no other drug did, the FDA approved its use for treatment-resistant schizophrenia, but required regular blood monitoring to detect changes in white blood cells before agranulocytosis developed. Clozapine's introduction in the United States in 1989 ushered in a new generation of antipsychotic medications. In December of 2002, clozapine was also approved for reducing the risk of suicide in schizophrenic or schizoaffective patients.

Although not FDA labeled for bipolar disorder, the drug has been shown in open studies to be effective for severe, psychotic, treatment-resistant, mixed, and rapid-cycling cases (e.g., Ciapparelli et al., 2003; Green et al., 2000). There has also been one randomized, but not placebo-controlled, trial of clozapine in acute mania (Barbini et al., 1997). Thirty hospitalized manic patients were treated with either clozapine or chlorpromazine (Thorazine) for 3 weeks. Clozapine-treated patients improved somewhat more rapidly but both drugs were equally effective at the end of 3 weeks. Clozapine has also been reported to reduce nicotine, alcohol, and drug use in schizophrenics (Drake et al., 2000).

Weight gain, sedation, dizziness, excessive salivation, constipation, and rapid heartbeat (tachycardia) are among the more common side effects. There is a 1.3 percent risk of agranulocytosis according to the *Physicians' Desk Reference*, which generally occurs between the second and fourth months of therapy. The onset is unpredictable. Some patients show a slow decline in white blood cells, whereas others have an abrupt drop. The onset is not related to dose. Weekly blood cell counts are therefore required for at least the first several months, but should probably be done indefinitely. Patients should immediately report the onset of lethargy, weakness, fever, sore throat, or any flu-like symptoms that might suggest infection. There is a risk of seizures associated with the use of clozapine.

Clozapine is available in 25 mg and 100 mg tablets. The starting dose is 25 mg per day at bedtime. Common doses range from 200 to 600 mg/day.

Olanzapine (Zyprexa) (Manufactured by Eli Lily)

Approved for use in schizophrenia in 1996, olanzapine became the first atypical antipsychotic to be FDA approved to treat acute mania. This occurred in the year 2000. It also got an FDA indication for the maintenance treatment of mania in 2004. It was only the third drug to receive such an indication (after lithium in 1974 and lamotrigine [Lamictal] in 2003).

Olanzapine is the most extensively studied atypical antipsychotic for bipolar disorder. It has been studied as monotherapy for acute mania, compared to lithium and divalproex in the treatment of acute mania, examined for its effectiveness as an adjunct to lithium and divalproex in acute mania and rapid cycling, studied as monotherapy for maintenance, and compared to lithium and divalproex for maintenance. It has also been studied for the treatment of bipolar depression. The drug's manufacturer has funded all these trials. Eli Lily has undoubtedly been hoping that olanzapine could pick up some of the share of the bipolar treatment market currently cornered by Abbott (manufacturers of divalproex–Depakote).

The studies indicating its effectiveness as monotherapy in the acute and maintenance treatment of mania have been reviewed in Vieta and Goikolea (2005), Dunner (2005), and Tohen et al. (2006). Discussed here are the trials comparing olanzapine to lithium and divalproex in both acute and maintenance treatment. The trials in which olanzapine was used as an adjunct to lithium or divalproex will be discussed in the final section of this chapter: "From Research to Practice: The Treatment of Acute Mania." The use of olanzapine for bipolar depression will be discussed in the next chapter.

Tohen et al. (2002a) found that olanzapine yielded greater mean improvement of mania ratings compared to divalproex in a 3-week, randomized, double-blind trial. The mean score for the divalproex group on the Young Mania Rating Scale

(YMRS) was only 3 points higher than for the olanzapine group, however. During the 3-week study, 47 percent of the patients treated with olanzapine achieved remission versus 34 percent of the divalproex patients, which was statistically significant.

In a study sponsored by Abbott (the manufacturer of divalproex), however, the drugs were equally effective in acute mania but divalproex-treated patients had fewer side effects (Zajecka et al., 2002). This was not a placebo-controlled trial, however, so it is impossible to determine if the drugs were truly effective or just equally ineffective.

Tohen et al. (2003) extended the treatment of the patients in the 2002 olanzapine versus divalproex study to 44 weeks. At the end of the 44 weeks, olanzapine-treated patients continued to show somewhat greater improvement in YMRS total scores than the divalproex patients and took considerably less time to remit (14 days vs. 62 days). But, there was no statistically significant difference in the rates of remission or relapse to mania or depression produced by the two drugs. The trial was not placebo controlled so it is not clear if the latter result implies equal effectiveness or equal ineffectiveness. In addition, about 85 percent of the participants in the study dropped out.

Tohen et al. (2005) compared olanzapine to lithium for relapse prevention in manic or mixed bipolar patients in a 52-week, randomized, double-blind trial. Overall, there was no statistically significant difference in relapse to a mood episode, but olanzapine was superior to lithium in preventing manic mixed-episode relapses in a secondary analysis. The patients continued on olanzapine had all achieved remission acutely with olanzapine and 60 percent of the patients in this study dropped out, so the degree to which the results can be generalized are limited.

Ketter et al. (2006) found that olanzapine was more effective in preventing relapse to mania or mixed episodes than lithium when given to bipolar I patients who had had no more than two previous manic or mixed episodes. This was a post-hoc analysis, however, so the results would need to be replicated in a prospective trial. Ghaemi (personal communication) pointed out that post-hoc analyses have a high likelihood of producing positive findings.

Sanger et al. (2003), in a secondary analysis of a placebo-controlled but non-randomized 3-week trial, found that olanzapine was effective in reducing manic symptoms in patients with a history of rapid cycling. The trial was not long enough, however, to determine if olanzapine was effective in reducing the rapid cycling.

Dizziness, dry mouth, and sedation are the more common side effects of this drug. Weight gain of 15 to 25 pounds in 1 year is not unusual with olanzapine (Meyer, 2004). Cavazzoni et al. (2006), in a retrospective Lily-sponsored study, reported that olanzapine does not increase the risk of EPS for patients with bipolar disorder compared to patients with schizophrenia. However, the study did not show that olanzapine was without risk of causing EPS. Guille et al. (2000) and

Ghaemi et al. (2006) have reported that olanzapine produces EPS, although the rate of EPS may be somewhat less than that seen with risperidone, ziprasidone, and aripiprazole.

Oral olanzapine is available in 2.5 mg, 5 mg, 7.5 mg, 10 mg, 15 mg, and 20 mg tablets. It is also available in orally disintegrating tablets (Zyprexa Zydis) in 5 mg, 10 mg, 15 mg, and 20 mg strengths. Oral olanzapine is administered once a day, generally beginning with 10 or 15 mg. Olanzapine is also available as an intramuscular injection.

Risperidone (Risperdal) (Manufactured by Janssen)

Risperidone was FDA approved in 1993 for the treatment of schizophrenia. It gained FDA approval in 2003 for acute mania. Risperidone has the potential for causing EPS at higher doses. The drug can cause significant weight gain, although not as much as clozapine and olanzapine. The risk of a patient developing the metabolic syndrome on risperidone is therefore somewhat less than with clozapine or olanxapine. Unlike other atypicals, however, it increases the hormone prolactin. Increased prolactin can cause breast lactation, breast enlargement, and disrupted menstrual function.

Vieta et al. (2001) did an open study of risperidone in 44 bipolar II patients presenting with hypomania. Risperidone appeared to be effective in this group, either in combination with mood stabilizers or when used alone. An earlier open study by Vieta et al. (1998) suggested risperidone might be of benefit in rapid-cycling patients.

Side effects of this drug include constipation or diarrhea, sedation, and dry mouth. Risperidone will be off-patent in 2007 and become available in generic form. The drug is available in .25 mg, .5 mg, 1 mg, 2 mg, 3 mg, and 4mg tablets. It is available in a 1 mg/ml oral solution, .5 mg, 1 mg, and 2 mg oral disintegrating tablets and a long-acting injectable form called Risperdal Consta. Starting dose is generally 1 mg per day. The common dose range is 2 to 6 mg/day.

Paliperidone ER (Invega)

This is the principal active metabolite of risperidone. It received FDA approval for the treatment of schizophrenia in December 2006. The main side effects include akathisia, tachycardia, and somnolence. The drug is being evaluated in an NIMH study as an add-on to lithium or divalproex for the treatment of mania and mixed bipolar episodes (visit www.clinicaltrials.gov).

Quetiapine (Seroquel) (Manufactured by AstraZeneca)

Quetiapine was FDA approved in 1997 for the treatment of schizophrenia and in 2004 for the treatment of mania. It was also approved for the treatment of bipolar depression in October of 2006 (see Chapter 7 for more details).

Quetiapine has a very low incidence of EPS. It can be quite sedating, however, and can cause dizziness and modest weight gain. The sedating qualities of the drug can be a useful side effect, however, when the entire dose is given at bed-time.

Stamouli and Lykcouras (2006) noted a previous case report of obsessive-compulsive disorder being induced by the use of quetiapine (Seroquel) and then reported on three cases of their own of de novo obsessive-compulsive disorder apparently induced by the drug.

The drug is available in 25 mg, 100 mg, 200 mg tablets, and a 300 mg caplet. Starting dose is generally 50 mg twice per day. Doses for mania range from 300 to 600 mg per day.

Ziprasidone (Geodon) (Manufactured by Pfizer)

Ziprasidone was FDA approved in 2001 for schizophrenia and 2004 for acute treatment of mania. It is a well-tolerated drug that generally has no effect on meta-bolic processes. It does not cause weight gain. Sleepiness, dizziness, nausea, and headache are the more common side effects. EPS, especially restlessness (akathisia) is possible. There is a risk of a change in heart rhythm known as prolongation of the QT interval. But Geodon has been prescribed to millions of people and there have been no reports of QT-related deaths.

Ziprazidone is available in 20 mg, 40 mg, 60 mg, and 80 mg capsules. Starting dose is generally 20 to 40 mg twice per day, with food. Typical doses range from 40 to 160 mg per day. It is also available as an intramuscular injection.

Aripiprazole (Abilify) (Manufactured by Otsuka America)

Aripiprazole was FDA approved in 2002 for schizophrenia and for the acute treatment of mania in 2004. It was also approved for the maintenance treatment of mania in 2005. It is unique in its complex effects on neurotransmitters and their receptors. It can block a dopamine receptor if it is overstimulated (acts as an antagonist) and stimulate a receptor to some degree when activity is needed (acts as a partial agonist; DeLeon et al., 2004).

Aripiprazole has minimal effect on metabolic processes and generally causes only slight weight gain in adults. Sleepiness is a common side effect and akathisia can be a problem, as well.

Aripiprazole is available in 5 mg, 10 mg, 15 mg, 20 mg, and 30 mg tablets. It is also available in a liquid preparation that delivers approximately 5 mg of aripiprazole per teaspoon. The starting dose is usually 15 mg. The typical dose range is 15 to 30 mg.

Atypical Antipsychotic Drugs under Investigation

A new generation of antipsychotics will be coming on the market over the next few years, including bifeprunox, arsenapine, iloperidone (Zomaril), and blonan-serin (Lonasen). These antipsychotics will differ in their neurotransmitter effects from most of the currently used atypical antipsychotics.

For example, bifeprunox is an atypical antipsychotic agent under development by Solvay Pharmaceuticals as a treatment for schizophrenia that has potential use in the treatment of bipolar disorder. It is being tested in an NIMH trial for schizophrenia (visit www.clinicaltrials.gov). Bifeprunox differs from most first-generation atypical antipsychotics in that it can decrease dopamine activity in one part of the brain while simultaneously increasing dopamine activity in other areas. In common with aripiprazole, bifeprunox also stimulates a specific serotonin receptor. This property may contribute to efficacy against the negative symptoms of schizophrenia. It apparently has a low incidence of EPS and is not likely to induce weight gain or adversely affect blood lipids or blood glucose levels.

High Dose Benzodiazepine Drugs

Lorazepam (Ativan) or clonazepam (Klonopin) are sometimes used for the treatment of acute mania because they have less of a side-effect burden than antipsychotic drugs (Modell et al., 1985). Bradwejn et al. (1990) found that in a controlled trial, lorazepam appeared more effective for treating acute mania than clonazepam. Lenox et al. (1992) found that lorazepam was as effective as haldol for manic agitation. On the other hand, Curtin and Schulz (2004) conducted a meta-analysis of studies on the effects of lorazepam and clonazepam in acute mania. They concluded that clonazepam has demonstrated efficacy in acute mania but that the evidence for lorazepam is inconclusive.

Although rare, some patients may become disinhibited on these drugs. That is, they may become more agitated and angry. This may particularly be the case for patients who had a childhood history of attention deficit hyperactivity disorder.

Calcium Channel Blockers

This class of drugs is used to treat high blood pressure, angina, and some irregularities of heart rhythm. Calcium channel blockers regulate calcium flow across cell membranes. Faulty mechanisms for regulating calcium ion levels within cells may be partially responsible for the symptoms of mania (Grunze, 2006). The two most widely studied drugs in this class are verapamil (Calan) and nimodipine (Nimotop). Amlodipine (Norvasc) and isradipine (DynaCirc) have been mentioned in the literature, as well.

Verapamil (Calan)

Open studies and case reports have suggested this drug might be useful in treating mania (e.g., Wisner et al., 2002). An open study by Barton and Gitlin (1987), however, showed it had no effect in acute mania but that it appeared to effectively treat two patients with antidepressant-induced hypomania, and was useful as a maintenance strategy in two of four patients.

Results of controlled trials of verapamil are mixed, as well. Dubovsky et al. (1986) found it helpful in five of seven acutely manic patients. None of these patients responded to placebo. Janicak et al. (1998), on the other hand, found there was no difference between verapamil and placebo in a trial of the drug in 32 patients with acute mania. A controlled trial of verapamil combined with magnesium oxide was more effective in acute mania than verapamil alone (Giannini et al., 2000). At least two controlled trials have compared verapamil to lithium. One showed it was equal to lithium (Garza-Trevino et al., 1992), but another demonstrated that lithium was superior (Walton et al., 1996).

Taken as a whole, these data suggest verapamil may be of some use to individual bipolar patients as an add-on treatment. However, it is not a first-line antimanic drug.

Nimodipine (Nimotop)

Open trials have demonstrated nimodipine to be effective in acute mania and in patients with rapid cycling (Brunet et al., 1990; Pazzaglia et al., 1993). A group of clinicians reported it was helpful in a pregnant patient who was not able to tolerate lithium (Yingling et al., 2002). Grunze et al. (1996) found that it might be considered as an alternative to antipsychotic drugs for prophylaxis.

In the only published controlled double-blind trial of nimodipine, Pazzaglia et al. (1993) found the drug to be helpful in ultra-rapid and ultradian (within the same day) cycling patients. In a later study, Pazzaglia et al. (1998), found that 4 of 14 partial responders to nimodipine improved significantly with the addition of carbamazepine.

In 2000, Goodnick stated that "nimodipine may have particular benefits for those diagnostic subclasses of bipolar disorder most resistant to therapy, e.g., ultra-rapid-cycling bipolars and brief recurrent depressions" (p. 165). The drug's short half-life and consequent need for multiple daily doses are a disadvantage, however (Grunze, 2006).

Tamoxifen (Nolvadex)

Research into the pathophysiology of mood disorders has expanded from understanding disordered communications *between* cells via intercellular neurotransmitters to what happens in the cell membrane and to signaling systems *inside* of cells after various molecules have attached to cell membrane receptors. Manji (1999) found that one of the many effects of both lithium and valproate, in spite of their being so structurally dissimilar, is inhibition of the intracellular signaling pathway known as protein kinase C (PKC). When Manji learned that tamoxifen, an estrogen receptor blocking drug, also inhibited PKC, he began to study its use in manic patients. He is currently conducting a placebo-controlled study of the drug in a National Institute of Mental Health (NIMH) sponsored study (visit www.clinicaltrials.gov).

Kulkarni (2006) reported that 13 women with mania or hypomania were treated with the drug in a 28-day, double-blind, placebo-controlled study. The women given tamoxifen showed significant improvement in symptoms of mania compared to those on placebo.

Mexiletine (Mexitil)

This is a medication used to treat patients with irregularities in heart rhythms. Schaffer et al. (2000) did a 6-week, open study of the drug in 20 subjects with rapid-cycling bipolar disorder who had failed to respond or were intolerant to lithium, valproic acid, and carbamazepine. Of 13 patients completing the trial, 8 were full or partial responders.

Opiates

Some researchers have suggested that faulty regulation of the brain's natural opiate system may be linked to pathological mood states and that compounds affecting this system could prove useful in the treatment of mania (Gold et al., 1982). Maremmani et al. (2006) describe some of the research showing that opiates have antidysphoric, anxiolytic, and antiaggressive effects. The use of opiates in the treatment of patients with mood disorders has been limited by their obvious potential for abuse.

The NIMH, however, is sponsoring a pilot, open-label study of Talwin, a combination of pentazocine (a narcotic) and naloxone, in acutely manic inpatients (visit www.clinicaltrials.gov). This combination of drugs may help modulate parts of the opiate system responsible for mania while reducing the risk for abuse.

From Research to Practice: The Treatment of Acute Mania

The initial treatment of acute euphoric mania is usually done on an inpatient basis. It generally involves the use of lithium or divalproex in combination with an atypical antipsychotic for severe mania and mixed states. For mild to moderate mania, lithium or divalproex might well be sufficient (American Psychiatric Association, 2002).

There is evidence that starting with an atypical antipsychotic alone might be appropriate in acute mania. Bowden et al. (2005b) showed quetiapine and lithium to be equivalent; Zajecka et al. (2002) found olanzapine and divalproex were equally effective in acute mania; Berk et al. (1999) showed olanzapine was equivalent to lithium; and Segal et al. (1998) showed risperidone equivalent to lithium in the treatment of mania.

Is there an advantage to combining an atypical antipsychotic and either lithium or divalproex in acute mania? Sachs et al. (2002, 2004) found that giving an atypical antipsychotic to patients hospitalized for a manic episode who were already on a mood stabilizer was effective in controlling mania. About a third of the patients in the Sachs et al. (2002) study were started on an atypical antipsychotic and mood stabilizer at the same time. In this group of patients, the benefit of the atypical antipsychotic was much less apparent.

In similar fashion, Yatham et al. (2003) found that 59 percent of patients already on lithium, divalproex, or carbamazepine for at least 2 weeks responded when given risperidone compared to 41 percent given a placebo. Risperidone did not help a great deal when it was started shortly after a mood stabilizer, however.

Tohen et al. (2002b) conducted a 6-week, double-blind, randomized, placebo-controlled trial of olanzapine given to manic or mixed patients who did not respond adequately to either lithium or divalproex. The addition of the olanzapine improved the outcome in these patients compared to continued lithium or divalproex monotherapy, but the decrease in mean Young Mania Rating Scale scores was only 4 points. In addition, the patients were treated with lithium and divalproex at relatively low serum levels for a brief period. Higher doses might have been effective over time.

Tohen et al. (2004) found there was no difference in the time to relapse into mania or depression for the combination of olanzapine and either lithium or divalproex compared to either lithium or divalproex alone. Patients taking olanzapine added to lithium or divalproex did, however, show some possible mild symptomatic benefits on secondary analysis (Ghaemi, personal communication). All the patients in this study achieved full remission with olanzapine acutely, so the results can be generalized only to this group (Perugi et al., 2006).

In patients with acute dysphoric mania (predominantly manic symptoms with depressive symptoms mixed in), the addition of olanzapine to ongoing lithium or valproate monotherapy significantly improved depressive symptoms, mania, and suicidality ratings in a secondary analysis of a double-blind, placebo-controlled study (Baker et al., 2004).

Lin et al. (2006) claim a 20 percent increase in response rates when a mood stabilizer and an atypical antipsychotic are combined. However, there is no clear evidence that the combination is more effective than a mood stabilizer alone in acutely manic or dysphoric patients who have never been treated with a mood stabilizer (Ghaemi, personal communication; Sachs et al., 2002). Moreover, the use of lithium and valproate at higher doses for longer periods might produce similar results as combination therapy.

Overall, the studies demonstrating olanzapine's superiority to lithium or divalproex either acutely or in maintenance are not entirely convincing. Any slight benefits that might be gained from using olanzapine alone as opposed to lithium or divalproex in acute mania or using olanzapine in combination with mood stabilizers may not be worth the risks of the metabolic syndrome, at least in mildly to moderately manic patients. However, olanzapine can, without question, be useful in rapidly calming severely dysphoric, anxious, and agitated bipolar patients who complain of racing thoughts. Atypical antipsychotics are being used more frequently as first-line treatments for mania in the United States than in Europe, where lithium and typical antipsychotics apparently remain the first-line choices (Bourin et al., 2005).

In mixed mania, the evidence most clearly supports the use of divalproex or a combination of divalproex and an atypical antipsychotic as first-line treatment. Swann et al. (1997) found that even a moderate level of depression in manic patients is a robust predictor of nonresponse to lithium and a predictor of a more favorable response to divalproex. In irritable or dysphoric mania, Swann et al. (2002) found that divalproex was more effective than lithium.

The treatment of rapid cycling can be especially difficult (Mackin & Young, 2004). There does not seem to be a clear advantage to any one agent. Although divalproex has been considered superior to lithium in the treatment of rapid-cycling patients, the available evidence indicates that this is not the case (Calabrese et al., 2005). Tondo et al. (2003) showed that divalproex, carbamazepine, and lithium are equivalent for the treatment of rapid cycling. Combinations of agents including anticonvulsants and atypical antipsychotics are often required (Post et al., 2000). Discontinuing antidepressants, which can promote cycling, is often helpful. Nimodipine and thyroid supplements should be considered. Supraphysiologic doses of thyroxine have been found to be helpful with rapid cycling (Bauer & Whybrow, 1990). For more on the relationship between thyroid functioning and bipolar disorder, see the section on thyroid augmentation in the following chapter. Kilzieh and Akiskal (1999) recommend that rapid-cycling patients avoid benzodiazepines and alcohol, caffeine, stimulants, exposure to bright light, and sleep deprivation.

The effective treatment of some acutely manic patients and the long-term treatment of many bipolar patients often requires more than one drug (polypharmacy). Polypharmacy is a common, and often necessary, practice in the treatment of patients with many chronic illnesses. At the 2003 Fifth International Conference on Bipolar Disorder, Gary Sachs, MD, a principal investigator involved in the Systematic Treatment and Effectiveness Program–Bipolar Disorder (STEP-BD), reported on medications used by bipolar patients upon entry into the program. Patients were being treated with an average of 4.2 medications. Less than 20 percent were on just one drug.

Polypharmacy is often needed because a substantial number of patients have symptoms that do not readily respond to lithium monotherapy or lithium combined with either valproate or carbamazepine (Post et al., 2006). Studies suggest that in community practice, lithium monotherapy is effective in only one-third of patients (Ghaemi, 2002).

Grof (2003) notes another reason for polypharmacy is the reluctance of clinicians and patients to stop a drug if it is partially effective. It is safer to continue using that drug—in terms of preventing the reemergence of symptoms—than it is to discontinue it and try another. Grof (2003) asserts that many bipolar patients can be adequately treated with one drug and without a trial-and-error strategy as long as a clinician is familiar with the indications that a particular medication is most likely to be the effective agent. Based on his understanding of the research literature and his experience, he makes the following suggestions: Lithium should be used for those patients with euphoric, episodic mania and a family history of bipolar disorder; lamotrigine for patients with nonepisodic course, atypical features, anxiety, and a family history of anxiety and substance use disorders; and olanzapine for a nonepisodic course with the presence of or history of psychosis, a family history of psychosis, and comorbid substance abuse.

Some clinicians might argue that Grof is being overly optimistic in his belief that properly chosen monotherapy can meet the treatment needs of most bipolar patients. A substantial number of patients remain ill, especially with some burden of depressive symptoms, even with intensive polypharmacy (Post et al., 2003). We do not have one pill that can effectively treat all the complex symptoms and comorbid conditions so characteristic of bipolar illness. It is also impossible, at this point, to determine which combination of medications is likely to help a particular patient. Thus, a great deal of reasoned trial and error with medication combinations has to take place. This process and the ultimate use of several medications can be frustrating and disturbing to many patients and their families. However, polypharmacy can be rational. For an expert and thorough review of this topic, the reader is referred to Ghaemi (2002) or the recent work by Post et al. (2006).

Ghaemi (personal communication) believes that much of the apparent need for polypharmacy in patients with bipolar disorder is due to the frequent and overly aggressive use of antidepressants. Antidepressants are cycle-inducing and destabilizing drugs for many bipolar patients (Calabrese et al., 2001; Goodwin & Jamison, 1990). Ghaemi (2002) states that the weight of the research evidence supports aggressive use of mood stabilizers, the frequent addition of atypical anti-psychotics and novel anticonvulsants, and only limited use of antidepressants.

Chang et al. (1998) reported that bipolar patients with mixed states have higher levels of thyroid abnormalities than manic patients and several studies have found a relationship between rapid cycling and various grades of hypothyroidism (Bauer, et al., 1990; Cowdry et al., 1983; Fagiolini et al., 2003; Kusalic, 1992). Oomen et al. (1996) found that early forms of autoimmune thyroid disease were highly significantly associated with rapid cycling in a large sample of psychiatric patients upon admission to the hospital. Post et al. (1997), however, found no relationship between thyroid hormone levels and rapid cycling.

As discussed in the section on the use of lithium, folate supplementation, preferably in the form of folinic acid or L-5-methyltetrahydrofolate (Metafolin), may be wise for patients taking lithium. The same may be true for patients taking anticonvulsant drugs. Sener et al. (2006) reported research indicating that some anticonvulsants interfere with the availability of folate.

A number of groups have developed treatment guidelines and algorithms for treating both the manic and depressive phase of bipolar disorder based on the available evidence and the consensus of experts. The American Psychiatric Association has guidelines on how to treat bipolar illness, of course (2002), but psychiatrists in the Lone Star State also have one of their own—the Texas Implementation of Medication Algorithms (TIMA; Suppes et al., 2005). The British have a set of guidelines (Goodwin, 2003) and psychiatrists on the continent have another (Vestergaard, 2004). The Canadians have a set of guidelines (CANMAT, 2005) and so do the Australians and New Zealanders (RANZCP, 2004). Each of these guidelines makes somewhat different recommendations. Some algorithms have been developed with the support of pharmaceutical companies. These algorithms have been scorned as nothing more than a marketing tool for the companies involved. A disadvantage of algorithms is that they can quickly become out-of-date. For an in-depth review of algorithms, the reader is referred to Perlis (2005).

Pharmacologic Treatment of Hypomania

Virtually all pharmacotherapy research done in bipolar disorder has been conducted on manic or bipolar I patients, even though those patients represent only a small portion of the bipolar spectrum. There are only a handful of studies that address the treatment of bipolar II disorder or hypomania with mood stabilizers. Most are open or observational trials (e.g., Jacobsen, 1993; Vieta et al., 2001; Vieta et al., 2002). There are very few controlled trials.

Greil et al. (1998) and Greil and Kleindienst (1999) found that there was a trend for carbamazepine to work better than lithium over a period of 2.5 years for bipolar II patients in a randomized, prospective, multicenter study.

Calabrese et al. (1999), in a randomized, double-blind, placebo-controlled study of a mix of bipolar I and II rapid-cycling patients, found that lamotrigine was modestly more effective than placebo in preventing relapse to hypomania (or depression) for 6 months. Only 15 patients in this study received lamotrigine alone. Another 60 were given lamotrigine as an adjunct to other medications.

Bowden et al. (2003) conducted an 18-month, placebo-controlled trial of lamotrigine in bipolar I patients with a recent manic or hypomanic episode. The lamotrigine was effective in preventing relapse to new mood episodes.

Dunner et al. (1982) found that lithium produced no significant reduction in hypomania compared to placebo over 33 months in 39 bipolar II patients.

Kane et al. (1982) did a 2-year, double-blind, randomized, placebo-controlled study that included 22 bipolar II patients on lithium alone, imipramine alone, and the combination of lithium and imipramine. Lithium alone prevented relapse to both hypomania and depression.

Euphoric hypomanic patients, who are feeling better than well, are not likely to seek help. Outpatient clinicians are most likely to see bipolar II patients with irritable hypomania or mixed depressions. These are patients who have predominantly depressive symptoms with some hypomanic features mixed in, such as pressured speech, racing thoughts, agitation, or hypersexuality along with various degrees of irritability or explosive temper. These patients' depressive episodes often emerge from a background cyclothymic temperament (Akiskal et al., 1995).

Given how little psychopharmacologic research has been done with bipolar II patients, treatment decisions for these patients must be based on what has worked for bipolar I manic patients, the results of open studies on the treatment of bipolar II disorder, and expert opinion. These all suggest that a mood stabilizer, particularly divalproex, should be the initial treatment, especially for mixed depressions with predominant dysphoric mood (Perugi et al., 2006). An atypical antipsychotic might be used, as well, particularly in patients with bipolar II mixed states or irritable hypomanic symptoms who do not respond to an adequate dose and duration of a mood-stabilizer monotherapy (Perugi et al., 2006; Vieta et al., 2005). Antidepressants should be avoided initially since they can increase irritability, promote rapid-cycling, and lead to refractory depression (see Chapter 7).

References

Akiskal, H. (1999). Affective disorders. In R. Berkow (Ed.), *Merck manual of diagnosis and therapy* (17th ed., pp. 1525–1544). Rathaway, NJ: Merck Research Labs.

Akiskal, H., Maser, J., Zeller, P., et al. (1995). Switching from "unipolar" to "bipolar II": An 11-year prospective study of clinical and temperamental predictors in 559 patients. *Archives of General Psychiatry, 52,* 114–123.

Allen, M., Hirschfeld, R., Wozniak, P., et al. (2006) Linear relationship of valproate serum concentration to response and optimal serum levels for acute mania. *American Journal of Psychiatry, 163*(2), 272–275.

Ananth, J., Parameswaran, S., Gunatilake, S., et al. (2004). Neuroleptic malignant syndrome and atypical antipsychotic drugs. *Journal of Clinical Psychiatry, 65*(4), 464–470.

Angst, F., Stassen, H., Clayton, P., et al. (2002). Mortality of patients with mood disorders: Follow-up over 34–38 years. *Journal of Affective Disorders, 68*(2–3), 167–181.

American Diabetes Association (ADA), American Psychiatric Association, American Association of Clinical Endocrinologists, & North American Association for the Study of Obesity. (2004). Consensus development conference on antipsychotic drugs and obesity and diabetes. *Journal of Clinical Psychiatry, 65*(2), 267–272.

American Psychiatric Association. (2002). *Practice guidelines for the treatment of patients with bipolar disorder (revision).* Washington, DC: Author.

Baker, R. W., Brown, E., Akiskal, H. S., Calabrese, J. R., Ketter, T. A., Schuh, L. M., et al. (2004). Efficacy of olanzapine combined with valproate or lithium in the treatment of dysphoric mania. *The British Journal of Psychiatry, 185,* 472–478.

Baldessarini, R., Tondo, L., Faedda, G., et al. (1996). Effects of the rate of discontinuing lithium maintenance treatment in bipolar disorders. *Journal of Clinical Psychiatry, 57*(10), 441–448.

Baldessarini, R., Tondo, L., & Hennen, J. (1999). Effects of lithium treatment and its discontinuation on suicidal behavior in bipolar manic-depressive disorders. *Journal of Clinical Psychiatry, 60*(Suppl. 2), 117–122.

Ballenger, J., & Post, R. (1980). Carbamazepine in manic-depressive illness: A new treatment. *American Journal of Psychiatry, 137,* 782–790.

Barbini, B., Scherillo, P., & Benedetti, F. (1997). Response to cloazpine in acute mania is more rapid than that of chlorpromazine. *International Clinical Psychopharmacology, 12,* 109–112.

Barclay, M. L., Brownlie, B. E., Turner, J. G., & Wells, J. E. (1994). Lithium associated thyrotoxicosis: A report of 14 cases, with statistical analysis of incidence. *Clinical Endocrinology, 40*(6), 759–764.

Barton, B., & Gitlin, M. (1987). Verapamil in treatment-resistant mania: An open trial. *Journal of Clinical Psychopharmacology, 7*(2), 101–103.

Bauer, M., & Whybrow, P. (1990). Rapid cycling bipolar affective disorder. II. Treatment of refractory rapid cycling with high-dose levothyroxine: A preliminary study. *Archives of General Psychiatry, 47*(5), 435–440.

Bellino, S., Paradiso, E., & Bogetto, F. (2005). Oxcarbazepine in the treatment of borderline personality disorder: A pilot study. *Journal of Clinical Psychiatry, 66*(9), 1111–1115.

Berk, M., Ichim, L., & Brook, S. (1999). Olanzapine compared to lithium in mania: A double-blind randomized controlled trial. *International Clinical Psychopharmacology, 14*(6), 339–343.

Bourin, M., Lambert, O., & Guitton, B. (2005). Treatment of acute mania—From clinical trials to recommendations for clinical practice. *Human Psychopharmacology, 20*(1), 15–26.

Bowden, C. (1995). Predictors of response to divalproex and lithium. *Journal of Clinical Psychiatry, 56,* 25–30.

Bowden, C., Brugger, A., Swann, A., & Calabrese, J. (1994). Efficacy of divalproex vs lithium and placebo in the treatment of mania. The Depakote Mania Study Group. *Journal of the American Medical Association, 271*(12), 918–924.

Bowden, C., Calabrese, J., McElroy, S., & Gyulai, L. (2000). A randomized, placebo-controlled 12-month trial of divalproex and lithium in treatment of outpatients with bipolar I disorder. Divalproex Maintenance Study Group. *Archives of General Psychiatry, 57*(5), 481–489.

Bowden, C., Collins, M., McElroy, S., et al. (2005). Relationship of mania symptomatology to maintenance treatment response with divalproex, lithium, or placebo. *Neuropsychopharmacology, 30*(10), 1932–1939.

Bowden, C., Grunze, H., Mullen, J., et al. (2005). A randomized, double-blind, placebo-controlled efficacy and safety study of quetiapine or lithium as monotherapy for mania in bipolar disorder. *Journal of Clinical Psychiatry, 66*(1), 111–121.

Bowden, C., & Singh, V. (2006). Valproate: Clinical pharmacological profile. In H. Akiskal & M. Tohen (Eds.), *Bipolar psychopharmacotherapy* (pp. 27–42). West Sussex, England: Wiley.

Bowden, C. L., Calabrese, J. R., Sachs, G., Yatham, L. N., Asghar, S. A., Hompland, M., et al. (2003). A placebo-controlled 18-month trial of lamotrigine and lithium maintenance treatment in recently manic or hypomanic patients with bipolar I disorder. *Archives of General Psychiatry, 60*(4), 392–400.

Bradwejn, J., Shriqui, C., Koszycki, D., et al. (1990). Double-blind comparison of the effects of clonazepam and lorazepam in acute mania. *Journal of Clinical Psychopharmacology, 10,* 403–408.

Braunig, P., & Kruger, S. (2003). Levetiracetam in the treatment of rapid-cycling bipolar disorder. *Journal of Psychopharmacology, 17*(2), 239–241.

Brunet, G., Cerlich, B., Robert, P., Dumas, S., Souetre, E., & Darcourt, G. (1990). Open trial of a calcium antagonist, nimodipine, in acute mania. *Clinical Neuropharmacology, 13*(3), 224–228.

Cade, J. (1949). Lithium salts in the treatment of psychotic excitement. *Medical Journal of Australia, 36,* 349–352.

Calabrese, J., Bowden, C., & McElroy, S. (1999). Spectrum of activity of lamotrigine in treatment-refractory bipolar disorder. *American Journal of Psychiatry, 56*(7), 1019–1023.

Calabrese, J., Shelton M., Rapport D., Youngstrom, E., et al. (2005). A 20-month, double-blind, maintenance trial of lithium versus divalproex in rapid-cycling bipolar disorder. *American Journal of Psychiatry, 162*(11), 2152–2161.

Calabrese, J. R., Shelton, M. D., Rapport, D. J., Kujawa, M., Kimmel, S. E., & Caban, S. (2001). Current research on rapid cycling bipolar disorder and its treatment. *Journal of Affective Disorders, 67*(1–3), 241–255.

Canadian Network for Mood and Anxiety Treatments (CANMAT). (2005). Guidelines for the management of patients with bipolar disorder: Consensus and controversies. *Bipolar Disorders, 7*(Suppl. 3), 5–69.

Carta, M., Hardoy, M., Hardoy, M., et al. (2003). The clinical use of gabapentin in bipolar spectrum disorders. *Journal of Affective Disorders, 75*(1), 83–91.

Cavazzoni, P. A., Berg, P. H., Kryzhanovskaya, L. A., Briggs, S. D., Roddy, T. E., Tohen, M., et al. (2006). Comparison of treatment-emergent extrapyramidal symptoms in patients with bipolar mania or schizophrenia during olanzapine clinical trials. *Journal of Clinical Psychiatry, 67*(1), 107–113.

Chang, K. D., Keck, P. E., Jr., Stanton, S. P., McElroy, S. L., Strakowski, S. M., & Geracioti, T. D., Jr. (1998). Differences in thyroid function between bipolar manic and mixed states. *Biological Psychiatry, 43*(10), 730–733.

Chengappa, K., Gershon, S., & Levine, J. (2001). The evolving role of topiramate among other mood stabilizers in the management of bipolar disorder. *Bipolar Disorders, 3*(5), 215–232.

Chengappa, K. N., Suppes, T., & Berk, M. (2004). Treatment of bipolar mania with atypical antipsychotics. *Expert Review of Neurotherapeutics, 4*(6 Suppl. 2), S17–25.

Ciapparelli, A., Dell'Osso, L., Bandettini di Poggio, A., et al. (2003). Clozapine in treatment-resistant patients with schizophrenia, schizoaffective disorder, or psychotic bipolar disorder: A naturalistic 48-month follow-up study. *Journal of Clinical Psychiatry, 64*(4), 451–458.

Cipriani, A., Pretty, H., Hawton, K., & Geddes, J. R. (2005). Lithium in the prevention of suicidal behavior and all-cause mortality in patients with mood disorders: A systematic review of randomized trials. *American Journal of Psychiatry, 162*(10), 1805–1819.

Cipriani, A., Rendell, J. M., & Geddes, J. R. (2006). Haloperidol alone or in combination for acute mania. *Cochrane Database Systematic Review, 3,* CD004362.

Coppen, A., & Abou-Saleh, M. T. (1982). Plasma folate and affective morbidity during long-term lithium therapy. *British Journal of Psychiatry, 141,* 87–89.

Coppen, A., Chaudhry, S., & Swade, C. (1986). Folic acid enhances lithium prophylaxis. *Journal of Affective Disorders, 10*(1), 9–13.

Coryell, W., Soloman, D., Leon, A., et al. (1998). Lithium discontinuation and subsequent effectiveness. *American Journal of Psychiatry, 155*(7), 895–898.

Cowdry, R. W., Wehr, T. A., Zis, A. P., & Goodwin, F. K. (1983). Thyroid abnormalities associated with rapid-cycling bipolar illness. *Archives of General Psychiatry, 40*(4), 414–420.

Curtin, F., & Schulz, P. (2004). Clonazepam and lorazepam in acute mania: A Bayesian meta-analysis. *Journal of Affective Disorders, 78*(3), 201–208.

DeLeon, A., Patel, N. C., & Crismon, M. L. (2004). Aripiprazole: A comprehensive review of its pharmacology, clinical efficacy, and tolerability. *Clinical Therapeutics, 26*(5), 649–666.

Denicoff, K. D., Smith-Jackson, E. E., Disney, E. R., Ali, S. O., Leverich, G. S., & Post, R. M. (1997). Comparative prophylactic efficacy of lithium, carbamazepine, and the combination in bipolar disorder. *Journal of Clinical Psychiatry, 58*(11), 470–478.

Dubovsky, S. L., Franks, R. D., Allen, S., & Murphy, J. (1986). Calcium antagonists in mania: A double-blind study of verapamil. *Psychiatry Research, 18*(4), 309–320.

Dunner, D. (2005). Safety and tolerability of emerging pharmacological treatments for bipolar disorder. *Bipolar Disorders, 7*, 307–325.

Dunner, D. L., Stallone, F., & Fieve, R. R. (1982). Prophylaxis with lithium carbonate: An update. *Archives of General Psychiatry, 39*(11), 1344–1345.

Drake, R., Xie, H., McHugo, G., et al. (2000) The effects of clozapine on alcohol and drug use disorders among patients with schizophrenia. *Schizophrenia Bulletin, 26*, 441–449.

Elias, M. (2006). Psychiatric drugs fare favorably when companies pay for studies. *USA Today,* May 25th, p. A1.

Elmslie, J., Silverstone, J., Mann, J., et al. (2000). Prevalence of overweight and obesity in bipolar patients. *Journal of Clinical Psychiatry, 61*, 179–184.

Ernst, C., & Goldberg, J. (2004). Antisuicidal properties of psychotropic drugs: A critical review. *Harvard Review of Psychiatry, 12*(1), 14–41.

Ertugrul, A., & Meltzer, H. Y. (2003). Antipsychotic drugs in bipolar disorder. *International Journal of Neuropsychopharmacology, 6*(3), 277–284.

Faedda, G., Tondo, L., Baldessarini, R., et al. (1993). Outcome after rapid vs gradual discontinuation of lithium treatment in bipolar disorders. *Archives of General Psychiatry, 50*(6), 448–455.

Fagiolini, A., Cook, D., Frank, E., & Kupfer, D. (2003, June12–14). Hypothyroidism in 175 patients with bipolar I disorder. Presented at the 5th International Conference on Bipolar Disorder, Pittsburgh, PA. Reported in *Bipolar Disorders, 5*(Suppl. 1), 47.

Frye, M., & Altshuler, L. (1997). Selection of initial treatment for bipolar disorder: Manic phase. *Modern Problems in Pharmacopsychiatry, 25*, 88–113.

Frye, M., Ketter, T., Kimbrell, T., et al. (2000). A placebo-controlled study of lamotrigine and gabapentin monotherapy in refractory mood disorders. *Journal of Clinical Psychopharmacology, 20*(6), 607–614.

Garza-Trevino, E. S., Overall, J. E., & Hollister, L. E. (1992). Verapamil versus lithium in acute mania. *American Journal of Psychiatry, 149*(1), 121–122.

Gelenberg, A. J., Kane, J. M., Keller, M. B., Lavori, P., Rosenbaum, J. F., Cole, K., et al. (1989). Comparison of standard and low serum levels of lithium for maintenance treatment of bipolar disorder. *New England Journal of Medicine, 321*(22), 1489–1493.

Ghaemi, N. (Ed.). (2002). *Polypharmacy in psychiatry.* New York: Dekker.

Ghaemi, S., & Goodwin, F. (2001). Gabapentin treatment of the non-refractory bipolar spectrum: An open case series. *Journal of Affective Disorders, 65*(2), 167–171.

Ghaemi, N., Ko, J., & Katzow, J. (2002). Oxcarbazepine treatment of refractory bipolar disorder: A retrospective chart review. *Bipolar Disorders, 4*, 70–74.

Ghaemi, S. N., Hsu, D. J., Rosenquist, K. J., Pardo, T. B., & Goodwin, F. K. (2006). Extrapyramidal side effects with atypical neuroleptics in bipolar disorder. *Progress in Neuropsychopharmacology and Biological Psychiatry, 30*(2), 209–213.

Giannini, A. J., Nakoneczie, A. M., Melemis, S. M., Ventresco, J., & Condon, M. (2000). Magnesium oxide augmentation of verapamil maintenance therapy in mania. *Psychiatry Research, 93*(1), 83–87.

Gold, M., Pottash, A., Sweeney, D., et al. (1982). Antimanic, antidepressant, and antipanic effects of opiates: Clinical, neuroanatomical, and biochemical evidence. *Annals of the New York Academy of Sciences, 398*(1), 140–150.

Goodnick, P. J. (2000). The use of nimodipine in the treatment of mood disorders. *Bipolar Disorders, 2*(3 Pt 1), 165–173.

Goodwin, F., & Jamison, K. (1990). *Manic-depressive illness.* New York: Oxford University Press.

Goodwin, G. (2003). Consensus Group of the British Association for Psychopharmacology. Evidence-based guidelines for treating bipolar disorder: Recommendations from the British Association for Psychopharmacology. *Journal of Psychopharmacology, 17*, 149–173.

Goodwin, G. M., Bowden, C. L., Calabrese, J. R., Grunze, H., Kasper, S., White, R., et al. (2004). A pooled analysis of 2 placebo-controlled 18-month trials of lamotrigine and lithium maintenance in bipolar I disorder. *Journal of Clinical Psychiatry, 65*(3), 432–441.

Green, A., Tohen, M., Patel, J., et al. (2000). Clozapine in the treatment of refractory psychotic mania. *American Journal of Psychiatry, 157*(6), 982–986.

Greil, W., & Kleindienst, N. (1999). Lithium versus carbamazepine in the maintenance treatment of bipolar II disorder and bipolar disorder not otherwise specified. *International Clinical Psychopharmacology, 14*(5), 283–285.

Greil, W., Kleindienst, N., Erazo, N., & Muller-Oerlinghausen, B. (1998). Differential response to lithium and carbamazepine in the prophylaxis of bipolar disorder. *Journal of Clinical Psychopharmacology, 18*(6), 455–460.

Grof, P. (2003) Selecting effective long-term treatment for bipolar patients: Monotherapy and combinations. *Journal of Clinical Psychiatry, 64*(Suppl. 5), 53–61

Grunze, H. (2006). Carbamazepine, other anticonvulsants and augmenting agents. In H. Akiskal & M. Tohen (Eds.), *Bipolar psychopharmacotherapy* (pp. 63–93). West Sussex, England: Wiley.

Grunze, H., Erfurth, A., Marcus, A., et al. (1999). Tiagabine appears not to be efficacious in the treatment of acute mania. *Journal of Clinical Psychiatry, 60*(11), 759–762.

Grunze, H., Langosch, J., Born, C., et al. (2003). Levetiracetam in the treatment of acute mania: An open add-on study with an on-off-on design. *Journal of Clinical Psychiatry, 64*(7), 781–784.

Grunze, H., Walden, J., Wolf, R., & Berger, M. (1996). Combined treatment with lithium and nimodipine in a bipolar I manic syndrome. *Progress in Neuropsychopharmacology and Biological Psychiatry, 20*(3), 419–426.

Guille, C. (1999). Gabapentin versus placebo as adjunctive treatment for acute mania and mixed states in Bipolar Disorders. Presented at the American Psychiatric Association Annual Meeting, NR10, 63.

Guille, C., Sachs, G. S., & Ghaemi, S. N. (2000). A naturalistic comparison of clozapine, risperidone, and olanzapine in the treatment of bipolar disorder. *Journal of Clinical Psychiatry, 61*(9), 638–642.

Gyulai, L., Bowden, C., McElroy, S., et al. (2003). Maintenance efficacy of divalproex in the prevention of bipolar depression. *Neuropsychopharmacology, 28*(7), 1374–1382.

Harris, M., Chandran, S., Chakraborty, N., & Healy, D. (2003). Mood-stabilizers: The archeology of the concept. *5*(6), 446–452.

Hartong, E. G., Moleman, P., Hoogduin, C. A., Broekman, T. G., & Nolen, W. A. (2003). Prophylactic efficacy of lithium versus carbamazepine in treatment-naive bipolar patients. *Journal of Clinical Psychiatry, 64*(2), 144–151.

Hasanah, C. I., Khan, U. A., Musalmah, M., & Razali, S. M. (1997). Reduced red-cell folate in mania. *Journal of Affective Disorders, 46*(2), 95–99.

Hayes, S. (1993). Barbiturate anticonvulsants in refractory affective disorders. *Annals of Clinical Psychiatry, 5*(1), 35–44.

Henry, C., & Demotes-Mainard, J. (2003). Avoiding drug-induced switching in patients with bipolar depression. *Drug Safety, 26*(5), 337–351.

Himmelhoch, J. (1994). On the failure to recognize lithium failure. *Psychiatric Annals, 24*(5), 241–250.

Hirschfeld, R., Allen, M., McEvoy, J., Keck, P., & Russell, J. (1999). Safety and tolerability of oral loading divalproex sodium in acutely manic bipolar patients. *Journal of Clinical Psychiatry, 60*(12), 815–818.

Hummel, B., Walde, J., Stampfer, R., et al. (2002) Acute antimanic efficacy and safety of oxcarbazepine in an open trial with an on-off-on design. *Bipolar Disorders, 4*, 412–417.

Jacobsen, F. (1993). Low-dose valproate: A new treatment for cyclothymia, mild rapid cycling disorders, and premenstrual syndrome. *Journal of Clinical Psychiatry, 54*(6), 229–234.

Janicak, P. G., Sharma, R. P., Pandey, G., & Davis, J. M. (1998). Verapamil for the treatment of acute mania: A double-blind, placebo-controlled trial. *American Journal of Psychiatry, 155*(7), 972–973.

Joffe, H., Cohen, L., Suppes, T., et al. (2006). Valproate is associated with new-onset oligomenorrhea with hyperandrogenism in women with bipolar disorder. *Biological Psychiatry, 59*(11), 1078–1086.

Kanba, S., Yagi, G., Kamijina, A., et al. (1994). The first open study of zonisamide, a novel anticonvulsant, shows efficacy in mania. *Progress in Neuro-psychopharmacology & Biological Psychiatry, 18*(4), 707–715.

Kane, J., Quitkin, F., Rifkin, A., et al. (1982). Lithium carbonate and imipramine in the prophylaxis of unipolar and bipolar II illness: A prospective, placebo-controlled comparison. *Archives of General Psychiatry, 39*(9), 1065–1069.

Kaufman, K. (1998). Adjunctive tiagabine treatment of psychiatric disorders: Three cases. *Annals of Clinical Psychiatry, 10*(4), 181–184.

Kaufman, K. (2004). Monotherapy treatment of bipolar disorder with levetiracetam. *Epilepsy and Behavior, 5*(6), 1017–1020.

Keck, P., & McElroy, S. (2006). A comparison of "second generation antipsychotics" in the treatment for bipolar disorder: Focus on cloazapine, quetiapine, ziprasidone and aripiprazole. In H. Akiskal & M. Tohen (Eds.), *Bipolar psychopharmacotherapy* (pp. 125–134). West Sussex, England: Wiley.

Ketter, T. A., Houston, J. P., Adams, D. H., Risser, R. C., Meyers, A. L., Williamson, D. J., et al. (2006). Differential efficacy of olanzapine and lithium in preventing manic or mixed recurrence in patients with bipolar I disorder based on number of previous manic or mixed episodes. *Journal of Clinical Psychiatry, 67*(1), 95–101.

Kilzieh, N., & Akiskal, H. S. (1999). Rapid-cycling bipolar disorder. An overview of research and clinical experience. *The Psychiatric Clinics of North America, 22*(3), 585–607.

Kleindienst, N., & Greil, W. (2000). Differential efficacy of lithium and carbamazepine in the prophylaxis of bipolar disorder: Results of the MAP study. *Neuropsychobiology, 42*(Suppl. 1), 2–10.

Koukopoulos, A., Kaliari, B., & Tondo, A. (1983). Rapid cyclers, temperament and antidepressants. *Comprehensive Psychiatry, 24*, 249–258.

Kulkarni, J., Garland, K., Scaffidi, A., et al. (2006). A pilot study of hormone modulation as a new treatment for mania in women with bipolar affective disorder. *Psychoneuroendocrinology, 31*(4), 543–547.

Kusalic, M. (1992). Grade II and grade III hypothyroidism in rapid-cycling bipolar patients. *Neuropsychobiology, 25*(4), 177–181.

Kushner, S., Khan, A., Lane, R., & Olson, W. (2006). Topiramate monotherapy in the management of acute mania: Results of four double-blind placebo-controlled trials. *Bipolar Disorders, 8*(1), 15–27.

Lenox, R. H., Newhouse, P. A., Creelman, W. L., & Whitaker, T. M. (1992). Adjunctive treatment of manic agitation with lorazepam versus haloperidol: A double-blind study. *Journal of Clinical Psychiatry, 53*(2), 47–52.

Lin, D., Mok, H., & Yatham, L. N. (2006). Polytherapy in bipolar disorder. *CNS Drugs, 20*(1), 29–42.

Loew, T. H., Nickel, M. K., Muehlbacher, M., Kaplan, P., Nickel, C., Kettler, C., et al. (2006). Topiramate treatment for women with borderline personality disorder: A double-blind, placebo-controlled study. *Journal of Clinical Psychopharmacology, 26*(1), 61–66.

Mackin, P., & Young, A. (2004). Rapid cycling bipolar disorder: Historical overview and focus on emerging treatments. *Bipolar Disorders, 6*, 523–529.

Maj, M., Pirozzi, R., & Magliano, L. (1995). Nonresponse to reinstituted lithium prophylaxis in previously responsive bipolar patients: Prevalence and predictors. *American Journal of Psychiatry, 152*(12), 1810–1811.

Malhi, G. S., Berk, M., Bourin, M., Ivanovski, B., Dodd, S., Lagopoulos, J., et al. (2005). Atypical mood stabilizers: A "typical" role for atypical antipsychotics. *Acta Psychiatrica Scandanavica,* Suppl(426), 29–38.

Manji, H., Bebchuk, J., Moore, G., et al. (1999). Modulation of CNS signal transduction pathways and gene expression by mood-stabilizing agents: Therapeutic implications. *Journal of Clinical Psychiatry, 60*(Suppl. 2), 27–39.

Maremmani, I., Perugi, G., Paeini, M., & Akiskal, H. (2006). Toward a unitary perspective on the bipolar spectrum and substance abuse: Opiate addiction as a paradigm. *Journal of Affective Disorders, 93*, 1–12.

McElroy, S., Arnold, L., & Altshuler, L. (2006). Bipolarity in women: Therapeutic issues.

In H. Akiskal & M. Tohen (Eds.), *Bipolar psychopharmacotherapy* (pp. 235–277). West Sussex, England: Wiley.

McElroy, S., Dessain, E., Pope, H., et al. (1991). Clozapine in the treatment of psychotic mood disorders, schizoaffective disorder and schizophrenia. *Journal of Clinical Psychiatry, 52,* 411–414.

McElroy, S., Kotwal, R., Hudson, J., et al. (2004a). Zonisamide in the treatment of binge-eating disorder: An open-label, prospective trial. *Journal of Clinical Psychiatry, 65*(1), 50–56.

McElroy, S., Shapira, N., & Arnold, L. (2004b) Topiramate in the long-term treatment of binge-eating disorder associated with obesity. *Journal of Clinical Psychiatry, 65*(11), 1463–1469.

McElroy, S., Suppes, T., Keck, P., et al. (2005). Open-label adjunctive zonisamide in the treatment of bipolar disorders: A prospective trial. *Journal of Clinical Psychiatry, 66*(5), 617–624.

McIntyre, R. S., Konarski, J. Z., Misener, V. L., & Kennedy, S. H. (2005). Bipolar disorder and diabetes mellitus: Epidemiology, etiology, and treatment implications. *Annals of Clinical Psychiatry, 17*(2), 83–93.

Meyer, J. (2004). Confronting the challenges in the management of bipolar disorder and schizophrenia with atypical antipsychotics. Presented at the 17th Annual Psychiatric and Mental Health Congress. San Diego, CA.

Mishory, A., Winokur, M., & Bersudsky, Y. (2003). Prophylactic effect of phenytoin in bipolar disorder: A controlled study. *Bipolar Disorders, 5*(6), 464–467.

Mishory, A., Yaroslavsky, Y., Bersudsky, Y., & Belmaker, R. (2000). Phenytoin as an antimanic anticonvulsant: A controlled study. *American Journal of Psychiatry, 157*(3), 463–465.

Modell, J. G., Lenox, R. H., & Weiner, S. (1985). Inpatient clinical trial of lorazepam for the management of manic agitation. *Journal of Clinical Psychopharmacology, 5*(2), 109–113.

Moore, G. J., Bebchuk, J. M., Wilds, I. B., Chen, G., & Manji, H. K. (2000). Lithium-induced increase in human brain grey matter. *Lancet, 356*(9237), 1241–1242.

Narasimhan, M., Gupta, S., & Masand, P. (2005). *Psychiatric Times,* August, 75–79.

Nasrallah, H. A., Churchill, C. M., & Hamdan-Allan, G. A. (1988). Higher frequency of neuroleptic-induced dystonia in mania than in schizophrenia. *American Journal of Psychiatry, 145*(11), 1455–1456.

Newcomer, J. W. (2004). Abnormalities of glucose metabolism associated with atypical antipsychotic drugs. *Journal of Clinical Psychiatry, 65*(Suppl. 18), 36–46.

Nickel, C., Tritt, K., & Muehlbacher, M. (2005). Topiramate treatment in bulimia nervosa patients: A randomized, double-blind, placebo-controlled trial. *International Journal of Eating Disorders, 38*(4), 295–300.

Oomen, H. A., Schipperijn, A. J., & Drexhage, H. A. (1996). The prevalence of affective disorder and in particular of a rapid cycling of bipolar disorder in patients with abnormal thyroid function tests. *Clinical Endocrinology, 45*(2), 215–223.

Pande, A., Crockatt, J., & Janney, C. (2000). Gabapentin in bipolar disorder: A placebo-controlled trial of adjunctive therapy. *Bipolar Disorders, 2,* 249–255.

Pazzaglia, P. J., Post, R. M., Ketter, T. A., Callahan, A. M., Marangell, L. B., Frye, M. A., et al. (1998). Nimodipine monotherapy and carbamazepine augmentation in patients with refractory recurrent affective illness. *Journal of Clinical Psychopharmacology, 18*(5), 404–413.

Pazzaglia, P. J., Post, R. M., Ketter, T. A., George, M. S., & Marangell, L. B. (1993). Preliminary controlled trial of nimodipine in ultra-rapid cycling affective dysregulation. *Psychiatry Research, 49*(3), 257–272.

Perlis, R. (2005). The role of pharmacologic treatment guidelines for bipolar disorder. *Journal of Clinical Psychiatry, 66*(Suppl. 3), 37–47.

Perlis, R. H., Welge, J. A., Vornik, L. A., Hirschfeld, R. M., & Keck, P. E., Jr. (2006). Atypical antipsychotics in the treatment of mania: A meta-analysis of randomized, placebo-controlled trials. *Journal of Clinical Psychiatry, 67*(4), 509–516.

Perugi, G., Ghaemi, N., & Akiskal, H. (2006). Diagnsotic and clinical management approaches to bipolar depression, bipolar II and their comorbidities. In H. Akiskal & M. Tohen (Eds.), *Bipolar psychopharmacotherapy* (pp. 193–234). West Sussex, England: Wiley.

Perugi, G., Toni, C., Frare, F., et al (2002). The effectiveness of adjunctive gapentin in resistant bipolar disorder. Is it due to anxious-alcohol abuse comorbidity? *Journal of Clinical Psychopharmacology, 22*, 584–591.

Post, R., Altshuler, L., & Frye, M. (2005). Preliminary observations on the effectiveness of levetiracetam in the open adjunctive treatment of refractory bipolar disorder. *Journal of Clinical Psychiatry, 66*(3), 370–374.

Post, R., Denicoff, K., Leverich, G., et al. (2003). Morbidity in 258 bipolar outpatients followed for 1 year with daily prospective ratings on the NIMH Life Chart Method. *Journal of Clinical Psychiatry, 64*, 680–690.

Post, R., Frye, M., Denicoff, K., et al. (2000). Emerging trends in the treatment of rapid cycling bipolar disorder: A selected review. *Bipolar Disorders, 2*(4), 305–315.

Post, R., Leverich, G., Altshuler, L., & Mikalaukas, K. Lithium-discontinuation-induced refractoriness: Preliminary observations. *American Journal of Psychiatry, 149*(12), 1727–1729.

Post, R., Speer, A., & Leverich, G. (2006). Complex combination therapy: The evolution toward rational polypharmacy in lithium-resistant bipolar illness. In H. Akiskal & M. Tohen (Eds.), *Bipolar psychopharmacotherapy* (pp. 135–167). West Sussex, England: Wiley.

Post, R. M., Kramlinger, K. G., Joffe, R. T., Roy-Byrne, P. P., Rosoff, A., Frye, M. A., et al. (1997). Rapid cycling bipolar affective disorder: Lack of relation to hypothyroidism. *Psychiatry Research, 72*(1), 1–7.

Pratoomsri, W., Yatham, L. N., Sohn, C. H., Solomons, K., & Lam, R. W. (2005). Oxcarbazepine add-on in the treatment of refractory bipolar disorder. *Bipolar Disorders, 7*(Suppl. 5), 37–42.

Rachid, F., Bertschy, G., Bondolfi, G., & Aubry, J. M. (2004). Possible induction of mania or hypomania by atypical antipsychotics: An updated review of reported cases. *Journal of Clinical Psychiatry, 65*(11), 1537–1545.

Raja, M., & Azzoni, A. (2003). Oxcarbazepine vs. valproate in the treatment of mood and schizoaffective disorders. *International Journal of Neuropsychopharmacology, 6*(4), 409–414.

Ranjan, S., Chandra, P. S., Chaturvedi, S. K., Prabhu, S. C., & Gupta, A. (2006). Atypical antipsychotic-induced akathisia with depression: Therapeutic role of mirtazapine. *Annals of Pharmacotherapy, 40*(4), 771–774.

Reinstein, M. (2001). Prospective open label comparison of oxcarbazepine and valproate. Proceedings of the APA Annual Meeting. New Orleans, LA.

Riegelman, R. (2005). *Studying a study and testing a test.* Philadelphia: Lippincott Williams & Wilkins.

Royal Australian and New Zealand College of Psychiatrists Clinical Practice (RANZCP) Guidelines Team for Bipolar Disorder. (2004). Australian and New Zealand clinical practice guidelines for the treatment of bipolar disorder. *Australian and New Zealand Journal of Psychiatry, 38,* 280–305.

Sachs, G., Chengappa, K., Suppes, T., Mullen, J., et al. (2004). Quetiapine with lithium or divalproex for the treatment of bipolar mania: A randomized, double-blind, placebo-controlled study. *Bipolar Disorders, 6,* 213–223.

Sachs, G., Grossman, F., Ghaemi, N., Okamato, A., & Bowden, C. (2002). Combination of a mood stabilizer with risperidone or haloperidol for treatment of acute mania: A double-blind, placebo-controlled comparison of efficacy and safety. *American Journal of Psychiatry, 159*(7), 1146–1154.

Sanger, T., Tohen, M., & Vieta E. (2003). Olanzapine in the acute treatment of bipolar I disorder with a history of rapid cycling. *Journal of Affective Disorders, 73,* 155–161.

Schaffer, A., Levitt, A. J., & Joffe, R. T. (2000). Mexiletine in treatment-resistant bipolar disorder. *Journal of Affective Disorders, 57*(1–3), 249–253.

Schaffer, L., Schaffer, C., & Caretto, J. (1999). The use of primodone in the treatment of refractory bipolar disorder. *Annals of Clinical Psychiatry, 11*(2), 61–66.

Schaffer, L., Schaffer, C., & Howe, J. (2002). An open case series on the utility of tiagabine as an augmentation in refractory bipolar outpatients. *Journal of Affective Disorders, 71*(1–3), 259–263.

Schou, M., & Grof, P. (2006). Lithium treatment: Focus on long-term prophylaxis. In H. Akiskal & M. Tohen (Eds.), *Bipolar psychopharmacotherapy* (pp. 9–26). West Sussex, England: Wiley.

Schou, M., Juel-Nielson N., Stroomgren, E., & Voldby H. (1954). The treatment of manic psychoses by administration of lithium salts. *Journal of Neurochemistry, 17*(4), 250–260.

Segal, J., Berk, M., & Brook, S. (1998). Risperidone compared with both lithium and haloperidol in mania: A double-blind randomized controlled trial. *Clinical Neuropharmacology, 21*(3), 176–180.

Sener, U., Zorlu, Y., Karaguzel, O., Ozdamar, O., Coker, I., & Topbas, M. (2006). Effects of common anti-epileptic drug monotherapy on serum levels of homocystine, vitamin B12, folic acid and vitamin B6. *Seizure, 15*(2), 79–85.

Shirzadi, A. A., & Ghaemi, S. N. (2006). Side effects of atypical antipsychotics: Extrapyramidal symptoms and the metabolic syndrome. *Harvard Review of Psychiatry, 14*(3), 152–164.

Simon, G. E., Von Korff, M., Saunders, K., Miglioretti, D. L., Crane, P. K., van Belle, G., et al. (2006). Association between obesity and psychiatric disorders in the US adult population. *Archives of General Psychiatry, 63*(7), 824–830.

Simon, N., Worthington, J., & Doyle, A. (2004). An open-label study of levetiracetam for the treatment of social anxiety disorder. *Journal of Clinical Psychiatry, 65*(9), 1219–1222.

Small, J., Klapper, M., Milstein, V., Marhenke, J., & Small, I. (1996). Comparison of therapeutic modalities for mania. *Psychopharmacology Bulletin, 32,* 623–627.

Stamouli, S., & Lykouras, L. (2006). Quetiapine-induced obsessive-compulsive symptoms: A series of five cases. *Journal of Clinical Psychopharmacology, 26*(4), 396–400.

Suppes, T., Baldessarini, R., Faedda, G., & Tohen, M. (1991). Risk of recurrence following discontinuation of lithium treatment in bipolar disorder. *Archives of General Psychiatry, 48*(12), 1082–1088.

Suppes, T., Chisholm, K., Dhavale, D., et al. (2002). Tiagabine in treatment refractory bipolar disorder: A clinical case series. *Bipolar Disorders, 4*(5), 283–289.

Suppes, T., Dennehy, E., & Hirschfeld, R. (2005). The Texas Implementation of Medication Algorithms: Update to the Algorithms for Treatment of Bipolar I Disorder. *Journal of Clinical Psychiatry, 66*, 870–886.

Swann, A., Bowden, C., Calabrese, J., et al. (2002) Pattern of response to divalproex, lithium, or placebo in four naturalistic subtypes of mania. *Neuropsychopharmacology, 26*, 530–536.

Swann, A. C., Bowden, C. L., Morris, et al. (1997). Depression during mania. Treatment response to lithium or divalproex. *Archives of General Psychiatry, 54*(1), 37–42.

Tansey, B. (2004). Huge penalty in drug fraud Pfizer settles felony case in Neurontin off-label promotion. *San Francisco Chronicle*, May 14th, p. C1.

Tohen, M., Baker, R. W., Altshuler, L. L., Zarate, C. A., Suppes, T., Ketter, T. A., et al. (2002). Olanzapine versus divalproex in the treatment of acute mania. *American Journal of Psychiatry, 159*(6), 1011–1017.

Tohen, M., Cambell, G., & Lin, D. (2006). Olanzapine in treatment for bipolar disorder. In H. Akiskal & M. Tohen (Eds.), *Bipolar psychopharmacotherapy* (pp. 86–103). West Sussex, England: Wiley.

Tohen, M., Chengappa, K., Suppes, T., et al. (2002). Efficacy of olanzapine in combination with valproate or lithium in the treatment of mania in patients partially nonresponsive to valproate or lithium monotherapy. *Archives of General Psychiatry, 59*, 62–69.

Tohen, M., Chengappa, K., Suppes, T., et al. (2004). Relapse prevention in bipolar I disorder: 18-month comparison of olanzapine plus mood stabiliser v. mood stabiliser alone. *British Journal of Psychiatry, 184*, 337–345.

Tohen, M., Greil, W., Calabreses, J., et al. (2005). Olanzapine versus lithium in the maintenance treatment of bipolar disorder: A 12-month, randomized, double-blind, controlled clinical trial. *American Journal of Psychiatry, 162*(7), 1281–1290.

Tohen, M., Ketter, T., Zarate, C., Suppes, T., et al. (2003) Olanzapine versus divalproex sodium for the treatment of acute mania and maintenance of remission: A 47-week study. *American Journal of Psychiatry, 160*(7), 1263–1271.

Tondo, L., Baldessarini, R., Floris, G., & Rudis, N. (1997). Effectiveness of restarting lithium treatment after its discontinuation in bipolar I and bipolar II disorders. *American Journal of Psychiatry, 154*(4), 548–550.

Tondo, L., Hennen, J., & Baldessarini, R. (2003). Rapid-cycling bipolar disorder: Effects of long-term treatments. *Acta Psychiatrica Scandinavica, 108*(1), 4–14.

Tremont, G., & Stern, R. A. (1997). Use of thyroid hormone to diminish the cognitive side effects of psychiatric treatment. *Psychopharmacology Bulletin, 33*(2), 273–280.

Tsai, S. Y., Lee, C. H., Kuo, C. J., & Chen, C. C. (2005). A retrospective analysis of risk and protective factors for natural death in bipolar disorder. *Journal of Clinical Psychiatry, 66*(12), 1586–1591.

Vestergaard, P. (2004). Guidelines for maintenance treatment for bipolar disorder: Are there discrepancies between European and North American recommendations? *Bipolar Disorders, 6,* 519–522.

Vieta, E., Gasto, C., Colom, F., Martinez, A., Otero, A., & Vallejo, J. (1998). Treatment of refractory rapid cycling bipolar disorder with risperidone. *Journal of Clinical Psychopharmacology, 18*(2), 172–174.

Vieta, E., Gasto, C., Colom, F., Reinares, M., Martinez-Aran, A., Benabarre, A., et al. (2001). Role of risperidone in bipolar II: An open 6-month study. *Journal of Affective Disorders, 67*(1–3), 213–219.

Vieta, E., & Goikolea, J. (2005) Atypical antipsychotics: Newer options for mania and maintenance therapy. *Bipolar Disorders, 7*(Suppl. 4), 21–33.

Vieta, E., Goikolea, J., & Martínez-Arán, A. (2006). A double-blind, randomized, placebo-controlled, prophylaxis study of adjunctive gabapentin for bipolar disorder. *Journal of Clinical Psychiatry, 67,* 473–477.

Vieta, E., Reinares, M., & Bourgeois, M. (2005). Bipolar I and bipolar II: A dichotomy? In A. Marneros & F. Goodwin (Eds.), *Bipolar disorder: Mixed states, rapid cycling and atypical forms* (pp. 88–108). Cambridge, MA: Cambridge University Press.

Vieta, E., Torrent, C., Garcia-Ribas, G., Gilabert, A., Garcia-Pares, G., Rodriguez, A., et al. (2002). Use of topiramate in treatment-resistant bipolar spectrum disorders. *Journal of Clinical Psychopharmacology, 22*(4), 431–435.

Walton, S. A., Berk, M., & Brook, S. (1996). Superiority of lithium over verapamil in mania: A randomized, controlled, single-blind trial. *Journal of Clinical Psychiatry, 57*(11), 543–546.

Waxmonsky, J. A., Thomas, M. R., Miklowitz, D. J., Allen, M. H., Wisniewski, S. R., Zhang, H., et al. (2005). Prevalence and correlates of tobacco use in bipolar disorder: Data from the first 2000 participants in the Systematic Treatment Enhancement Program. *General Hospital Psychiatry, 27*(5), 321–328.

Weisler, R., Kalali, A., Ketter, T., et al. (2004). A multicenter, randomized, double-blind, placebo-controlled trial of extended-release carbamazepine capsules as monotherapy for bipolar disorder patients with manic or mixed episodes. *Journal of Clinical Psychiatry, 65*(4), 478–484.

Weisler, R., Keck, P., Swann, A., et al. (2005). Extended-release carbamazepine capsules as monotherapy for acute mania in bipolar disorder: A multicenter, randomized, double-blind, placebo-controlled trial. *Journal of Clinical Psychiatry, 66*(3), 323–330.

Wisner, K. L., Peindl, K. S., Perel, J. M., Hanusa, B. H., Piontek, C. M., & Baab, S. (2002). Verapamil treatment for women with bipolar disorder. *Biological Psychiatry, 51*(9), 745–752.

Yatham, L., Grossman, F., Augustyns, I., et al. (2003). Mood stabilisers plus risperidone or placebo in the treatment of acute mania. International, double-blind, randomised controlled trial. *British Journal of Psychiatry, 182,* 141–147.

Yazici, O., Kora, K., Polat, A., & Saylan, M. (2004). Controlled lithium discontinuation in bipolar patients with good response to long-term lithium prophylaxis. *Journal of Affective Disorders, 80*(2–3), 269–271.

Yingling, D. R., Utter, G., Vengalil, S., & Mason, B. (2002). Calcium channel blocker, nimodipine, for the treatment of bipolar disorder during pregnancy. *American Journal of Obstetrics and Gynecology, 187*(6), 1711–1712.

Young, A. H., & Newham, J. I. (2006). Lithium in maintenance therapy for bipolar disorder. *Journal of Psychopharmacology, 20*(Suppl. 2), 17–22.

Zajecka, J., Weisler, R., Sachs, G., et al. (2002) A comparison of the efficacy, safety, and tolerability of divalproex sodium and olanzapine in the treatment of bipolar disorder. *Journal of Clinical Psychiatry, 63,* 1148–1155.

Zarate, C. A., Jr., & Tohen, M. (2004). Double-blind comparison of the continued use of antipsychotic treatment versus its discontinuation in remitted manic patients. *American Journal of Psychiatry, 161*(1), 169–171.

CHAPTER 7

The Problem of Bipolar Depression

The Controversy Over the Use of Antidepressants in the Treatment of Bipolar Depression

Bipolar I patients spend 68 percent of the time they are ill in the depressed phase of their illness, while bipolar II patients spend 92 percent of the time they are ill in the depressed phase of their illness (Judd, 2002; Judd et al., 2003). In addition, the depressive episodes in bipolar disorder last longer than manic episodes (Thase, 2005) and are responsible for more impairment in work and family role responsibilities than the manic phase (Calabrese et al., 2004). Finally, the vast majority of suicides occur during depressive and mixed phases of the illness.

Despite the enormous clinical impact of bipolar depression, it has, until recently, received little research and clinical attention. A MEDLINE clinical queries search of the term "bipolar depression" returned only 15 references from 1987 to 1991. From 1992 until 1996 there were just 31 new references. Interest in this most impairing phase of bipolar disorder is now growing rapidly, however. By the 1997 to 2001 period, the number of new references to the condition had grown to 106. From 2002 through the first 4 months of 2006 alone, the number of references jumped to 209.

But we still have little controlled research to guide the treatment of bipolar depression. Nolen (2005) notes, for instance, that despite over 1,000 randomized, controlled trials of antidepressants for depression, there have been only 12 for bipolar depression. Of the 12 trials of antidepressants for bipolar depression reviewed by Gijsman et al. (2004), only 5 were placebo controlled.

The role of antidepressants in treating bipolar depression has been a source of heated debate among psychiatrists. European experts and some researchers in the United States (e.g., Altshuler et al., 2001; Amsterdam & Shults, 2005b; Grunze,

179

2005; Joffe et al., 2005; Moller & Grunze, 2000; Moller et al., 2001) contend that antidepressants are an effective and necessary treatment for acute bipolar depression, that their long-term use in bipolar patients has been shown to prevent depressive relapse, and that the concerns over induction of mania are overstated, especially when an antidepressant is combined with a mood stabilizer. They also assert that mood stabilizers have not been shown to have the antidepressant efficacy of antidepressants. Grunze (2005) asserts that "inappropriate treatment of bipolar depression [use of mood stabilizers without antidepressants] may leave patients at high risk of suicide and increased chronicity of symptoms; effective therapy [an antidepressant] should, therefore, be provided as early as possible" (p. 17).

While acknowledging that antidepressants can be an effective acute treatment for bipolar depression, other experts point to a number of problems associated with these drugs in acute and especially in maintenance treatment. They argue that antidepressant-induced switching is a serious adverse, albeit infrequent, effect that cannot be ignored (e.g., El-Mallakh & Karippot, 2003; Ghaemi et al., 2003a; Goldberg & Ghaemi, 2005; Perugi et al., 2006) and that switching is only one of several risks associated with the use of antidepressants in bipolar patients. Table 7.1 lists possible adverse outcomes when antidepressants are used in patients with bipolar depression.

While not opposed to the use of antidepressants, these researchers contend that, overall, the risks of using them routinely for bipolar depression outweigh the benefits. They believe antidepressants should be reserved for patients who do

TABLE 7.1

Adverse Events Associated With the Use of Antidepressants in Patients with Bipolar Depression

- Induction of mania or hypomania

- Induction or worsening of mixed states (agitation, anger, suicidal ideation or behavior, racing thoughts, insomnia)

- Induction or worsening of rapid cycling, sometimes with less severe depressive episodes

- Mood lability: irregularly occurring, brief, but discrete periods of irritability, depressed mood, lack of motivation

- Short-term nonresponse to antidepressants more common in bipolar than unipolar depression (Ghaemi et al., 2004)

- Long-term loss of response (tachyphalaxis) more common in bipolar than unipolar depression (Ghaemi et al., 2004)

- Refractory depression in spite of high doses of antidepressants or antidepressant combinations not respond to lithium, anticonvulsants, atypical antipsychotics, or combinations of these agents and that antidepressants should generally be discontinued shortly after remission, unless an individual patient repeatedly relapses after discontinuation.

Akiskal, Ghaemi, Perugi, and others provide a detailed and compelling analysis of the evidence that supports their views. Some of the points they make regarding the treatment of acute bipolar depression are:

- Studies showing switch rates with antidepressants comparable to placebo are misleading due to a number of methodological problems including, but not limited to, small sample size and measurement biases such as a lack of sensitivity to ego-syntonic hypomania. Small sample size makes it unlikely that a difference between placebo and active drug for an infrequent event like switch into hypomania will be detected. There are many case reports, case series, and well-conducted observational studies indicating that concerns about hypomanic switch in bipolar patients on antidepressants are warranted. In addition, switches into mania and hypomania have been reported with non-pharmacologic antidepressant treatments such as bright light therapy, sleep deprivation, and sleep phase advance (Goodwin & Jamison, 1990).

- There are no controlled trials demonstrating that antidepressants are more effective than lithium alone.

- The one adequately powered, controlled trial that compared antidepressants to therapeutic doses of lithium found antidepressants produced no added benefit (Nemeroff et al., 2001). (The federally funded Systematic Treatment Enhancement Program for Bipolar Disorder is currently conducting a trial to determine whether a mood stabilizer plus an antidepressant is more effective than a mood stabilizer alone.)

- Lithium is far from being an inappropriate or inadequate treatment for suicidal patients. In fact, lithium is one of only two drugs that has been definitively shown to dramatically reduce suicide risk (e.g., Cipriani et al., 2005). The evidence that antidepressants protect against suicide is weaker.

- Evidence indicates that antidepressants not only do not protect bipolar individuals from developing chronic depressive symptoms, but that they actually *increase* the likelihood that they will develop chronic depressive states (see the section on long-term use of antidepressants later in this chapter for details).

- Mood-stabilizing drugs provide some protection against the risk of hypomanic switch associated with antidepressants but do not eliminate it (e.g., Henry et al., 2001; Leverich et al., 2006).

- Lithium, anticonvulsants, and atypical antipsychotics have been shown to have acute antidepressant properties in bipolar patients with minimal risk of inducing hypomania or causing rapid cycling (e.g., quetiapine: Calabrese et al., 2004; divalproex: Davis et al., 2005). These drugs should be used as first-line treatment in bipolar depression.

Other Issues Regarding Antidepressant Treatment of Bipolar Depression

Are the SSRI antidepressants safe to use in bipolar patients and less likely to cause switch to hypomania than tricyclic antidepressants? What about Effexor and Wellbutrin?

It seems to have become accepted clinical wisdom that there is less risk of inducing hypomania in depressed bipolar patients with SSRI antidepressants than with tricyclics. In fact, there is very little data to support that contention and most of the data is from studies on the use of paroxetine (Paxil). Young et al. (2000), for instance, found that a group of bipolar depressed patients on lithium or valproate did equally well when either paroxetine (Paxil) or a second mood stabilizer was added. In a study of paroxetine, imipramine, or placebo in bipolar depressed patients treated with lithium, patients treated with paroxetine showed a lower rate of switch than patients on imipramine (Nemeroff et al., 2001). Shelton and Stahl (2004) found that 1 of 10 bipolar depressed patients receiving paroxetine in addition to a mood stabilizer became mildly hypomanic. We have to note, however, that all the patients in these trials were treated with mood stabilizers. Even then, some of the paroxetine-treated patients had a hypomanic switch. The most that can be concluded from these studies is that paroxetine in combination with a mood stabilizer is associated with a low rate of switch. No statement can be made about the safety of paroxetine as monotherapy in bipolar depression.

Other studies indicate that the SSRIs citalopram (Celexa) and escitalopram (Lexapro), while effective in the acute treatment of bipolar depression are certainly not free of the risk of inducing hypomania, even when patients are on a mood stabilizer. Schafer et al. (2006) reported that 1 patient out of 10 treated with citalopram (Celexa) added to mood stabilizer therapy switched to hypomania. Fonseca et al. (2006) found that 4 out of 20 depressed bipolar patients on a mood stabilizer given adjunctive escitalopram (Lexapro) had a manic or hypomanic switch. One had to be hospitalized for the emergence of suicidal ideation and psychosis.

Parker et al. (2006) reported on a randomized, double-blind, placebo-controlled cross-over study of 10 healthy, adult, medication-naïve bipolar II patients (with minimal alcohol or drug use, no suicidal ideation, and no significant personality disorder) treated with escitalopram (Lexapro) for 3 months. They found that the escitalopram led to a reduction in depression without a worsening of the course of illness. But they also wrote that the drug appeared to have mood-stabilizing effects in this sample of bipolar II patients because some patients had a small reduction in the frequency of hypomania. The four patients with the best outcomes, however, either repeatedly relapsed to depression, had repeated hypomanias, or continued to cycle between hypomania and depression. Moreover, the small sample size and the short period of observation leave the validity and generalizability of the results in doubt (Ghaemi, personal communication). To conclude that escitalopram can act as a mood stabilizer in bipolar II patients based on this data would be stretching the meaning of the term.

Studies by Peet (1994) and Amsterdam et al. (1998) found that SSRIs are less likely to cause switch than tricyclics. Boerlin et al. (1998) treated 29 bipolar I patients, who had a total of 79 depressive episodes, with fluoxetine (Prozac), tricyclics or MAOIs. Hypomanic switch occurred in 28 percent of the antidepressant-treated depressive episodes. Fluoxetine-treated patients had the lowest rate of switch.

By contrast, Henry et al. (2001) found that switch rates for bipolar patients on TCAs and SSRIs were equal in a 6-week, nonrandomized prospective study. Ghaemi et al. (2003b), in an analysis of 155 trials of TCAs, SSRIs, bupropion (Wellbutrin), and other modern antidepressants in 41 patients, found no significant differences between SSRIs and TCAs. Overall, Perugi et al. (2006) estimate a 20 percent switch rate in bipolar patients treated with SSRIs.

Data from a number of open, uncontrolled studies indicate bupropion is associated with a low rate of switch (Erfurth et al., 2002; Haykal & Akiskal 1990; Shopsin, 1983; Wilens et al., 2003; Wright et al., 1985). Haykal and Akiskal (1990) reported on the use of bupropion added to lithium and/or thyroid supplements in four female and two male treatment-refractory bipolar II patients with at least 2 years of rapid cycling. Three female and one male patient had a sustained, dramatic response with no development of hypomania and without the reemergence of rapid cycling.

In terms of controlled studies, McIntyre et al. (2002) reported on a single-blind comparison of bupropion and the anticonvulsant topiramate (Topamax) in patients already on lithium or valproate. They found that both compounds produced the same response rates. The Sachs et al. (1994) randomized trial is most often cited as evidence for bupropion's low rate of switch compared to a tricyclic (11% vs. 50%). Although the results were statistically significant, the sample was very small (nine patients treated with bupropion, ten treated with the tricyclic).

There have been case reports of hypomania and mixed states being associated with the use of bupropion in bipolar patients (Masand & Stern, 1993; Zubieta & Demitrack, 1991). In addition, Fogelson et al. (1992) found that 6 of 11 patients with bipolar depression experienced manic or hypomanic episodes that necessitated discontinuation of bupropion. Five of the six patients who had manic episodes had been stabilized on lithium and carbamazepine or valproate prior to the addition of bupropion.

Recently, Leverich et al. (2006) reported the results of a 1-year study in which 150 patients with bipolar I disorder or bipolar II disorder participated in a total of 228, 10-week randomized trials of bupropion, sertraline (Zoloft), or venlafaxine

(Effexor) added to mood-stabilizer treatment. Patients in 87 of these trials continued treatment with these drugs for up to 1 year. In this study, venlafaxine had the highest rate of switch. Bupropion was associated with the onset of hypomania but it did so at a lower rate than venlafaxine and sertraline.

Taken as a whole, these data suggest that bupropion may, in fact, cause a lower rate of switch into hypomania than other antidepressants. However, it is obviously not free of the risk of switching bipolar patients into hypomania. Unfortunately, in my experience, it tends to be used as if this were the case. Since it is impossible to predict which patients will switch into hypomania, using it alone in patients with bipolar depression or in those of uncertain polarity may be unwise.

Researchers with the Systematic Treatment Enhancement Program for Bipolar Disorder (STEP-BD) are conducting a randomized, double-blind trial comparing an SSRI to bupropion in 300 bipolar depressed patients. Results are expected soon.

What role do monoamine oxidase inhibitor (MAOI) antidepressants play in the treatment of bipolar depression?

The initial mechanism of action for tricyclic and SSRI antidepressants is blocking reuptake of neurotransmitters such as serotonin and norepinephrine into the cells that produced them. MAOIs have few direct effects on reuptake. They work by inhibiting the enzymes that break down serotonin, norepinephrine, and dopamine. An MAOI was the first compound found to have antidepressant properties. Researchers were investigating the effectiveness of the MAOI isocarboxazid (Marplan) in treating tuberculosis. Although isocarboxazid did not help patients with their tuberculosis, the researchers noticed the drug did have a mood-elevating effect.

MAOIs work particularly well in patients with atypical depression symptoms (oversleeping, for instance). Many bipolar patients, when depressed, have atypical symptoms. Whether for this reason or other reasons not known, MAOIs work quite well for anergic bipolar depressed patients. There are problems, however. Certain foods, such as aged cheese, beer, and cold remedies, when combined with MAOIs can cause dangerous hypertension and possible stroke. MAOIs can also induce hypomania and mania. There are no studies indicating that MAOIs induce less switching than other antidepressants.

The FDA recently approved a transdermal patch for the administration of the MAOI selegiline (Emsam). Transdermal administration does not cause the hypertension and stroke risk associated with oral use of an MAOI. The selegiline patch has not yet been tested in patients with bipolar depression.

What about the new antidepressant duloxetine (Cymbalta)?

Duloxetine, like venlafaxine, is an inhibitor of the reuptake of both serotonin and norepinephrine. Venlafaxine is a much more potent inhibitor of the reuptake of serotonin than norepinephrine, however. Duloxetine is a more balanced inhibitor of the reuptake of these neurotransmitters. The clinical impact of this difference has yet to be determined, but duloxetine may have a lower risk of raising blood pressure than venlafaxine (Thase et al., 2005).

Although there have been reports that the drug caused only a low rate of switch in a variety of patients (Dunner et al., 2005; Viktrup et al., 2004), as of January, 2007, there were no studies on the use of duloxetine in strictly bipolar patients designed to examine rates of switch. Given its potent norepinephrine reuptake properties, caution in the use of this drug in bipolar patients is warranted. Desarkar et al. (2007) reported a case of induction of ultra-rapid cycling in a bipolar depressed adolescent given duloxetine.

Are there any factors predicting which patients are likely to have antidepressant-induced switch?

Table 7.2 lists the factors that have been found to predict antidepressant-induced switch in bipolar patients.

TABLE 7.2

Factors Associated with Antidepressant-Induced Switch in Bipolar Patients

- Premorbid hyperthymic temperament (Henry et al., 2001)
- Bipolar family history (Goldberg & Truman, 2003)
- Initial episode of bipolar disorder was depressed (Serretti et al., 2003)
- Multiple antidepressant trials (Truman et al., 2003)
- Absence of lithium (Henry & Demotes-Mainard, 2003)
- Previous antidepressant-induced hypomania (Tamada et al., 2004)
- Mixed features, dysphoria (Bottlender et al., 2004; Koukopoulos & Koukopoulos, 1999; Mallakh et al., 2003)
- Mutation in the serotonin transporter gene (Mundo et al., 2001)
- History of rapid cycling (Truman et al., 2003)
- Bipolar I diagnosis (Altshuler et al., 2006; Ketter et al., 2005; Leverich et al., 2006)[a]
- Higher number of past manic episodes (Boerlin et al., 1998)[a]
- Substance abuse (Goldberg & Whiteside, 2002)[a]
- Early age of onset of depression (Nasrallah et al., 1982)[a]
- Women, especially those with low normal thyroid functioning (Papadimitriou et al., 2005)[a]

[a] Some studies have not found an association between the factor noted and antidepressant-induced switch.

Should bipolar patients who respond to acute antidepressant therapy continue to take antidepressants to prevent depressive relapse?

At first, it would seem sensible to keep bipolar patients who respond to antidepressants on these drugs to prevent depressive relapse. But, the research evidence indicates that antidepressants do not prevent relapse to depression. In fact, some evidence indicates they *worsen* the course of illness in many bipolar patients.

Some experts point to studies like that of Altshuler et al. (2001), a retrospective chart review of bipolar patients on antidepressants followed for 1 year. This study reported a high rate of depressive relapse in patients who discontinued antidepressants, suggesting that bipolar patients should remain on antidepressants. Perugi et al. (2006), however, note that noncontrolled observational studies such as this one do not take account of a number of confounding variables that could dramatically alter the results. Even if taken at face value, however, the Altshuler study found that only a small subset of bipolar patients—about 15 percent—benefited from long-term treatment.

A more recent study by Fu et al. (2006) would seem, at first glance, to provide evidence that antidepressants should be continued in bipolar patients who respond acutely to antidepressant therapy. They looked at information on 589 bipolar patients, drawn from a managed-care claims database, taking second-generation antidepressants (including SSRIs) after remission from a depressive episode. They compared the risk of depressive relapse for patients who took antidepressants for more than 6 months to those who discontinued antidepressants shortly after remission. They found that continuous antidepressant therapy for 6 months or more was associated with a lower risk of depressive relapse.

This study is a nonrandomized, retrospective, observational study. Fu and colleagues were able to control for some confounding variables. But they had no information on a number of other critical variables that, if taken into account, could have altered the results. Thus the results may be valid or they may be misleading (Ghaemi, personal communication). In addition, at follow-up, only about 20 percent of the patients remained on antidepressants. According to Ghaemi's analysis, even if the results are valid, the data from this study support the use of antidepressants for no more than 9 to 12 months, and then only in a small percentage of the individuals studied.

Perugi and his colleagues point to the lack of *controlled* trials showing that antidepressants prevent depressive relapse. Moreover, they point to the Ghaemi et al. (2001) review, which found seven controlled trials where antidepressants were *not* more effective in the prevention of depressive relapse than lithium alone. For instance, a double-blind study by Prien et al. (1984) showed that a group of bipolar patients stabilized on lithium and imipramine who continued to take both drugs had the same rate of depressive relapse after a year as patients who just took lithium. Perugi and his colleagues also cite the Quitkin et al. (1981) study showing that antidepressants actually *worsened* the course of illness in a group of bipolar patients.

Data from randomized and controlled trials are considered to hold more validity than observational studies such as the ones by Altshuler and Fu. The study with the most clinical weight and validity regarding continued antidepressant treatment in bipolar patients is the on-going 5-year randomized trial being conducted by Ghaemi and his colleagues. In this study, patients initially stabilized on a combination of mood stabilizers (mostly lithium) and antidepressants (mostly SSRIs) were openly randomized to continue or discontinue antidepressants. Four years into this trial, the patients continuing antidepressants have not had fewer depressive episodes and, in fact, appear to have had more mood episodes over follow-up than the group that stopped antidepressants (Ghaemi et al., 2005; Ghaemi, personal communication).

Other studies, as well, have suggested that antidepressants adversely alter the course of bipolar illness. Leverich et al. (2006) found that only 23.3 percent of bipolar patients on a mood stabilizer and an antidepressant had a sustained antidepressant response in the continuation phase in the absence of a switch. A study by Bauer et al. (2003) demonstrated that bipolar patients taking antidepressants were depressed *more* often than bipolar patients not on antidepressants. (It is not clear if severity of depression was controlled for in this study. If it was not, then the results could have another explanation: more severely depressed patients more often received antidepressant medication.) Wehr et al. (1988) found that at the time of the onset of rapid cycling, 37 of 51 patients were taking antidepressant drugs and that the continuation of rapid cycling was associated with antidepressant drug therapy in 26 of the patients.

Indirect evidence of the lack of efficacy of antidepressants in preventing depressive relapse may be found in a 1999 study by Perry and colleagues. Patients who learned to recognize early signs of developing mania and got early treatment (presumably with mood stabilizers or antipsychotics) significantly increased time to the next manic relapse and reduced the number of relapses they suffered. But there was no significant effect on prevention of depressive relapse when patients recognized prodromes of impending depression and then got treatment with antidepressants. This may have been due to other factors, of course, such as depressive prodromes perhaps being harder to recognize, but it does at least suggest antidepressants may not be the treatment of choice for depressive relapse in bipolar patients.

Is there a link between suicidal behavior and the use of SSRIs or venlafaxine (Effexor)?

An increase in suicidality in some patients was noted shortly after the introduction of fluoxetine (Prozac; Teicher et al., 1990). This issue has recently resurfaced with regard to the use of SSRIs in children and adolescents.

At least four possible explanations have been proposed to explain the phenomenon:

1. SSRIs can, in fact, cause suicidal preoccupation and behavior in some children (Fergusson et al., 2005).

2. SSRIs do not cause suicidal behavior. Suicide is a naturally occurring risk in these patients (Isacsson et al., 2005).

3. SSRIs may lead to suicidal behavior because the drug induces extreme restlessness and agitation (an akathisia-like extrapyramidal reaction; Tueth, 1994).

4. A subset of patients who become suicidal on SSRIs are bipolar. The drugs induce or worsen mixed states, thereby increasing the risk of suicide (Rihmer & Akiskal, 2006).

Data have been published that, at first glance, would appear to rule out this fourth possibility. Bauer et al. (2006) reported that of 2,000 participants followed for 18 months in the Systematic Treatment Enhancement Program for Bipolar Disorder (STEP-BD), 24 developed new-onset suicidal ideation and two patients attempted suicide. The researchers found no association between onset of suicidal ideation or attempts and initiation of antidepressant treatment.

Does this prove that clinicians do not need to worry about antidepressants increasing the risk of suicide in bipolar patients? Not at all. First, this study was not a controlled trial designed to see if antidepressant monotherapy in patients with bipolar disorder increased the risk of suicide. It was an observational study with no placebo control and no correction for any confounding factors. Second, in all likelihood, very few patients were on antidepressant monotherapy. Over 70 percent of the first 500 alone were on lithium, divalproex, or carbamazepine and a substantial proportion of this number were also on novel anticonvulsants and atypical antipsychotics (Ghaemi et al., 2006a). It is likely that these reduced, to some degree, the extent to which antidepressants contributed to the agitated, mixed states most clearly associated with high suicide risk.

Do bipolar patients who have been treated with antidepressants and had adverse effects, including the alteration of the natural course of their illness, fully respond to subsequent mood-stabilizer treatment? Is the natural course of their illness restored?

This question remains largely unanswered. We know, however, that a patient who develops rapid cycling on an antidepressant can be more treatment-resistant (Bowden et al., 2000). We also know that bipolar patients treated with antidepressants can develop chronic depressive symptoms and associated morbidity (Bauer et al., 2003; Goodwin & Jamison, 1990). Koukopoulos et al. (1983) found a robust effect of lithium in rapid-cycling patients who had never been exposed to tricyclics. Finally, Winsberg et al. (2001) found divalproex more effective in bipolar depression in patients never exposed to antidepressants. These studies underscore the critical importance of getting the diagnosis right and making sure patients do not get prematurely exposed to antidepressants.

The debate over the use of antidepressants in bipolar depression undoubtedly will continue. On one hand, the evidence indicates antidepressants should not be used routinely in bipolar depression, even in those on lithium or anticonvulsants (these drugs do not provide complete protection against adverse outcomes). On the other hand, a small percentage of bipolar patients—perhaps 15 to 20 percent (Altshuler et al., 2001; Ghaemi & Goodwin, 2001b; Perugi et al., 2006)—may do reasonably well on antidepressants and some may need them to prevent depressive relapse. The problem is this: We cannot reliably identify this group of patients ahead of time.

There is another concern. Even when bipolar patients do well on antidepressants in the short run, some develop problems months, and even years, later that resemble early-onset adverse outcomes. I have seen several such patients in my practice who have responded initially to antidepressant therapy, but who go on to have intermittent, spontaneous episodes of anergic depression or periods of marked irritability.

For example, a patient who came to me for psychotherapy was in the midst of an anergic depression. He had a history of high energy and productivity, but was put on Prozac several years prior to his consultation with me during a previous episode of anergic depression. He had an excellent response to it and may, in fact, have had a mild, euphoric hypomania. He stopped the drug after several years and then restarted it after a relapse to another anergic depressive episode. He had only a minimal response. Over the course of the next few years, he was tried on four different antidepressants. All of these trials produced the same result: a slight easing of his depression without remission. The patient was on sertraline (Zoloft) when I first saw him. He was able to work, but was far from well. This chronic, refractory depression is a condition Goodwin and Jamison (1990) mentioned as a possible outcome of antidepressant treatment of a bipolar patient. I referred the patient to a new psychiatrist, who initially added lithium to the sertraline. The patient had a rapid and dramatic response. Although this dramatic response to the addition of lithium can occur in unipolar patients only partially responsive to antidepressants, it occurs more frequently in bipolar patients (Himmelhoch, 1994). The sertraline was slowly tapered and discontinued with no loss of antidepressant response. In this case, the patient's premorbid high energy and productivity, subsequent anergic depressions, and multiple antidepressant failures should have suggested a bipolar diathesis.

I had another patient who had a previous hospitalization for a major depressive episode. She could not recall how doctors had diagnosed her but she did remember she was treated with lithium and ECT. She discontinued the lithium after discharge. She started 20 mg of fluoxetine (Prozac) several years later under the care of another psychiatrist during a depressive episode with pronounced atypical features. She did well for a few years, although some bursts of productivity suggested she might have had hypomanic episodes. Then, quite suddenly, the fluoxetine stopped working. The psychiatrist gradually increased the fluoxetine to 80 mg per day but she did not respond. He added bupropion and slowly titrated it to a high dose. No response. The fluoxetine was stopped and she was started on venlafaxine in addition to the bupropion. She had a partial response that she lost after a few months. Eighteen months after the initial increase in fluoxetine, she remained ill but managed to avoid hospitalization. She sought consultation with another physician who added lithium to the antidepressant mix. The patient responded dramatically to the addition of the lithium. The second psychiatrist in this case should have been alerted to the possibility of a bipolar diathesis and the need for mood-stabilizing medication by the brief hypomanic episodes, the atypical features, and the multiple antidepressant failures (and, of course, the prior use of lithium).

There are also a number of case examples and case series reported in the literature on late-onset adverse outcomes with antidepressants. El-Mallakh and Karippot (2005), for instance, describe a common pattern of response seen in bipolar patients given antidepressants. They described six depressed bipolar I patients who responded to initial antidepressant treatment, but whose depression returned over time. Depressive symptoms, they wrote, "would transiently improve with dose increase or change of agents" (p. 267). After at least 3 years of antidepressant treatment, however, these patients developed "a triad of dysphoric mood, irritability, and middle insomnia. . . . Ultimately, the dysphoria and associated symptoms became chronic and resulted in dysfunction. Concomitant mood stabilizer did not appear to alter this pattern. Discontinuation of antidepressants was associated with a slow and gradual improvement in these symptoms over the ensuing year" (p. 267).

Ghaemi et al. (2004) have published data regarding late-onset loss of response to antidepressants. They analyzed clinical records for the outcomes of antidepressant trials in 41 patients with bipolar depression and in 37 with unipolar depression. They found that long-term tolerance to antidepressants (late-onset loss of response) occurred 3.4 times as often in bipolar as unipolar patients. Relapse into depression upon antidepressant discontinuation occurred 4.7 times less often in bipolar than in unipolar depression. Modern antidepressants, in general, did not have lower rates of negative outcomes than tricyclic antidepressants. Fluoxetine was the antidepressant most often associated with late-onset loss of response (Ghaemi, personal communication).

Phelps (2005) described a patient with dysthymia and recurrent depressions and "no recognizable features of mania or hypomania" (p. 277). She was apparently diagnosed as having a unipolar depression and put on an antidepressant. She remained euthymic for 7 years. She then lost response to the antidepressant and a short time later developed an agitated dysphoria on an increased dose. The antidepressant was discontinued and restarted 1 year later with a recurrence of the agitation. The patient was treated with an atypical antipsychotic and lithium, but did not get better until the antidepressant was discontinued.

One could reasonably argue that the prescription of antidepressant mono-therapy in these cases was appropriate given the longer-term effectiveness of the drugs. The problems that developed cannot be definitively linked to the antidepressants given the amount of time that passed since initiation of the drugs. This would be somewhat reassuring had the initial choice of antidepressant monotherapy been based on a proper diagnosis and a careful weighing of all the pharmacologic options. But these clinicians apparently never considered the diagnosis of bipolar depression or the possible need for lithium, anticonvulsants, or antipsychotics.

The first rule is to do no harm. It could be considered malpractice when a patient is harmed by a clinician's failure to consider a diagnosis of bipolar disorder and by his or her indiscriminate use of antidepressant medication. That thousands of lawsuits have not been filed against clinicians who have made these mistakes can only be attributed to both patients and malpractice lawyers being unaware of this issue.

Pharmacologic Options for Treating Bipolar Depression

The empirical evidence for the pharmacologic treatment of bipolar depression has been expertly reviewed by Perugi et al. (2006). Following is a summary of findings on the usefulness of drugs available in the United States for the treatment of bipolar depression.

Lithium

Lithium has been found to be modestly effective for the acute treatment of bipolar depression (Perugi et al., 2006). Ghaemi and Goodwin (2001b) found it was also useful for the prevention of new depressive episodes, but Bowden et al. (2003) and Calabrese et al. (2003) have reported that lithium was not superior to placebo in delaying onset of a new depressive episode.

The ideal blood level for treatment of bipolar depression has been a topic of some debate. Gelenberg et al. (1989) found that patients maintained at 0.8 to 1.2 mEq/L had lower relapse rates than those whose blood levels were maintained at 0.4 to 0.6 mEq/L. But patients also have more side effects at the higher level, which leads to greater noncompliance. The researchers did not look at the relapse rate for blood levels between 0.6 and 0.8 mEq/L, where side effects are minimal. Perugi et al. (2006) assert that bipolar depression responds better to higher doses and blood levels of lithium. Ghaemi (personal communication), a coauthor of the Perugi article, states that "some patients may benefit from low levels of lithium, but most seem to need standard levels (about 0.8)."

A number of other experts on bipolar disorder have indicated that lower levels are preferable. Goodwin and Jamison (1990), for instance, recommended reducing the dose of lithium for maintenance to the point where side effects almost disappear or until a blood level of 0.6 to 0.7 mEq/L is reached. Himmelhoch

(1994) wrote that commonly accepted maintenance levels in the United States are too high. He cited his own research indicating that anergically depressed bipolar patients respond better to low doses of lithium (450 to 600 mg per day) and low serum levels (0.35 to 0.65 mEq/L). Finally, Schou and Grof (2006) note that European doctors generally keep the maintenance blood level between 0.4 and 0.8 mEq/L.

Patients are often anxious to discontinue lithium because of side effects, because they feel better and believe they no longer need treatment, or because the idea of needing a drug for life is narcissistically wounding. Clinicians should inform them that there is a high probability of relapse to mania and an increased risk of suicide if they choose to discontinue the drug (Baldessarini et al., 1999; Suppes et al., 1991). A slow discontinuation of the drug (2 to 4 weeks as opposed to 1 day to 2 weeks) can reduce the risk of immediate relapse (Baldessarini et al., 1996; Faedda et al., 1993). But even patients who have been stable for many years on lithium and who discontinue the drug gradually may run a high risk of relapse within a year of stopping it (Yazici et al., 2004).

According to studies by Post et al. (1992) and Maj et al. (1995), patients who stop lithium may not respond to it, or respond to it as well, if they decide to restart it. Tondo et al. (1997) and Coryell et al. (1998), on the other hand, found no evidence that lithium was not as effective after restarting it. Ghaemi (personal communication) states that Post's data indicates a lack of response after lithium rechallenge in only 5 to 10 percent of patients.

Divalproex (Manufactured by Abbott)

Divalproex has not been extensively tested in the treatment of acute bipolar depression. However, its efficacy in the treatment of bipolar depression has been examined in three small, randomized, and controlled trials. In the first trial, Sachs and Collins (2001) randomly assigned 45 patients with bipolar depression to treatment with either divalproex or placebo. Divalproex was effective in 45 percent of the patients compared to 28 percent for those treated with placebo, but the results were not statistically significant because of the small sample size. The second, Davis et al. (2005), was an 8-week, double-blind, placebo-controlled, randomized clinical trial in 25 outpatients with bipolar I depression. The investigators found divalproex effective in reducing the symptoms of depression and anxiety. The third, Dunn et al. (2006), replicated the findings of the Davis study. In a 6-week, double-blind, randomized, controlled trial of divalproex in 21 depressed patients with bipolar I, II, and NOS disorders, the drug provided acute antidepressant and anxiolytic benefit compared to placebo. The investigators noted that the design of the study might have enhanced drug versus placebo benefits, however.

Gyulai et al. (2003) did a study of divalproex as a maintenance treatment for the prevention of depressive relapse in a 52-week, randomized, double-blind, parallel-group, multicenter trial. Divalproex improved several dimensions of depressive morbidity and reduced the probability of depressive relapse in bipolar disorder, particularly in patients who had responded to divalproex when manic, and among patients with a more severe course of illness.

There have been two studies of divalproex that, while not directly addressing the issue of efficacy in bipolar depression, have some important clinical implications: Stoner et al. (2001) reported a search of the literature for bipolar or schizoaffective patients on divalproex revealed that those who required the addition of an antidepressant had significantly lower serum valproate levels than those who did not require an antidepressant. The study suggests that relatively high blood levels of valproate are needed for an antidepressant effect. Winsberg et al. (2001) found divalproex was more effective in bipolar depression in patients never exposed to antidepressants. This suggests that mistakenly treating bipolar patients with antidepressants may not be a benign or easily repaired mistake.

In summary, two of three randomized, controlled trials support the use of divalproex for the treatment of acute bipolar depression. Unlike antidepressants, it poses no risk of inducing hypomania or contributing to an increase in the rate of cycling. It can be especially helpful in the treatment of patients with bipolar II mixed states (Perugi et al., 2006). These patients often have considerable irritability and/or explosive tempers. The drug's disadvantages include the need for blood monitoring of drug levels to avoid toxicity and to check liver functioning, along with its propensity to cause weight gain.

Divalproex ER (extended release) is being studied in NIMH trials for bipolar depression and in a trial in which it will be combined with aripiprazole (Abilify) for treatment of refractory bipolar depression (visit www.clinicaltrials.gov).

Lamotrigine (Lamictal) (Manufactured by Glaxo)

Lamotrigine is an anticonvulsant drug, FDA approved as an add-on for seizure treatment in 1994. Investigators noted that it improved mood in patients being treated for epilepsy. It was FDA labeled for maintenance treatment of bipolar disorder in 2003 after studies showed it prevented new mood episodes in patients with bipolar I disorder. It is more effective in preventing relapse to depression than mania (Goodwin et al., 2004).

Glaxo Smith Kline has not sought FDA approval for lamotrigine for the acute treatment of bipolar depression, however, because the company has not been able to produce data showing it is effective for that condition. In fact, there have been several trials demonstrating that it is *not* more effective than placebo in acute bipolar depression (GSK, data on file; Ghaemi, personal communication).

Calabrese et al. (1999) is the study most often cited regarding the effectiveness of lamotrigine in bipolar depression. Although the drug showed a trend for improving depression scores in the type of data analysis required by the FDA, the results were not statistically significant. The difference between placebo and lamotrigine in another method of data analysis showed the drug to be modestly effective, but the FDA does not accept this particular method as proof of efficacy (Ghaemi, personal communication). Moreover, the difference between placebo and lamotrigine in this data analysis (four points on the 17-item Hamilton Depression Rating Scale), although statistically significant, was not particularly impressive. Other studies have shown the same modest degree of benefit with lamotrigine (Brown et al., 2006; Calabrese et al., 2000; Nierenberg et al., 2006).

Given all this, the enthusiasm for lamotrigine's use in bipolar depression appears excessive. To what then can we attribute this enthusiasm? One factor is publication bias. That is, studies with positive findings get submitted and published while negative studies do not get submitted. The pharmaceutical industry has set up a web site (www.clinicalstudyresults.org) for the publication of all studies, including negative ones, but pharmaceutical manufacturers are not required to post negative studies on the site.

Another factor for lamotrigine's popularity is that clinicians have no drug for bipolar depression that is as well-tolerated as lamotrigine. Except for the possibility of a rash and the rare life-threatening skin condition called Stevens-Johnson syndrome, the drug is generally well-tolerated (although headache, nausea, and insomnia have been reported). It is not sedating and, most importantly, it does not cause weight gain. The drug is also easy for patients and doctors to use. There is no need for regular blood tests to check the level of the drug in the bloodstream (although such a test is available). There is also no need to regularly check the functioning of various organ systems as is necessary for other anticonvulsants (although some physicians may request occasional blood work to check for elevation of liver enzymes). Finally, there appears to be less stigma attached to using the drug than there is with lithium, divalproex, or the atypical antipsychotics.

Although the enthusiasm for lamotrigine may be excessive, ruling out the use of the drug in acute bipolar depression may be unwise. There are, after all, indications it may be of modest benefit in some patients. Manning et al. (2005), Preston et al. (2004), and Pinto and Akiskal (1998) have presented data from open trials suggesting it may be useful in patients with personality disorder traits that overlap or are comorbid with soft forms of bipolar disorder. We have, as well, the results of a pilot trial by Schaffer et al. (2006). He and his colleagues did a 12-week, randomized, double-blind pilot trial comparing the addition of lamotrigine or citalopram in 20 bipolar depressed patients on mood-stabilizer medication. Each treatment group experienced a statistically significant reduction in depressive symptoms. (Unfortunately, the lack of a placebo control and the small number of patients raises questions about the validity of the finding.)

Given its tolerability and ease of use, lamotrigine might be a reasonable first choice in outpatients who are functioning reasonably well; are not severely depressed, agitated, or suicidal; or if they strongly object to using mood stabilizers or antipsychotics requiring blood work and those with a potentially high side-effect burden. It might also be preferable to start with lamotrigine in patients with such a profile if their depression is of uncertain polarity. Lamotrigine has less risk than antidepressants of adversely affecting the course of illness in patients who may have a bipolar diathesis, although there have been case reports of it inducing hypomania (e.g. Margolese et al., 2003).

Indications for starting a depressed bipolar patient on lamotrigine rather than lithium might also include the presence of comorbid anxiety, panic attacks, or substance abuse and those patients with family histories of major depression (as opposed to clear-cut bipolar I or II disorder), panic, and substance abuse (Grof, 2003; Passmore et al., 2003).

Dosages of lamotrigine must be increased slowly to minimize the risk of rash and Stevens-Johnson syndrome. Patients are usually started on 25 mg of lamotrigine and titrated to 200 mg per day over 4 to 6 weeks. Some physicians prescribe the drug in higher doses but there is no randomized data to suggest this is effective. Lamotrigine is being tested in NIMH-sponsored trials for bipolar depression, including a trial comparing it to venlafaxine and another comparing it to lithium (visit www.clinicaltrials.gov).

Other Anticonvulsants

Carbamazepine (Tegretol: Manufactured by Novartis; Equetro: Manufactured by Shire) The FDA approved an extended-release form of carbamazepine (Equetro) for manic and mixed states in 2004. There is very little data on the use of carbamazepine in bipolar depression Most reports on the acute or long-term antidepressant efficacy of carbamazepine are anecdotal or come from uncontrolled studies. The one exception is the Post et al. (1986) trial. In this double-blind study of acute antidepressant efficacy, carbamazepine was shown to be mildly to moderately helpful in 32 of 35 patients.

Oxcarbazepine (Trileptil) (Manufactured by Novartis) There are no controlled studies on the use of oxcarbazepine in bipolar depression. A variety of noncontrolled studies have found it to be useful in the treatment of bipolar depression when used as an add-on agent, however (e.g., Benedetti et al., 2004; Ghaemi et al., 2002; Pratoomsri et al., 2005). Raja and Azzoni (2003) compared 27 inpatients with mood or schizoaffective disorders on oxcarbazepine to 27 matched patients on valproate and found similar efficacy on a number of measures.

More recently, Bellino et al. (2005) conducted a study of oxcarbazepine in 17 borderline patients. Four patients did not complete the study because of noncompliance. The 13 patients who completed the study had a statistically significant response on a number of measures including the Hamilton Rating Scales for Depression and the Borderline Personality Disorder Severity Index.

There is too little evidence to recommend oxcarbazepine as a first-line treatment for bipolar depression.

Phenytoin (Dilantin) Phenytoin has been studied in the treatment of bipolar disorder (see chapter on treatment of mania) but not specifically for bipolar depression. A double-blind, but not placebo–controlled, study of 33 patients with a major depressive episode (polarity unspecified) by Nemets et al. (2005), however, showed that phenytoin was equivalent to fluoxetine in efficacy.

Gabapentin (Neurontin) (Manufactured by Warner-Lambert, now a subsidiary of Pfizer) Open trials of gabapentin for bipolar depression have been positive. Ghaemi and Goodwin (2001a), for instance, reported that in an uncontrolled study of gabapentin either alone or as an adjunct, the drug appeared moderately effective in treating bipolar depression. Wang et al. (2002) found adjunctive gabapentin was effective in an open trial in patients with mild to moderate bipolar depression.

The results of controlled trials, by contrast, have been mixed. On one hand, Guille (1999) found that depressive symptoms improved with the drug in a small, add-on, double-blind, placebo-controlled trial. More recently, Vieta et al. (2006) conducted a randomized, 1-year, add-on prophylactic trial of gabapentin in 13 euthymic bipolar I and II patients versus 12 taking placebo. The gabapentin group did somewhat better than the placebo group as measured by the Clinical Global Impressions Scale for Bipolar Illness, Modified. There were no new depressive symptoms in the gabapentin group, but there were also none in the placebo group. On the other hand, Frye et al. (2000) compared gabapentin to lamotrigine and placebo. In treatment refractory patients, gabapentin was not effective for depressive symptoms.

The most important role for gabapentin in the treatment of bipolar patients may be as an add-on treatment in bipolar patients with comorbid social phobia and panic disorder (e.g., Perugi et al., 2002).

The drug may cause some weight gain but is generally very well tolerated. It is not metabolized by the liver and is excreted unchanged in the urine.

Topiramate (Topamax) (Manufactured by Ortho-McNeil) Topiramate was FDA approved for the treatment of certain types of seizure disorders in 1999. McIntyre et al. (2002) compared topiramate to bupropion when added to lithium in a small, randomized, single-blind study of their efficacy in treating acute bipolar depression. Topiramate was equal to bupropion. Later, McIntyre et al. (2005) found topiramate to be effective in a 16-week, open trial when used as an add-on in 109 bipolar I and II outpatients. Eleven percent of patients withdrew because of adverse effects.

Nickel et al. (2005) found topiramate effective in reducing depressive symptoms and anger in a group of women in a placebo-controlled, double-blind study. The same group of researchers found topiramate to be helpful in a double-blind, placebo-controlled study for women meeting diagnostic criteria for borderline personality disorder (Loew et al., 2006).

Topiramate is one of the few psychotropics that can cause weight loss. It can therefore be useful in bipolar patients who are overweight or who have gained weight on other drugs. For the same reason, it may a useful drug for the bipolar patients who binge-eat or who are bulimic (McElroy et al., 2004; Nickel et al., 2005).

There can be problems with tolerability. Among other side-effects, it can cause significant cognitive dysfunction, leading some clinicians to dub the medication *Dope-amax*.

Levetiracetam (Keppra) (Manufactured by UCB) Levetiracetam was FDA approved as an adjunctive treatment for certain types of seizure disorders in 1999. There are no controlled studies of its use in bipolar depression.

In terms of open studies, Post et al. (2005) used levetiracetam in 34 patients who had various symptoms including depression ($N = 13$) despite ongoing treatment with mood stabilizers. Five of these 13 patients met criteria for remission. Simon et al. (2004) found levetiracetam to be helpful in 20 adult outpatients who had a primary diagnosis of social anxiety disorder (some of whom had comorbid depression). Braunig and Kruger (2003) reported improved symptoms of depression in two patients with rapid-cycling bipolar disorder who were treated with add-on levetiracetam.

Felbamate (Felbatol) (Manufactured by Wallace Laboratories) Since the anticonvulsant lamotrigine reduces glutamatergic neurotransmission, a group of clinicians investigated the usefulness of felbamate in bipolar depression, which also reduces glutamatergic neurotransmission. An FDA trial of this anticonvulsant was completed in March 2006. The results have not yet been published.

Felbamate can suppress the blood-cell forming function of bone marrow and cause liver failure. Because these conditions are potentially fatal, its use in patients with epilepsy has been restricted to those with severe, refractory seizures.

Zonisamide (Zonegran) (Manufactured by Elan) Zonisamide was FDA approved as an adjunctive treatment for certain types of seizure disorders in 1999. It was developed in Japan and a group of Japanese researchers were the first to report on its effects in mania.

Zonisamide has been the subject of an increasing number of open studies in bipolar patients, perhaps because of its ability to cause significant weight loss. There have been no controlled studies in the treatment of patients with bipolar depression. In the most recent study, Ghaemi et al. (2006b) conducted an open-label, prospective, nonrandomized, 8-week study in 20 (10 men, 10 women) depressed bipolar patients (17 type I, 2 type II, 1 NOS). No patients were manic or in a mixed state. Previous treatments were continued during the study. Ten patients withdrew from the study because of adverse effects, mostly nausea/vomiting, cognitive impairment, and sedation. One patient experienced increased suicidal ideation, and one patient experienced hypomania. Mean Montgomery Asberg Depression Rating Scale scores decreased by a statistically significant mean of 8.4 points in those completing the study.

Anand et al. (2005) studied the effects of open-label, add-on zonisamide in 10 patients with bipolar depression who had not tolerated or not responded to other treatments. Five of eight patients who completed 8 weeks of the study had more than a 50 percent decrease in the Hamilton Rating Scale for Depression.

McElroy et al. (2005) evaluated the effects of open-label, adjunctive zonisamide in a group of 62 bipolar patients with various symptoms including depression in a prospective 8-week acute trial followed by a 48-week continuation trial. Twenty-two patients with depressive symptoms at the start of the study showed significant reductions in those symptoms in the acute phase. Only nine patients entered the continuation phase but the antidepressant effect was mostly maintained in these individuals. Of six patients who were initially euthymic, four entered the continuation phase. Two of them developed depressive symptoms. Twenty of the original 62 patients discontinued zonisamide for worsening mood symptoms.

Baldassano et al. (2004) did a retrospective chart review of 12 depressed bipolar I or II patients treated with adjunctive zonisamide. Six patients responded. Four patients discontinued the therapy, two because of sedation and two for lack of efficacy.

McElroy et al. (2004) reported that zonisamide was effective in reducing binge-eating frequency in eight of fifteen outpatients with binge-eating disorder during an open-label, prospective trial. One subject discontinued zonisamide because of lack of response, two for lack of adherence, and four for side effects.

Although this drug looks promising as a treatment for bipolar depression, it appears from these open studies that it may carry a significant side effect burden. Since it is a sulfa drug, those with sulfa allergy should not use it.

Atypical antipsychotics

Quetiapine (Seroquel) (Manufactured by Astra Zeneca) Quetiapine was FDA approved for the treatment of bipolar depression in October of 2006. It is only the second drug to receive approval for bipolar depression (the other is Symbyax). Calabrese et al. (2005b) reported that in an 8-week, double-blind, placebo-controlled study, quetiapine (at doses of 300 or 600 mg/day) was effective and well-tolerated in 542 outpatients with bipolar I ($N = 360$) or II ($N = 182$) disorder experiencing a major depressive episode.

Quetiapine also appears to be effective in bipolar depressed patients with rapid-cycling and perhaps mixed states (Calabrese et al., 2005b; Keck et al., 2005). Hirschfeld et al. (2006) reported that quetiapine was effective in treating anxiety symptoms in bipolar I depression. The data in patients with bipolar II were not as convincing, but the sample of bipolar II patients was half that of the bipolar I sample.

The antidepressant effect size in bipolar I patients was much larger for quetiapine than either olanzapine (0.91–1.09 vs. .32) or olanzapine plus fluoxetine (Symbyax; Calabrese et al., 2005a), suggesting that quetiapine may be a particularly promising drug for use in patients with bipolar depression.

The drug's advantages include less weight gain than that caused by olanzapine and a low rate of akathisia and other EPS. Its main side effects are sedation and somnolence. These may be quite problematic initially in depressed, bipolar spectrum outpatients. Low initial doses and a slow titration are often required. Acutely manic hospitalized patients, however, may be able to tolerate much more rapid and aggressive titration of the drug (Hatim et al., 2006). The somnolence can be a useful side effect for agitated patients with initial insomnia when the drug is given at bedtime (as it typically is).

Stamouli and Lycouras (2006) noted a previous case report of obsessive-compulsive disorder being induced by the use of quetiapine (Seroquel) and then reported on three cases of their own of de novo obsessive-compulsive disorder apparently induced by the drug.

Olanzapine and the Olanzapine/Fluoxetine Combination (Symbyax) (Manufactured by Lily) The olanzapine/fluoxetine (Zyprexa/Prozac) combination was the first drug to be FDA-approved for the treatment of acute bipolar depression. Someone has said Symbyax should have been named Zypzac.

Olanzapine is the most studied atypical antipsychotic for bipolar depression. The manufacturer has sponsored all of the trials. Tohen et al. (2003) did randomized, double-blind, placebo, 8-week controlled trials of olanzapine and the olanzapine/fluoxetine combination in 833 bipolar depressed patients at 84 sites in 13 countries. The olanzapine/fluoxetine combination was clearly more effective than placebo but the olanzapine alone was only slightly better than placebo. The difference between olanzapine and placebo was statistically significant because of the huge sample size, but the effect size was very small and confined mostly to sleep and appetite symptoms (olanzapine's side effects include sedation, sleepiness, and increased appetite; Perugi et al., 2006). Perugi et al. (2006) and Ghaemi (personal communication) state that olanzapine alone has no clinically meaningful benefit in bipolar depression. Indeed, Shelton et al. (2005) showed that an olanzapine/fluoxetine combination did not differ significantly from fluoxetine alone in a group of depressed patients who had not responded to previous SSRI treatment. The olanzapine/fluoxetine combination appears to have a switch rate similar to placebo (Amsterdam & Shults, 2005a; Keck et al., 2005), which Perugi et al. (2006) believe may justify its use in bipolar depression. However, the studies on rate of switch were only 8 weeks in duration and did not look for any of the other possible adverse outcomes associated with antidepressants in bipolar patients that have been previously discussed.

The olanzapine/fluoxetine combination is not FDA approved for maintenance treatment of bipolar depression. Corya et al. (2006), however, reported on a 6-month open-label trial of olanzapine and olanzapine/fluoxetine in 376 depressed bipolar I patients. The majority of patients who entered the study in nonremission achieved remission. The overall rate of depressive relapse was 27.4 percent. Nearly six percent of the patients switched into mania. Since the trial lacked a placebo control, however, the significance of this rate of switch cannot be determined.

As with olanzapine alone, olanzapine/fluoxetine can promote substantial weight gain. This may be one reason it has not become a popular treatment for bipolar depression (Shelton, 2006). Along with the weight gain come elevated nonfasting blood glucose and cholesterol levels. The olanzapine/fluoxetine combination is also associated with a higher rate of nausea and diarrhea than olanzapine alone.

Other Atypical Antipsychotics

It is not yet known if risperidone, aripiprazole, and ziprasidone are effective in treating acute bipolar depression. There are some studies reporting efficacy of risperidone in bipolar depression, but they all lack placebo controls.

Shelton and Stahl (2004), for instance, randomly assigned 30 patients with bipolar I or II disorder, depressed phase, who were receiving a stable dose of a mood stabilizer to 12 weeks of double-blind treatment with risperidone (plus placebo), paroxetine (plus placebo), or the combination of risperidone and paroxetine. All were modestly effective. The small sample size makes it difficult to know if the improvement with risperidone was actually due to the risperidone. The study was meant as a pilot study, and the small effect size prompted the manufacturer not to do a larger study (Ghaemi, personal communication). A 6-week open study of the addition of risperidone to other treatments in 95 schizoaffective patients, bipolar type, decreased Hamilton Depression Rating Scale scores a mean of 6.6 points (Vieta et al., 2001). Finally, Janicak et al. (2001) conducted a three-site, randomized, double-blind, 6-week trial of risperidone (up to 10 mg/day) or haloperidol (up to 20 mg/day) in 62 patients (29 depressed type; 33 bipolar type). Risperidone produced a mean decrease of 13 points from the baseline on the Hamilton Depression Rating Scale compared with an 8-point decrease with haloperidol. In those patients who had more severe depressive symptoms risperidone produced at least a 50 percent mean improvement in 12 (75%) of 16 patients in comparison to 8 (38%) of 21 patients receiving haloperidol. Although the substantial drop in the Hamilton score for risperidone, especially compared to haloperidol, suggests acute efficacy for risperidone, the absence of a placebo control makes definitive conclusions impossible.

Muller-Siechender et al. (1998) compared risperidone alone to haloperidol plus a tricyclic antidepressant in patients with psychotic depression (either schizoaffective or unipolar patients). The risperidone monotherapy was less effective than the haloperidol plus tricyclic, although a post hoc analysis suggested that perhaps risperidone was more effective in the schizoaffective depressed subgroup (Ghaemi, personal communication).

There have been no controlled trials of aripiprazole or ziprasidone specifically for the acute treatment of patients with bipolar depression. However, secondary measures of depression symptoms in studies testing the drugs' effectiveness in treatment of manic and mixed episodes suggest possible antidepressant effects. In addition, ziprasidone and aripiprazole augmentation of various selective serotonin reuptake inhibitors has been reported to be effective in refractory unipolar depression, but only in open-label studies (Nemeroff, 2005). Finally, Ketter et al. (2006) administered open, adjunctive aripiprazole to 30 depressed bipolar, treatment-resistant outpatients. Aripiprazole appeared to be useful in the 16 patients who completed the study.

Theoretically, aripiprazole and ziprasidone's ability to modulate serotonin and norepinephrine neurotransmission would suggest they might have acute antidepressant properties (Ghaemi, personal communication). In fact, ziprasidone's multiple effects on serotonin neurotransmission may be why the drug has most frequently been reported to induce manic and hypomanic switch in bipolar patients (Rachid, 2004).

Stimulants and Modafinil (Provigil)

Carlson et al. (2004) retrospectively reviewed the cases of eight consecutive patients they treated (five with bipolar I and three with bipolar II) who received adjunctive stimulants (either methylphenidate or amphetamine). The primary target symptoms of stimulant therapy were residual depression and medication-induced sedation. The eight patients had moderate clinical improvement in their target symptoms and substantial improvement overall. There was no evidence of stimulant-induced switching or abuse.

Fernandes and Petty (2003) reported on two bipolar patients with a recently remitted depressive episode who they treated with the narcolepsy drug modafinil for hypersomnia. The patients had a decrease in hypersomnia and improvement in their level of functioning with no adverse effects or mood changes.

These are reports of acute treatment. Stimulants and modafinil cannot be assumed to be safe and effective for maintenance treatment of bipolar patients. Both stimulant drugs and modafinil have been associated with the induction of mania and hypomania in children (Faedda et al., 2004; Ranjan & Chandra, 2005; Vorspan et al., 2005).

Experimental Drugs

RU-486 (Mifepristone) (Mifeprex) This drug blocks the action of progesterone and is used to terminate a pregnancy. But it also blocks the action of cortisol. Cortisol is a so-called glucocorticoid hormone produced by a portion of the adrenal gland. It regulates a number of metabolic processes, is anti-inflammatory, and can suppress immune function. Blood levels of cortisol may become elevated in response to psychological stress. High levels of cortisol (hypercortisolemia) can cause or contribute to cognitive impairment and depression. A number of medications in addition to mifepristone, can suppress hypercortisolemia. Mifepristone and these other drugs are therefore called antiglucocorticoids. Antiglucocorticoids have been used to treat depression, psychotic depression, and may be useful for individuals with histories of childhood abuse, since abuse can cause chronic hypercortisolemia. Pharmaceutical companies are working on developing new antidepressant drugs that work by suppressing the action of cortisol. In a placebo-controlled double-blind study, Young et al. (2004) found that mifepristone had modest antidepressant effects in bipolar patients. It is under study in an NIMH-funded trial (see www.clinicaltrials.gov).

Riluzole (Rilutek)   Riluzole has several pharmacologic actions including the inhibition of the excitatory neurotransmitter glutamate. It is FDA labeled to treat Lou Gehrig's disease (amyotrophic lateral sclerosis—ALS). Zarate et al. (2005), in an open trial, reported that the drug was effective and well tolerated by 14 patients with bipolar depression who were already taking lithium. No hypomanic switches occurred.

Riluzole is under study in an NIMH-funded trial (see www.clinicaltrials.gov).

Memantine (Namenda)   Memantine is FDA approved for the treatment of Alzheimer's disease or dementia. It is under study in an NIMH-funded trial (see www.clinicaltrials.gov) for the treatment of depressed bipolar patients who have not fully responded to lamotrigine (Lamictal).

Pramipexole (Mirapex) and Ropinirole (Requip)   Pramipexole is a drug that acts like the neurotransmitter dopamine (dopamine agonist). It is FDA labeled to treat Parkinson's disease. Two uncontrolled studies (Perugi et al., 2001; Sporn et al., 2000) using pramipexole as an adjunct to mood stabilizers and antidepressants in treatment of refractory bipolar patients found the drug to be a safe and effective antidepressant. Goldberg et al. (2004), in a small, randomized, double-blind, placebo-controlled trial of pramipexole used as an adjunct to either lithium or valproate also found the drug to be safe and effective. A small, double-blind, placebo-controlled study of pramipexole in depressed, bipolar II patients on lithium or valproate by Zarate et al. (2004) had similar findings. The two controlled trials reported some cases of hypomania associated with the use of pramipexole, but the Zarate study reported patients on placebo also had hypomanias.

Ropinirole (Requip), a drug used to treat restless legs syndrome, is also a dopamine agonist. Perugi et al. (2001) treated some of the patients in their open study with ropinirole.

Both pramipexole and ropinirole are being tested in NIMH-funded studies for the treatment of bipolar depression (see www.clinicialtrials.gov).

Thyroid Augmentation

The pituitary gland, located at the base of the brain, produces a compound called thyroid stimulating hormone (TSH), which tells the thyroid gland to produce two thyroid hormones: thyroxine (T4) and triiodothyronine (T3).

The amounts of TSH, T4, and T3 that are being produced by the pituitary and thyroid glands can be measured with blood tests. T4 can be measured in two forms: total T4 and free T4. Free T4 is the physiologically active form of thyroxine. It is not bound to protein in the blood and can therefore enter target tissues to exert its effects. It is thought by many physicians to be a more accurate measure of thyroxine function.

The range of normal values listed for these hormones on lab reports may vary from one lab to the next. However, a common set of ranges is shown in Table 7.3.

Physicians look for below normal values of T3 and T4, but above normal TSH values, to diagnose an underactive thyroid. The pituitary gland monitors the levels of T4 and T3 in circulation. If the levels are low, the pituitary gland secretes increased amounts of TSH telling the thyroid to produce more T4 and T3. There are three levels of severity or grades of hypothyroidism. The grade of hypothyroidism is determined by which thyroid hormone value or values are out of range.

The connection between thyroid hormone levels and the course of bipolar illness has been studied and debated for decades (Whybrow, 1994). Researchers disagree on the extent to which bipolar patients are prone to have or develop thyroid abnormalities (Muller-Oerlinghausen & Bauer, 2003). Nevertheless, abnormal and low normal thyroid hormone levels have been tied to a number of difficult-to-treat forms of bipolar disorder (Chang et al., 1998; Fagiolini et al., 2003), including treatment-refractory bipolar depression (Cole et al., 2002; Frye et al., 1999). Women may be more vulnerable to the mood-altering and somatic effects of thyroid dysfunction than men. They tend to respond better to thyroid augmentation (Hendrick et al., 1998). In addition, the immune systems of bipolar patients have been found to produce higher levels of antibodies against thyroid tissue than the immune systems of healthy individuals and of patients with other psychiatric disorders (e.g., Kupka et al., 2002).

It is unlikely that clinicians, especially those in outpatient practice, will be consulted by patients who have any grade of unrecognized hypothyroidism (patients who have an elevated TSH value or T3/T4 values that are below the normal range). Patients' physicians will typically have discovered the abnormalities and treated them or referred them to an endocrinologist.

TABLE 7.3

Normal Thyroid Hormone Values

Hormone	Range
TSH	0.4 to 4.0 mIU/L (mili-International Units per liter of blood)
Total T4	4.5 to 12 mcg/dl (micrograms per deciliter of blood)
Free T4	0.8 to 1.8 ng/dl (nanograms per deciliter of blood)
Total T3	70 to 195 ng/dl

Note: See text for explanations of thyroid hormone abbreviations.

Clinicians will, however, frequently see depressed bipolar patients who have *low normal* T4 levels or *high normal* TSH levels (Goodwin & Jamison, 1990). Their internists or endocrinologists will be satisfied with these levels because they are in the normal range. However, low normal T4 levels and high normal TSH levels may not be optimal for some bipolar patients. Cole et al. (2002), for example, have found that bipolar patients with T4 levels below the median value of the range and TSH values above the median value for the range have poorer treatment outcomes compared to patients with above median T4 values and below median TSH values. They estimate that as many as three-quarters of bipolar patients have thyroid levels that are not optimal for achieving euthymia. Lack of elevation in TSH levels may not be a very good indicator of thyroid dysfunction in bipolar patients. TRH, a hormone made by part of the brain called the hypothalamus, stimulates secretion of TSH from the pituitary gland. Severely ill bipolar patients have deficient TRH signaling of the pituitary and reduced TSH response (Larsen et al., 2004).

Clinicians will typically see bipolar depressed patients with suboptimal but normal thyroid values from one of three groups: (a) those who have never had their thyroid levels checked because their physicians have not seen specific signs or symptoms of hypothyroidism; (b) patients who have been diagnosed with hypothyroidism and are taking thyroid medication (Synthroid or Cytomel) at a dose sufficient to put their T4 level in the low normal range; (c) patients who have had thyroid tests and been informed by their doctor that they do not need thyroid supplements because their levels, while somewhat low, do not support a diagnosis of hypothyroidism. Some of these patients may already be on lithium.

When patients from the last two groups are asked about results of any recent thyroid tests, they will report they have been told their levels are normal. Clinicians need to ask depressed bipolar patients to bring in copies of recent test results so that low normal T4 values or high normal TSH values can be considered in planning treatment. Table 7.4 lists clinical factors associated with suboptimal thyroid functioning in bipolar patients.

Goodwin and Jamison (1990) state that low normal thyroid hormone values

TABLE 7.4

Clinical Factors Associated with Suboptimal Thyroid Functioning in Bipolar Patients

- Perimenopausal women or women over the age of 50
- Rapid cycling
- Treatment-refractory depression
- Fatigue, lethargy, weight gain
- Problems with memory or concentration
- Use of lithium

justify a trial of thyroid supplementation in depressed bipolar patients. Nonmedically trained therapists may have difficulty, however, in persuading physicians
to consider thyroid augmentation. Some options for the nonmedically trained
clinician to consider in working with the patient's physicians are: Gather research
reports on thyroid supplementation in mood disordered patients and give them
to the patient, psychiatrist, and endocrinologist. The therapist can also ask the
psychiatrist to speak to the endocrinologist about the use of supplemental thyroxine. The therapist might also suggest to the patient that he or she present the
literature on thyroid supplementation to their psychiatrist and endocrinologist
when asking them to consider supplementation.

In my experience, psychiatrists hesitate to give bipolar patients with low normal T4 values thyroid supplements. They understandably prefer to leave management of thyroid function to endocrinologists. But many endocrinologists may
themselves be hesitant to prescribe thyroid supplements when hormone values
are in the normal range

When psychiatrists or endocrinologists do prescribe thyroid supplements, they
may not be willing to prescribe the doses needed to boost patients' T4 levels
into the high normal range, especially when thyroxine supplements dramatically reduce TSH values. Physicians are typically concerned about suppression
of natural thyroid function and hypermetabolic responses (e.g., increased heart
rate) to high doses of exogenous thyroxine. However, Bauer et al. (2002b) have
found that healthy controls and depressed patients respond differently to high
doses of thyroxine; depressed patients do not get hypermetabolic symptoms on
these doses.

Physicians are also concerned about the possibility of high T4 levels contributing to a decrease in bone mineral density in older women. While recommending
bone mineral density monitoring for patients on large doses of thyroxine, Gyulai
et al. (2001) and Bauer et al. (2004) found that bone mineral density was not affected to a significant degree in mood-disordered patients. A number of studies by
Bauer et al. (e.g., 2002a, 2005) have found that very high (supraphysiologic) doses
of supplemental thyroxine (400 to 500 mcg per day—sufficient to raise T4 levels
to 150 percent of normal) are effective in treating rapid-cycling and treatment-
resistant bipolar patients. Afflelou et al. (1997) have found similar results with
very high doses of thyroxine.

Thyroid indices need to be monitored and thyroid supplements may need
to be used in patients on lithium since lithium can suppress thyroid function.
The risk for hypothyroidism induced by lithium is especially high in women
over the age of 50 (Kirov et al., 2005). Thyroid supplements may be helpful in
patients on lithium who have recovered substantially from bipolar depression
but are lethargic, fatigued, gaining weight, and having problems with memory or
concentration. Clinicians need to be careful not to mistake these symptoms for
treatment-refractory depression symptoms. A reduction in the dose of lithium
may also be needed if these symptoms persist (Himmelhoch, 1994).

One final note: Szuba et al. (2005) found in a controlled trial that administering thyrotropin releasing hormone (TRH) at night was a rapidly acting and effective antidepressant for depressed bipolar I and II patients.

Folate, B Vitamin Supplementation, and Homocysteine

Folates are forms of a B vitamin involved in many biochemical pathways critical to human health, including the synthesis of monoamine neurotransmitters such as serotonin and norepinephrine. Homocysteine is a molecule produced by the metabolism of the dietary amino acid methionine. Increased plasma homocysteine is a functional marker of both folate and vitamin B12 deficiency and is a risk factor for atherosclerosis, dementia, and depression. Oral folic acid supplements are used to decrease serum homocysteine levels and to protect against atherosclerosis.

Low folate, B12, and B6 levels have been found in studies of depressive patients (Hvas et al., 2004; Tiemeier et al., 2002). Coppen and Abou-Saleh (1982) reported that patients on lithium with lower plasma folate concentration had higher affective morbidity. Coppen et al. (1986) found that folic acid enhanced lithium prophylaxis. Folate deficiency may contribute to depression but depression can also contribute to folate deficiency through poor diet. Researchers have suggested that folate deficiency and depression have reciprocal effects on each other. A vicious circle can occur whereby depression contributes to and is exacerbated by folate deficiency (Alpert & Fava, 1997). Low folate levels are associated with a poor response to antidepressants and predict relapse (Papakostas et al., 2004). Treatment with folic acid improves response to antidepressants (Coppen & Bailey, 2000) and high vitamin B12 status may be associated with better treatment outcome (Hintikka et al., 2003).

Durand et al. (2003) recommend that B12 levels should be tested when a patient has treatment-resistant depression, dementia, psychosis, or risk factors for malnutrition such as alcoholism or advancing age, malabsorption, gastrointestinal surgery, or a strict vegetarian diet. B12 deficiency can be checked for with a serum B12 test or, when results of this are equivocal, measurement of serum methylmalonic acid. High levels of serum methylmalonic acid are a very sensitive measure of compromised B12 status.

Increased homocysteine levels were positively correlated with length of current major depressive episode and HAM-D-17 scores in depressed patients with anger attacks but not in those without anger attacks (Fraguas et al., 2006). Anger attacks in a patient with a major depressive episode suggest the possibility of a bipolar spectrum illness.

Some people have a gene mutation (polymorphism) that interferes with folate chemistry. In fact, individuals with depression, psychotic mood disorders, and perhaps bipolar disorder have a greater incidence of this polymorphism (methylenetetrahydrofolate reductase—MTHFR) than the general population (Coppen & Bolander-Gouaille, 2005; Reif et al., 2005). This suggests that mood-disordered patients may have a metabolic problem with folate chemistry that contributes, at least in part, to their illness.

Folic acid is the form of folate commonly used to fortify foods and sold in vitamin stores. Individuals with a MTHFR polymorphism from each parent will not be able to utilize folic acid supplements. Folinic acid (5-formyl-tetrahydrofolate) or L-5-methyltetrahydrofolate (Metafolin) will be needed since they can be metabolized by individuals with the polymorphism.

Four hundred mcg of folinic acid or Metafolin (the RDA) or higher should be used. Although these are available over the counter, folinic acid is also available as a prescription with the name Leucovorin (contains 5 mg of folinic acid). Up to 1 mg per day of B12 can be taken, preferably in sublingual form, since some people may have trouble absorbing B12 swallowed in pill form. It may also be preferable to use the metabolite of vitamin B6, P5P. Although the risk of toxicity with B vitamin supplementation is low (Hathcock, 1997), patients should check with their physicians before starting these supplements, especially if they are on phenytoin (Dilantin).

From Research to Practice: Pharmacologic Treatment of Bipolar Depression in Outpatient Settings

A clinician in outpatient practice is most likely to see bipolar patients who are in depressive mixed states or patients with atypical depressive features (particularly oversleeping). Patients who are oversleeping should have their premorbid histories evaluated for periods of high energy and productivity. These periods may not have been clearly hypomanic. Rather, they may have been a reflection of hyperthymic temperament, cyclothymic temperament, or irregular, unstable borderline-like states. A substantial proportion of patients with mixed episodes may have multiple comorbidities including panic attacks and impulse-control problems such as episodic alcohol abuse, explosive tempers, overspending, eating disorders, hypersexuality, and sexual compulsions.

If the therapist is not licensed to prescribe medication, he or she will need to refer the patient to a psychiatrist or nurse practitioner, preferably to one with a special interest or expertise in bipolar disorder. Except in areas not served by a psychiatrist or nurse practitioner, the therapist should not refer patients with suspected bipolar spectrum illnesses to family physicians, internists, or obstetricians/gynecologists for psychopharmacologic treatment. The misdiagnosis of bipolar spectrum illnesses as unipolar depression is very common in primary care settings (Ghaemi et al., 2006c). In addition, even if accurately diagnosed, bipolar patients require more frequent and intensive contact with a physician, particularly when suicidal, than general practitioners can provide.

Surprisingly, therapists may find that psychiatrists without a special interest in bipolar disorder are often not aware of the markers for bipolar spectrum illnesses (Ghaemi et al., 2006c; Marneros & Goodwin, 2005). If the patient does not have a clear-cut history of hypomania, simply telling these psychiatrists you believe the patient may be bipolar has, in my experience, often resulted in the patient being diagnosed as unipolar and being given a prescription for an antidepressant. The therapist should therefore send the consulting psychiatrist or nurse practitioner a written summary of the findings that support a diagnosis of bipolar disorder. Findings to report may include the presence of mixed or atypical symptoms, premorbid hyperthymia, early age of onset of depression, or an extensive family history of depression or mood instability. Concerns about the use of antidepressant monotherapy could be expressed, as well.

If the consulting psychiatrist states that it is not clear the patient has a bipolar disorder but acknowledges that it is possible, the patient may be given bupropion, since it is considered safer for bipolar patients than other antidepressants. Why, however, when there is doubt about the diagnosis, do psychiatrists not err on the side of caution and prescribe lithium or an anticonvulsant? This may be because antidepressants are better tolerated than lithium and anticonvulsants, more easily managed, and more readily accepted by patients. There is less stigma associated with the use of antidepressants and considerable fear about the use of lithium and atypical antipsychotics. Patients often believe that the use of these drugs implies they are "crazy."

The nonmedically trained therapist may also see patients with undiagnosed bipolar spectrum illness who are already on antidepressant monotherapy when they come for an initial consultation. These patients may have already been tried on several antidepressants with suboptimal results. The therapist may find the patient is in a chronic, partially remitted, or mixed depressive state. In these cases, the therapist might suggest to the psychiatrist that the patient be given a trial of low-dose lithium. This may result in the lifting of the depression in as little as 12 to 48 hours, although a response can take up to 2 weeks (Himmelhoch, 1994).

The following treatment guidelines for antidepressant-naive patients or patients who are currently not taking antidepressants are based on the work of Perugi et al. (2006).

It is best to avoid antidepressant monotherapy, especially in patients with agitated and mixed depressive states. If a patient is on an antidepressant and is still depressed or if he or she is in a mixed state or rapid cycling, antidepressants should be discontinued. Discontinuation of an antidepressant in a patient who is in a mixed state will often lead to improvement (Koukopoulos & Koukopoulos, 1999). Rarely, rapid discontinuation of an antidepressant in a bipolar patient can result in hypomanic switch (Andrade, 2004).

Monotherapy, with either lithium, divalproex, or perhaps lamotrigine (Lamictal), is the appropriate starting point for patients with mild to moderate anergic bipolar depression and/or mild irritability. This is now the standard of care (American Psychiatric Association, 2002).

The evidence for the efficacy of lamotrigine in acute bipolar depression is not very strong and it can take some time to titrate the drug to an effective dose. However, the fact that it is a well tolerated and easy to manage drug and that it may be effective for some patients with bipolar depression makes it a reasonable place to start for mildly to moderately depressed outpatients with minimal functional impairment.

Indications for starting a mildly depressed, minimally functionally impaired bipolar patient on lamotrigine rather than lithium might include the presence of comorbid anxiety, panic attacks, or substance abuse and the absence of a clear-cut family history of bipolar disorder (Grof, 2003; Passmore et al., 2003).

Should an antidepressant be used in conjunction with a mood stabilizer in severe bipolar depression? This would certainly have been the approach recommended years ago (Goodwin & Jamison, 1990). However, with the many pharmacologic options now available, the use of an atypical antipsychotic and lithium, lamotrigine, or divalproex would be a safer initial strategy. Lithium might be preferable in patients who are at risk of suicide.

Divalproex and/or atypical antipsychotics should be used for those frequently encountered depressed outpatients with prominent agitation, irritability, and explosive temper (mixed states).

Thyroid augmentation sufficient to raise the patients' free T4 levels to the upper quartile of the normal range should be considered, especially in older women with low normal thyroid hormone values or in those on lithium. Folate augmentation, at least, and probably B12 and B6 supplementation are wise to improve antidepressant and mood-stabilizing effects of drugs and to protect cardiovascular health.

Bupropion (Wellbutrin) or paroxetine (Paxil) are the antidepressants that might be appropriate if other approaches fail. The patient might be most protected against switch by the concomitant use of lithium (Henry & Demotes-Mainard, 2003).

Medication options for treating comorbid conditions include gabapentin (Neurotin) for anxiety and social phobia, topiramate (Topamax) or zonisamide (Zonegran) for binge-eating or obesity, divalproex for panic attacks or migraine, atypical antipsychotics for psychosis and the atypicals risperidone (Risperdal) or aripiprazole (Abilify) for obsessive-compulsive disorder.

The reader should consult Ghaemi (2002) and Post et al. (2006) for a complete discussion of polypharmacy in bipolar illness.

References

Afflelou, S., Auriacombe, M., Cazenave, M., et al. (1997). Administration of high dose levothyroxine in treatment of rapid cycling bipolar disorders. Review of the literature and initial therapeutic application apropos of 6 cases. *Encephale, 23*(3), 209–217.

Alpert, J., & Fava, M. (1997). Nutrition and depression: The role of folate. *Nutrition Reviews, 55*(5), 145–149.

Altshuler, L., Kiriakos, L., Calcagno, J., et al. (2001). The impact of antidepressant discontinuation versus antidepressant continuation on 1-year risk for relapse of bipolar depression: A retrospective chart review. *Journal of Clinical Psychiatry, 62,* 612–616.

Altshuler, L. L., Suppes, T., Black, D. O., et al. (2006). Lower switch rate in depressed patients with bipolar II than bipolar I disorder treated adjunctively with second-generation antidepressants. *American Journal of Psychiatry, 163*(2), 313–315.

Amsterdam, J., Garcia-Espana, F., & Fawcett, J. (1998). Efficacy and safety of fluoxetine in treating bipolar II major depressive episode. *Journal of Clinical Psychopharmacology, 8,* 435–440.

Amsterdam, J., & Shults, J. (2005a). Comparison of fluoxetine, olanzapine, and combined fluoxetine plus olanzapine initial therapy of bipolar type I and type II major depression—lack of manic induction. *Journal of Affective Disorders, 87*(1), 121–130.

Amsterdam, J., & Shults, J. (2005b). Fluoxetine monotherapy of bipolar type II and bipolar NOS major depression: A double-blind, placebo-substitution, continuation study. *International Clinical Psychopharmacology, 20*(5), 257–264.

Anand, A., Bukhari, L., Jennings, S., et al. (2005). A preliminary open-label study of zonisamide treatment for bipolar depression in 10 patients. *Journal of Clinical Psychiatry, 66*(2), 195–198.

Andrade, C. (2004). Antidepressant-withdrawal mania: A critical review and synthesis of the literature. *Journal of Clinical Psychiatry, 65,* 987–993.

American Psychiatric Association. (2002). *Practice guidelines for the treatment of patients with bipolar disorders.* Washington, DC: Author.

Baldassano, C., Ghaemi, S., Chang, A., et al. (2004). Acute treatment of bipolar depression with adjunctive zonisamide: A retrospective chart review. *Bipolar Disorders, 6*(5), 432–434.

Baldessarini, R., Tondo, L., Faedda, G., et al. (1996). Effects of the rate of discontinuing lithium maintenance treatment in bipolar disorders. *Journal of Clinical Psychiatry, 57*(10), 441–448.

Baldessarini, R. J., Tondo, L., & Hennen, J. (1999). Effects of lithium treatment and its discontinuation on suicidal behavior in bipolar manic-depressive disorders. *Journal of Clinical Psychiatry, 60*(Suppl 2), 77–84, 111–116.

Bauer, M., Baur, H., Berghofer, A., et al. (2002a). Effects of supraphysiological thyroxine administration in healthy controls and patients with depressive disorders. *Journal of Affective Disorders, 68*(2–3), 285–294.

Bauer, M., Berghofer, A., Bschor, T., et al. (2002b). Supraphysiological doses of L-thyroxine in the maintenance treatment of prophylaxis-resistant affective disorders. *Neuropsychopharmacology, 27*(4), 620–628.

Bauer, M., Fairbanks, L., Berghofer, A., et al. (2004). Bone mineral density during maintenance treatment with supraphysiological doses of levothyroxine in affective disorders: A longitudinal study. *Journal of Affective Disorders, 83*(2–3), 183–190.

Bauer, M., London, E. D., Rasgon, N., et al. (2005). Supraphysiological doses of levothyroxine alter regional cerebral metabolism and improve mood in bipolar depression. *Molecular Psychiatry, 10*(5), 456–469.

Bauer, M., Rasgon, N., Grof, P., et al. (2003, June 12–14). Mood patterns in patients with bipolar disorder: Influence of antidepressants. 5th International Conference on Bipolar Disorder. Pittsburgh, PA. Reported in *Bipolar Disorders, 5*(Suppl. 1), 31.

Bauer, M., Wisniewski, S., Marangell, L., et al. (2006). Are antidepressants associated with new-onset suicidality in bipolar disorder? A prospective study of participants in the Systematic Treatment Enhancement Program for Bipolar Disorder (STEP-BD). *Journal of Clinical Psychiatry, 67*(1), 48–55.

Bellino, S., Paradiso, E., & Bogetto, F. (2005). Oxcarbazepine in the treatment of borderline personality disorder: A pilot study. *Journal of Clinical Psychiatry, 66*(9), 1111–1115.

Benedetti, A., Lattanzi, L., Pini, S., Musetti, L., Dell'Osso, L., & Cassano, G. B. (2004). Oxcarbazepine as add-on treatment in patients with bipolar manic, mixed or depressive episode. *Journal of Affective Disorders, 79*(1–3), 273–277.

Boerlin, H., Gitlin, M., & Zoellner, L. (1998). Bipolar depression and antid-depressasnt induced mania: A naturalistic study. *Journal of Clinical Psychiatry, 59*, 374–379.

Bottlender, R., Sato, T., Kleindienst, N., Strauss, A., & Moller, H. J. (2004). Mixed depressive features predict maniform switch during treatment of depression in bipolar I disorder. *Journal of Affective Disorders, 78*(2), 149–152.

Bowden, C., Calabrese, J., Sachs, G., et al (2003). A placebo-controlled 18-month trial of lamotrigine and lithium maintenance treatment in recently manic or hypomanic patients with bipolar I disorder. *Archives of General Psychiatry, 60*, 392–400.

Bowden, C. L., Lecrubier, Y., Bauer, M., et al. (2000). Maintenance therapies for classic and other forms of bipolar disorder. *Journal of Affective Disorders, 59*(Suppl 1), S57–S67.

Braunig, P., & Kruger, S. (2003). Levetiracetam in the treatment of rapid-cycling bipolar disorder. *Journal of Psychopharmacology, 17*(2), 239–241.

Brown, E. B., McElroy, S. L., Keck, P. E., Jr., Deldar, A., Adams, D. H., Tohen, M., et al. (2006). A 7-week, randomized, double-blind trial of olanzapine/fluoxetine combination versus lamotrigine in the treatment of bipolar I depression. *Journal of Clinical Psychiatry, 67*(7), 1025–1033.

Calabrese, J., Bowden, C., & Sachs, G. (1999). A double-blind placebo-controlled study of lamotrigine monotherapy in outpatients with bipolar I depression. *Journal of Clinical Psychiatry, 60*, 79–88.

Calabrese, J. R., Elhaj, O., Gajwani, P., & Gao, K. (2005a). Clinical highlights in bipolar depression: Focus on atypical antipsychotics. *Journal of Clinical Psychiatry, 66*(Suppl 5), 26–33.

Calabrese, J. R., Hirschfeld, R. M., Frye, M. A., & Reed, M. L. (2004). Impact of depressive symptoms compared with manic symptoms in bipolar disorder: Results of a U.S. community-based sample. *Journal of Clinical Psychiatry, 65*(11), 1499–1504.

Calabrese, J. R., Keck, P. E., Jr., Macfadden, W., Minkwitz, M., Ketter, T. A., Weisler, R. H., et al. (2005b). A randomized, double-blind, placebo-controlled trial of quetiapine in the treatment of bipolar I or II depression. *American Journal of Psychiatry, 162*(7), 1351–1360.

Calabrese, J. R., Suppes, T., Bowden, C. L., Sachs, G. S., Swann, A. C., McElroy, S. L., et al. (2000). A double-blind, placebo-controlled, prophylaxis study of lamotrigine in rapid-cycling bipolar disorder. Lamictal 614 Study Group. *Journal of Clinical Psychiatry, 61*(11), 841–850.

Calabrese, R., Bowden, C., Sachs, G., et al. (2003). A placebo-controlled 18-month trial of lamotrigine and lithium maintenance treatment in recently depressed patients with bipolar I disorder. *Journal of Clinical Psychiatry, 64*, 1013–1024

Carlson, P. J., Merlock, M. C., & Suppes, T. (2004). Adjunctive stimulant use in patients with bipolar disorder: Treatment of residual depression and sedation. *Bipolar Disorder, 6*(5), 416–420.

Chang, K., Keck, P., Jr., Stanton, S., et al. (1998). Differences in thyroid function between bipolar manic and mixed states. *Biological Psychiatry, 43*(10), 730–733.

Cipriani, A., Pretty, H., Hawton, K., & Geddes, J. R. (2005). Lithium in the prevention of suicidal behavior and all-cause mortality in patients with mood disorders: A systematic review of randomized trials. *American Journal of Psychiatry, 162*(10), 1805–1819.

Cole, D., Thase, M., Mallinger, A., et al. (2002). Slower treatment response in bipolar depression predicted by lower pretreatment thyroid function. *American Journal of Psychiatry, 159*(1), 116–121.

Coppen, A., & Abou-Saleh, M. T. (1982). Plasma folate and affective morbidity during long-term lithium therapy. *British Journal of Psychiatry, 141,* 87–89.

Coppen, A., & Bailey, J. (2000). Enhancement of the antidepressant action of fluoxetine by folic acid: A randomised, placebo controlled trial. *Journal of Affective Disorders, 60*(2), 121–130.

Coppen, A., & Bolander-Gouaille, C. (2005). Treatment of depression: Time to consider folic acid and vitamin B12. *Journal of Psychopharmacology, 19*(1), 59–65.

Coppen, A., Chaudhry, S., & Swade, C. (1986). Folic acid enhances lithium prophylaxis. *Journal of Affective Disorders, 10*(1), 9–13.

Corya, S. A., Perlis, R. H., Keck, P. E., Jr., Lin, D. Y., Case, M. G., Williamson, D. J., et al. (2006). A 24-week open-label extension study of olanzapine-fluoxetine combination and olanzapine monotherapy in the treatment of bipolar depression. *Journal of Clinical Psychiatry, 67*(5), 798–806.

Coryell, W., Solomon, D., Leon, A. C., Akiskal, H. S., Keller, M. B., Scheftner, W. A., et al. (1998). Lithium discontinuation and subsequent effectiveness. *American Journal of Psychiatry, 155*(7), 895–898.

Davis, L., Batolucci, A., & Petty, F. (2005). Divalproex in the treatment of bipolar depression: A placebo-controlled study. *Journal of Affective Disorders, 85*(3), 259–266.

Desarker, P., Bakhla, A., & Sinha, V. (2007). Duloxetine-induced ultrarapid cycling in an adolescent with bipolar depression. *Journal of Clinical Psychopharmacology, 27*(1), 115–116.

Dunn, R., Gilmer, W., Fleck, J., et al. (2006, May 20–25). Divalproex monotherapy for acute bipolar depression: A double-blind, randominzed, placebo-controlled trial. Poster presented at the 159th Annual Meeting of the American Psychiatric Association, Toronto, Canada.

Dunner, D. L., D'Souza, D. N., Kajdasz, D. K., Detke, M. J., & Russell, J. M. (2005). Is treatment-associated hypomania rare with duloxetine: Secondary analysis of controlled trials in non-bipolar depression. *Journal of Affective Disorders, 87*(1), 115–119.

Durand, C., Mary, S., Brazo, P., & Dollfus, S. (2003). Psychiatric manifestations of vitamin B12 deficiency: A case report. *Encephale, 29*(6), 560–565.

El-Mallakh, R., & Karippot, A. (2005). Antidepressant-associated chronic irritable dysphoria (acid) in bipolar disorder: A case series. *Journal of Affective Disorders, 84*(2-3), 267–272.

Erfurth, A., Michael, N., Stadtland, C., & Arolt, V. (2002). Bupropion as add-on strategy in difficult-to-treat bipolar depressive patients. *Neuropsychobiology, 45*(Suppl. 1), 33–36.

Faedda, G., Tondo, L., Baldessarini, R., et al. (1993). Outcome after rapid vs gradual discontinuation of lithium treatment in bipolar disorders. *Archives of General Psychiatry, 50*(6), 448–455.

Faedda, G. L., Baldessarini, R. J., Glovinsky, I. P., & Austin, N. B. (2004). Treatment-emergent mania in pediatric bipolar disorder: A retrospective case review. *Journal of Affective Disorders, 82*(1), 149–158.

Fagiolini, A., Cook, D., Frank, E., & Kupfer, D. (2003, June 12–14). Hypothyroidism in 175 patients with bipolar I disorder. Paper presented at the 5th International Conference on Bipolar Disorder, Pittsburgh, PA. Reported in *Bipolar Disorders, 5*(Suppl. 1), 47.

Fergusson, D., Doucette, S., Glass, K. C., et al. (2005). Association between suicide attempts and selective serotonin reuptake inhibitors: Systematic review of randomised controlled trials. *British Medical Journal, 330*(7488), 396.

Fernandes, P. P., & Petty, F. (2003). Modafinil for remitted bipolar depression with hypersomnia. *Annals of Pharmacotherapy, 37*(12), 1807–1809.

Fogelson, D. L., Bystritsky, A., & Pasnau, R. (1992). Bupropion in the treatment of bipolar disorders: The same old story? *Journal of Clinical Psychiatry, 53*(12), 443–446.

Fraguas, R., Jr., Papakostas, G., Mischoulon, D., et al. (2006). Anger attacks in major depressive disorder and serum levels of homocysteine. *Biological Psychiatry, 60*(3), 270–274.

Frye, M., Denicoff, K., Bryan, A., et al. (1999). Association between lower serum free T4 and greater mood instability and depression in lithium-maintained bipolar patients. *American Journal of Psychiatry, 156*(12), 1909–1914.

Frye, M. A., Ketter, T. A., Kimbrell, T. A., Dunn, R. T., Speer, A. M., Osuch, E. A., et al. (2000). A placebo-controlled study of lamotrigine and gabapentin monotherapy in refractory mood disorders. *Journal of Clinical Psychopharmacology, 20*(6), 607–614.

Fu, A. Z., Christensen, D. B., Hansen, R. A., & Liu, G. G. (2006). Second-generation antidepressant discontinuation and depressive relapse in adult patients with bipolar depression: Results of a retrospective database analysis. *Clinical Therapy, 28*(6), 979–989.

Gelenberg, A., Kane, J., Keller, M., et al. (1989). Comparison of standard and low serum levels of lithium for maintenance treatment of bipolar disorder. *New England Journal of Medicine, 32*(22), 1489–1493.

Ghaemi, N. (2002). *Polypharmacy in psychiatry.* New York: Dekker.

Ghaemi, N., Ko, J., & Katzow, J. (2002). Oxcarbazepine treatment of refractory bipolar disorder: A retrospective chart review. *Bipolar Disorders, 4,* 70–74.

Ghaemi, S., El-Mallakh, R., Baldassano, C., & Ostacher, M. (2005, June 16–18). A randomized clinical trial of efficacy and safety of long-term antidepressant use in bipolar disorder. Presented at the 6th International Conference on Bipolar Disorder, Pittsburgh, PA. Reported in *Bipolar Disorders, 7*(Suppl. 2), 59.

Ghaemi, S., Hsu, D., Soldani, R., & Goodwin, F. (2003a). Antidepressants in bipolar disorder: The case for caution. *Bipolar Disorders, 5,* 421–433.

Ghaemi, S., Lenox, M., Baldessarini, R., et al. (2001). Effectiveness and safety of long-term antidepressant treatment in bipolar disorder. *Journal of Clinical Psychiatry, 62,* 565–569.

Ghaemi, S., Rosenquist, K., Ko, J., et al (2003b, June 12–14). Effects of newer and older antidepressants in bipolar depression. Paper presented at the 5th International Conference on Bipolar Disorder. Pittsburgh, PA. Reported in *Bipolar Disorders, 5*(Suppl. 1), 49.

Ghaemi, S., Saggase, J., & Goodwin, F. (2006c). Diagnosis of bipolar depression. In R. El-Mallakh & S. Ghaemi (Eds.), *Bipolar Depression: A comprehensive guide* (pp. 3–36). Washington, DC: American Psychiatric Publishing.

Ghaemi, S. N., & Goodwin, F. K. (2001a). Gabapentin treatment of the non-refractory bipolar spectrum: An open case series. *Journal of Affective Disorders, 65*(2), 167–171.

Ghaemi, S. N., & Goodwin, F. K. (2001b). Long-term naturalistic treatment of depressive symptoms in bipolar illness with divalproex vs. lithium in the setting of minimal antidepressant use. *Journal of Affective Disorders, 65*(3), 281–287.

Ghaemi, S. N., Hsu, D. J., Thase, M. E., Wisniewski, S. R., Nierenberg, A. A., Miyahara, S., et al. (2006a). Pharmacological treatment patterns at study entry for the first 500 STEP-BD participants. *Psychiatr Serv, 57*(5), 660–665.

Ghaemi, S. N., Rosenquist, K. J., Ko, J. Y., Baldassano, C. F., Kontos, N. J., & Baldessarini, R. J. (2004). Antidepressant treatment in bipolar versus unipolar depression. *American Journal of Psychiatry, 161*(1), 163–165.

Ghaemi, S. N., Zablotsky, B., Filkowski, M. M., Dunn, R. T., Pardo, T. B., Isenstein, E., et al. (2006b). An open prospective study of zonisamide in acute bipolar depression. *Journal of Clinical Psychopharmacology, 26*(4), 385–388.

Gijsman, H. J., Geddes, J. R., Rendell, J. M., Nolen, W. A., & Goodwin, G. M. (2004). Antidepressants for bipolar depression: A systematic review of randomized, controlled trials. *American Journal of Psychiatry, 161*(9), 1537–1547.

Goldberg, J., & Truman, C. (2003). Antidepressant induced mania: An overview of current controversies. *Bipolar Disorders, 5*(6), 407–420.

Goldberg, J., & Whiteside, J. (2002) The association between substance-abuse and anti-depressant-induced mania in bipolar disorder: A preliminary study. *Journal of Clinical Psychiatry, 63*, 791–795.

Goldberg, J. F., Burdick, K. E., & Endick, C. J. (2004). Preliminary randomized, double-blind, placebo-controlled trial of pramipexole added to mood stabilizers for treatment-resistant bipolar depression. *American Journal of Psychiatry, 161*(3), 564–566.

Goldberg, J. F., & Nassir Ghaemi, S. (2005). Benefits and limitations of antidepressants and traditional mood stabilizers for treatment of bipolar depression. *Bipolar Disorder, 7*(Suppl. 5), 3–12.

Goodwin, F., & Jamison, K. (1990). *Manic-depressive illness.* New York: Oxford University Press.

Goodwin, G. M., Bowden, C. L., Calabrese, J. R., Grunze, H., Kasper, S., White, R., et al. (2004). A pooled analysis of 2 placebo-controlled 18-month trials of lamotrigine and lithium maintenance in bipolar I disorder. *Journal of Clinical Psychiatry, 65*(3), 432–441.

Grof, P. (2003). Selecting effective long-term treatment for bipolar patients: Monotherapy and combinations. *Journal of Clinical Psychiatry, 64*(Suppl. 5), 53–61.

Grunze, H. (2005). Reevaluating therapies for bipolar depression. *Journal of Clinical Psychiatry, 66*(Suppl. 5), 17–25.

Guille, C. (1999). Gabapentin vs placebo as adjunctive treatment for acute mania and mixed states in bipolar disorders. Annual meeting of the American Psychiatric Association.

Gyulai, L., Bauer, M., Garcia-Espana, F., Hierholzer, J., Baumgartner, A., Berghofer, A., et al. (2001). Bone mineral density in pre- and post-menopausal women with affective disorder treated with long-term L-thyroxine augmentation. *Journal of Affective Disorders, 66*(2–3), 185–191.

Gyulai, L., Bowden, C. L., McElroy, S. L., Calabrese, J. R., Petty, F., Swann, A. C., et al. (2003). Maintenance efficacy of divalproex in the prevention of bipolar depression. *Neuropsychopharmacology, 28*(7), 1374–1382.

Hathcock, J. (1997). Vitamins and minerals: efficacy and safety. *American Journal of Clinical Nutrition, 66*(2), 427–437.

Hatim, A., Habil, H., Jesjeet, S. G., Low, C. C., Joseph, J., Jambunathan, S. T., et al. (2006). Safety and efficacy of rapid dose administration of quetiapine in bipolar mania. *Human Psychopharmacology, 21*(5), 313–318.

Haykal, R. F., & Akiskal, H. S. (1990). Bupropion as a promising approach to rapid cycling bipolar II patients. *Journal of Clinical Psychiatry, 51*(11), 450–455.

Hendrick, V., Altshuler, L., & Whybrow, P. (1998). Psychoneuroendocrinology of mood disorders. The hypothalamic-pituitary-thyroid axis. *Psychiatric Clinics of North America, 21*(2), 277–292.

Henry, C., & Demotes-Mainard, J. (2003). Avoiding drug-induced switching in patients with bipolar depression. *Drug Safety, 26*(5), 337–351.

Henry, C., Sorbara, F., Lacoste, J., Gindre, C., & Leboyer, M. (2001). Antidepressant-induced mania in bipolar patients: Identification of risk factors. *Journal of Clinical Psychiatry, 62*(4), 249–255.

Himmelhoch, J. (1994). On the failure to recognize lithium failure. *Psychiatric Annals, 24*(5), 241–250.

Hintikka, J., Tolmunen, T., Tanskanen, A., & Viinamaki, H. (2003). High vitamin B12 level and good treatment outcome may be associated in major depressive disorder. *BMC Psychiatry, 3,* 17.

Hirschfeld, R., Weisler, R., Shane, R., et al. (2006). Quetiapine in the treatment of anxiety in patients with bipolar I or II depression: A secondary analysis from a randomized, double-blind, placebo-controlled study. *Journal of Clnical Psychiatry, 67,* 355–362.

Hvas, A. M., Juul, S., Bech, P., & Nexo, E. (2004). Vitamin B6 level is associated with symptoms of depression. *Psychotherapy and Psychosomatics, 73*(6), 340–343.

Isacsson, G., Holmgren, P., & Ahlner, J. (2005). Selective serotonin reuptake inhibitor antidepressants and the risk of suicide: A controlled forensic database study of 14,857 suicides. *Acta Psychiatrica Scandanavica, 111*(4), 286–290.

Janicak, P. G., Keck, P. E., Jr., Davis, J. M., Kasckow, J. W., Tugrul, K., Dowd, S. M., et al. (2001). A double-blind, randomized, prospective evaluation of the efficacy and safety of risperidone versus haloperidol in the treatment of schizoaffective disorder. *Journal of Clinical Psychopharmacology, 21*(4), 360–368.

Joffe, R. T., MacQueen, G. M., Marriott, M., & Young, L. T. (2005). One-year outcome with antidepressant–treatment of bipolar depression. *Acta Psychiatrica Scandanavica, 112*(2), 105–109.

Judd, L. (2002). The long-term natural history of the weekly symptomatic status of bipolar I disorder. *Archives of General Psychiatry, 59*(6), 530–537.

Judd, L., Akiskal, H., Schettler, P., et al. (2003). A prospective investigation of the naturla history of the long-term weeekly symptomatic status of bipolar II disorder. *Archives of General Psychiatry, 60,* 261–269.

Keck, P. E., Jr., Corya, S. A., Altshuler, L. L., Ketter, T. A., McElroy, S. L., Case, M., et al. (2005). Analyses of treatment-emergent mania with olanzapine/fluoxetine combination in the treatment of bipolar depression. *Journal of Clinical Psychiatry, 66*(5), 611–616.

Ketter, T., Calabrese, J., Bowden, C., et al. (2005, June 16–18). Differential role of adjunctive antidepressants in bipolar II vs. bipolar I disorder. Paper presented at the 6th International Conference on Bipolar Disorder, Pittsurgh, PA. Reported in *Bipolar Disorders, 7*(Suppl. 2), 23.

Ketter, T. A., Wang, P. W., Chandler, R. A., Culver, J. L., & Alarcon, A. M. (2006). Adjunctive aripiprazole in treatment-resistant bipolar depression. *Annals of Clinical Psychiatry, 18*(3), 169–172.

Kirov, G., Tredget, J., Rhys, J., et al. (2005). A cross-sectional and a prospective study of thyroid disorders in lithium-treated patients. *Journal of Affective Disorders, 87*(2–3), 313–317.

Koukopoulos, A., Kaliari, B., & Tondo, A. (1983). Rapid cyclers, temperament and antidepressants. *Comprehensive Psychiatry, 24,* 249–258.

Koukopoulos, A., & Koukopoulos, A. (1999). Agitated depression as a mixed state and the problem of melancholia. *Psychiatric Clinics of North America, 22,* 547–564.

Kupka, R. W., Nolen, W. A., Post, R. M., McElroy, S. L., Altshuler, L. L., Denicoff, K. D., et al. (2002). High rate of autoimmune thyroiditis in bipolar disorder: Lack of association with lithium exposure. *Biological Psychiatry, 51*(4), 305–311.

Larsen, J. K., Faber, J., Christensen, E. M., Bendsen, B. B., Solstad, K., Gjerris, A., et al. (2004). Relationship between mood and TSH response to TRH stimulation in bipolar affective disorder. *Psychoneuroendocrinology, 29*(7), 917–924.

Leverich, G. S., Altshuler, L. L., Frye, M. A., Suppes, T., McElroy, S. L., Keck, P. E., Jr., et al. (2006). Risk of switch in mood polarity to hypomania or mania in patients with bipolar depression during acute and continuation trials of venlafaxine, sertraline, and bupropion as adjuncts to mood stabilizers. *American Journal of Psychiatry, 163*(2), 232–239.

Loew, T. H., Nickel, M. K., Muehlbacher, M., Kaplan, P., Nickel, C., Kettler, C., et al. (2006). Topiramate treatment for women with borderline personality disorder: A double-blind, placebo-controlled study. *Journal of Clinical Psychopharmacology, 26*(1), 61–66.

Maj, M., Pirozzi, R., & Magliano, L. (1995). Nonresponse to reinstituted lithium prophylaxis in previously responsive bipolar patients: Prevalence and predictors. *American Journal of Psychiatry, 152*(12), 1810–1811.

Marneros, A., & Goodwin, F. (2005). Bipolar disorders beyond major depression and euphoric mania. In A. Marneros & F. Goodwin (Eds.), *Bipolar disorders: Mixed states, rapid cycling and atypical forms* (pp. 1–44). New York: Cambridge University Press.

Manning, J., Haykal, R., Connor, P., et al. (2005). Sustained remission with lamotrigine augmentation or monotherapy in female resistant depressives with mixed cyclothymic-dysthymic temperament. *Journal of Affective Disorders, 84*(2–3), 259–266.

Margolese, H., Beauclair, L., Szkrumelak, N., & Chouinard, G. (2003). Hypomania induced by adjunctive lamotrigine. *American Journal of Psychiatry, 160*(1), 183-184.

Masand, P., & Stern, T. A. (1993). Bupropion and secondary mania. Is there a relationship? *Annals of Clinical Psychiatry, 5*(4), 271–274.

McElroy, S., Kotwal, R., Hudson, J., et al. (2004). Zonisamide in the treatment of binge-eating disorder: An open-label, prospective trial. *Journal of Clinical Psychiatry, 65*(1), 50–56.

McElroy, S., Suppes, T., Keck, P., et al. (2005). Open-label adjunctive zonisamide in the treatment of bipolar disorders: A prospective trial. *Journal of Clinical Psychiatry, 66*(5), 617–624.

McIntyre, R., Mancini, D., McCann, S., et al. (2002) Topiramate versus bupropion SR when added to mood stabilizer therapy for the depressive phase of bipolar disorder: A preliminary single-blind study. *Bipolar Disorders, 4,* 207–213.

McIntyre, R. S., Riccardelli, R., Binder, C., & Kusumakar, V. (2005). Open-label adjunctive topiramate in the treatment of unstable bipolar disorder. *Canadian Journal of Psychiatry, 50*(7), 415–422.

Moller, H., Bottlender, R., Grunze, H., et al. (2001). Are antidepressants less effective in the acute treatment of bipolar I compared to unipolar depression? *Journal of Affective Disorders, 67,* 141–146.

Moller, H., Grunze, H., et al. (2000). Have some guidelines for the treatment of acute bipolar depression gone too far in the restriction of antidepressants? *European Archives of Psychiatry and Clinical Neurosciences, 250*(2), 57–68.

Muller-Oerlinghausen, B., & Bauer, M. (2003, June 12–14). Somatic comorbidity: New insights into the link between the thyroid system and bipolar disorder. Paper presented at the 5th International Conference on Bipolar Disorder, Pittsburgh, PA. Reported in *Bipolar Disorders, 5*(Suppl. 1), 20.

Muller-Siechender F., Muller, M., Hillert, A., et al. (1998). Risperidone versus haloperidol and amitriptyline in the treatment of patients with a combined psychotic and depressive syndrome. *Journal of Clinical Psychopharmacology, 18,* 111–120.

Mundo, E., Walker, M., Cate, T., Macciardi, F., & Kennedy, J. L. (2001). The role of serotonin transporter protein gene in antidepressant-induced mania in bipolar disorder: Preliminary findings. *Archives of General Psychiatry, 58*(6), 539–544.

Nasrallah, H., Lyskowski, J., & Schroeder, D. (1982). TCA-induced mania: differences between switchers and nonswitchers. *Biological Psychiatry, 17*(2), 271–274.

Nemeroff, C., Evans, D., & Gyulai, L. (2001). Double-blind, placebo-controlled comparison of imipramine and paroxetine in the treatment of bipolar depression. *American Journal of Psychiatry, 158,* 906–912.

Nemeroff, C. B. (2005). Use of atypical antipsychotics in refractory depression and anxiety. *Journal of Clinical Psychiatry, 66*(Suppl. 8), 13–21.

Nemets, B., Bersudsky, Y., & Belmaker, R. H. (2005). Controlled double-blind trial of phenytoin vs. fluoxetine in major depressive disorder. *Journal of Clinical Psychiatry, 66*(5), 586–590.

Nickel, C., Lahmann, C., Tritt, K., Muehlbacher, M., Kaplan, P., Kettler, C., et al. (2005). Topiramate in treatment of depressive and anger symptoms in female depressive patients: A randomized, double-blind, placebo-controlled study. *Journal of Affective Disorders, 87*(2–3), 243–252.

Nierenberg, A. A., Ostacher, M. J., Calabrese, J. R., Ketter, T. A., Marangell, L. B., Miklowitz, D. J., et al. (2006). Treatment-resistant bipolar depression: A STEP-BD equipoise randomized effectiveness trial of antidepressant augmentation with lamotrigine, inositol, or risperidone. *American Journal of Psychiatry, 163*(2), 210–216.

Nolen, W. A. (2005). Lack of evidence in the treatment of important subgroups of depression. *Ned Tijdschr Geneeskd, 149*(27), 1498–1501.

Papadimitriou, G., Calabrese, J., Dikeos, D., & Christodoulou, G. (2005). Rapid cycling bipolar disorder: biology and pathogenesis. *International Journal of Neuropsychopharmacology, 8*(2), 281–292.

Papakostas, G. I., Petersen, T., Mischoulon, D., Ryan, J. L., Nierenberg, A. A., Bottiglieri,

T., et al. (2004). Serum folate, vitamin B12, and homocysteine in major depressive disorder, Part 1: Predictors of clinical response in fluoxetine-resistant depression. *Journal of Clinical Psychiatry, 65*(8), 1090–1095.

Parker, G., Tully, L., Olley, A., & Hadzi-Pavlovic, D. (2006). SSRIs as mood stabilizers for Bipolar II Disorder? A proof of concept study. *Journal of Affective Disorders, 92*(2-3), 205–214.

Passmore, M. J., Garnham, J., Duffy, A., MacDougall, M., Munro, A., Slaney, C., et al. (2003). Phenotypic spectra of bipolar disorder in responders to lithium versus lamotrigine. *Bipolar Disorder, 5*(2), 110–114.

Peet, M. (1994). Induction of mania with selective serotonin reuptake inhibitors and tricyclic anti-depressants. *British Journal of Psychiatry, 164,* 549–550.

Perugi, G., Ghaemi, S., & Akiskal, H. (2006). Diagnostic and clinical mangagement approaches to bipolar depression, bipolar II and their co-morbidities. In H. Akiskal & M. Tohen (Eds.), *Bipolar psychopharmacotherapy* (pp. 193–234). West Sussex, England: Wiley.

Perugi, G., Toni, C., Frare, F., et al (2002). The effectiveness of adjunctive gapentin in resistant bipolar disorder. Is it due to anxious-alcohol abuse comorbidity? *Journal of Clinical Psychopharmacology, 22,* 584–591.

Perugi, G., Toni, C., Ruffolo, G., Frare, F., & Akiskal, H. (2001). Adjunctive dopamine agonists in treatment-resistant bipolar II depression: An open case series. *Pharmacopsychiatry, 34*(4), 137–141.

Phelps, J. R. (2005). Agitated dysphoria after late-onset loss of response to antidepressants: A case report. *Journal of Affective Disorders, 86*(2–3), 277–280.

Pinto, O. C., & Akiskal, H. S. (1998). Lamotrigine as a promising approach to borderline personality: An open case series without concurrent DSM-IV major mood disorder. *Journal of Affective Disorders, 51*(3), 333–343.

Post, R., Altshuler, L., & Frye, M. (2005). Preliminary observations on the effectiveness of levetiracetam in the open adjunctive treatment of refractory bipolar disorder. *Journal of Clinical Psychiatry, 66*(3), 370–374.

Post, R., Speer, A., & Leverich, G. (2006). Complex combination therapy: The evolution toward rational polypharmacy in lithium-resistant bipolar illness. In H. Akiskal & M. Tohen (Eds.), *Bipolar psychopharmacotherapy* (pp. 135–167). West Sussex, England: Wiley.

Post, R. M., Leverich, G. S., Altshuler, L., & Mikalauskas, K. (1992). Lithium-discontinuation-induced refractoriness: Preliminary observations. *American Journal of Psychiatry, 149*(12), 1727–1729.

Post, R. M., Uhde, T. W., Roy-Byrne, P. P., & Joffe, R. T. (1986). Antidepressant effects of carbamazepine. *American Journal of Psychiatry, 143*(1), 29–34.

Pratoomsri, W., Yatham, L. N., Sohn, C. H., Solomons, K., & Lam, R. W. (2005). Oxcarbazepine add-on in the treatment of refractory bipolar disorder. *Bipolar Disorders, 7*(Suppl 5), 37–42.

Prien, R., Kupfer, D., & Mansky, P. (1984). Drug therapy in the prevention of recurrences in unipolar and bipolar affective disorders. *Archives of General Psychiatry, 41*(11), 1096–1104.

Preston, G. A., Marchant, B. K., Reimherr, F. W., Strong, R. E., & Hedges, D. W. (2004). Borderline personality disorder in patients with bipolar disorder and response to lamotrigine. *Journal of Affective Disorders, 79*(1-3), 297–303.

Quitkin, F. M., Kane, J. M., Rifkin, A., Ramos-Lorenzi, J. R., Saraf, K., Howard, A., et al. (1981). Lithium and imipramine in the prophylaxis of unipolar and bipolar II depression: A prospective, placebo-controlled comparison [proceedings]. *Psychopharmacology Bulletin, 17*(1), 142–144.

Rachid, F., Bertschy, G., Bondolfi, G., & Aubry, J. M. (2004). Possible induction of mania or hypomania by atypical antipsychotics: An updated review of reported cases. *Journal of Clinical Psychiatry, 65*(11), 1537–1545.

Raja, M., & Azzoni, A. (2003). Oxcarbazepine vs. valproate in the treatment of mood and schizoaffective disorders. *International Journal of Neuropsychopharmacology, 6*(4), 409–414.

Ranjan, S., & Chandra, P. S. (2005). Modafinil-induced irritability and aggression? A report of 2 bipolar patients. *Journal of Clinical Psychopharmacology, 25*(6), 628–629.

Reif, A., Pfuhlmann, B., & Lesch, K. P. (2005). Homocysteinemia as well as methylenetetrahydrofolate reductase polymorphism are associated with affective psychoses. *Progress in Neuropsychopharmacology and Biological Psychiatry, 29*(7), 1162–1168.

Rihmer, Z., & Akiskal, H. (2006). Do antidepressants t(h)reat(en) depressives? Toward a clinically judicious formulation of the antidepressant-suicidality FDA advisory in light of declining national suicide statistics from many countries. *Journal of Affective Disorders, 94*(1-3), 3–13.

Sachs, G., & Collins, M. (2001). A placebo-controlled trial of divalproex sodium in acute bipolar depression. Paper presented at the 40th meeting of the American College of Neuropsychopharmacology, Waikola, Hawaii.

Sachs, G. S., Lafer, B., Stoll, A. L., Banov, M., Thibault, A. B., Tohen, M., et al. (1994). A double-blind trial of bupropion versus desipramine for bipolar depression. *Journal of Clinical Psychiatry, 55*(9), 391–393.

Schaffer, A., Zuker, P., & Levitt, A. (2006). Randomized, double-blind pilot trial comparing lamotrigine versus citalopram for the treatment of bipolar depression. *Journal of Affective Disorders, 96*(1-2), 95–99.

Schou, M., & Grof, P. (2006). Lithium treatment: Focus on long-term prophylaxis. In H. Akiskal & M. Tohen (Eds.), *Bipolar psychopharmacotherapy* (pp. 9–26). West Sussex, England: Wiley.

Serretti, A., Artioli, P., Zanardi, R., & Rossini, D. (2003). Clinical features of antidepressant associated manic and hypomanic switches in bipolar disorder. *Progress in Neuropsychopharmacology and Biological Psychiatry, 27*(5), 751–757.

Shelton, R. C. (2006). Olanzapine/fluoxetine combination for bipolar depression. *Expert Review of Neurotherapeutics, 6*(1), 33–39.

Shelton, R. C., & Stahl, S. M. (2004). Risperidone and paroxetine given singly and in combination for bipolar depression. *Journal of Clinical Psychiatry, 65*(12), 1715–1719.

Shelton, R. C., Williamson, D. J., Corya, S. A., Sanger, T. M., Van Campen, L. E., Case, M., et al. (2005). Olanzapine/fluoxetine combination for treatment-resistant depression: A controlled study of SSRI and nortriptyline resistance. *Journal of Clinical Psychiatry, 66*(10), 1289–1297.

Shopsin, B. (1983). Bupropion's prophylactic efficacy in bipolar affective illness. *Journal of Clinical Psychiatry, 44*(5 Pt 2), 163–169.

Simon, N., Worthington, J., & Doyle, A. (2004). An open-label study of levetiracetam for the treatment of social anxiety disorder. *Journal of Clinical Psychiatry, 65*(9), 1219–1222.

Sporn, J., Ghaemi, S. N., Sambur, M. R., Rankin, M. A., Recht, J., Sachs, G. S., et al. (2000). Pramipexole augmentation in the treatment of unipolar and bipolar depression: A retrospective chart review. *Annals of Clinical Psychiatry, 12*(3), 137–140.

Stamouli, S., & Lykouras, L. (2006). Quetiapine-induced obsessive-compulsive symptoms: A series of five cases. *Journal of Clinical Psychopharmacology, 26*(4), 396–400.

Stoner, S., Worrel, J., & Vlach, D. (2001). Retrospective analysis of serum valproate levels and need for an antidepressant drug. *Pharmacotherapy, 21*(7), 850–854.

Suppes, T., Baldessarini, R., Faedda, G., & Nolen, W. (1991). Risk of recurrence following discontinuation of lithium treatment of bipolar disorder. *Archives of General Psychiatry, 48*, 1082–1088.

Szuba, M. P., Amsterdam, J. D., Fernando, A. T., III, Gary, K. A., Whybrow, P. C., & Winokur, A. (2005). Rapid antidepressant response after nocturnal TRH administration in patients with bipolar type I and bipolar type II major depression. *Journal of Clinical Psychopharmacology, 25*(4), 325–330.

Tamada, R. S., Issler, C. K., Amaral, J. A., Sachs, G. S., & Lafer, B. (2004). Treatment emergent affective switch: A controlled study. *Bipolar Disorder, 6*(4), 333–337.

Teicher, M., Glod, C., & Cole, J. (1990). Emergence of intense suicidal preoccupation during fluoxetine treatment. *American Journal of Psychiatry, 147*(2), 207–210.

Thase, M. E. (2005). Bipolar depression: Issues in diagnosis and treatment. *Harvard Review of Psychiatry, 13*(5), 257–271.

Thase, M. E., Tran, P. V., Wiltse, C., Pangallo, B. A., Mallinckrodt, C., & Detke, M. J. (2005). Cardiovascular profile of duloxetine, a dual reuptake inhibitor of serotonin and norepinephrine. *Journal of Clinical Psychopharmacology, 25*(2), 132–140.

Tiemeier, H., van Tuijl, H. R., Hofman, A., Meijer, J., Kiliaan, A. J., & Breteler, M. M. (2002). Vitamin B12, folate, and homocysteine in depression: The Rotterdam Study. *American Journal of Psychiatry, 159*(12), 2099–2101.

Tohen, M., Vieta, E., Calabrese, J., Ketter, T. A., Sachs, G., Bowden, C., et al. (2003). Efficacy of olanzapine and olanzapine-fluoxetine combination in the treatment of bipolar I depression. *Archives of General Psychiatry, 60*(11), 1079–1088.

Tondo, L., Baldessarini, R. J., Floris, G., & Rudas, N. (1997). Effectiveness of restarting lithium treatment after its discontinuation in bipolar I and bipolar II disorders. *American Journal of Psychiatry, 154*(4), 548–550.

Truman, C., Baldassano, C., Goldberg, J., et al. (2003). History of antidepressant-induced mania in the STEP 500. Poster #29 at the APA annual meeting. San Francisco, CA.

Tueth, M. (1994). Revisiting fluoxetine (Prozac) and suicidal preoccupations. *Journal of Emergency Medicine, 12*(5), 685–687.

Vieta, E., Herraiz, M., Fernandez, A., Gasto, C., Benabarre, A., Colom, F., et al. (2001). Efficacy and safety of risperidone in the treatment of schizoaffective disorder: Initial results from a large, multicenter surveillance study. Group for the Study of Risperidone in Affective Disorders (GSRAD). *Journal of Clinical Psychiatry, 62*(8), 623–630.

Vieta, E., Manuel Goikolea, J., Martinez-Aran, A., Comes, M., Verger, K., Masramon, X., et al. (2006). A double-blind, randomized, placebo-controlled, prophylaxis study of adjunctive gabapentin for bipolar disorder. *Journal of Clinical Psychiatry, 67*(3), 473–477.

Viktrup, L., Perahia, D. G., & Tylee, A. (2004). Duloxetine treatment of stress urinary incontinence in women does not induce mania or hypomania. *Primary Care Companion to the Journal of Clinical Psychiatry, 6*(6), 239–243.

Vorspan, F., Warot, D., Consoli, A., Cohen, D., & Mazet, P. (2005). Mania in a boy treated with modafinil for narcolepsy. *American Journal of Psychiatry, 162*(4), 813–814.

Wang, P. W., Santosa, C., Schumacher, M., Winsberg, M. E., Strong, C., & Ketter, T. A. (2002). Gabapentin augmentation therapy in bipolar depression. *Bipolar Disorder, 4*(5), 296–301.

Wehr, T., Sack, D., Rosenthal, N., & Cowdry, R. (1988). Rapid cycling affective disorder: contributing factors and treatment responses in 51 patients. *American Journal of Psychiatry, 145*(2), 179–184.

Whybrow, P. C. (1994). The therapeutic use of triiodothyronine and high dose thyroxine in psychiatric disorder. *Acta Medica Austriaca, 21*(2), 47–52.

Wilens, T. E., Prince, J. B., Spencer, T., Van Patten, S. L., Doyle, R., Girard, K., et al. (2003). An open trial of bupropion for the treatment of adults with attention-deficit/hyperactivity disorder and bipolar disorder. *Biological Psychiatry, 54*(1), 9–16.

Winsberg, M. E., DeGolia, S. G., Strong, C. M., & Ketter, T. A. (2001). Divalproex therapy in medication-naive and mood-stabilizer-naive bipolar II depression. *Journal of Affective Disorders, 67*(1-3), 207–212.

Wright, G., Galloway, L., Kim, J., Dalton, M., Miller, L., & Stern, W. (1985). Bupropion in the long-term treatment of cyclic mood disorders: Mood stabilizing effects. *Journal of Clinical Psychiatry, 46*(1), 22–25.

Yazici, O., Kora, K., Polat, A., & Saylan, M. (2004). Controlled lithium discontinuation in bipolar patients with good response to long-term lithium prophylaxis. *Journal of Affective Disorders, 80*(2-3), 269–271.

Young, A. H., Gallagher, P., Watson, S., Del-Estal, D., Owen, B. M., & Ferrier, I. N. (2004). Improvements in neurocognitive function and mood following adjunctive treatment with mifepristone (RU-486) in bipolar disorder. *Neuropsychopharmacology, 29*(8), 1538–1545.

Young, L. T., Joffe, R. T., Robb, J. C., MacQueen, G. M., Marriott, M., & Patelis-Siotis, I. (2000). Double-blind comparison of addition of a second mood stabilizer versus an antidepressant to an initial mood stabilizer for treatment of patients with bipolar depression. *American Journal of Psychiatry, 157*(1), 124–126.

Zarate, C. A., Jr., Payne, J. L., Singh, J., Quiroz, J. A., Luckenbaugh, D. A., Denicoff, K. D., et al. (2004). Pramipexole for bipolar II depression: A placebo-controlled proof of concept study. *Biological Psychiatry, 56*(1), 54–60.

Zarate, C. A., Jr., Quiroz, J. A., Singh, J. B., Denicoff, K. D., De Jesus, G., Luckenbaugh, D. A., et al. (2005). An open-label trial of the glutamate-modulating agent riluzole in combination with lithium for the treatment of bipolar depression. *Biological Psychiatry, 57*(4), 430–432.

Zubieta, J. K., & Demitrack, M. A. (1991). Possible bupropion precipitation of mania and a mixed affective state. *Journal of Clinical Psychopharmacology, 11*(5), 327–328.

CHAPTER 8

Psychosocial Treatments

Matt is a 28-year-old, married carpenter with a 3-month-old daughter and 3-year old son, Matt, Jr. He has always loved working with his hands. His relationship with his wife, Sue, who is sensitive and emotionally overreactive, has been stormy from the start. Matt, Jr. has not outgrown his terrible-twos. His crying, complaining, and demanding are almost more than his parents can tolerate at times.

Matt was diagnosed with bipolar disorder 8 years ago. For the last 3 years he has been stable on a combination of lithium, Depakote, and Seroquel. He had been in individual therapy up until a year ago with a young therapist at a community mental health center. The therapist had been kind and helpful but not able to provide education or guidance to him or his wife about his illness. Matt saw a psychiatrist once every 2 months for 10 to 15 minutes.

He had recently been working a lot of overtime. He was also busy a few nights a week with side work and on the weekends with home construction projects. He was getting less sleep since the baby was born. He decided to cut down his Seroquel because it was leaving him feeling very groggy in the morning. He soon found he had more energy, needed less sleep, and got more work done. After a few weeks, he decided to stop it altogether. He was feeling fine and had never liked the idea of being on medication (he felt ashamed of his illness and thought he should be able to handle his problems on his own). He then decided to cut down on the lithium and Depakote since they were causing him to gain weight.

Within a week his wife noticed he was becoming increasingly irritable, agitated, and critical. He constantly complained that she was not doing enough to keep the house clean. She responded to this criticism with a gripe of her own. He was becoming a nasty s.o.b. again. She also blamed him for their son's increasingly out-of-control behavior. Matt's doctor had once briefly explained to her that Matt's irritable, demanding behavior was a manifestation of his illness and could be used to gauge how he was doing. But she had difficulty recalling that when he was attacking her. For the most part, she really believed that he had a nasty personality. After all, hadn't he been like this since they first met?

Matt started staying out late at night with his friends and began drinking more heavily. Sue, not knowing what to do and feeling frantic, began attacking him for being a lousy husband and father. Matt retaliated with attacks of his own. Sue complained to Matt's parents, who lived near by, that their son was being irresponsible. One day, when Matt and his family were visiting his parents, his mother criticized him for being selfish by staying out at night. She began to lecture him about how a father should be at home with his children at night. He cursed at her, told her to mind her business, and stormed out of the house. His father came after him, yelling at him not to talk to his mother that way.

The next day, Matt felt very depressed. He had no motivation and began sleeping 14 hours a day. He went to work, but was barely able to function otherwise. He could not muster the interest or the energy to do side work or to work on his house. He decided that carpentry had lost its luster for him. He no longer enjoyed it and thought he would have to find a new career.

Research on psychosocial treatments for bipolar illness has been virtually nonexistent up until recently. Medical interventions, of course, form the foundation of treatment for bipolar illness. But even with expert psychopharmacologic intervention, relapses, residual symptoms, and lingering psychosocial and occupational impairments are common in patients with this disorder. Patients with mood disorders in general and bipolar illness in particular have central nervous systems that are poorly buffered against stress and are easily destabilized. A variety of positive and negative biopsychosocial stressors can destabilize patients and lead to relapse: antidepressant medication, loss of sleep because of a new-born child or a family medical emergency, job promotion, and living with relatives who are highly critical are some examples. Bipolar patients also introduce sources of stress into their lives by not taking medication as prescribed, staying out late and losing sleep, using alcohol or drugs, becoming involved in arguments with family members or having extramarital affairs. One would expect that psychotherapy, by helping bipolar patients avoid impulsive, self-destructive behavior, resolve interpersonal problems, cope with stress, and adhere to medication regimens would provide some benefit.

Several psychosocial interventions (shown in Table 8.1) have now been shown in empirical trials to improve medication compliance and reduce relapse and hospitalization rates when added to ongoing treatment with medication (Otto & Miklowitz, 2004). A meta-analysis of eight recent adjunctive psychosocial thera-

TABLE 8.1

Psychosocial Treatments for Bipolar Disorder

- Psychoeducation
- Family-focused treatment
- Interpersonal and social-rhythm therapy
- Integrated family and IPSRT therapy
- Cognitive-behavioral therapy and behavioral activation
- Life Goals Program

---

pies studies, for instance, found about a 40 percent reduction in relapse rates when active interventions are compared to standard treatment alone (Scott, Colom et al., 2006).

The empirically tested psychosocial treatments to be discussed here have, for the most part, been found effective only as *maintenance* treatments. With the exception of some data from cognitive-behavioral therapy trials for the treatment of bipolar depression (e.g., Zaretsky et al., 1999), there is no evidence to suggest that they are effective in the *acute* treatment of mania, hypomania, or depression. In fact, the research evidence indicates family-focused treatment and interpersonal social-rhythm therapy are *ineffective in acute treatment.*

Some practitioners have also attempted to use cognitive techniques to help patients modify aspects of hypomanic thinking and behavior (e.g., Leahy, 2004), but there are no controlled studies indicating that this is possible. Preliminary research evidence suggests that cognitive therapy is not effective in patients who are hypomanic (Lam et al., 2005b).

Psychosocial Treatments for Bipolar Disorder

Psychoeducation

Matt received almost no information about his illness, its treatment, the risks associated with discontinuing medication, how to forestall relapse, or how to manage symptoms. Most of the research on psychosocial treatment of bipolar disorder in general and the importance of psychoeducation in particular has been done just since the early 1990s.

Education about bipolar illness and its treatment is a critical component of every psychosocial treatment empirically validated. A review of the literature shows that researchers and clinicians have delivered psychoeducation in individual, marital, family, and group formats (Frank, 2005). Psychoeducation is a key component of the two most well researched and widely used psychosocial treatments for bipolar disorder: family-focused treatment and interpersonal social-rhythm therapy.

Although this intervention is educational in focus, it serves a psychotherapeutic function, as well. By helping a patient understand that a bipolar diagnosis, for instance, does not imply he or she is crazy, it may help him or her more readily accept needed treatment. By informing the patient that lethargy and lack of motivation do not reflect laziness but are symptoms of bipolar depression, the therapist can help reduce the patient's guilt and shame. Psychoeducation may also change how parents, spouse, and siblings view patient's problems (from a character defect or personality disorder to a manifestation of an illness), thereby setting the stage for working with the patient in a less hostile and more supportive way. Psychoeducation may also help modify dysfunctional beliefs about the implications of using medication (e.g., "Lithium is for crazy people").

Clarkin et al. (1988) developed a family intervention for patients hospitalized for various disorders including bipolar illness. Their method focused on helping patients and their families accept the reality of their disorders and the need for ongoing treatment, identify stressful events that may have acted as precipitants for relapse, modify family relationships, and learn ways to cope with future stresses and episodes of illness.

In 1998, Clarkin and his colleagues tested a psychoeducational marital intervention for bipolar patients and their spouses. The sample was composed of middle-aged couples that had been married for an average of 17 years. Patients were randomly assigned to receive either medication management ($N = 23$) or medication management plus the marital intervention with their spouses ($N = 19$) for an 11-month period. Couples in the experimental group had 25 sessions at a usual rate of one session a week for the first 10 sessions then bimonthly for the remaining 15 sessions. Although there was no impact of the intervention on patients' symptoms, medication adherence was better in the combined treatment as was overall patient functioning. The medication plus marital intervention group received substantially more professional attention than the medication alone group, so it is possible that the extra time and attention and not the content of the intervention could have been the decisive factor in improved patient functioning (Clarkin et al., 1998).

Perry et al. (1999) randomly assigned 69 patients with bipolar disorder who had had a relapse in the previous 12 months to either (a) routine care and seven to twelve individual sessions of psychoeducation focused on recognizing and seeking help for prodromal symptoms or (b) routine care alone. Patients were followed for 18 months. Patients who recognized manic prodromes and sought early treatment significantly increased time to the next manic relapse and reduced the number of relapses they suffered. Recognizing prodromal symptom of depression and getting early treatment with an antidepressant did not significantly affect depressive relapses. This may have been due to the fact that depressive prodromes were harder to recognize. But it is an interesting finding in light of the findings on the failure of antidepressant medications to prevent relapse to depression in bipolar patients (see Chapter 7). Patients in the psychoeducation group showed improved social functioning and job performance.

Colom, Vieta, and their colleagues in Spain have done the most work in recent years on the role of psychoeducation in the treatment of patients with bipolar disorder. Their study (Colom et al., 2003) is the only randomized, controlled trial of group psychoeducation for bipolar patients. The program focuses on helping patients detect the onset of prodromal symptoms, enhance their compliance with treatment, and increase lifestyle regularity.

The program consists of 21 group sessions that provide information on the following: the nature of bipolar illness, its symptoms, precipitants, course, outcome, and treatment; the importance of compliance with medication and the dangers associated with discontinuation of medication; the risks of alcohol and drug use; detection and management of prodromal symptoms; and life-style regularity, stress management, and problem-solving. Discussion of the material by group members is encouraged (Colom & Vieta, 2006).

Colom and his colleagues tested their program with 120 bipolar I and II outpatients being treated with medication who were in remission for at least 6 months prior to the study. Roughly a third of the patients in both groups had made suicide attempts and three quarters had psychotic features. The control group had had a mean of nearly nine previous episodes and the psychoeducation group had had more than ten. Patients in each group had a mean of roughly two previous hospitalizations. Patients were randomly assigned to 21 sessions of group psychoeducation or 21 sessions of nonstructured group meetings and followed for 2 years (patients remained on medications but did not receive any additional psychological help).

Results were reported as follows: "Group psychoeducation significantly reduced the number of relapsed patients and the number of recurrences per patient, and increased the time to depressive, manic, hypomanic, and mixed recurrences. The number and length of hospitalizations per patient were also lower in patients who received psychoeducation" (p. 402). During the treatment phase, 60 percent of the control group relapsed and 38 percent of the psychoeducation group relapsed ($p = .01$). The difference in relapse rates was statistically significant, however, only for hypomanic and depressive episodes, not manic or mixed states. At 2-year follow-up, 92 percent of the control group had relapsed and 67 percent of the psychoeducation group had relapsed ($p < .001$). Differences in relapse rates were significant for hypomanic, depressive, and mixed episodes but not manic episodes.

Family-Focused Treatment

Matt's story is an example of how bipolar disorder is an illness that adversely affects a patient's relationships with spouse, children, and parents and whose course and outcome can, in turn, be adversely affected by criticism, hostility, or overinvolvement of these family members.

Family-focused therapy of bipolar disorder was developed by David Miklowitz, PhD, and his colleagues at the University of Colorado at Boulder. His research initially focused on the impact critical and intrusive comments (referred to as expressed emotion or EE) had on remission and relapse in schizophrenic patients. He then turned to studying the relationship between high EE and the course of bipolar illness. In a prospective study, he and his colleagues found that high family EE predicted relapse in bipolar patients who were not in treatment (Miklowitz et al., 1988). For patients in treatment with either family-focused treatment or a less intensive crisis management approach, Kim and Miklowitz (2004) found that those with relatives who made frequent critical comments had higher levels of mania and depression over a 2-year follow-up.

Miklowitz and Goldstein (1990) adapted family psychoeducational, communication skills training, and problem-solving skills training designed to reduce relapse in schizophrenic patients to families with a bipolar member. This work led to the development of a formal, manual-based treatment for bipolar patients and their families aimed at improving the long-term course of bipolar illness (Miklowitz, 1996; Miklowitz & Goldstein, 1997).

Family-focused treatment consists of 21 sessions spread over 9 months. Initial sessions are scheduled on a weekly basis. Patients and spouses or families are seen together. The treatment is divided into 3 phases: The first seven sessions or so involve psychoeducation. Patients and their parents or spouses are given information on bipolar disorder and the need for continued medications and stress management. They learn how to identify prodromal symptoms of mania and depression and discuss a plan for dealing with these should they arise. This includes practicing appropriate ways of discussing the problem with the patient that keep stress and hostile communications at a minimum. The next phase, comprising seven to ten sessions, is aimed at developing communication skills to reduce EE and improve the emotional climate in the home. Through role-playing and practice, patients are taught how to listen actively, express themselves in constructive ways, and request change. In the last phase, patients and families are taught rational problem-solving skills: specifying the problem, developing possible solutions, evaluating pros and cons of the various solutions, and planning for implementation. Families are given homework assignments and are asked to practice at home the skills learned in sessions.

The steps involved in administering family-focused treatment are specific and detailed. This has allowed the treatment to be tested in randomized trials. Miklowitz et al. (2003a) randomly assigned 101 bipolar patients to family-focused treatment and pharmacotherapy or a less frequent and intense crisis management intervention and pharmacotherapy. The family-focused treatment lasted 9 months and the pharmacotherapy continued throughout the study. Both groups were followed for 2 years. Fifty-two percent of the patients undergoing family-focused treatment did not relapse over the 2 years whereas only 17 percent of those in the clinical management group did not relapse. Patients treated with family-focused treatment showed greater reductions in depressive symptoms but only after 6 months of treatment. They also had better compliance with medication.

Miklowitz et al. (2005) found that patients who were more distressed by their relatives' criticisms had more severe depressive and manic symptoms and proportionately fewer days well during the study year than patients who were less distressed by criticisms. Interestingly, patients who reported that their relatives became more upset by the their criticisms had less severe depressive symptoms at follow-up. This could be taken as evidence for the adaptive value or defensive function of irritability. Perhaps the best defense really is a good offense (or, at least, being offensive).

Were the superior results seen with family-focused treatment due to greater frequency and intensity of professional contact rather than the specific effects of the treatment? The results of another 2-year randomized trial suggest not. Rea et al. (2003) assigned 53 bipolar, manic patients to family-focused therapy and medication or to equally intensive individual educational therapy and medication. The individual therapy included many elements of family-focused therapy but family members were not involved. Patients in family-focused therapy had lower rates of relapse (28%) and rehospitalization (12%) than patients in individual therapy (60% and 60%, respectively), but only during a 1-year posttreatment interval. There were no differences between the groups during the first year of treatment.

What was not clear from these trials was the mechanism by which family interventions contributed to more favorable outcomes: was it by educating patients and families about bipolar illness, improving family relationships, increasing compliance with medication, or something else? A further analysis in the Miklowitz trial indicated that treatment-related improvements in family communication skills were associated primarily with reductions in patients' depressive symptoms. Improved family communication had less impact on manic symptoms. Adherence to medication mediated the effects of the psychosocial interventions on mania symptoms.

Family-focused treatment may be well suited for working with families with a teen or adult-child patient at home. Miklowitz has, in fact, developed a treatment protocol for conducting family-focused therapy for adolescents with bipolar disorder. A small-scale, open treatment trial involving 20 bipolar adolescents found that the combination of family-focused treatment and mood-stabilizing medications was associated with improvements in depression symptoms, mania symptoms, and behavior problems over 1 year (Miklowitz et al., 2004).

Interpersonal and Social-Rhythm Therapy

> Matt was never told how important it is for bipolar patients to keep their daily routines regular. Maintaining a regular sleep/wake schedule is especially critical for patients with bipolar disorder. If a bipolar patient oversleeps, he or she will reinforce depression. If he or she does not get enough sleep, he or she runs the risk of reinforcing or developing a manic episode.

In 1988, Ehlers and colleagues proposed that a disruption of social rhythms can result in instability of biological rhythms and could be responsible for triggering the onset of a major depressive episode in vulnerable individuals. In 1997, Frank (who had coauthored the 1988 paper with Ehlers) and her colleagues reported the development of a psychosocial intervention for patients with bipolar I disorder that focused on promoting the regularity of daily routines. Frank also coauthored studies in 1998 and again in 2000 demonstrating a connection between life events that disrupt sleep/wake rhythms in bipolar patients and the development of mania (Malkoff-Schwartz et al., 1998, 2000). Bipolar patients apparently may have a genetically derived, biological-based vulnerability to mood instability when the sleep/wake cycle is disrupted. Mood disorders in general can be viewed as a problem in buffering the central nervous system against stress.

Administered in conjunction with medications, interpersonal and social-rhythm therapy (IPSRT) combines the basic principles of Klerman et al.'s (1984) interpersonal psychotherapy for depression (found effective in the treatment of unipolar depression) with behavioral techniques to help patients modify both biological and psychosocial factors that affect circadian rhythms and the sleep-wake cycle. The basis of the therapy is "the conviction that regularity of social routines and stability of interpersonal relationships have a protective effect in recurrent mood disorders" (Frank et al., 2005). Frank and her colleagues believe there are three ways in which new episodes of illness get started: (a) nonadherence to medication; (b) interpersonal stress and changes in social role; and (c) disruptions of social rhythms. The last two may exert their effects not only directly but through disruptions of the sleep/wake cycle, as well.

In the initial phase of treatment, the therapist meets with the patient weekly for three to five sessions. The focus is on history taking (particularly with an emphasis on establishing a connection between interpersonal problems, disruption of social rhythms, and symptoms), education, an assessment of the patient's interpersonal relationships (using an instrument called the Interpersonal Inventory), an assessment of the regularity of social routines (using an instrument referred to as the Social Rhythm Metric), and, finally, the selection of an interpersonal problem area. Five interpersonal problem areas are identified: unresolved grief, role transitions, interpersonal role disputes, interpersonal deficits, and grief over the loss of the healthy self.

In the intermediate phase, the focus is on helping the patient achieve some regularity in social rhythms, particularly in his or her sleep/wake schedule, and on intervening in the interpersonal problem area. The patient will be helped to recognize maladaptive patterns of interaction with others and to develop new approaches to interpersonal problem solving. Sessions may occur weekly, biweekly, or monthly.

In the maintenance phase, the focus is on helping the patient learn how to deal with challenges to the maintenance of regular social rhythms and further work on improving interpersonal relationships.

Readers are referred to Frank's (2005) book on IPSRT for more details on implementing the method.

One controlled study of IPSRT has been reported (Frank et al., 2005). In this study, IPSRT with pharmacotherapy was compared to an intensive clinical management (ICM) treatment with pharmacotherapy in 175 acutely ill patients with bipolar I disorder. Intensive clinical management included support; education about bipolar disorder, medications, and sleep hygiene; inquiry about symptoms and medication side effects; management of medication side effects; identification and management of prodromal symptoms including the use of rescue medications; and 24-hour on-call service. Patients were randomly assigned to one of four treatments: acute and maintenance IPSRT, acute and maintenance ICM, acute IPSRT followed by maintenance ICM, or acute ICM followed by maintenance IPSRT. The maintenance phase of the study lasted 2 years.

IPSRT and ICM were virtually identical in terms of the proportion of patients achieving remission. In addition, the two treatments did not differ in time to remission and there were no differences among the treatments in patients' average levels of depression or mania. However, patients treated with IPSRT in the acute phase who were able to stabilize their daily routines experienced longer survival time without a new affective episode and were more likely to remain well for the full 2 years of the preventive maintenance phase. Intensive clinical management was superior to IPSRT in patients with many medical problems and high levels of anxiety. The authors speculated that these patients might have found it difficult to put aside their somatic focus and turn their attention to the work of IPSRT. Participants who were married at baseline had significantly better long-term outcomes than those who were not. Patients who were married were overrepresented in the acute IPSRT arms of the study. IPSRT appears to work best for the married patient without substantial medical comorbidity or anxiety. Such patients may not be the norm in general outpatient practice.

An issue for clinicians to keep in mind is that young people have a great deal of difficulty stabilizing their routines, especially their sleep/wake cycles. In fact, they seem quite adept at introducing sources of stress and instability in their lives. Many of them do not like regularity. They are perhaps easily bored and seek stimulation in ways that add chaos to their lives: keeping odd hours, using drugs, and being involved in tempestuous love affairs, for example. The median age of the patients in the IPSRT study was roughly 35. IPSRT may not be the most appropriate treatment for teens or young adults. Motivational interviewing techniques might be useful in getting these patients more interested in regulating their routines.

Integrated Family and IPSRT Therapy

Miklowitz et al. (2003b) did an open trial of combined or integrated family and individual therapy (IFIT) in 30 bipolar I and II patients compared to 70 patients who received medication, limited family education, and crisis management. Integrated family and individual therapy was composed of sessions of individual IPSRT alternating with sessions of family therapy. All patients were on medication. Over the course of 1 year, the IFIT-treated patients had greater improvement in depressive symptoms (but not on manic symptoms) and longer periods without symptoms.

Cognitive-Behavioral Therapy and Behavioral Activation

Matt could have used some help in modifying his dysfunctional beliefs about his illness and the implications of using medication for his disorder. This may not have entirely convinced him that his symptoms were nothing to be ashamed of or that medication was not a crutch. However, it might have helped forestall his rash decision to discontinue medication.

Cognitive therapy was developed by Beck et al. (1979) for the treatment of unipolar depression. Beck's therapy is geared toward relieving depression in two ways: recognition and modification of inaccurate, dysfunctional thoughts (automatic negative thoughts) and scheduled activities to test dysfunctional thoughts, improve a sense of mastery, and bring pleasure (behavioral activation). Cognitive-behavioral therapy (CBT) has also been tested in the treatment of patients with bipolar disorder (e.g., Lam et al., 2003; Scott et al., 2001; Zaretsky et al., 1999). Modest improvements in depressive symptoms, social functioning, and decreased rates of relapse have been reported.

More recently, Lam et al. (2005a) published the 2-year follow-up data from a trial of cognitive therapy for relapse prevention in bipolar patients. He and his colleagues randomly assigned 103 patients with bipolar I disorder suffering from frequent relapses into a cognitive therapy plus medication group or a control condition of medication only. Over 30 months, the cognitive therapy group had a better outcome in terms of time to relapse. However, the effect of relapse prevention was mainly in the first year—cognitive therapy had no significant effect in relapse reduction over the last 18 months of the study. The cognitive therapy group did have longer periods of wellness, better mood ratings, and social functioning, however

Scott, Paykel, and colleagues (2006) did an 18-month, multicenter, randomized-controlled trial of CBT in 253 patients with bipolar disorder. More than half of the patients had a recurrence by 18 months, with no significant differences between groups. Lam (2006) noted with concern that the results of the study were at odds with the positive findings of other studies of cognitive therapy in patients with bipolar disorder. He criticized Scott on two counts: First, the patients in the Scott study were apparently a mixed group of relatively well and acutely ill patients, some of whom may not have been on medication. Lam pointed out that this made it likely that the study would not show benefit. Second, Lam criticized Scott for drawing conclusions about the ineffectiveness of cognitive therapy for patients with many episodes of illness on the basis of a post-hoc analysis.

Ball et al. (2006) randomly assigned 52 patients with bipolar I or II disorder to a 6-month trial of either CBT or treatment as usual (TAU), with both treatment groups also receiving mood stabilizers. In this trial, the researchers added emotive techniques derived largely from Gestalt therapy to the usual repertoire of cognitive interventions. These techniques were geared towards helping patients experience emotions or emotional memories associated with dysfunctional beliefs. At the end of the trial, patients treated with CBT had less severe depression scores. There was a substantial difference on a measure of illness severity in favor of the CBT group at follow-up.

Readers interested in learning more about CBT of bipolar disorder are referred to Basco and Rush (2005).

Studies in patients with unipolar depression indicate that the behavioral activation component in CBT may be the key to alleviating depression (Jacobson et al., 1996; Dimidjian et al., 2006; Martell et al., 2004). Both Martell and Dimidjian found that behavioral activation was equivalent to medication and superior to the full CBT program. In fact, in the Martell study, cognitive therapy performed no better than pill placebo.

Behavioral activation has been developed into a treatment in its own right for depression (Addis & Martell, 2004; Martell et al., 2001). The inactivity and lack of motivation so characteristic of bipolar depression suggest that behavioral activation might be a useful intervention for patients with this condition (Colom & Vieta, 2006).

However, caution in attempting to apply the method to patients with bipolar depression is warranted. Patients with bipolar depression can have a very difficult time overcoming their inertia, perhaps more so than unipolar depressed patients. If patients cannot activate themselves, the therapy could prove demoralizing. No specific data exist to support this concern, but a parallel can be found in the treatment of unipolar patients. An analysis of data from patients treated in the National Institute of Mental Health Treatment of Depression Collaborative Research Program found that patients with low social dysfunction did best in interpersonal psychotherapy and patients with low cognitive dysfunction did better in CBT (Sotsky et al., 1991). This suggests that trying to get patients to change in areas that are most problematic for them may not be productive. Perhaps bipolar depressed patients with less inertia might do better with behavioral activation than patients with a great deal of inertia.

Life Goals Program

Matt's functioning might have been improved by helping him focus on taking small steps toward getting back into his formerly rewarding side work and home construction projects. This kind of activity might begin to reverse his growing conviction that such work could no longer bring him pleasure.

Bauer and McBride (1996) have developed a structured manual-based group psychotherapy program for bipolar patients being treated through the U.S. Veterans Administration called the Life Goals Program. The aims of the program are to improve patient participation in medical treatment and to assist patients in achieving at least one social, occupational, or leisure goal that has been disrupted by their illness. Patients identify a goal and then develop a series of small, discrete steps they can take to achieve that goal, then implement these steps. This obviously bears a close resemblance to behavioral activation therapy. The manual for the Life Goals Program was published in 1996.

In 1998 Bauer and McBride undertook a program feasibility study and found that many patients actively participated in the program and the majority were able to work toward and achieve a goal (Bauer et al., 1998). In 2002, Simon and other colleagues, including Bauer, reported that they had designed and implemented a study to evaluate the Life Goals Program. The program was combined with a number of other interventions including monthly telephone monitoring by a nurse (Simon et al., 2002). Four hundred forty one patients were randomized to either the intervention or usual care (presumably medication visits and crisis intervention). Simon et al. (2005) reported that, during the first year of the study, participants assigned to the intervention group had significantly lower mean mania ratings and had spent approximately one-third less time in hypomanic or manic episodes. Mean depression ratings across the entire follow-up period did not differ significantly between the two groups, but the intervention group showed a greater decline in depression ratings over time.

Simon and his colleagues published results of the 2-year follow-up in 2006. The Life Goals Program reduced the mean level of mania symptoms and the time with mania symptoms but there was no significant effect on mean level of depressive symptoms or time with depressive symptoms. Benefits of the intervention were found only in a subgroup of 343 persons with clinically significant mood symptoms at the baseline assessment (Simon et al., 2006). Bauer et al. (2006) reported improvements in patients' social role function and mental quality of life, but reductions in mean manic and depressive symptoms were not significant.

Readers interested in learning more about the Life Goals Program are referred to Bauer and McBride (1996).

Self-Help Support Groups

Self-help was the second most common form of psychosocial intervention sought by the first 500 patients enrolled in the Systematic Treatment Enhancement Program for Bipolar Disorder (Lembke et al., 2004). It can obviously be a source of support for patients and can help dramatically reduce the guilt and shame associated with having bipolar illness. It can also be an important source for information about bipolar illness and its treatment. Support by members of the group may give relatives a break and help improve family relationships.

The Depression and Bipolar Support Alliance (formerly the National Depressive and Manic-Depressive Association) is a nonprofit, patient-run organization that provides information, advocacy, and support for those dealing with bipolar illness and depression. They have over 1,000 support groups throughout the United States.

Support groups also exist for the families of bipolar patients. The National Alliance for the Mentally Ill sponsors many such groups through their more than 1,100 nation-wide affiliates. Patients should be encouraged to check with their county mental health association to locate other resources in their communities.

Other Forms of Psychosocial Intervention

This chapter has focused on the kinds of psychotherapy that can be provided by outpatient clinicians on a once a week or less basis. However, many other levels of care and types of service exist that are often essential for helping patients with bipolar illness. These include intensive outpatient and partial hospitalization, vocational skills training and counseling, supported or supervised employment opportunities, longer-term residential treatment, and assertive community treatment (ACT) teams. Day-treatment programs should be considered for patients who are having substantial trouble functioning in several domains of life or who need more structure and support than can be provided in outpatient treatment.

From Research to Practice: Psychosocial Treatment

Combining psychosocial interventions with medication improves outcome in the treatment of patients with bipolar disorder. The combination provides greater benefit than medication alone in terms of increased time between episodes, fewer days in the hospital, and decreased risk of relapse. The benefits in acute treatment and in reducing the severity of depression and mania are much less clear.

The methods that have been described have demonstrated efficacy, for the most part, only in bipolar I patients treated at research centers. Whether these approaches can be used with equally beneficial results by therapists in agency or private practice who are dealing with patients who have multiple comorbidities (especially those with alcohol or drug abuse) or soft bipolar spectrum illnesses has not been determined. At this point, there is little evidence that any one of these treatments is superior to another. However, one study suggests that family psychoeducation may be important to clinical outcome. Rea et al. (2003) compared family-focused psychoeducational treatment to an individually-focused treatment for recently hospitalized manic patients. They found that patients in family-focused treatment were less likely to be rehospitalized during a 2-year study period and experienced fewer relapses over the 2 years. They did not, however, differ from patients in individual treatment in their likelihood of a first relapse.

Additional guidance for clinicians should come from the National Institute of Mental Health's Systematic Treatment Enhancement Program for Bipolar Disorder (STEP-BD). STEP-BD is the largest treatment study ever conducted for patients with bipolar disorder. It is a long-term outpatient study that has been conducted at 19 sites around the country. The study completed its data collection on September 30, 2005, with a total enrollment of 4,361 participants. The aim of the program is to find out which treatments, or combinations of them, are most effective for treating episodes of depression and mania and for preventing relapse. STEP-BD is evaluating not only medication treatments but is also studying and comparing all the psychosocial interventions described in this chapter. The first results on psychosocial treatments will be published soon.

Taking what seems to be helpful from each method and applying it to patients to whom the clinician believes it best applies is a reasonable approach at this stage of our knowledge. There is no research indicating that mixing and matching of methods dilutes their effectiveness. In fact, there is some research indicating that adhering to manual-based treatment guidelines does not improve outcome, at least in family-focused therapy (Weisman et al., 2002). Surprisingly, in the Weisman study, patients who relapsed and were hospitalized rated their therapists as more competent in conducting the problem-solving module of family-focused treatment than patients who did not relapse.

Therapists should perhaps be cautious about having too much therapeutic zeal, at least initially, with very depressed or dysfunctional bipolar patients. Pushing them too hard to make changes they feel they may not have the energy or ability to make could result in iatrogenic worsening of depressive symptoms.

Table 8.2 lists the key findings of the psychosocial treatment research described in this chapter.

TABLE 8.2

Summary of Key Points from Psychosocial Treatment Research

- Educate patients and their families about bipolar illness and its treatment.
- Explore blocks to accepting the diagnosis and using medication.
- Reduce hostility and criticism in marital and family interactions.
- Teach patient and family communication and problem-solving skills.
- Have patient track the connection between irregular daily rhythms and symptoms.
- Help patient maintain consistent sleep.
- Help patients learn to identify and manage dysfunctional thoughts.
- Help patients learn to assert themselves, learn communication, and interpersonal problem-solving skills.
- Help patients grieve loss of healthy self.
- Help patients learn to recognize and seek help for prodromal symptoms.
- Encourage patients to test the value of taking small steps toward achieving modest goals.

References

Addis, M., & Martell, C. (2004). *Overcoming depression one step at a time: The new behavioral activation approach to getting your life back.* Oakland, CA: New Harbinger Publications.

Ball, J., Mitchell, P., Corry, J., et al. (2006). A randomized controlled trial of cognitive therapy for bipolar disorder: Focus on long-term change. *Journal of Clinical Psychiatry, 67*(2), 277–286.

Basco, M., & Rush, A. (2005). *Cognitive-behavioral therapy for bipolar disorder* (2nd ed.). New York: Guilford

Bauer, M., & McBride, L. (1996). *Structured group psychotherapy for bipolar disorder: The life goals program.* New York: Springer

Bauer, M., McBride, L., Chase, C., et al. (1998). Manual-based group psychotherapy for bipolar disorder: a feasibility study. *Journal of Clinical Psychiatry, 59*(9), 449–455.

Bauer, M., McBride, L., Williford, W., et al. (2006). Collaborative care for bipolar disorder: Part II. Impact on clinical outcome, function, and costs. *Psychiatric Services, 57*(7), 937–945.

Beck, A., Rush, A., Shaw, B., & Emery, G. (1979). *Cognitive therapy of Depression.* New York: Guilford.

Clarkin, J., Carpenter, D., Hull, J., et al. (1998). Effects of psychoeducational intervention for married patients with bipolar disorder and their spouses. *Psychiatric Services, 49*(4), 531–533.

Clarkin, J. F., Haas, G. L., & Glick, I. D. (Eds.). (1988). *Affective disorders and the family: Assessment and treatment.* New York: Guilford

Colom, F., & Vieta, E. (2006). The pivotal role of psychoeducation in the long-term treatment of bipolar disorder. In H. Akiskal & M. Tohen (Eds.), *Bipolar psychopharmacotherapy* (pp. 333–345). West Sussex, England: Wiley.

Colom, F., Vieta, E., Martinez-Aran, A., Reinares, M., Goikolea, J. M., Benabarre, A., et al. (2003). A randomized trial on the efficacy of group psychoeducation in the prophylaxis of recurrences in bipolar patients whose disease is in remission. *Archives of General Psychiatry, 60*(4), 402–407.

Dimidjian, S., Hollon, S. D., Dobson, K. S., Schmaling, K. B., Kohlenberg, R. J., Addis, M. E., et al. (2006). Randomized trial of behavioral activation, cognitive therapy, and antidepressant medication in the acute treatment of adults with major depression. *Journal of Consult Clinical Psychology, 74*(4), 658–670.

Ehlers, C. L., Frank, E., & Kupfer, D. J. (1988). Social zeitgebers and biological rhythms. A unified approach to understanding the etiology of depression. *Archives of General Psychiatry, 45*(10), 948–952.

Frank, E. (2005). *Treating bipolar disorder: A clinicians guide to interpersonal and social rhythm therapy.* New York: Guilford

Frank, E., Hlastala, S., Ritenour, A., Houck, P., Tu, X. M., Monk, T. H., et al. (1997). Inducing lifestyle regularity in recovering bipolar disorder patients: Results from the maintenance therapies in bipolar disorder protocol. *Biological Psychiatry, 41*(12), 1165–1173.

Frank, E., Kupfer, D. J., Thase, M. E., Mallinger, A. G., Swartz, H. A., Fagiolini, A. M., et al. (2005). Two-year outcomes for interpersonal and social rhythm therapy in individuals with bipolar I disorder. *Archives of General Psychiatry, 62*(9), 996–1004.

Jacobson, N., Dobson, K., Truax, P., et al. (1996) A component analysis of cognitive-behavioral treatment for depression. *Journal of Consulting and Clinical Psychology, 64*, 295–304.

Kim, E. Y., & Miklowitz, D. J. (2004). Expressed emotion as a predictor of outcome among bipolar patients undergoing family therapy. *Journal of Affective Disorders, 82*(3), 343–352.

Klerman, G., Weissman, M., Rounsaville, B., & Cevron, E. (1984). *Interpersonal psychotherapy of Depression.* New York: Basic Books.

Lam, D. (2006). What can we conclude from studies on psychotherapy in bipolar disorder? Invited commentary on. Cognitive-behavioural therapy for severe and recurrent bipolar disorders. *British Journal of Psychiatry, 188*, 321–322.

Lam, D., Watkins, E., & Haywood, P. (2003). A randomized, controlled study of cognitive therapy for relapse prevention for bipolar affective disorder: Outcome of the first year. *Archives of General Psychiatry, 60*, 145-152.

Lam, D., Wright, K., & Sham, P. (2005b). Sense of hyper-positive self and response to cognitive therapy in bipolar disorder. *Psychological Medicine, 35*(1), 69–77.

Lam, D. H., Hayward, P., Watkins, E. R., Wright, K., & Sham, P. (2005a). Relapse prevention in patients with bipolar disorder: Cognitive therapy outcome after 2 years. *American Journal of Psychiatry, 162*(2), 324–329.

Leahy, R. (2004). Cognitive therapy. In S. Johnson & R. Leahy (Eds.), *Psychological treatment of bipolar disorder* (pp. 139–161). New York: Guilford.

Lembke, A., Miklowitz, D. J., Otto, M. W., Zhang, H., Wisniewski, S. R., Sachs, G. S., et al. (2004). Psychosocial service utilization by patients with bipolar disorders: Data from the first 500 participants in the Systematic Treatment Enhancement Program. *Journal of Psychiatric Practice, 10*(2), 81–87.

Malkoff-Schwartz, S., Frank, E., Anderson, B., Sherrill, J. T., Siegel, L., Patterson, D., et al. (1998). Stressful life events and social rhythm disruption in the onset of manic and depressive bipolar episodes: A preliminary investigation. *Archives of General Psychiatry, 55*(8), 702–707.

Malkoff-Schwartz, S., Frank, E., Anderson, B. P., Hlastala, S. A., Luther, J. F., Sherrill, J. T., et al. (2000). Social rhythm disruption and stressful life events in the onset of bipolar and unipolar episodes. *Psychological Medicine, 30*(5), 1005–1016.

Martell, C., Addis, M., & Dimidjian, S. (2004) Finding the action in behavioral activation: The search for empirically supported interventions and mechanisms of change. In S. Hayes, V. Follette, & M. Linehan (Eds.), *Mindfulness and acceptance: Expanding the cognitive-behavioral tradition* (pp. 152–167). New York: Guilford.

Martell, C., Addis, M., Jascobson, N., & Addis, M. (2001). *Depression in context: Strategies for guided action.* New York: W.W. Norton

Miklowitz, D. (1996). Psychotherapy in combination with drug treatment for bipolar disorder. *Journal of Clinical Psychopharmacology, 16*(2 Suppl. 1), 56S–66S.

Miklowitz, D., & Goldstein, M. (1997). *Bipolar disorder: A family focused treatment approach.* New York: Guilford.

Miklowitz, D. J., George, E. L., Axelson, D. A., Kim, E. Y., Birmaher, B., Schneck, C., et al. (2004). Family-focused treatment for adolescents with bipolar disorder. *Journal of Affective Disorders, 82*(Suppl. 1), S113–128.

Miklowitz, D. J., George, E. L., Richards, J. A., Simoneau, T. L., & Suddath, R. L. (2003a). A randomized study of family-focused psychoeducation and pharmacotherapy in the outpatient management of bipolar disorder. *Archives of General Psychiatry, 60*(9), 904–912.

Miklowitz, D. J., & Goldstein, M. J. (1990). Behavioral family treatment for patients with bipolar affective disorder. *Behavior Modification, 14*(4), 457–489.

Miklowitz, D. J., Goldstein, M. J., Nuechterlein, K. H., Snyder, K. S., & Mintz, J. (1988). Family factors and the course of bipolar affective disorder. *Archives of General Psychiatry, 45*(3), 225–231.

Miklowitz, D. J., Richards, J. A., George, E. L., Frank, E., Suddath, R. L., Powell, K. B., et al. (2003b). Integrated family and individual therapy for bipolar disorder: Results of a treatment development study. *Journal of Clinical Psychiatry, 64*(2), 182–191.

Miklowitz, D. J., Wisniewski, S. R., Miyahara, S., Otto, M. W., & Sachs, G. S. (2005). Perceived criticism from family members as a predictor of the one-year course of bipolar disorder. *Psychiatry Research, 136*(2-3), 101–111.

Otto, M. W., & Miklowitz, D. J. (2004). The role and impact of psychotherapy in the management of bipolar disorder. *CNS Spectrum, 9*(11 Suppl. 12), 27–32.

Perry, A., Tarrier, N., Morris, R., et al. (1999). Randomised controlled trial of efficacy of teaching patients with bipolar disorder to identify early symptoms of relapse and obtain treatment. *BMJ, 318*, 149–153.

Rea, M. M, Tompson, M., Miklowitz, D. J., Goldstein, M. J., Hwang, S., & Mintz, J. (2003). Family focused treatment vs individual treatment for bipolar disorder: Results of a randomized clinical trial. *Journal of Consulting and Clinical Psychology, 71*, 482–492.

Scott, J., Colom, F., & Vieta, E. (2006). A meta-analysis of relapse rates with adjunctive psychological therapies compared to usual psychiatric treatment for bipolar disorders. *International Journal of Neuropsychopharmacology*, pp. 1–7.

Scott, J., Garland, A., & Moorhead, S. (2001). A pilot study of cognitive therapy in bipolar disorders. *Psychological Medicine, 31*(3), 459–467.

Scott, J., Paykel, E., Morriss, R., Bentall, R., Kinderman, P., Johnson, T., et al. (2006). Cognitive-behavioural therapy for severe and recurrent bipolar disorders: Randomised controlled trial. *British Journal of Psychiatry, 188*, 313–320.

Simon, G. E., Ludman, E., Unutzer, J., & Bauer, M. S. (2002). Design and implementation of a randomized trial evaluating systematic care for bipolar disorder. *Bipolar Disorder, 4*(4), 226–236.

Simon, G. E., Ludman, E. J., Bauer, M. S., Unutzer, J., & Operskalski, B. (2006). Long-term effectiveness and cost of a systematic care program for bipolar disorder. *Archives of General Psychiatry, 63*(5), 500–508.

Simon, G. E., Ludman, E. J., Unutzer, J., Bauer, M. S., Operskalski, B., & Rutter, C. (2005). Randomized trial of a population-based care program for people with bipolar disorder. *Psychological Medicine, 35*(1), 13–24.

Sotsky, S. M., Glass, D. R., Shea, M. T., Pilkonis, P. A., Collins, J. F., Elkin, I., et al. (1991). Patient predictors of response to psychotherapy and pharmacotherapy: Findings in the NIMH Treatment of Depression Collaborative Research Program. *American Journal of Psychiatry, 148*(8), 997–1008.

Weisman, A., Tompson, M. C., Okazaki, S., Gregory, J., Goldstein, M. J., Rea, M., et al. (2002). Clinicians' fidelity to a manual-based family treatment as a predictor of the one-year course of bipolar disorder. *Family Process, 41*(1), 123–131.

Zaretsky, A. E., Segal, Z. V., & Gemar, M. (1999). Cognitive therapy for bipolar depression: A pilot study. *Canadian Journal of Psychiatry, 44*(5), 491–494.

CHAPTER 9

Nonpharmacologic Approaches

The nonpharmacologic approaches to symptoms of mania and bipolar depression discussed in this chapter are *not*, with the exception of electroconvulsive therapy, viable alternatives to medication. At best, they could be considered potential adjunctive treatments. Most reports of their usefulness are based on findings from non-randomized, non-controlled trials. Patients should *not* self-administer these without professional guidance. Table 9.1 lists the nonpharmacologic treatments that have been reported as helpful in the treatment of mania, hypomania, and mixed states. Table 9.2 lists nonpharmacologic treatments that have been reported as helpful for bipolar depression.

Electroconvulsive Therapy (ECT)

Jack Nicholson in *One Flew Over the Cuckoo's Nest* is what typically comes to mind when ECT is mentioned. The common view is that it is a dangerous and barbaric procedure that destroys an individual's identity and intellectual abilities. Quite the contrary. The only true danger from the procedure lies in the use of anesthesia—a danger shared by all medical procedures requiring anesthesia. Patients are given medication to prevent muscle contractions and convulsions. The *convulsive* part of the therapy refers to the electrically induced seizure activity in the brain.

Electroconvulsive therapy is often more rapidly effective and has fewer side effects than medication. Patients can experience problems with memory and other cognitive impairments following the procedure. Physicians administering ECT can lessen cognitive side effects by making adjustments in the procedure, such as using right unilateral ECT (electrode placed only on the right side of the patient's head) versus bilateral ECT (electrodes placed on both sides of the patient's head). But severe mood disorders, particularly bipolar disorder, can also produce cognitive impairments. Some patients report improved cognitive abilities following successful ECT. Electroconvulsive therapy is the single most effective

TABLE 9.1

Nonpharmacologic Approaches: Mania, Hypomania, and Mixed States

- Darkness
- Magnesium
- Medroxyprogesterone
- Reducing vanadium
- GABA
- Megavitamins/minerals
- Melatonin

TABLE 9.2

Nonpharmacologic Approaches: Bipolar Depression

- Bright light
- Partial sleep deprivation, sleep phase advance
- Omega-3 essential fatty acids
- Dietary amino acids and their metabolites
- Folate and B vitamins
- Zinc
- Reproductive hormones and DHEA
- Inositol
- Vagus nerve stimulation
- Repetitive transcranial magnetic stimulation
- Megavitamins/minerals
- Exercise, yoga, and qigong

treatment available for manic, severely melancholic, psychotic, rapid-cycling, agitated, violent, or suicidal individuals with unipolar or bipolar disorder. It is also effective in complex, difficult to treat conditions such as mania with delirium (confusion and disorientation; Fink, 2006).

Electroconvulsive therapy has been relegated to a treatment of last resort, which is unfortunate given the relapse rate and disability associated with even expert psychopharmacologic treatment of bipolar illness. Electroconvulsive therapy is not only an effective acute treatment but is also helpful as a continuation treatment to maintain remission. There does not appear to be any cumulative damage to cognitive capacities with repeated ECT treatments. Acute or continuation ECT can be combined with medication, although anticonvulsants are typically discontinued during the procedure. Lithium can be continued, but typically at lower dosages to avoid post-ECT complications. Those wishing to learn more about ECT can read Fink (2002) or Abrams (2002).

Repetitive Transcranial Magnetic Stimulation (rTMS)

This procedure involves passing a powerful electromagnet over specific areas of the skull. The rapidly changing magnetic field generates small electrical pulses in the prefrontal cortex of the brain, an area that regulates mood. Patients generally report they feel few sensations from rTMS other than mild contractions in the scalp muscles. The procedure is currently used only in research settings and is still considered experimental.

A meta-analysis of rTMS studies in affective disorders found a modest, statistically significant antidepressant effect after 2 weeks of daily treatment (Simons & Dierick, 2005). Open trials have suggested the procedure can be helpful in the treatment of mania (e.g., Saba et al., 2004). A double-blind, controlled trial of rTMS in 20 patients showed the procedure was effective after 2 weeks in patients with bipolar depression (Dolberg et al., 2002). Other controlled studies on rTMS in mania and bipolar depression, however, have been negative (Kapstan et al., 2003; Nahas et al., 2003). TMS has been reported to induce mania in some patients (Sakkas et al., 2003).

Rohan et al. (2004) reported that echo-planar magnetic resonance spectroscopic imaging (EP-MRSI), a diagnostic imaging procedure that uses a magnetic field, produced mood improvements in patients with bipolar disorder that were similar to those seen with rTMS.

Vagus Nerve Stimulation (VNS)

Vagus nerve stimulation is a recently FDA-approved treatment for refractory major depression. It is delivered with a device implanted in a patient's chest that applies a small electrical current to the vagus nerve. Bajbouj et al. (2006) reported on the VNS treatment of a 60-year-old woman with rapid-cycling bipolar disorder. Although there was no effect on hypomanic symptoms, the investigators reported a decrease in severity and duration of depression symptoms.

Bright Light

Individuals with seasonal affective disorder (SAD), winter type, become depressed during fall or winter and improve in the spring. Some individuals have hypomanic or manic episodes during the spring or summer and are part of the bipolar spectrum of illnesses. Bright light administered in the morning can produce antidepressant effects in SAD patients in as little as 1 to 2 days and it may be effective in some patients with nonseasonal depression, as well (Golden et al., 2005; Goodwin & Jamison, 1990). Bright light can be an effective treatment for acute nonseasonal bipolar depression (Bauer, 1993; Deltito et al., 1991; Liebenluft et al., 1995).

However, the safety and effectiveness of bright light as a maintenance treatment for patients with bipolar depression remains in question. Bright light treatment of patients with bipolar disorder has been associated with the development of agitation, irritability, hypomania, and suicidal ideation (Liebenluft et al., 1995; Praschak-Rieder et al., 1997). That is, it can induce mixed states. Morning bright light may be particularly destabilizing for bipolar patients (Sit et al., 2005). In the Liebenluft study, three of five bipolar patients given morning bright light had to discontinue it because of mood instability. Three of five patients given midday bright light improved and presumably did not experience mood instability or the induction of mixed states.

Unfortunately, for most patients who work normal business hours, using a light box to get midday bright light is not practical. Use of a light visor might solve this logistical problem but could obviously create some embarrassment for the patient. A more workable solution might be for the patient to take a brisk lunch-time walk to get the benefits of both sunlight and exercise.

Darkness

If bright light can treat depression, can darkness treat mania? It appears so. Wehr et al. (1998) treated a rapid-cycling bipolar patient with enforced darkness from 6 pm to 8 am. The patient had previously slept very irregular hours and for varying lengths of time. His mania subsided and his mood stabilized fairly quickly with this treatment. No medications were used. The period of darkness was later reduced to 10 hours per night.

In 1999, Wirz-Justice et al. conducted a similar study with a treatment-refractory bipolar I rapid-cycling patient on divalproex. The patient was treated initially with a 10-hour dark/rest period (later extended to 14 hours). Rapid cycling stopped immediately. Depression gradually improved when midday bright light was added. Near-euthymia was attained after light therapy was shifted to the morning. The investigators made no mention of problems with agitation or hypomania with morning bright light.

The Wehr and Wirz-Justice findings were replicated in a controlled case series done by Italian researchers (Barbini et al., 2005). Sixteen bipolar inpatients with mania were treated with enforced darkness from 6 pm to 8 am each night for 3 consecutive days. When compared to a control group of matched bipolar patients receiving treatment as usual, the group treated with darkness had a significantly faster decrease in mania, provided they were treated within 2 weeks from the onset of the manic episode. If not, darkness therapy had no effect. Responders needed lower doses of antimanic drugs and were discharged earlier from the hospital.

For hundreds of thousands of years, humans and their ancestors have gone to bed when the sun went down. Wehr and colleagues (1998) note that "the modern practice of using artificial light to extend waking activities into the nighttime hours might be expected to precipitate or exacerbate bipolar illness" (p. 822). Manic, mixed, or rapid-cycling outpatients, particularly teens or young adults, who like to hang out with their friends until 2 am (and then sleep through midday), or who are fond of late-night TV or surfing the internet, will likely not commit to 14 hours a night of enforced darkness. However, the studies cited in this section do suggest that such patients should be encouraged to at least experiment with consistent exposure to darkness at night and bright light at midday. Patients who are vulnerable to the disruptive effects of odd-hour exposures to darkness and light may become motivated to change their habits, particularly if it means using fewer medications, once they experience the benefits of a regular sleep schedule.

Manipulation of the Sleep-Wake Cycle

Loss of sleep (from extraordinary work requirements, exam preparation, family medical emergencies, late-night parties, psychological stress, medications, or illicit drug use or withdrawal) can precipitate mania in some individuals with bipolar disorder (Wehr et al., 1987). Treating insomnia in a developing or breakthrough manic or hypomanic episode with a benzodiazepine drug such as clonazepam (Klonopin) can abort the development of such an episode by helping the patient fall asleep (Goodwin & Jamison, 1990).

Melatonin, a hormone derived from serotonin and secreted from the pineal gland, helps regulate the sleep-wake cycle. It may help ease insomnia in bipolar patients when added to standard medications. Bersani and Garavini (2000), in an open clinical trial, administered 3 mg of melatonin to eleven manic bipolar patients on antimanic drugs whose insomnia had not responded to benzodiazepines. All patients had longer duration of sleep, as well as a reduction in the severity of manic symptoms, after 1 month of melatonin treatment. However, Liebenluft et al. (1997), in a placebo-controlled, double-blind study, found that 10 mg of melatonin per night for 12 weeks had no significant effect on mood or sleep in 5 patients with rapid-cycling bipolar disorder.

Conversely, a night of total or second-half of the night sleep deprivation will produce dramatic or partial improvement in 60 percent of patients with severe depression (Pflug & Tolle, 1971; Schilgen & Tolle, 1980). (One cannot help but wonder if the early morning awakening that some severely depressed patients experience is a natural homeostatic mechanism designed to bring about remission.) Unfortunately, the antidepressant effect of sleep deprivation is often not sustained if the patient takes a nap or then gets 1 or 2 nights of normal sleep.

Researchers have tried various strategies to sustain the effects of total or partial sleep deprivation. One effective strategy is referred to as sleep phase advance. Following a night of sleep deprivation, patients go to bed at 5 pm and get up at 12 am. These times are advanced an hour on each subsequent night until the individual is going to bed at 10 or 11 pm and getting up at 5 or 6 am. There are several reports of this procedure in the literature including, for example, the study by Berger et al. (1997). A few groups of researchers have experimented with an abbreviated, 3-day sleep phase advance and found that it is effective (e.g., Voderholzer et al., 2003). In this procedure a patient is allowed to sleep from, say, 5 pm until midnight on the first day following sleep deprivation with daily shift backs of 2 hours for the next 2 nights.

Antidepressant effects of sleep deprivation may also be sustained or enhanced with the use of lithium, either alone or in combination with sleep phase advance (Baxter et al., 1986; Benedetti et al., 2001). Smeraldi et al. (1999) added the serotonergic receptor antagonist drug pindolol (Visken) to sleep deprivation therapy for a group of bipolar patients. The medication was found to be significantly more effective than placebo in producing remission.

Combining bright light and sleep deprivation may also help sustain the effects of sleep deprivation (Loving et al., 2002; Neumeister et al., 1996). Benedetti et al. (2005) found bright light was effective in sustaining the antidepressant effects of sleep deprivation in depressed bipolar patients. Some evidence suggests total sleep deprivation leads to better clinical effects in bipolar than unipolar patients (Barbini et al., 1998). But there is also a problem with using sleep deprivation and sleep phase advance procedures in bipolar patients. As with every other antidepressant strategy for bipolar patients, these procedures can induce hypomania and mania in some patients (Colombo et al., 1999; Wehr et al., 1982). The rate of induction of hypomania or mania in bipolar depressed patients treated with sleep deprivation differed substantially in the Wehr and Colombo studies. The high rate of switch in the Wehr study could possibly be accounted for by the rapid-cycling status of the patients.

Omega-3 Essential Fatty Acids

A major component of all cell membranes are compounds called phospholipids. Essential fatty acids are a part of cell-membrane phospholipids. Several varieties of fatty acids, including those labeled omega-3 and omega-6, are considered essential because they must be consumed in the diet. The human body cannot synthesize them from other dietary components. The two main omega-3 fatty acids are eicosapentanoic acid (EPA) and docoahexaenoic acid (DHA).

An absence of omega-3 fatty acids and an overabundance of omega-6 fatty acids in the diet leads to adverse functional changes in cell membranes, including cell membranes in the brain. The typical diet in the United States is very low in omega-3 fatty acids, which are found in fish, wild game, walnuts, and flaxseed and very high in omega-6 fatty acids from cereal grains, vegetable oils derived from these grains, and cattle and chickens fed an omega-6 laden diet of cereal products.

This lopsided omega-6–omega-3 ratio has been linked to a variety of chronic maladies including cardiovascular disease, inflammatory disease, autoimmune disease (Simopoulos, 2006), asthma, as well as depression and bipolar illness. Studies have revealed, for instance, a significant decrease of omega-3 fatty acids and/or an increase of the omega-6–omega-3 ratio in the red blood cell (rbc) membranes of depressed individuals (Peet et al., 1998). RBC fatty acid content is thought to reflect the fatty acid content of brain cell membranes. Low levels of a particular omega-3 fatty acid called DHA have been linked to postpartum depression (Hibbeln, 2002). Sobczak et al. (2004) found that relatives of patients with bipolar disorder have increased total omega-6 fatty acid content of their phospholipids. In the same study, lower total omega-3 fatty acids in phospholipids were associated with lower mood. Noaghiul and Hibbeln (2003) have found that greater seafood consumption correlates with lower prevalence of bipolar disorders in a cross-national study. Of course, these correlations do not prove that omega-3 fatty acids protect against bipolar disorder or depression, but they are suggestive. Omega-3 fatty acids are also the precursors of anti-inflammatory molecules, while omega-6s are the basis for proinflammatory compounds in the human body. Individuals with depression often have an activation of the inflammatory response system (Colin et al., 2006).

These findings raise the intriguing possibility that the symptoms of a number of psychiatric disorders might respond to treatment with omega-3 fatty acids found in fish oil supplements. Peet and Stokes (2005) note that five of six double-blind, placebo-controlled trials in schizophrenia, and four of six such trials in depression, have reported therapeutic benefit from omega-3 fatty acids particularly when EPA is added to existing psychotropic medication. Peet and Stokes also report that combined omega-3 and omega-6 fatty acids have been found helpful for attention-deficit hyperactivity disorder. Zanarini and Frankenburg (2003), in a double-blind, placebo-controlled study, reported that 1 gram per day of ethyl-EPA was effective in diminishing aggression as well as the severity of depressive symptoms.

There has been one open and three controlled studies with omega-3 fatty acids in bipolar disorder. Stoll et al. (1999) did a 4-month, double-blind, placebo-controlled study, comparing omega-3 fatty acids (roughly 6 grams of EPA and 3 grams of DHA) versus placebo (olive oil), in addition to usual treatment, in 30 patients with bipolar disorder. The omega-3 fatty acid group had a significantly longer period of remission than the placebo group. In addition, for nearly every other outcome measure, the omega-3 fatty acid group performed better than the placebo group.

Osher et al. (2005), in an open-label study, treated 12 bipolar I depressed outpatients with 1.5 to 2 grams/day of EPA for up to 6 months. Eight of the 10 patients who completed at least 1 month of follow-up achieved a 50 percent or greater reduction on a measure of depressive symptoms.

Frangou et al. (2006) did a 4-month, double-blind study of individuals with bipolar depression who were randomly assigned to adjunctive treatment with placebo ($n = 26$) or either 1 gram per day ($n = 24$) or 2 grams per day ($n = 25$) of ethyl-EPA. Significant improvement was noted with the 1 gram per day ethyl-EPA treatment compared with placebo on a measure of depression. Interestingly, there was no apparent benefit of 2 grams over 1 gram of ethyl-EPA per day. There was no apparent benefit of the active treatments for mania.

Keck et al. (2006) conducted a 4-month, randomized, placebo-controlled, adjunctive trial of 6 grams per day of ethyl-eicosapentanoate (a form of EPA) in the treatment of 59 patients with bipolar depression and rapid-cycling bipolar disorder. Subjects were receiving mood-stabilizing medications at therapeutic doses or plasma concentrations. There were no significant differences on any outcome measure between the EPA and placebo groups.

There has been a great deal of speculation as to why the Keck et al. trial might have been negative (in addition to the obvious conclusion that EPA is not effective in the treatment of patients with bipolar disorder). Chiu et al. (2005), based in part on a reanalysis of Stoll's data, state that the main effect of omega-3 fatty acids are in bipolar depression and not mania. The results of the Faragou trial support that contention. Perhaps the inclusion of rapid-cycling patients in the Keck study biased the results. Or perhaps the investigators used too large a dose of EPA in the absence of any DHA. Finally, the subject's consumption of omega-6 fatty acids could have nullified the increased omega-3 intake.

In summary, there is not enough data to recommend that omega-3s be used as first-line monotherapy for patients with bipolar disorder, especially if patients are predominantly manic or rapid cycling (Marangell et al., 2006). However, given that omega-3s are a naturally occurring substance critical for overall human health, are well-tolerated, and may be of some benefit to patients with bipolar depression, it would seem reasonable to have most bipolar patients add it to their treatment regimen. Current evidence suggests the omega-3 with the best results for patients with depression and bipolar disorder is EPA. Marangell et al. (2003) gave DHA to patients with depression and found it was not effective. The difficulty lies in determining the right dose of EPA. The body's minimal requirement for health is only around 350 mg per day of EPA, although high omega-6 intake may increase the need to ten times that amount according to Hibbeln et al. (2006). Based on current studies, patients might best start with a modest dose of 1 to 2 grams per day of EPA for 3 or 4 months and then increase the dose until they respond or run out of patience and money (fish oil supplements are fairly expensive). Reducing intake of saturated fat, trans-fat, and omega-6 fatty acids (primarily by cutting back on grain products) might be prudent.

Since fish-oil supplements are not FDA regulated, patients will have to be careful about the supplement they choose. Some cheaper supplements may be tainted with mercury or pesticide residues or not have the amount of EPA stated on the label. Those interested in obtaining omega-3 supplements that have been tested and approved by an independent laboratory may visit www.consumerlab.com for a list of those supplements. The best values in fish-oil supplements can be found with flavored liquid forms. There is a theoretical risk of increased blood-clotting time with the use of high-dose fish oils. Individuals with clotting problems or who are on blood-thinning drugs (anticoagulants) such as warfarin (Coumadin) should check with their physicians before using fish-oil supplements.

What about flax oil? Flax oil is a plant-based source of omega-3 fatty acids and is less expensive than fish oil. To my knowledge, there have been no studies on the use of flaxseed oil to treat bipolar disorder. In addition, the omega-3 fatty acid in flaxseed is in the form of alpha-linoleic acid (ALA). An enzyme in the human body converts ALA to EPA. It's probably best to take EPA directly and not have to rely on the body's capacity to convert ALA to EPA.

Some epidemiologic studies have found that high flax oil consumption is correlated with prostate cancer. Other studies have not found such a relationship. It is impossible to determine if the positive correlation represents causation. There are too many uncontrolled variables in these studies to be able to make much use of them. In fact, some evidence suggests that flaxseed may actually help in fighting prostate cancer (Demark-Wahnefried et al., 2004; Lin et al., 2002).

A food supplement known as lecithin is composed of a key phospholipid component of cell membranes called phosphatidylcholine. Cohen et al. (1982) reported that lecithin was effective in treating mania in five of six patients in a double-blind placebo-controlled trial. Stoll et al. (1996), in an open study, found that five of six rapid-cycling bipolar outpatients being treated with lithium had a substantial reduction in mania and four patients had a marked reduction in all mood symptoms when given choline, a component of phosphatidylcholine High intake of lecithin or choline, however, may produce acute gastrointestinal distress, sweating, salivation, and anorexia.

Inositol

Inositol is an isomer of glucose. That is, a molecule of inositol has the same number and kinds of atoms as glucose but they are arranged in a different way. Inositol is an important component of chemical communication systems *within* cells (second-messenger systems). Serotonin is a component of a first-messenger system. It handles messages *between* cells.

The results of adding inositol to standard treatments in patients with bipolar depression have been mixed. An Israeli group first studied inositol as a treatment for unipolar depression and found it to be an effective antidepressant (Levine et al., 1995). A small open study suggested it was useful for bipolar depression when added to standard mood-stabilizing medication (Chengappa et al., 2000). A more recent small, placebo-controlled trial produced highly variable results

(Evins et al., 2006). Of nine subjects receiving inositol, two had greater than 50 percent worsening of scores on the Hamilton Depression Rating Scale, three had no change, and four had greater than 50 percent improvement. Those who had worsening in depressive symptoms apparently had more mixed features at baseline (irritability, disruptive/aggressive behavior). Nierenberg et al. (2006) did an open-label comparison of adjunctive inositol to lamotrigine and to risperidone in 66 subjects who were nonresponsive to a combination of adequate doses of mood stabilizers plus at least one antidepressant. No differences were found between any two compounds in rate of recovery. Recovery rates were very low for all three treatments. The antidepressants used in this study may have contributed to treatment resistance.

Oddly, the therapeutic effect of lithium on mania may be due to the *depletion* of inositol via inhibition of an enzyme. Shaldubina et al. (2006) reported that an inositol *deficiency* diet had a major effect in reducing the severity of affective disorder in 10 of 15 manic patients within the first 7 to 14 days of treatment.

Based on the results of the Evins study, inositol should be avoided in patients who are irritable or in mixed states. It would be interesting to see the results of a study comparing inositol in bipolar depressed patients with atypical versus mixed features

Dietary Amino Acids and Their Metabolites

Tryptophan is the amino acid precursor of the neurotransmitter serotonin. Goodwin and Jamison (1990) discussed four double-blind clinical trials of its use in mania and noted that three had positive results. Sharma and Barrett (2001) reported that 2 grams per day of tryptophan stabilized the mood of a 40 year-old rapid-cycling patient who had been unresponsive to combinations of mood stabilizers.

SAMe is a metabolite of the amino acid methionine. It can be an effective antidepressant when used in high doses (1600 mg/day or more), although there is a risk the compound will induce mania in bipolar depressed patients (Williams et al., 2005).

The amino acids tyrosine and phenylalanine have been used to treat patients with unipolar depression. No studies on their use in bipolar depression could be located. Tyrosine is the amino acid precursor of the neurotransmitter dopamine. Antipsychotic drugs work in manic patients, in part, by blocking excess activity of dopamine. McTavish et al. (2001) reported that giving manic patients a diet based on a tyrosine-depleted mixture can ease symptoms of mania.

Folate and B Vitamins

Please refer to the section on folate, B vitamins, and homocysteine on page 206 in Chapter 7.

Vitamin D3

Gloth et al. (1999) reported that 100,000 IU of vitamin D per day was effective in reducing scores on the Hamilton Depression scale in 8 subjects with seasonal affective disorder.

Magnesium and Zinc

Calcium is considered an excitatory element. Mania may somehow be related to problems in the regulation of calcium ion flow across cell membranes. Drugs such as nimodipine (Nimtop) are called calcium-channel blockers because they dampen the flow of calcium ions into cells. Nimodipine is helpful in treating rapid-cycling bipolar illness (see Chapter 6 for more information on nimodipine). Magnesium also regulates calcium ion flow in neuronal calcium channels. In essence, it is a natural calcium-channel blocker. Epidemiological studies have suggested that a substantial portion of the population does not get enough magnesium (Sales & Pedrosa, 2006).

Chouinard et al. (1990) treated nine severe rapid-cycling bipolar patients with magnesium aspartate hydrochloride (Magnesiocard) in an open-label study for a period up to 32 weeks with good results. An open study showed that seven of ten patients treated with intravenous magnesium sulphate who had severe, therapy-resistant manic agitation had marked improvement on the Clinical Global Impression scale (Heiden et al., 1999). Giannini et al. (2000) found that a combination of magnesium oxide and the calcium-channel blocking drug verapamil (Calan) was more effective than verapamil alone in treating mania. Eby and Eby (2006) presented case histories of depressed patients with mixed or agitated symptoms such as anxiety, irritability, and insomnia successfully treated with magnesium glycinate or taurinate.

Nowak et al. (2003) found that adding 25 mg of zinc per day to ongoing antidepressant therapy was beneficial for 6 unipolar depressed patients. Nowak et al. (2005) reported low serum zinc levels in some patients with depression. To my knowledge, there are no studies on the use of zinc in bipolar patients.

Reproductive Hormones and DHEA

Estradiol, a reproductive hormone, has been shown in several studies to be effective for depression in perimenopausal women (e.g., Soares et al., 2001). Although no studies of estradiol in bipolar depression could be located, a small, open study of estradiol in patients with postpartum psychosis—a condition thought to be related to bipolar disorder—was found (Ahokas, 2000). Estradiol levels drop after childbirth, which may affect multiple neurotransmitter systems. In the Ahokas study, ten women with florid postpartum psychosis and very low levels of estradiol were treated with bioidentical, sublingual 17beta-estradiol for 6 weeks. Symptoms were reversed in all patients.

Kumar et al. (2003) gave transdermal estradiol to 29 women with preexisting bipolar or schizoaffective illness, beginning 48 hours after delivery, to see if estradiol could reduce the rate of relapse. Although the estradiol did not reduce relapse rates, of 12 women who relapsed, those who had taken the highest dose of estradiol needed less subsequent psychotropic medication and were discharged sooner than those who had taken either of the two lower doses. Kulkarni et al. (2006) reported that medroxyprogesterone acetate was superior to placebo in reducing symptoms of mania or hypomania in 13 women with bipolar disorder.

Testosterone and DHEA (a steroid hormone produced by the adrenal glands) levels decline with advancing age. Both testosterone and DHEA have been used to treat depression in middle-aged men (Schmidt et al., 2005; Shamlian & Cole, 2006), but there have been no studies on their use in bipolar depression. There have been several case reports of both triggering mania, however (e.g., Kline & Jaggers, 1999; Weiss et al., 1999).

Reducing Vanadium

Vanadium is a trace metallic element that may have some etiologic role in bipolar disorder. Raised levels of vanadium have been reported in plasma in mania and depression and raised hair levels reported in mania. Lithium has been reported to inhibit the functioning of vanadium (Naylor, 1984).

Naylor states that reducing vanadium through changes in diet (avoiding foods rich in vanadium including black pepper, mushrooms, shellfish, and parsley) or reducing the effect of vanadium with various compounds including vitamin C, methylene blue, or EDTA can be helpful in bipolar disorder.

Miscellaneous Nutritional Approaches

Gamma-aminobutyric acid (GABA) is an amino acid that is available over the counter. It is also a major inhibitory neurotransmitter in the nervous system. Divalproex (Depakote) may work, in part, by increasing the concentration of GABA in critical areas of the brain. There have been scattered anecdotal reports that supplements of GABA might be helpful for the agitation, irritability, and insomnia associated with mixed bipolar disorder.

There have also been anecdotal reports that very low doses of lithium in the form of lithium orotate are useful for patients with bipolar disorder. There have been no studies to support these claims, however.

There has been one small, open study and a case series with the use of a megavitamin/mineral preparation for bipolar disorder (Kaplan et al., 2001; Popper, 2001). The reports claim a number of patients were able to remain well without use of medication while taking the supplement.

Readers interested in learning more about alternative approaches to bipolar disorder might wish to consult Marohn (2003).

Exercise, Yoga, and Qigong

Studies have found that cardiovascular exercise of at least moderate intensity carried out several times per week over many weeks can be effective in treating patients with mild to moderate major depressive disorder (Dunn et al., 2005). Exercise may perform as well as antidepressant medication in some depressed patients. Babyak et al. (2000), for instance, studied 156 adult volunteers with major depressive disorder for 6 months after being randomly assigned to a 4-month course of aerobic exercise, sertraline therapy, or a combination of exercise and sertraline. At the end of the initial 4 months, patients in all three groups exhibited significant improvement with a comparable proportion of remitted patients in each group. Without a placebo condition, it is impossible to tell if the treatments themselves were responsible for the results. The passage of time or the extra attention from staff that patients get in exercise programs might be important factors. After 10 months, however, remitted subjects in the exercise group had significantly lower relapse rates than subjects in the medication group. Resistance training (weight lifting) has also been found to be an effective treatment for major depression or dysthymia, at least for individuals age 60 and older (Singh et al., 1997).

Pilkington et al. (2005) found positive results for yoga in five randomized controlled trials for patients with depression but noted that variation in forms of yoga utilized, severity of symptoms, and reporting of trial methodology made it difficult to draw firm conclusions. Janakiramaiah et al. (2000) did an interesting uncontrolled study comparing Sudarshan Kriya Yoga (SKY) to ECT and the tricyclic antidepressant medication imipramine (Tofranil) in 45 hospitalized melancholic depressed patients. Remission rates at the end of the trial for ECT, imipramine, and SKY were 93, 73, and 67 percent, respectively.

A study by Tsang et al. (2006) of a meditative movement exercise called qigong demonstrated that 16 weeks of the practice could relieve depression and improve self-efficacy and personal well being among elderly persons with chronic physical illness and depression.

Although there are no controlled trials on the use of exercise to treat symptoms of bipolar depression, there is no reason to believe exercise might not be of equal benefit in bipolar patients. Rather, the problem is getting bipolar patients to exercise. Patients in exercise studies are monitored, supervised, and spurred on by staff, often on inpatient units. Getting bipolar depressed outpatients, who can be paralyzed with lethargy and fatigue, to exercise on their own may be virtually impossible. Perhaps patients should consider hiring a personal trainer along with (or instead of) a psychotherapist. There have been reports in the press of therapists who conduct psychotherapy while the patient is performing aerobic exercise.

References

Abrams, R. (2002). *Electroconvulsive therapy.* New York: Oxford University Press.

Ahokas, A., Aito, M., & Rimon, R. (2000). Positive treatment effect of estradiol in postpartum psychosis: A pilot study. *Journal of Clinical Psychiatry, 61*(3), 166–169.

Babyak, M., Blumenthal, J., Herman, S., et al. (2000). Exercise treatment for major depression: Maintenance of therapeutic benefit at 10 months. *Psychosomatic Medicine, 62*(5), 633–638.

Bajbouj, M., Danker-Hopfe, H., Heuser, I., & Anghelescu, I. (2006). Long-term outcome of vagus nerve stimulation in rapid-cycling bipolar disorder. *Journal of Clinical Psychiatry, 67*(5), 837–838.

Barbini, B., Benedetti, F., Colombo, C., et al. (2005). Dark therapy for mania. *Bipolar Disorders, 7*(1), 98–101.

Barbini, B., Colombo, C., Benedetti, F., et al. (1998). The unipolar-bipolar dichotomy and the response to sleep deprivation. *Psychiatry Research, 79*(1), 43–50.

Bauer, M. (1993). Summertime bright-light treatment of bipolar major depressive episodes. *Biological Psychiatry, 33*(8-9), 663–665.

Baxter, L., Liston, E., & Schwartz, J. (1986). Prolongation of the antidepressant response to partial sleep deprivation by lithium. *Psychiatry Research, 19*(1), 17–23.

Benedetti, F., Barbini, B., & Campori, E. (2001). Sleep phase advance and lithium to sustain the antidepressant effect of total sleep deprivation in bipolar depression: new findings supporting the internal coincidence model? *Journal of Psychiatric Research, 35*(6), 323–329.

Benedetti, F., Barbini, B., & Fulgosi, M. (2005). Combined total sleep deprivation and light therapy in the treatment of drug-resistant bipolar depression: Acute response and long-term remission rates. *Journal of Clinical Psychiatry, 66*(12), 1535–1540.

Berger, M., Vollmann, J., Hohegan, F., et al. (1997). Sleep deprivation combined with consecutive sleep phase advance as a fast-acting therapy in depression: An open pilot trial in medicated and unmedicated patients. *American Journal of Psychiatry, 154*(6), 870–872.

Bersani, G., & Garavini, A. (2000). Melatonin add-on in manic patients with treatment resistant insomnia. *Progress in Psychopharmacology and Biological Psychiatry, 24*(2), 185–191.

Chengappa, K., Levine, J., Gershon, S., et al. (2000). Inositol as an add-on treatment for bipolar depression. *Bipolar Disorders, 2*(1), 47–55.

Chiu, C., Huang, S., Chen, C., & Su, K. (2005). Omega-3 fatty acids are more beneficial in the depressive phase than in the manic phase in patients with bipolar I disorder. *Journal of Clinical Psychiatry, 66*(12), 1613–1614.

Chouinard, G., Beauclair, L., Geiser, R., & Etienne, P. (1990). A pilot study of magnesium aspartate hydrochloride (Magnesiocard) as a mood stabilizer for rapid cycling bipolar affective disorder patients. *Progress in Neuropsychopharmacology and Biological Psychiatry, 14*(2), 171–180.

Cohen, B., Lipiski, J., & Altesman, R. (1982). Lecithin in the treatment of mania: double-blind, placebo-controlled trials. *American Journal of Psychiatry, 139*(9), 1162–1164.

Colin, A., Reggers, J., Castronovo, V., & Ansseau, M. (2003). Lipids, depression and suicide. *Encephale, 29*(1), 49–58.

Colombo, C., Benedetti, F., Barbini, B., et al. (1999). Rate of switch from depression into mania after therapeutic sleep deprivation in bipolar depression. *Psychiatry Research, 86*(3), 267–270.

Deltito, J., Moline, M., Pollack, C., et al. (1991). Effects of phototherapy on non-seasonal unipolar and bipolar spectrum disorders. *Journal of Affective Disorders, 23*(4), 231–237.

Demark-Wahnefried, W., Robertson, C., & Walther, P. (2004). Pilot study to explore effects of low-fat, flaxseed-supplemented diet on proliferation of benign prostatic epithelium and prostate-specific antigen. *Urology, 63*(5), 900–904.

Dolberg, O., Dannon, P., Schreiber, S., & Grunhaus, L. (2002). Transcranial magnetic stimulation in patients with bipolar depression: a double blind, controlled study. *Bipolar Disorders, 4*(Suppl. 1), 94–95.

Dunn, A., Trivedi, M., Kampert, J., et al. (2005). Exercise treatment for depression: efficacy and dose response. *American Journal of Preventive Medicine, 28*(1), 1–8.

Eby, G., & Eby, K. (2006). Rapid recovery from major depression using magnesium treatment. *Medical Hypotheses, 67*(2), 362–370.

Evins, A., Demopulos, C., Yovel, I., Culhane, M., Ogutha, J., Grandin, L. D., et al. (2006). Inositol augmentation of lithium or valproate for bipolar depression. *Bipolar Disorder, 8*(2), 168–174.

Fink, M. (2002). *ECT: Healing mental illness.* New York: Oxford University Press

Fink, M. (2006). ECT in therapy-resistant mania: Does it have a place? *Bipolar Disorders, 8*(3), 307.

Frangou, S., Lewis, M., & McCrone, P. (2006). Efficacy of ethyl-eicosapentaenoic acid in bipolar depression: Randomised double-blind placebo-controlled study. *British Journal of Psychiatry, 188*, 46–50.

Giannini, A. J., Nakoneczie, A. M., Melemis, S. M., Ventresco, J., & Condon, M. (2000). Magnesium oxide augmentation of verapamil maintenance therapy in mania. *Psychiatry Research, 93*(1), 83–87.

Gloth, F., 3rd, Adam, W., & Hollis, B. (1999). Vitamin D vs broad spectrum phototherapy in the treatment of seasonal affective disorder. *Journal of Nutrition, Health and Aging, 3*(1), 5–7.

Golden, R. N., Gaynes, B. N., Ekstrom, R. D., Hamer, R. M., Jacobsen, F. M., Suppes, T., et al. (2005). The efficacy of light therapy in the treatment of mood disorders: A review and meta-analysis of the evidence. *American Journal of Psychiatry, 162*(4), 656–662.

Goodwin, F., & Jamison, K. (1990). *Manic-depressive illness.* New York: Oxford University Press.

Heiden, A., Frey, R., Presslich, O., Blasbichler, T., Smetana, R., & Kasper, S. (1999). Treatment of severe mania with intravenous magnesium sulphate as a supplementary therapy. *Psychiatry Research, 89*(3), 239–246.

Hibbeln, J. R. (2002). Seafood consumption, the DHA content of mothers' milk and prevalence rates of postpartum depression: A cross-national, ecological analysis. *Journal of Affective Disorders, 69*(1-3), 15–29.

Hibbeln, J. R., Nieminen, L. R., Blasbalg, T. L., Riggs, J. A., & Lands, W. E. (2006). Healthy intakes of n-3 and n-6 fatty acids: Estimations considering worldwide diversity. *American Journal of Clinical Nutrition, 83*(6 Suppl.), 1483S–1493S.

Janakiramaiah, N., Gangadhar, B. N., Naga Venkatesha Murthy, P. J., Harish, M. G., Subbakrishna, D. K., & Vedamurthachar, A. (2000). Antidepressant efficacy of Sudarshan Kriya Yoga (SKY) in melancholia: A randomized comparison with electroconvulsive therapy (ECT) and imipramine. *Journal of Affective Disorders, 57*(1-3), 255–259.

Kaplan, B. J., Simpson, J. S., Ferre, R. C., Gorman, C. P., McMullen, D. M., & Crawford, S. G. (2001). Effective mood stabilization with a chelated mineral supplement: An open-label trial in bipolar disorder. *Journal of Clinical Psychiatry, 62*(12), 936–944.

Kaptsan, A., Yaroslavsky, Y., Applebaum, J., Belmaker, R. H., & Grisaru, N. (2003). Right prefrontal TMS versus sham treatment of mania: A controlled study. *Bipolar Disorders, 5*(1), 36–39.

Keck, P. E., Jr., Mintz, J., McElroy, S. L., Freeman, M. P., Suppes, T., Frye, M. A., et al. (2006). Double-blind, randomized, placebo-controlled trials of ethyl-eicosapentanoate in the treatment of bipolar depression and rapid cycling bipolar disorder. *Biological Psychiatry, 60*(9), 1020–1022.

Kline, M. D., & Jaggers, E. D. (1999). Mania onset while using dehydroepiandrosterone. *American Journal of Psychiatry, 156*(6), 971.

Kulkarni, J., Garland, K. A., Scaffidi, A., Headey, B., Anderson, R., de Castella, A., et al. (2006). A pilot study of hormone modulation as a new treatment for mania in women with bipolar affective disorder. *Psychoneuroendocrinology, 31*(4), 543–547.

Kumar, C., McIvor, R. J., Davies, T., Brown, N., Papadopoulos, A., Wieck, A., et al. (2003). Estrogen administration does not reduce the rate of recurrence of affective psychosis after childbirth. *Journal of Clinical Psychiatry, 64*(2), 112–118.

Leibenluft, E., Feldman-Naim, S., Turner, E., et al. (1997). Effects of exogenous melatonin administration and withdrawal in five patients with rapid-cycling bipolar disorder. *Journal of Clinical Psychiatry, 61*(3), 215.

Leibenluft, E., Turner, E. H., Feldman-Naim, S., Schwartz, P. J., Wehr, T. A., & Rosenthal, N. E. (1995). Light therapy in patients with rapid cycling bipolar disorder: Preliminary results. *Psychopharmacology Bulletin, 31*(4), 705–710.

Levine, J., Barak, Y., Gonzalves, M., Szor, H., Elizur, A., Kofman, O., et al. (1995). Double-blind, controlled trial of inositol treatment of depression. *American Journal of Psychiatry, 152*(5), 792–794.

Lin, X., Gingrich, J. R., Bao, W., Li, J., Haroon, Z. A., & Demark-Wahnefried, W. (2002). Effect of flaxseed supplementation on prostatic carcinoma in transgenic mice. *Urology, 60*(5), 919–924.

Loving, R. T., Kripke, D. F., & Shuchter, S. R. (2002). Bright light augments antidepressant effects of medication and wake therapy. *Depress Anxiety, 16*(1), 1–3.

Marangell, L. B., Martinez, J. M., Zboyan, H. A., Kertz, B., Kim, H. F., & Puryear, L. J. (2003). A double-blind, placebo-controlled study of the omega-3 fatty acid docosahexaenoic acid in the treatment of major depression. *American Journal of Psychiatry, 160*(5), 996–998.

Marangell, L. B., Suppes, T., Ketter, T. A., Dennehy, E. B., Zboyan, H., Kertz, B., et al. (2006). Omega-3 fatty acids in bipolar disorder: Clinical and research considerations. *Prostaglandins Leukot Essential Fatty Acids, 75*(4–5), 315–321.

Marohn, S. (2003). *The natural medicine guide to bipolar disorder.* Charlottesville, VA: Hampton Roads.

McTavish, S. F., McPherson, M. H., Harmer, C. J., Clark, L., Sharp, T., Goodwin, G. M., et al. (2001). Antidopaminergic effects of dietary tyrosine depletion in healthy subjects and patients with manic illness. *British Journal of Psychiatry, 179*, 356–360.

Nahas, Z., Kozel, F. A., Li, X., Anderson, B., & George, M. S. (2003). Left prefrontal transcranial magnetic stimulation (TMS) treatment of depression in bipolar affective disorder: A pilot study of acute safety and efficacy. *Bipolar Disorder, 5*(1), 40–47.

Naylor, G. J. (1984). Vanadium and manic depressive psychosis. *Nutrition Health, 3*(1-2), 79–85.

Neumeister, A., Goessler, R., Lucht, M., Kapitany, T., Bamas, C., & Kasper, S. (1996).

Bright light therapy stabilizes the antidepressant effect of partial sleep deprivation. *Biological Psychiatry, 39*(1), 16–21.

Nierenberg, A., Ostacher, M., Calabrese, J., et al. (2006). Treatment-resistant bipolar depression: A STEP-BD equipoise randomized effectiveness trial of antidepressant augmentation with lamotrigine, inositol, or risperidone. *American Journal of Psychiatry, 163*(2), 210–216.

Noaghiul, S., & Hibbeln, J. R. (2003). Cross-national comparisons of seafood consumption and rates of bipolar disorders. *American Journal of Psychiatry, 160*(12), 2222–2227.

Nowak, G., Szewczyk, B., & Pilc, A. (2005). Zinc and depression. An update. *Pharmacological Research, 57*(6), 713–718.

Osher, Y., Bersudsky, Y., & Belmaker, R. H. (2005). Omega-3 eicosapentaenoic acid in bipolar depression: Report of a small open-label study. *Journal of Clinical Psychiatry, 66*(6), 726–729.

Peet, M., Murphy, B., Shay, J., & Horrobin, D. (1998). Depletion of omega-3 fatty acid levels in red blood cell membranes of depressive patients. *Biological Psychiatry, 43*(5), 315–319.

Peet, M., & Stokes, C. (2005). Omega-3 fatty acids in the treatment of psychiatric disorders. *Drugs, 65*(8), 1051–1059.

Pflug, B., & Tolle, R. (1971). Disturbance of the 24-hour rhythm in endogenous depression and the treatment of endogenous depression by sleep deprivation. *International Pharmacopsychiatry, 6*(3), 187–196.

Pilkington, K., Kirkwood, G., Rampes, H., & Richardson, J. (2005). Yoga for depression: The research evidence. *Journal of Affective Disorders, 89*(1-3), 13–24.

Popper, C. W. (2001). Do vitamins or minerals (apart from lithium) have mood-stabilizing effects? *Journal of Clinical Psychiatry, 62*(12), 933–935.

Praschak-Rieder, N., Neumeister, A., Hesselmann, B., Willeit, M., Barnas, C., & Kasper, S. (1997). Suicidal tendencies as a complication of light therapy for seasonal affective disorder: A report of three cases. *Journal of Clinical Psychiatry, 58*(9), 389–392.

Rohan, M., Parow, A., Stoll, A. L., Demopulos, C., Friedman, S., Dager, S., et al. (2004). Low-field magnetic stimulation in bipolar depression using an MRI-based stimulator. *American Journal of Psychiatry, 161*(1), 93–98.

Saba, G., Rocamora, J. F., Kalalou, K., Benadhira, R., Plaze, M., Lipski, H., et al. (2004). Repetitive transcranial magnetic stimulation as an add-on therapy in the treatment of mania: A case series of eight patients. *Psychiatry Research, 128*(2), 199–202.

Sakkas, P., Mihalopoulou, P., Mourtzouhou, P., et al. (2003). Induction of mania by rTMS: Report of two cases. *European Psychiatry, 18*(4), 196–198.

Sales, C. H., & Pedrosa Lde, F. (2006). Magnesium and diabetes mellitus: Their relation. *Clinical Nutrition, 25*(4), 554–562.

Schilgen, B., & Tolle, R. (1980). Partial sleep deprivation as therapy for depression. *Archives of General Psychiatry, 37*(3), 267–271.

Schmidt, P. J., Daly, R. C., Bloch, M., Smith, M. J., Danaceau, M. A., St Clair, L. S., et al. (2005). Dehydroepiandrosterone monotherapy in midlife-onset major and minor depression. *Archives of General Psychiatry, 62*(2), 154–162.

Shaldubina, A., Stahl, Z., Furszpan, M., Regenold, W. T., Shapiro, J., Belmaker, R. H., et al. (2006). Inositol deficiency diet and lithium effects. *Bipolar Disorder, 8*(2), 152–159.

Shamlian, N. T., & Cole, M. G. (2006). Androgen treatment of depressive symptoms in older men: A systematic review of feasibility and effectiveness. *Canadian Journal of Psychiatry, 51*(5), 295–299.

Sharma, V., & Barrett, C. (2001). Tryptophan for treatment of rapid-cycling bipolar disorder comorbid with fibromyalgia. *Canadian Journal of Psychiatry, 46*(5), 452–453.

Simons, W., & Dierick, M. (2005). Transcranial magnetic stimulation as a therapeutic tool in psychiatry. *World Journal of Biological Psychiatry, 6*(1), 6–25.

Simopoulos, A. (2006). Evolutionary aspects of diet, the omega-6/omega-3 ratio and genetic variation: nutritional implications for chronic diseases. *Biomedicine and Pharmacotherapy, 60*(9), 502–507.

Singh, N. A., Clements, K. M., & Fiatarone, M. A. (1997). A randomized controlled trial of progressive resistance training in depressed elders. *Journal of Gerontology 52*(1), M27–35.

Sit, D., Hanusa, B., Terman, M., & Wisner, K. (2005). Light therapy for bipolar disorder. *Bipolar Disorders, 7*(Suppl. 2), 101 (Poster 227).

Smeraldi, E., Benedetti, F., Barbini, B., Campori, E., & Colombo, C. (1999). Sustained antidepressant effect of sleep deprivation combined with pindolol in bipolar depression. A placebo-controlled trial. *Neuropsychopharmacology, 20*(4), 380–385.

Soares, C. N., Almeida, O. P., Joffe, H., & Cohen, L. S. (2001). Efficacy of estradiol for the treatment of depressive disorders in perimenopausal women: A double-blind, randomized, placebo-controlled trial. *Archives of General Psychiatry, 58*(6), 529–534.

Sobczak, S., Honig, A., Christophe, A., Maes, M., Helsdingen, R. W., De Vriese, S. A., et al. (2004). Lower high-density lipoprotein cholesterol and increased omega-6 polyunsaturated fatty acids in first-degree relatives of bipolar patients. *Psychological Medicine, 34*(1), 103–112.

Stoll, A. L., Sachs, G. S., Cohen, B. M., Lafer, B., Christensen, J. D., & Renshaw, P. F. (1996). Choline in the treatment of rapid-cycling bipolar disorder: Clinical and neurochemical findings in lithium-treated patients. *Biological Psychiatry, 40*(5), 382–388.

Stoll, A. L., Severus, W. E., Freeman, M. P., Rueter, S., Zboyan, H. A., Diamond, E., et al. (1999). Omega 3 fatty acids in bipolar disorder: A preliminary double-blind, placebo-controlled trial. *Archives of General Psychiatry, 56*(5), 407–412.

Tsang, H. W., Fung, K. M., Chan, A. S., Lee, G., & Chan, F. (2006). Effect of a qigong exercise programme on elderly with depression. *International Journal of Geriatric Psychiatry, 21*(9), 890–897.

Voderholzer, U., Valerius, G., Schaerer, L., Riemann, D., Giedke, H., Schwarzler, F., et al. (2003). Is the antidepressive effect of sleep deprivation stabilized by a three day phase advance of the sleep period? A pilot study. *European Archives of Psychiatry and Clinical Neuroscience, 253*(2), 68–72.

Wehr, T., Goodwin, F., Wirz-Justice, A., et al. (1982).48-hour sleep-wake cycle in manic-depressive illness: Naturalistic observations and sleep-deprivation experiments. *Archives of General Psychiatry, 39,* 559–565.

Wehr, T. A., Sack, D. A., & Rosenthal, N. E. (1987). Sleep reduction as a final common pathway in the genesis of mania. *American Journal of Psychiatry, 144*(2), 201–204.

Wehr, T. A., Turner, E. H., Shimada, J. M., Lowe, C. H., Barker, C., & Leibenluft, E. (1998). Treatment of rapidly cycling bipolar patient by using extended bed rest and darkness to stabilize the timing and duration of sleep. *Biological Psychiatry, 43*(11), 822–828.

Weiss, E. L., Bowers, M. B., Jr., & Mazure, C. M. (1999). Testosterone-patch-induced psychotic mania. *American Journal of Psychiatry, 156*(6), 969.

Williams, A. L., Girard, C., Jui, D., Sabina, A., & Katz, D. L. (2005). S-adenosylmethionine (SAMe) as treatment for depression: A systematic review. *Clinical and Investigative Medicine, 28*(3), 132–139.

Wirz-Justice, A., Quinto, C., Cajochen, C., et al. (1999). A rapid-cycling bipolar patient treated with long nights, bedrest, and light. *Biological Psychiatry, 45*(8), 1075–1077.

Zanarini, M. C., & Frankenburg, F. R. (2003). Omega-3 fatty acid treatment of women with borderline personality disorder: A double-blind, placebo-controlled pilot study. *American Journal of Psychiatry, 160*(1), 167–169.

CHAPTER 10

Identification and Management of Suicide Risk

There are two kinds of clinicians: Those who have had a patient commit suicide and those who will.

Ninety percent of those who commit suicide have psychiatric illnesses. The majority—60 to 80 percent—have a major mood disorder (Fawcett, 2001; Goodwin, 1999). The lifetime risk of suicide in patients with mood disorders is between 2 and 15 percent and 15 to 20 percent in patients with mood disorders who have been hospitalized (Bostwick & Pankratz, 2000). Estimates of the lifetime suicide completion rate for bipolar patients have ranged from 9 to 60 percent with a weighted mean of nearly 19 percent across 31 studies of over 9,000 bipolar patients (Goodwin, 1999). This represents a 30-fold increased risk of suicide in bipolar patients over the general population. Baldessarini et al. (2006) stated that patients with bipolar disorder have a 60-fold increased risk of suicide over the general population. Table 10.1 lists statistics on suicide in the United States.

There have been scores of studies on suicide, but the majority of them have focused on either the characteristics of individuals with suicidal ideation or risk factors that identify those who will attempt suicide. But at least 80 percent of bipolar patients have thoughts of suicide (Valtonen et al., 2005) and 25 to 50 percent of them will attempt suicide (Goodwin & Jamison, 1990; Valtonen et al., 2005). While suicide attempts are certainly important for the clinician to try to prevent (especially since they are a risk factor for later completed suicide), clinicians need information on patients who are at the highest risk of completing suicide in the near future. Researchers have discovered that suicide attempters and completers are distinct populations (Moskos et al., 2004; Paris, 2006).

TABLE 10.1

Suicide in the United States

Suicide took the lives of 30,622 people in 2001 (CDC, 2004). It is the eleventh leading cause of death overall in the United States (CDC, 2004).

It is the third leading cause of death in 15–24 year olds (Anderson & Smith, 2003).

Five to 6 percent of annual suicides occur in hospitals (Busch et al., 2003).

Males are four times more likely to die from suicide than females (CDC, 2004).

Suicide is the eighth leading cause of death for U.S. men (Anderson & Smith 2003).

Suicide rates for women fell between 1965 and 1999 (Levi et al., 2003).

The highest suicide rates were for white men over age 85 (CDC, 2004; DHHS, 1999).

In 1996, white males accounted for 73 percent of all suicides (DHHS, 1999).

Sixty percent of male suicides in 2001 were from guns (Anderson & Smith, 2003).

Suicide rates in western states are higher than the national average (DHHS, 1999).

Suicides are most frequent in the spring (Goodwin & Jamison, 1990).

Identification of Patients with Mood Disorders Who Are at Risk of Committing Suicide in the Near Term

In a study of 954 psychiatric patients with major affective disorders (both unipolar and bipolar) panic attacks, severe anxiety, diminished concentration, anhedonia, alcohol abuse, and insomnia were associated with suicide *within 1 year* (Fawcett et al., 1990). McGirr et al. (2007) also found insomnia to be a risk factor for suicide completion in patients with major depressive disorder.

Other researchers have found an association between substance abuse and increased risk of suicide, as well. Wilcox et al. (2004) reviewed studies on substance abuse and suicide published through 2002. They found many studies that linked alcohol abuse to increased suicide risk and some studies that linked opioid abuse and dependence to suicide. The association of suicide and other drug use disorders (e.g., cocaine, cannabis) was less clear. Dumais et al. (2005) compared 104 male suicide completers with 74 living depressed male patients and found that substance abuse increased the risk of suicide completion in depressed patients. Sher (2006) found that partner-relationship disruptions were strongly associated with suicidal behavior in individuals with alcoholism.

Fawcett and his colleagues (1990) also found that severe hopelessness and a history of previous suicide attempts were associated with suicide completion, but not in the short-term. Rather, they were associated with suicide after 1 year. Many studies have shown a clear connection between suicide attempts, self-harm (a concept that includes suicide attempts but also includes nonsuicidal acts such as self-mutilation), and the risk of eventual suicide (e.g., Brown et al., 2000; Crandall et al., 2006; DeMoore et al., 1996; Hawton & Fagg, 1988; Kuo and Gallo, 2005; Owens et al., 2002).

The Hawton/Fagg and Owens studies show a 50- to 100-fold increase in eventual suicide in those who have made attempts. Cooper et al. (2005) cite research showing that approximately one-half of persons who die by suicide have a history of self-harm, while two-thirds of those in younger age groups who commit suicide have such a history.

In contrast to Fawcett et al.'s data, Hawton and Fagg (1988) found the highest risk of suicide in those with attempts came within 6 months of an episode of self-harm. In line with this are the data by Cooper et al. (2005) indicating that deliberate self-harm is a predictor of suicide completion in the near term. Their 4-year prospective study of 7,968 emergency room patients who engaged in deliberate self-harm (psychiatric diagnoses not reported) indicated an elevated rate of suicide within 6 months of the episode of self-harm.

Increased risk of suicide is an issue to which clinicians may need to attend for as long as they are working with some patients. Suominen et al. (2004) followed 100 consecutive self-poisoning patients in Helsinki, Finland, and found that the increased risk of suicide lasted for the entire 37 years of follow-up. Individuals with multiple episodes of deliberate self-harm have been found to be at greater risk of eventual suicide than individuals with only one reported incident of deliberate self-harm (Zahl & Hawton, 2004).

Clinicians also need to keep in mind that suicidality runs in families, independent of depression and other psychopathology (Kim et al., 2005; Lieb et al., 2005; Qin et al., 2002). Table 10.2 lists risk factors for suicide completion within one year that have been reported in the literature. Table 10.3 is a summary of other risk factors associated with suicide and suicide attempts.

Some research suggests that strong religious beliefs (Dervic et al., 2006, 2004), being a parent (Qin & Mortensen, 2003), and for men, strong social support (Houle, 2004) decrease the risk of suicide.

Suicide Completion Risk Factors in Bipolar Patients

Do people with bipolar disorder commit suicide more often than those with unipolar disorder? Rihmer and Kiss (2002), based on a review of population and clinical studies, concluded that individuals with bipolar disorders are at higher risk of attempted and completed suicide than those with unipolar major depression. Bipolar II patients were found to have the highest risk of all.

TABLE 10.2

Risk Factors for Suicide Completion within One Year in Patients with Mood Disorders

- Panic attacks, severe anxiety
- Poor concentration
- Insomnia
- Anhedonia
- Alcohol and drug abuse
- Family history of completed suicide
- History of self-harm, suicide attempt

TABLE 10.3

Other Risk Factors for Suicide and Suicide Attempts

- Recent adverse life events, such as loss (Isometsa, 2005; Qin, 2006)
- Childhood neglect and abuse (Enns et al., 2006)
- Physicians, dentists (Alexander, 2001; Arnetz et al., 1987; Stack, 2004)
- Medical illness, especially if age 50+ or with multiple illnesses (Druss & Pincus, 2000; Hendin, 1999)
- Social isolation (Duberstein et al., 2004)
- Psychosis (Black et al., 1988; Simpson & Jamison, 1999)
- Communication of intent to family and professionals (Isometsa, 2005)
- History of psychiatric hospitalization (Qin, 2006)
- Recent hospital admission or discharge, especially if hospital stay was short (Hoyer et al., 2004; Qin & Nordentoft, 2005)
- Impulsive-aggressive behaviors, hostility (Dumais et al., 2005; Michaelis et al., 2004)
- Attempts in which the individual expected to die (Gibb et al., 2005)
- Attempts using violent or highly lethal means (Forster, 1994; Skogman et al., 2004)
- Attempts after which subjects state they wished they had died (Henriques et al., 2005)
- High degree of impairment, total symptom load (in youth; Foley et al., 2006)
- Refractory or recurrent depression (Oquendo et al., 2006)
- Biological markers: Hypothalamic-pituitary-adrenal axis hyperactivity (Coryell et al., 2006)
- Low serum cholesterol (Coryell et al., 2006)

On the other hand, Angst and Preisig (1995) followed 406 patients with various forms of affective disorder for several decades. Forty-five of these patients committed suicide. At 35-year follow-up, the rates of suicide for unipolar and bipolar patients were equal, but at 44 years unipolar depressives had the highest rate of suicide (Angst et al., 2005). Osby et al. (2001), in a Swedish population-based study, found that suicide completion was higher in unipolar than bipolar patients. Bipolar and unipolar individuals had similar suicide completion rates in a clinical study of hospitalized patients conducted by Bottlender et al. (2000). Bipolar patients, however, attempted suicide more often.

Rihmer and Kiss's conclusions are based on an analysis of the entire literature while Angst and Bottlender's conclusions are based on the study of much smaller clinical samples. Osby's results are compelling, however, given that they were derived from a large, population-based study. Varying definitions of bipolar disorder across studies, however, make it difficult to draw firm conclusions about the incidence of suicide in unipolar versus bipolar patients.

More importantly, the results of these studies comparing the suicide rate in unipolar versus bipolar patients may be misleading since the researchers did not differentiate between patients in mixed states from those with anergic depression. McGirr et al. (2007) found that atypical symptoms such as appetite and weight gain along with hypersomnia (symptoms common in lethargic, bipolar depressed patients) are *not* associated with increased suicidal risk. On the other hand, patients in bipolar mixed states are at high risk for suicide completion (Tondo et al., 1999; Valtonen et al., 2006). Balazs et al. (2006) noted the very high prevalence of mixed states among 100 depressed suicide attempters. The vast majority were irritable, distractible, and agitated. In 650 consecutive Italian private practice patients seen for major depression and interviewed with a structured diagnostic instrument, Akiskal and Benazzi (2006) found that suicidal ideation was significantly associated with agitation, irritability, and racing/crowded thoughts. The researchers concluded that bipolar II depressive mixed states were the main diagnostic substrate for the occurrence of suicidality. Table 10.4 lists risk factors for suicide completion specifically for bipolar patients.

TABLE 10.4

Suicide Risk Factors in Patients with Bipolar Disorder

- Depressive mixed states: irritability, agitation, racing/crowded thoughts
- Alcohol and drug abuse (Isometsa, 2005)
- First 10 years after diagnosis (Fagiolini et al., 2004; Tsai et al., 2002)
- History of suicide attempts (Hawton et al., 2005)
- Hopelessness (Hawton et al., 2005)
- Family history of completed suicide (Rihmer & Kiss, 2002)

Management of Suicide Risk

Although it is impossible to predict which individual patient will commit suicide, the risk that a patient will do so can be reduced by close monitoring of risk factors and aggressive treatment (Angst et al., 2005). The risk a patient with bipolar disorder will commit suicide fluctuates depending on factors such as the stage of illness, the occurrence of adverse life events, the type and severity of the symptoms, and the degree of support the patient feels is available from family, spouse, and others.

Clinicians should periodically assess risk with each of their patients, especially when a patient becomes depressed, is faced with a crisis or major loss, and during prolonged periods of demoralization and hopelessness. Therapists need to consciously remind themselves to be vigilant for the signs of a suicidal crisis in patients with whom they have been working for years. In such cases, therapists tend to assume that patients will turn to them for help if they begin feeling suicidal. However, when patients decide to commit suicide, therapists may well cease to be viewed as allies.

Questions about suicidal ideation, intent, plans, or available means do not, by themselves, constitute an adequate assessment of suicide risk. First, while individuals with a plan are more likely to make a suicide attempt than those without a plan, a large percentage of suicide attempts are unplanned (Borges et al., 2006). Second, a discussion of ideation, intent, plan, and means alone does not take into account the factors that have been clearly linked to completed suicide. Clinicians working with depressed and bipolar patients must assess the risk factors previously listed for suicide completion within 1 year.

Combinations of agitated, hostile, or depressive mixed states; insomnia; and substance abuse are particularly dangerous. Even when patients deny suicidal ideation, intent, or plan, the presence of these factors should lead clinicians to consider additional treatment measures. The presence or absence of the specific risk factors previously discussed should be noted and an overall assessment of risk should be documented (e.g., low, moderate, high).

If risk is rated as moderate or high, the clinician should formulate a plan to deal with the increased risk of suicide. The plan can include the following:

- *Thorough* assessment of the known risk factors for suicide completion.
- Seeing the patient more frequently.
- Scheduling regular phone contact with the patient.
- Instructing family and friends not to leave the patient alone.
- Having patient and family remove means of committing suicide (removing firearms and pills).
- Instructing the patient or family to call if necessary.

- Treating severe anxiety, agitation, and insomnia with medication.
- Using lithium.
- Referring the patient for electroconvulsive therapy.
- Addressing alcohol and drug abuse.
- In a crisis: Asking family or the police to take the patient to the emergency room.
- Giving information to the emergency room physician or social worker.

Fortunately, some of the factors that make the greatest contribution to the near-term risk of suicide (severe anxiety, insomnia, and agitation) are treatable. Lithium, anticonvulsants, and antidepressants may not take effect for weeks. But benzodiazepine drugs such as clonazepam have immediate anxiolytic and hypnotic effects. In substance-abusing patients or in patients with severe agitation mixed states or explosive anger, atypical antipsychotics can quickly reduce agitation and help patients sleep.

There is substantial evidence that lithium is associated with major sustained reductions in self-harm, suicide attempts, and risk of suicide (Baldessarini et al., 2006). Baldessarini et al. (2001), in a review of the results of 33 studies, found a 13-fold lower rate of completed and attempted suicide in patients treated with lithium. Such benefits have not been convincingly demonstrated with other commonly used medications, including antidepressants. Lithium reduces premature death in bipolar patients not only from suicide but from all medical causes, as well (Cipriani et al., 2005). In spite of this, it is not the most commonly prescribed medication for depressed, suicidal patients. Antidepressants are the most commonly prescribed medication, despite the evidence discussed in Chapter 7 that they are not only ineffective in maintenance treatment of bipolar depression, but that they contribute to mood instability (Goldberg et al., 2005).

Clozapine (Clozaril), an atypical antipsychotic, is the only other drug that has been shown to clearly reduce suicide risk. It is FDA approved for that purpose in schizophrenic patients. This suggests other atypical antipsychotics may be useful in reducing suicide risk, as well (Sharma, 2003).

Some therapists in outpatient settings and nurses on in-patient units make use of a contract for safety with suicidal patients. Patients are asked for assurances they will contact the clinician or staff before acting on suicidal impulses. There is no evidence to support the use of these contracts and they are obviously of no value when working with patients who abuse alcohol or other drugs, or who are psychotic (Egan, 1997). They are of dubious value when patients' insight, impulse control, and judgment are impaired by their illness. In some cases, they may be useful when used together with the other risk-management strategies listed. Using them alone, as the sole means of risk management, is a serious mistake.

A good overview of how to assess the short-term risk of suicide can be found in Forster (1994). Simons and Hales (2006) offer a comprehensive accounting of risk assessment and management in their book.

Some Principles of Psychotherapy with Suicidal Patients

No aspect of work with bipolar patients raises more anxiety for therapists than suicide. The anxiety is based, consciously, on concern for patients, feelings of helplessness, and concern about being blamed for patients' suicide. Unconsciously, anxiety may sometimes be linked to wishes to be rid of these patients in some way (including wishes the patients would kill themselves). These conscious and unconscious pressures can lead therapists to make one of two mistakes with patients: failing to attend to suicide risk or making extraordinary efforts to comfort or save the patient.

Goodwin and Jamison (1990) cite work by Cassem suggesting that therapists must have the capacity to hear, tolerate, and reflect understanding of patients' desperation, anguish, and rage while avoiding premature attempts to soothe them. They also cite West, who noted that suicidal patients may initially seem unresponsive to therapists' efforts, but often later acknowledge that the efforts were comforting.

Empirical evidence on which psychosocial treatment methods are effective with suicidal patients is sparse. From a review of 17 randomized, controlled studies on psychosocial treatments aimed at ameliorating psychosocial risk factors for suicide, Gray and Otto (2001) identified three strategies with some evidence of efficacy: (a) helping patients seek emergency care at times of distress; (b) training patients in problem-solving strategies; and (c) intensive rehearsal of cognitive, social, emotional-labeling, and distress-tolerance skills.

Since Gray and Otto's review, Rucci et al. (2002) have published data on the effectiveness of interpersonal social rhythm therapy in reducing suicide attempts. Linehan et al. (2006) have published data showing dialectical behavior therapy is effective in reducing suicide risk. Readers interested in getting detailed information on how to work with suicidal patients from other theoretical perspectives can turn to: Brown et al. (2005) for a cognitive-behavioral approach, Busch et al. (2004) for a psychodynamic perspective, or Guthrie et al. (2001) for a combined psychodynamic-interpersonal approach.

Following is a summary of principles from these approaches to the suicidal patient:

- Tolerate the patient's anguish and your anxiety. Reflect feelings.
- Assess for factors associated with suicide-completion risk.
- Explore the context in which suicidal impulses arise.
- Explore the patient's reasons for wanting to commit suicide.
- Explore what has kept the patient from killing him or herself.

- Point out that feelings are not facts. Depression distorts thinking and the ability to accurately assess reality.

- Point out that hopelessness is a feeling and not necessarily a reflection of reality.

- Explain that once depression is treated, the patient will feel better *even if problems do not get better.*

- Help patient become mindful of depressive thinking.

- Help patient consider other, less permanent solutions than suicide.

- Always look to support self-esteem and reduce unrealistic self-criticism or shame.

- When applicable, discuss how self-worth is not tied to success or some other goal.

- When applicable, discuss how not being loved by another does not make one unlovable.

- Help patient distract him- or herself from depressive rumination through constructive or potentially soothing activity.

- Monitor your level of frustration. Excessive frustration may be a signal a patient's covert anger needs to be explored.

References

Akiskal, H. & Benazzi, F. (2006). Does the FDA proposed list of possible correlates of suicidality associated with antidepressants apply to an adult private practice population? *Journal of Affective Disorders, 94*(1-3), 105–110.

Alexander, R. E. (2001). Stress-related suicide by dentists and other health care workers. Fact or folklore? *Journal of the American Dental Association, 132*(6), 786–794.

Anderson, R., & Smith, B. (2003). Deaths: Leading causes for 2001. *National Vital Statistics Report, 52*(9), 1–86.

Angst, J., Angst, F., Gerber-Werder, R., & Gamma, A. (2005). Suicide in 406 mood-disorder patients with and without long-term medication: A 40 to 44 years' follow-up. *Archives of Suicide Research, 9*(3), 279–300.

Angst, J., & Preisig, M. (1995). Outcome of a clinical cohort of unipolar, bipolar and schizoaffective patients. Results of a prospective study from 1959 to 1985. *Schweiz Archives of Neurological Psychiatry, 146*(1), 17–23.

Arnetz, B. B., Horte, L. G., Hedberg, A., & Malker, H. (1987). Suicide among Swedish dentists. A ten-year follow-up study. *Scandinavian Journal of Social Medicine, 15*(4), 243–246.

Balazs, J., Benazzi F., Rihmer Z., et al. (2006). The close link between suicide attempts and mixed (bipolar) depression: Implications for suicide prevention. *Journal of Affective Disorders, 91*(2-3): 133–138.

Baldessarini, R., Pompili, M., & Tondo, L. (2006). Suicide in bipolar disorder: Risks and management. *CNS Spectrum, 11*(6), 465–471.

Baldessarini, R. J., Tondo, L., & Hennen, J. (2001). Treating the suicidal patient with bipolar disorder: Reducing suicide risk with lithium. *Annals of the New York Academy of Sciences, 932,* 24–38.

Black, D. W., Winokur, G., & Nasrallah, A. (1988). Effect of psychosis on suicide risk in 1,593 patients with unipolar and bipolar affective disorders. *American Journal of Psychiatry, 145*(7), 849–852.

Borges, G., Angst, J., Nock, M. K., Ruscio, A. M., Walters, E. E., & Kessler, R. C. (2006). A risk index for 12-month suicide attempts in the National Comorbidity Survey Replication (NCS-R). *Psychological Medicine,* pp. 1–11.

Bostwick, J., & Pankratz, V. (2000). Affective disorders and suicide risk: A reexamination. *American Journal of Psychiatry, 157,* 1925–1932.

Bottlender, R., Jager, M., Strauss, A., & Moller, H. J. (2000). Suicidality in bipolar compared to unipolar depressed inpatients. *European Archives of Psychiatry and Clinical Neuroscience, 250*(5), 257–261.

Brown, G., Beck, A., Steer, R., & Grisham, J. (2000). Risk factors for suicide in psychiatric outpatients: A 20-year prospective study. *Journal of Consulting and Clinical Psychology, 68,* 371–377.

Brown, G., Ten Have, T., & Henriques, G. (2005). Cognitive therapy for the prevention of suicide attempts: A randomized controlled trial. *Journal of the American Medical Association, 294*(5), 563–570.

Busch, F., Rudden, M., & Shapiro, T. (2004). *Psychodynamic treatment of depression.* Washington, DC: APA Press.

Busch, K. A., Fawcett, J., & Jacobs, D. G. (2003). Clinical correlates of inpatient suicide. *Journal of Clinical Psychiatry, 64*(1), 14–19.

Centers of Disease Control (CDC). (2004). National Center for Injury Prevention and Control Web-based Injury Statistics Query and Reporting System (WISQARS). Retrieved from http://www.cdc.gov/ncipc/wisqars/default.htm

Cipriani, A., Pretty, H., Hawton, K., & Geddes, J. R. (2005). Lithium in the prevention of suicidal behavior and all-cause mortality in patients with mood disorders: A systematic review of randomized trials. *American Journal of Psychiatry, 162*(10), 1805–1819.

Cooper, J., Kapur, N., Webb, R., Lawlor, M., Guthrie, E., Mackway-Jones, K., et al. (2005). Suicide after deliberate self-harm: A 4-year cohort study. *American Journal of Psychiatry, 162*(2), 297–303.

Coryell, W., Young, E., & Carroll, B. (2006). Hyperactivity of the hypothalamic-pituitary-adrenal axis and mortality in major depressive disorder. *Psychiatry Research, 142*(1), 99–104.

Crandall, C., Fullerton-Gleason, L., Aguero, R., & LaValley, J. (2006). Subsequent suicide mortality among emergency department patients seen for suicidal behavior. *Academic Emergency Medicine, 13*(4), 435–442.

De Moore, G. M., & Robertson, A. R. (1996). Suicide in the 18 years after deliberate self-harm a prospective study. *British Journal of Psychiatry, 169*(4), 489–494.

Dervic, K., Oquendo, M. A., Currier, D., Grunebaum, M. F., Burke, A. K., & Mann, J. J. (2006). Moral objections to suicide: Can they counteract suicidality in patients with cluster B psychopathology? *Journal of Clinical Psychiatry, 67*(4), 620–625.

Dervic, K., Oquendo, M. A., Grunebaum, M. F., Ellis, S., Burke, A. K., & Mann, J. J.

(2004). Religious affiliation and suicide attempt. *American Journal of Psychiatry, 161*(12), 2303–2308.

Department of Health and Human Services (DHHS). (1999). The Surgeon General's call to action to prevent suicide. Retrieved from http://www.surgeongeneral.gov/library/calltoaction/default.htm.

Druss, B., & Pincus, H. (2000). Suicidal ideation and suicide attempts in general medical illnesses. *Archives of Internal Medicine, 160*(10), 1522–1526.

Duberstein, P. R., Conwell, Y., Conner, K. R., Eberly, S., Evinger, J. S., & Caine, E. D. (2004). Poor social integration and suicide: Fact or artifact? A case-control study. *Psychological Medicine, 34*(7), 1331–1337.

Dumais, A., Lesage, A. D., Alda, M., Rouleau, G., Dumont, M., Chawky, N., et al. (2005). Risk factors for suicide completion in major depression: A case-control study of impulsive and aggressive behaviors in men. *American Journal of Psychiatry, 162*(11), 2116–2124.

Egan, M. P. (1997). Contracting for safety: A concept analysis. *Crisis, 18*(1), 17–23.

Enns, M. W., Cox, B. J., Afifi, T. O., de Graaf, R., Ten Have, M., & Sareen, J. (2006). Childhood adversities and risk for suicidal ideation and attempts: A longitudinal population-based study. *Psychological Medicine, 36*(12), 1769–1778.

Fagiolini A., Kupfer D., Rucci P., et al. (2004). Suicide attempts and ideation in patients with bipolar I disorder. *Journal of Clinical Psychiatry, 65*(4), 509–514.

Fawcett, J. (2001). Treating impulsivity and anxiety in the suicidal patient. *Annals of the New York Academy of Sciences, 932,* 94–102, 102–105.

Fawcett, J., Scheftner, W., Fogg, L., et al. (1990). Time-related predictors of suicide in major affective disorder. *American Journal of Psychiatry, 147*(9), 1189–1194.

Foley, D. L., Goldston, D. B., Costello, E. J., & Angold, A. (2006). Proximal psychiatric risk factors for suicidality in youth: The Great Smoky Mountains Study. *Archives of General Psychiatry, 63*(9), 1017–1024.

Forster, P. (1994). Accurate assessment of short-term suicide risk in a crisis. *Psychiatric Annals, 24*(11), 571–578.

Gibb, S. J., Beautrais, A. L., & Fergusson, D. M. (2005). Mortality and further suicidal behaviour after an index suicide attempt: A 10-year study. *Australian and New Zealand Journal of Psychiatry, 39*(1-2), 95–100.

Goldberg, J. F., Allen, M. H., Miklowitz, D. A., Bowden, C. L., Endick, C. J., Chessick, C. A., et al. (2005). Suicidal ideation and pharmacotherapy among STEP-BD patients. *Psychiatric Services, 56*(12), 1534–1540.

Goodwin, F., & Jamison, K. (1990). *Manic-depressive illness.* New York: Oxford University Press.

Goodwin, F. K. (1999). Anticonvulsant therapy and suicide risk in affective disorders. *Journal of Clinical Psychiatry, 60*(Suppl. 2): 89–93, 111–116.

Gray, S. M., & Otto, M. W. (2001). Psychosocial approaches to suicide prevention: Applications to patients with bipolar disorder. *Journal of Clinical Psychiatry, 62*(Suppl. 25), 56–64.

Guthrie, E., Kapur, N., Mackway-Jones, K., et al. (2001). Randomised controlled trial of brief psychological intervention after deliberate self-poisoning. *British Medical Journal, 323,* 135–138.

Hawton, K., & Fagg, J. (1988). Suicide, and other causes of death, following attempted suicide. *British Journal of Psychiatry, 152,* 359–366.

Hawton, K., Sutton, L., Haw, C., Sinclair, J., & Harriss, L. (2005). Suicide and attempted suicide in bipolar disorder: A systematic review of risk factors. *Journal of Clinical Psychiatry, 66*(6), 693–704.

Hendin, H. (1999). Suicide, assisted suicide, and medical illness. *Journal of Clinical Psychiatry, 60*(Suppl. 2): 46–50, 51–42, 113–116.

Henriques, G., Wenzel, A., Brown, G. K., & Beck, A. T. (2005). Suicide attempters' reaction to survival as a risk factor for eventual suicide. *American Journal of Psychiatry, 162*(11), 2180–2182.

Houle, J. (2004). Help seeking, social support and gender roles in men who attempted suicide. *Journal of Affective Disorders, 78*(3), 209–217.

Hoyer, E. H., Olesen, A. V., & Mortensen, P. B. (2004). Suicide risk in patients hospitalized because of an affective disorder: A follow-up study, 1973–1993. *Journal of Affective Disorders, 78*(3), 209–217.

Isometsa, F. (2005). Suicide in bipolar I disorder in Finland: psychological autopsy findings from the National Suicide Prevention Project in Finland. *Archives of Suicide Research, 9*(3), 251–260.

Kim, C. D., Seguin, M., Therrien, N., Riopel, G., Chawky, N., Lesage, A. D., et al. (2005). Familial aggregation of suicidal behavior: A family study of male suicide completers from the general population. *American Journal of Psychiatry, 162*(5), 1017–1019.

Kuo, W. H., & Gallo, J. J. (2005). Completed suicide after a suicide attempt. *American Journal of Psychiatry, 162*(3), 633.

Levi, F., La Vecchia, C., Lucchini, F., Negri, E., Saxena, S., Maulik, P. K., et al. (2003). Trends in mortality from suicide, 1965–99. *Acta Psychiatrica Scand, 108*(5), 341–349.

Lieb, R., Bronisch, T., Hofler, M., Schreier, A., & Wittchen, H. U. (2005). Maternal suicidality and risk of suicidality in offspring: Findings from a community study. *American Journal of Psychiatry, 162*(9), 1665–1671.

Linehan, M., Comtois, K., & Murray, A. (2006). Two-year randomized controlled trial and follow-up of dialectical behavior therapy vs. therapy by experts for suicidal behaviors and borderline personality disorder. *Archives of General Psychiatry, 63*(7), 757–766.

McGirr, A., Renaud, J., Seguin, M., et al. (2007). An examination of *DSM-IV* depressive symptoms and risk for suicide completion in major depressive disorder: A psychological autopsy study. *Journal of Affective Disorders, 97*(1-3), 203–209.

Michaelis, B. H., Goldberg, J. F., Davis, G. P., Singer, T. M., Garno, J. L., & Wenze, S. J. (2004). Dimensions of impulsivity and aggression associated with suicide attempts among bipolar patients: A preliminary study. *Suicide Life Threat Behavior, 34*(2), 172–176.

Moskos, M. A., Achilles, J., & Gray, D. (2004). Adolescent suicide myths in the United States. *Crisis, 25*(4), 176–182.

Oquendo, M. A., Currier, D., & Mann, J. J. (2006). Prospective studies of suicidal behavior in major depressive and bipolar disorders: What is the evidence for predictive risk factors? *Acta Psychiatrica Scand, 114*(3), 151–158.

Osby, U., Brandt, L., Correia, N., Ekbom, A., & Sparen, P. (2001). Excess mortality in bipolar and unipolar disorder in Sweden. *Archives of General Psychiatry, 58*(9), 844–850.

Owens, D., Horrocks, J., & House, A. (2002). Fatal and non-fatal repetition of self-harm. Systematic review. *British Journal of Psychiatry, 181,* 193–199.

Paris, J. (2006). Predicting and preventing suicide: Do we know enough to do either? *Harvard Review of Psychiatry, 14*(5), 233–240.

Qin, P. (2006). Life events, hospitalization and suicide: What comes first? *Psychiatria Danubina, 18*(Suppl. 1), 76.

Qin, P., Agerbo, E., & Mortensen, P. B. (2002). Suicide risk in relation to family history of completed suicide and psychiatric disorders: A nested case-control study based on longitudinal registers. *Lancet, 360*(9340), 1126–1130.

Qin, P., & Mortensen, P. B. (2003). The impact of parental status on the risk of completed suicide. *Archives of General Psychiatry, 60*(8), 797–802.

Qin, P., & Nordentoft, M. (2005). Suicide risk in relation to psychiatric hospitalization: Evidence based on longitudinal registers. *Archives of General Psychiatry, 62*(4), 427–432.

Rihmer, Z., & Kiss, K. (2002). Bipolar disorders and suicidal behavior. *Bipolar Disorders,* (Suppl. 1), 21–25.

Rucci, P., Frank, E., Kostelnik, B., et al. (2002). Suicide attempts in patients with bipolar I disorder during acute and maintenance phases of intensive treatment with pharmacotherapy and adjunctive psychotherapy. *American Journal of Psychiatry, 159,* 1160–1164.

Sharma, V. (2003). Atypical antipsychotics and suicide in mood and anxiety disorders. *Bipolar Disorder, 5*(Suppl. 2), 48–52.

Sher, L. (2006). Alcoholism and suicidal behavior: A clinical overview. *Acta Psychiatrica Scand, 113*(1), 13–22.

Simons, R. & Hales, R. (Eds.). (2006). *The American psychiatric publishing textbook of suicide assessment and management.* Washington, DC: APA Press.

Simpson, S. G., & Jamison, K. R. (1999). The risk of suicide in patients with bipolar disorders. *Journal of Clinical Psychiatry, 60*(Suppl. 2), 53–56, 75–56, 113–116.

Skogman, K., Alsen, M., & Ojehagen, A. (2004). Sex differences in risk factors for suicide after attempted suicide-a follow-up study of 1052 suicide attempters. *Social Psychiatry and Psychiatric Epidemiology, 39*(2), 113–120.

Stack, S. (2004). Suicide risk among physicians: A multivariate analysis. *Archives of Suicide Research, 8*(3), 287–292.

Suominen, K., Isometsa, E., Suokas, J., Haukka, J., Achte, K., & Lonnqvist, J. (2004). Completed suicide after a suicide attempt: A 37-year follow-up study. *American Journal of Psychiatry, 161*(3), 562–563.

Tondo, L., Baldessarini, R. J., Hennen, J., Minnai, G. P., Salis, P., Scamonatti, L., et al. (1999). Suicide attempts in major affective disorder patients with comorbid substance use disorders. *Journal of Clinical Psychiatry, 60*(Suppl. 2), 63–69, 75–66, 113–116.

Tsai, S. Y., Kuo, C. J., Chen, C. C., & Lee, H. C. (2002). Risk factors for completed suicide in bipolar disorder. *Journal of Clinical Psychiatry, 63*(6), 469–476.

Valtonen, H., Suominen, K., Mantere, O., Leppamaki, S., Arvilommi, P., & Isometsa, E. T. (2005). Suicidal ideation and attempts in bipolar I and II disorders. *Journal of Clinical Psychiatry, 66*(11), 1456–1462.

Valtonen, H. M., Suominen, K., Mantere, O., et al. (2007). Suicidal behaviour during different phases of bipolar disorder. *Journal of Affective Disorders, 97*(1-3), 101–107.

Wilcox, H. C., Conner, K. R., & Caine, E. D. (2004). Association of alcohol and drug use disorders and completed suicide: An empirical review of cohort studies. *Drug Alcohol Depend, 76*(Suppl.), S11–19.

Zahl, D. L., & Hawton, K. (2004). Repetition of deliberate self-harm and subsequent suicide risk: Long-term follow-up study of 11,583 patients. *British Journal of Psychiatry, 185*, 70–75.

CHAPTER 11

Child and Early Adolescent Bipolar Disorder: An Emerging Diagnosis

Carolyn Colwell, LCSW

Introduction

Childhood bipolar disorder, in a little more than a decade, has gone from a somewhat obscure, infrequent diagnosis to the cover of *TIME* magazine and the subject of millions of dollars of research sponsored by the National Institutes of Health (Kluger, Song, & Simon, 2002; NIMH, 2006a).

Is it a diagnosis d'jour? Or is there a previously underrecognized group of children and early adolescents struck by some form of this serious mental illness? Or is it as rare as it's always been historically? Is bipolar disorder different in children than adults? Or is it sometimes confused with similar but different childhood conditions?

To date, the research on child-onset bipolar disorder has resulted in little consensus or clarity on these and other questions.

From the second century AD until now, the idea that children can have mania has swung back and forth from recognition to denial to acceptance. Aretaeus of Cappadocia wrote in 150 AD that "in those periods of life with which much heat and blood are associated, persons are most given to mania, namely those about puberty, young men, and such as possess general vigor." He is considered to have provided the first description of bipolar adolescents (Child and Adolescent Bipolar Foundation, 2006, p. 1). The historical record on bipolar disorder in adolescents and prepubertal children however, appears to have been quiet until the late eighteenth century, Glovinsky (2002) reports. In his 2002 work, Glovinsky quotes a medical text published in 1798 that tells the story of a male infant who was described in 1763 as "raving mad . . . he possessed so much strength in his legs and arms, that four women could, at times, with difficulty restrain him. These paroxysms either ended in indescribable laughter . . . or else he tore in anger everything near him, cloaths, linen, bed, furniture, even thread when he could get hold of it . . . he would get on the benches and table, and even attempt to climb the walls" (p. 7).

Almost 150 years later, Theodor Ziehen, a German psychiatrist, noted in his 1926 textbook that mania alternates with melancholia in children. He described, "pathological jocularity . . . accelerated . . . thinking . . . and increased psychomotoractivity" as three major symptoms. Ziehen (2004) also talked about how childhood mania is hard to diagnose but that "sudden onset" and a "pathological lack of fatigue and sleep" are keys to distinguishing it from normal childhood behavior (pp. 213, 216).

The godfather of modern psychiatry, Emil Kraepelin, a few years earlier validated the concept of mania in children. In his 1921 text, reprinted as *Manic Depressive Insanity and Paranoia,* Kraepelin reported mania was "rare" in children. He found that of 903 people studied only 0.4 percent had a first attack of manic depressive insanity, as bipolar disorder was called then, at the age of 10 or younger.

From the 1920s to 1960 in America the debate continued among those arguing for the existence of rare childhood onset, those who theorized that it didn't exist at all, others finding that 15 or so was the frequent age of onset among youths (Glovinsky, 2002).

In the United States, the idea that children can have manic depression or bipolar disorder didn't gain much recognition until the 1970s. Then some psychiatric pioneers described cases of childhood mania and depression, a few doctors created sets of diagnostic criteria, and some children began to receive the new miracle drug, lithium.

By 1980, childhood bipolar disorder was becoming accepted as a possible diagnosis. The breakthrough moment for pediatric bipolar disorder came in 1995. That year, *The Journal of the American Academy of Child and Adolescent Psychiatry* published more than a dozen articles on the illness, including a special section in its June issue.

A month later in the same journal, Janet Wozniak, MD, and her colleagues (1995) at Massachusetts General Hospital caused a stir. Their study of 262 consecutively referred children aged 12 and under, revealed that 16 percent of them met *DSM-III-R* criteria for mania and that 42 of those 43 children met criteria for ADHD. They concluded that further research was needed because the high comorbidity of ADHD raised the question of whether the children with mania had ADHD or bipolar disorder or both. But they said their findings showed that mania may be fairly common among children referred for psychiatric problems.

Suddenly things changed. Kids had the bipolar label too with an ever-increasing frequency. Among the wards of Illinois counties, 11 percent were diagnosed as bipolar in 1998 (Youngstrom, Findling, Youngstrom, & Calabrese, 2005).

In 2000, filling "the gaps in treatment knowledge" for child and adolescent bipolar disorder became part of NIMH's broader drive to "encourage" research on bipolar disorder, according to the then director (Hyman, 2000, p. 440).

That same year a group of experts and researchers sat down at an NIMH roundtable on prepubertal bipolar disorder and agreed "a diagnosis of bipolar disorder, using *DSM* criteria, is possible in prepubertal children" (p. 871). In other words, childhood bipolar exists and could be identified. Importantly, the experts also found that there is a significant group of children who don't meet full *DSM-IV* criteria for bipolar I or II but who are "severely impaired by symptoms of mood instability." This second, larger, more heterogeneous group with some bipolar symptoms was identified as having bipolar disorder not otherwise specified (BP NOS; NIMH, 2001, p. 871).

In 2006, Axelson and colleagues, whose research is part of the NIMH study "The Course and Outcome of Bipolar Youth (COBY)," called for renewed attention to this illness. "It is becoming more apparent that pediatric BP [Bipolar] is a significant public health problem" (p. 1139). COBY, as of this writing, is the largest study of pediatric bipolar disorder among clinically referred children from 7 to 17 (NIMH, 2006b).

The research on pediatric bipolar disorder so far hasn't provided the hoped for results regarding agreement on characteristics, diagnosis, prevalence, or other issues in part because of a variety of problems. These include small sample sizes; the use of different population samples with different age groups, settings, and time frames; different diagnostic criteria, definitions, and classifications; the predominant use of Caucasian subjects from higher socioeconomic status levels; and an insufficient number of longitudinal, prospective, double-blind, random, and/or placebo-controlled studies.

Data specifically on children 12 and under is limited to nonexistent because most studies do not segregate results for prepubertal children from adolescents. Generally, mania and bipolar disorders in older adolescents look similar to adult bipolar disorder, while children and early adolescents may have somewhat different presentations, according to some experts.

Epidemiology

The epidemiology of pediatric bipolar disorder is important to mental health professionals because it gives clinicians an estimate of how likely they are to encounter a case of bipolar disorder in their practices.

The *prevalence* of bipolar disorder in children 12 and under in the general population hasn't been determined. Estimates in clinical populations of children 12 and under and early adolescents remain controversial. Several factors add to the confusion, for example: Are researchers talking about *DSM-IV* bipolar I disorder (BP I)? Or are they using broader definitions of the bipolar spectrum, including bipolar II disorder (BP II), cyclothymia, and/or subsyndromal symptoms of mood instability? Are patients selected randomly from clinical intakes? Or are children clinically referred, after being diagnosed with or suspected of having a bipolar disorder?

On one hand, experts such as Gabrielle Carlson, MD, maintain that *DSM-IV* BP I in young children remains very rare. Carlson is professor of psychiatry and pediatrics at the State University of New York at Stony Brook's School of Medicine and director of child and adolescent psychiatry. "The younger the child, the rarer the condition" (Carlson, 2005b, p. 336). "However, there is no disputing the fact that a substantial number of preadolescent children have symptoms of mania, usually superimposed on a number of diverse developmental and psychiatric conditions" (Carlson, 2005b, p. 334).

Carlson (2005b) adds that, in part, "The bipolar controversy is about how far we can bend criteria that were originally developed from the experience of Emil Kraepelin (1921) . . . to fit children whose development may alter the meaning of those criteria" (p. 336). The lives of psychiatrically ill people often don't "fit neatly into the classes created for them" so that there has been a tendency to "broaden and bend criteria so they fit the people seen" or develop "the concept of a spectrum" or "define subtypes" (Carlson, 2005b, p. 335).

On the other hand, Joseph Biederman, MD (2006), argues that "pediatric mania may not be rare, but difficult to treat" (p. 279). Biederman is a Harvard professor of psychiatry and serves as Chief of Clinical Research in Pediatric Psychopharmacology at Massachusetts General Hospital, as well as Chief of its Adult ADHD Program.

Some experts point to the recent surveys in which some adults diagnosed with bipolar disorders retrospectively claim they experienced bipolar symptoms before the age of 13. These experts conclude those reports are a possible indication of a higher rate of bipolar conditions in children than expected.

Zoe A. Kyte and Carlson (2006), however, cast doubts about the reliability and validity of such retrospective reports. They don't give much weight to this recall, because of "the high rates of comorbidity in BPD, particularly in childhood" that may not be taken into account in making such judgments. In addition, the lack of co-informant confirmation "increases the likelihood of false negative life histories" (p. 1199).

Geography apparently makes a difference in how frequently childhood bipolar disorders may be diagnosed. In mid-2006, the mother of a 9-year-old Canadian girl who was previously diagnosed with bipolar disorder by her Calgary psychiatrist said she was told by workers at an Alberta hospital that her daughter didn't have bipolar disorder because that "condition is not possible in children" (Canadian Broadcasting Corporation, 2006, p. 1).

In England, a prominent psychiatric hospital over a recent 10-year period reportedly found no cases of mania or pediatric bipolar disorders in 2,500 children aged 10 and under (Soutullo et al., 2005).

In a Brazilian study, 7.2 percent of the 35 outpatients under 15 received a bipolar diagnosis according to modified *DSM-IV* criteria (Soutullo et al., 2005).

How frequently bipolar disorder occurs in American children and adolescents is an unresolved question. The 1996 Great Smokey Mountains epidemiological study of 4,500 North Carolina children who were 9, 11, and 13 years old found no BP I (Costello et al., 1996; Pavuluri, Birmaher, & Naylor, 2005). At this writing, there appears to be no epidemiological study of children 12 and under.

For adolescents, an epidemiological study of a random sample of 1,709 Oregon high school students from 14 to 18 years showed about a 1 percent lifetime incidence of bipolar disorders, including BP I but mostly BP II and cyclothymia. An additional 5.7 percent were categorized as "core positive" or a having a broadly defined BP NOS. These youths were severely impaired by subsyndromal symptoms (Lewinsohn, Klein, & Seeley, 1995, p. 457).

The incidence in smaller clinical populations is a different story, especially if the sample includes the loosely defined BP NOS and/or subsyndromal symptoms of mood instability. In these bipolar not otherwise specified and subsyndromal cases, there is a question whether these bipolar-like conditions correlate with adult bipolar disorder and even whether these bipolar-like illnesses will carry into adulthood as classic adult bipolar disorder. That is not to say, however, that clinical samples of early-onset *DSM-IV* BP I do not exist. For example, Craney and Geller (2003) found the mean age of onset for a first episode was 6.8 yrs (SD 3.4) in a clinical sample of 93 BP I prepubertal and early adolescent patients.

Where children and adolescents are combined in clinical samples, prevalence ranges from 2 to 15 percent, Birmaher and Axelson (2005) report. The numbers vary according to diagnostic criteria, methodology, and other factors. Birmaher and Axelson are professors of psychiatry at the University of Pittsburgh and investigators for the NIMH COBY study.

To prevent over and under diagnosis, E. A. Youngstrom recommends that mental health professionals look at base rates for early-onset bipolar disorder as a "starting probability" for a diagnosis. Youngstrom is an associate professor of psychology at the University of North Carolina at Chapel Hill. It's important to know "how often different diagnoses occur in a setting similar to where one works" (Youngstrom, & Duax, 2005, p. 713). Youngstrom suggests checking recently published research to find prevalence data for a similar sample to serve as benchmarks, taking into account geography, demographics, diagnostic methodology, and type of clinical setting. However, "bipolar disorder is probably rare in children before puberty," he cautions, concurring with Carlson and others (Youngstrom & Duax, 2005, p. 712).

The type of patients in a given practice also affects the likelihood of a patient presenting with child bipolar disorder. A practice that works with a large number of ADHD youngsters, as noted previously, has a higher chance of seeing a bipolar child or adolescent, since estimates of bipolar youth with ADHD reach as high as 60 to 90 percent (Biederman, 2006).

To put those percentages in context, NIMH in 2005 reported that half of all lifetime cases of mental illness begin by age 14, adding that when treatment is delayed the illness often becomes more severe and comorbid mental illnesses develop. The research also revealed that "mental disorders are quite common; 26 percent of the general population [of all ages] reported that they had symptoms sufficient for diagnosing a mental disorder during the past 12 months" (NIMH, 2005, p. 2).

If there has been a real increase in bipolar conditions in children at younger ages in recent decades rather than just an increase in diagnoses, there is one hypothesis that might explain it: genetic anticipation. That is the "idea that with every generation the disorder is showing up at an earlier age with increased severity," explains Kiki Chang, MD, whose team at Stanford University is researching this concept (Pederson, 2003). "Pediatric BP may become a more serious problem in the future, because of the age of onset of BP may be getting younger in more recent birth cohorts," adds the COBY phenomenology study (Axelson et al., 2006, p. 1139).

SES and ethnicity factors may be skewing the current epidemiology on child and adolescent bipolar disorder. Many of the child bipolar studies so far have been done on samples of children and adolescents of mostly Caucasian European heritage. Research populations usually are heavily drawn from the mid and higher SES levels where parents are most likely to bring their bipolar child to clinicians' attention.

It seems likely then, that significant population groups of American children may not be counted in attempts to quantify this illness.

Phenomenology

Childhood-onset bipolar disorder not only is less common than the adolescent or adult condition, it may look different as well. Manic symptoms may have a longer duration. They often are more severe. They often rapidly shift in a short space of time from manic to depressed to manic (Axelson et al., 2006; Birmaher et al., 2006; Geller, Tillman, & Craney, 2004).

Getting a picture of what prepubertal bipolar disorder looks like is made more difficult by the fact that some of the manic symptoms described in the *DSM-IV* are unlikely to be expressed in the same way in childhood. For example, few children engage in spending sprees or make foolish business investments or take off on wild trips to Paris. These are common examples of adult manic behavior that meet the *DSM-IV*'s criteria for "excessive involvement in pleasurable activities that have a high potential for painful consequences" (American Psychiatric Association, 1994, p. 332).

Consequently, Geller and other investigators have researched how child and early adolescent expression of the hallmark *DSM-IV* manic symptoms may be described. Their examples follow:

Elation: Measuring a normal level of happiness in children may be like deciding how much is too much ice cream for a birthday party. However, Craney and Geller (2003, p. 246) offer a measure: How appropriate is the elation to the context and how impairing is the elation to behavior? They compare a *normal* child being happy during a Disneyland vacation with a manic 7-year-old boy being suspended from school because of constant clowning and giggling in class and being asked to leave church because of similar behaviors. Almost 90 percent of Craney and Geller's PEA-BP (Prepubertal Early Adolescent) bipolar subjects reported elated moods in their 2003 study, as compared with 13.6 percent of those with ADHD and none from community controls (p. 246).

Grandiosity: Playing can be grandiose. A child may insist that he knows how to teach the class better than his elementary school teacher. If a child said that while playing school, it wouldn't be grandiose, Geller and Craney explain. If he or she actually told that to a teacher in class, it would be (Craney & Geller, 2003; Kupfer, Findling, Geller, & Ghaemi, 2002).

Carlson (2005b) offers that there also can be a correlation between age, developmental level, and grandiosity. For example, it might be a normal fantasy for a very young child to think she can fly, but not for a 7-year-old who should have better reality testing. Another thing to look for is that "children with learning disabilities were less likely than children without learning disabilities to understand that the impossible things portrayed in cartoons were truly impossible," Carlson adds (p. 339).

Other caveats regarding assessment are reports that (a) abused children may have more grandiose and unrealistic responses than children who have not been abused; and, (b) that hyperactive ADHD boys may inflate and "over estimate their competence in areas in which they were most impaired" (Carlson, 2005b, p. 339).

Also determining whether a child's statements are grandiose may take some additional probing. Another example Carlson (2005b, p. 338) gives is of children bragging about their prowess in sports, which parents may describe as grandiose, but adds that additional questioning about a child's view of his or her attributes may reveal "the child wishes he or she had those attributes but doesn't really *think* he or she had those attributes."

Super powers is another term for children's manic grandiosity used by Kowatch, Fristad, and others. These special powers are different from fantasy in that children persist in their self-delusion in spite of contrary external evidence (Kowatch & Fristad, 2006).

In their 1994 article, Geller, Fox, and Clark raise an interesting question about whether bullying in some cases might be "a developmental age-specific manifestation of grandiosity" (p. 467).

Irritability: This is the most controversial of the major mood symptoms ("elevated, expansive or irritable") in the first *DSM-IV* criteria for mania (American Psychiatric Association 1994, p. 332). Some regard irritability as the primary and only symptom needed to satisfy the first *DSM-IV* criteria for mania in children. For example, Biederman (2006) argues that manic children often are not elated or euphoric. Instead, he says they may suffer from severe affective storms with severe irritability and "prolonged and aggressive temper outbursts" (p. 280). The 2005 *Treatment Guidelines for Children and Adolescents with Bipolar Disorder: Child Psychiatric Workgroup on Bipolar Disorder* describe manic irritability as "extreme rages or meltdowns over trivial matters," giving the example of children's "1 to 2-hour tantrum after being asked to tie their shoes" (Kowatch et al., 2005, p. 216).

Ellen Leibenluft, MD, agrees irritability is a key characteristic of pediatric bipolar disorder. She and two colleagues write, "This irritability, which is characterized by extreme, often physical, responses to frustration and other negative emotional stimuli, is one of the most impairing symptoms of the illness. Although irritability occurs in adults with euphoric and mixed mania, both its prevalence and its severity appear to be more marked in juvenile, as compared with adult, BPD" (Leibenluft, Charney, & Pine, 2003, p. 1010). Leibenluft is chief of the affective disorders unit in the Pediatrics and Developmental Neuropsychology Branch at NIMH's Mood and Anxiety Disorders Program.

Others accept that irritability is frequently present but don't believe it's pathognomonic. For example, Barbara Geller, MD, has pointed out that 97.9 percent of bipolar children and early adolescents are irritable and elated at the same time and "the fact that irritability is a symptom of numerous disorders is a possible impediment in diagnosis" (Kupfer et al., 2002, p. 3). Geller, a professor of psychiatry at Washington University, has been a frequent investigator in pediatric bipolar research sponsored by NIMH.

Other conditions with symptoms of irritability include: major depressive disorder, dysthymic disorder, oppositional defiant disorder, anxiety disorders schizophrenia, ADHD, pervasive developmental disorder, posttraumatic stress disorder, and intermittent explosive disorder (Kowatch et al., 2005; Youngstrom et al., 2005).

Rage has increasingly been connected with childhood bipolar disorder, but often inappropriately, according to Carlson and Meyer (2006); rages "may occur in mania, but they are not synonymous with or exclusive to it." They remark that parents inaccurately may describe a child's "anger attack" as a "mood swing." In a survey of rages and tantrums among 318 consecutively referred families, Carlson and Meyer (2006) found that "bipolar spectrum disorders were diagnosed in less than 25 percent of either raging or tantruming children" (p. 958).

Highly aggressive behavior is considered by some to be the key characteristic of a child or adolescent bipolar condition and by others to be part of comorbid oppositional defiant or conduct disorder, or merely aggressive behavior. In a presentation to the 6th International Conference on Bipolar Disorder, Findling said about 2 percent of children "come into this world swinging," as they are born "profoundly aggressive." He added, "that's not bipolarity" (Findling, 2005). Findling is codirector for the Bipolar Disorder Research Center at Case Western Reserve University.

Flight of ideas/racing thoughts: Flight of ideas means "constantly shifting from one idea to another" through a rapid stream of words in which "ideas tend to be connected" (Sadock & Sadock, 2003, p. 309). Racing thoughts are "the speeding up of mental functioning" (Miklowitz, 2002, p. 23).

Craney and Geller (2003) report flight of ideas and racing thoughts are the third most common *DSM-IV* symptom of mania in children and early adolescents that does not overlap with ADHD criteria. Among 93 bipolar subjects with an average age of 10 years old, 71 percent experienced flight of ideas and/or racing thoughts as compared with only 9.9 percent of the matched ADHD subjects and 0 percent of the community controls. In a separate study of a similar age group diagnosed with bipolar disorder, Faedda and his coinvestigators found 78 percent had racing thoughts (Faedda, Baldessarini, Glovinsky, & Austin, 2004). The recent larger COBY study on phenomenology found 75.5 percent of BP I subjects with an average age of 12 experienced racing thoughts and 80 percent had flight of ideas (Axelson et al., 2006).

Nonbipolar children or early adolescents won't have flights of ideas or racing thoughts, while those with bipolar disorder will give specific descriptions of the phenomena, according to Craney and Geller. For example, children might make statements like: "My thoughts broke the sound barrier in my mind" or, "It's like an Energizer Bunny in my head" (Craney & Geller, 2003, p. 247).

Others, however, recommend that clinicians be alert to the possibility of confusing language disorders with pressured speech or the flight of ideas (Youngstrom et al., 2005b).

Decreased need for sleep: The emphasis is on *need.* A child with ADHD may have trouble sleeping but may wake up tired. A bipolar child may sleep little or not at all and have plenty of energy to bounce through the next day. Roughly 40 percent of prepubertal children and early adolescents with mania experience a decreased need for sleep, Craney and Geller (2003) reported in their phenomenology study of PEAs with BP I.

In bipolar adults, sleep deprivation has been associated with triggering mania and changes in sleep routines have been associated with mood swings (Rao, 2003).

A small recent study on child bipolar disorder and sleep suggests that sleep history and sleep studies may become an important part of making a pediatric bipolar diagnosis. This controlled, 2-year study of 438 5- to 7-year-olds demonstrated that the small number ($n = 13$, 2.97%) identified with childhood bipolar disorder had significant differences in sleep. The differences were: less sleep efficiency, percentage of time in REM sleep, total time in REM sleep, and more time in stage 3 sleep, as well as more nightmares, more morning headaches, and trouble falling asleep. The bipolar children showed a little more than six times the number of awakenings than their controls, but not at a statistically significant level. These results suggest "the possibility of a specific sleep-disorder pattern associated with PBD [pediatric bipolar disorder]" (Mehl et al., 2006, p. 196).

As a child and adolescent counterpart to the *DSM-IV*'s criteria for "excessive involvement in pleasurable activities that have a high potential for painful consequences" (American Psychiatric Association, 1994, p. 332), Geller and colleagues have identified some commonly found symptoms that represent similarly poor judgment at the child and early adolescent level. They are daredevil acts, silliness, uninhibitedly seeking people, and hypersexuality.

Hypersexuality was found in 43 percent of a child and early adolescent sample (average age 10.9) who met *DSM-IV* criteria for mania or hypomania with elation and/or grandiosity (Geller et al., 2000). The COBY phenomenological data for a sample with a slightly higher mean age of 12.7 found a similar percentage of its BP I sample (48.6%) experienced hypersexuality during the most severe lifetime episode (Axelson et al., 2006). Faedda and his coinvestigators found a slightly lower percentage (31.7%) of hypersexuality at evaluation in a pediatric bipolar sample with a mean age of 10.6 (Faedda et al., 2004).

Often hypersexuality in this age group is associated with sexual abuse, but in the study by Geller's group only 1 of the 93-member manic or hypomanic group had a history of being sexually abused. Geller and company report their data are based on multiple interviews of children, mothers, and others (Geller et al., 2000). Similarly, in Faedda's sample no history of sexual abuse was reported (Faedda et al., 2004).

What does hypersexuality look like in prepubertal children? Geller and Tillman describe it as "flirtatious or sexualized behaviors that are both age- and situation-inappropriate" (2004, p. 2).

Other phenomenon associated with prepubertal bipolar disorder include rapid cycling, mixed mania, psychosis, suicidality, hypersensitivity, poor social skills, and family conflict. (Family conflict is described in the discussion of treatment.)

Cycling and Mixed Mania: The course of BP I with an onset before age 13 *typically* involves multiple mood swings in 1 day. In those cases, there appears to be a short, or almost no, return to baseline along with chronic mood instability (Kowatch & Fristad, 2006, p. 221).

Geller and colleagues, in their four-year prospective outcome study of 86 prepubertal children and early adolescents meeting *DSM-IV* criteria for BP I, found high rates of cycling and mixed mania. Over the course of the study, 88.4 percent experienced mania mixed with major depression, dysthymia, or minor depression. Rapid cycling occurred in 88.4 percent of these cases, the majority of which experienced multiple daily mood changes (77.9%). The sample of boys and girls had a mean age at intake of 10.8 years plus or minus 2.7 years (Geller, Tillman, Craney, & Bolhofner, 2004, p. 462).

In a slightly older sample, followed for a shorter period, COBY data show a slightly lower rate of mixed/rapid cycling. Its 2-year-longitudinal data indicates that mixed/rapid-cycling fluctuations on a weekly basis affected 28.9 percent of the child/adolescent subjects with BP I, as compared with 5.9 percent of BP I adult subjects. The age range for the COBY child adolescent subjects ranged from 7 to 17 with a mean age of 13 (Birmaher et al., 2006).

Conceptualizing how much more frequently children and adolescents with BP I have cycling or mixed mania than adults depends upon the definitions used. According to the *DSM-IV* (which does not include separate criteria for bipolar spectrum children and adolescents) "at least four episodes of a mood disturbance in the last 12 months" is the definition of rapid cycling (American Psychiatric Association, 1994).

A child or early adolescent with BP I might experience that many mood swings in an hour or a day, therefore, Geller and other experts describe these youngsters as having ultra-rapid cycling or ultradian cycling.

To Geller and Tillman an episode refers "to the entire length of illness." Cycling "refers to mood changes during an episode." Ultrarapid cycling involves mood changes "every few days." Ultradian cycling means mood changes "that occur at least once daily" (Geller et al., 2004, p. 461).

Mixed mania or mixed episodes are defined by the *DSM-IV* as the experience of having both manic and major depressive symptoms "nearly every day" over a period of at least one week (American Psychiatric Association, 1994, p. 335). Given many children's ultradian cycling, it appears that the concept of cycling and mixed mania may overlap. Geller points out that in one study she and her investigators found a mean of 3 episodes a day occurred during ultradian cycling. She adds that "at one point a child may appear to be elated, bouncy, hyperenergetic, and silly and the next moment, without any observable reason, the same child will have marked psychomotor retardation and serious suicidality" (Kupfer et al., 2002, p. 3).

The frequent mixed mania and cycling contribute to the severity of symptoms that occur in children and adolescents with BP I.

Psychosis: Being out of touch with reality can occur with bipolar disorder. Youngsters with the illness sometimes may sound psychotic without really crossing that threshold, according to Findling and colleagues (Findling, Kowatch, & Post, 2003). For example, a child with bipolar disorder might occasionally think he or she hears voices or sees strange shadows at night, rather than having *prominent* hallucinations or delusions (Findling et al., 2003).

If a child or adolescent has a true psychotic episode, it most likely will be when other bipolar symptoms are most severe and it will be mood congruent. In other words, while manic, a youngster might think he or she has special powers or have delusions of grandeur. Or, while depressed, he or she might have delusions of worthlessness or hear derogatory auditory hallucinations, according to Findling and colleagues.

If these psychotic thoughts are just a feature of the bipolar disorder, they will occur during periods of disturbed moods. If a patient experiences them also during euthymic or relatively stable periods, then he or she may have schizoaffective disorder, a combination of mood disorders and schizophrenia (Findling et al., 2003).

According to COBY data, 44.1 percent of children and adolescents from 7 to 17 years old with BP I have psychotic symptoms, compared with only 21.1 with BP II, and 21.7 with BP NOS (Birmaher et al., 2006).

Suicidality: Survival is another important aspect of the longitudinal course of pediatric bipolar disorder. Children and adolescents with bipolar disorder are at risk for suicidal behavior. Recent results of a COBY study of 405 mostly Caucasian youths from ages 7 to 17 show that 32 percent had made at least one suicide attempt in their lifetimes (Goldstein et al., 2005).

No suicide attempt in this sample population was successful as of September 2005, when the study was submitted for publication.

Goldstein and her coinvestigators (2005) reported that "findings from the present study indicate that pediatric bipolar patients at highest risk for suicide attempt include those who are older, with a lifetime history of mixed episodes, psychotic features, and BP-I, co-morbid substance use, panic disorder, non-suicidal self-injurious behavior, family history of suicide attempt, history of hospitalization, and history of physical and/or sexual abuse" (p. 533).

In adult populations, a high risk of suicidality has been reported for patients with BP II. The investigators suggest that was not true in this study perhaps because of the small percentage of BP II subjects (7%) or because BP II "may be an unstable diagnostic category" for children and adolescents as "20 percent go on to develop BP-I" (Goldstein et al., 2005, p. 532).

There was no significant relationship between attempts and conduct disorder or oppositional defiant disorder, and attempters "were significantly less likely" to have a lifetime diagnosis of ADHD (Goldstein et al., 2005, p. 530). Additionally, there was no statistically significant connection in this study between a family history of suicide completion or attempts, and pediatric attempters.

The mean age of attempters was 13.7, plus or minus 3.1 years. The mean age of nonattempters was 12.3 plus or minus 3.1. The study reported that "younger patients . . . were less likely to have attempted suicide than older adolescents" probably because of "a complex interaction of developmental, psychological and family factors" (Goldstein et al., 2005, p. 532).

Data on successful suicide attempts among American children with bipolar disorder who are 12 and under is not available at the time of this writing.

Poor social skills seem to be another phenomenon among children and early adolescents with bipolar disorders. No or few friends as well as poor psychosocial skills were found in sample population of 93 children and early adolescents 7 to 16 years old with *DSM-IV* bipolar disorder with and without comorbid ADHD (Geller et al., 2000).

A seeming lack of ability to relate well to others has new scientific grounding.

Recent research shows a neurological basis for early adolescents having trouble accurately reading the emotions in human faces. According to the small NIMH study, cognitive misperceptions caused these youths to interpret the neutral faces as more hostile and to have more fearful emotional responses to them than did controls. The study is limited because it could not control for medication in the 22 mostly BP I subjects with a mean age of 14.2. Nor did the researchers ascertain the possible involvement of comorbid disorders. However, this study may point the way to an eventual greater understanding of the difficulties bipolar youth endure (Rich & Vinton, 2006).

Another NIMH study of 40 outpatients diagnosed primarily with *DSM-IV* BP I and a mean age of 12.9 showed similar deficits in accurately recognizing facial emotions in adults and children. In addition, they "performed more poorly" than controls in the "formulation of socially appropriate responses to interpersonal situations" (McClure et al., 2005, p. 1649).

Switching: Pediatric bipolar may be the outcome of an evolutionary course that starts at various developmental stages. For example, childhood unipolar depression may become pediatric bipolar disorder. Or a child may start out diagnosed with attention deficit hyperactivity disorder (ADHD), obsessive-compulsive disorder (OCD), or an anxiety disorder and slowly show the signs of bipolar disorder. In a way ADHD, OCD, or anxiety some day may be looked at as antecedents of a bipolar condition, while now they are only conditions comorbid to bipolar disorder.

Some experts report that a first episode of pediatric bipolar disorder may be depressive, although the condition may not be recognized until the child has a manic episode (Kupfer et al., 2002).

Geller found that 50 percent of prepubertal subjects with major depression, who were followed for 10 years, switched to bipolar disorder. One prominent factor related to the switching was a parent or grandparent with bipolar disorder. "Clinicians need to look carefully at the young, depressed patient who has a bipolar family history to assess for manifestations of mania that can occur in children," she warns (Kupfer et al., 2002 p. 5).

NIMH (2000) describes the symptoms of depression that occur during pediatric bipolar disorder as: persistent sadness or irritability, anhedonia, changes in appetite or weight, difficulties sleeping, psychomotor agitation or retardation, low energy, problems with concentration, and repeated thoughts about death or dying.

Within childhood bipolar disorder there also may be a progression from a milder to a more severe form of the illness. For example, recent COBY data revealed that 25 percent of those initially classified as BP NOS switched to BP I or BP II during the follow-up period (Birmaher et al., 2006).

Comorbid Conditions

Childhood bipolar disorder seldom occurs by itself. Attention deficit, anxiety, conduct, oppositional defiant, or obsessive-compulsive disorders are frequent companions.

"[I]n the real world, children don't simply have bipolar disorder, they have multiple comorbidities," Gabrielle A. Carlson, MD, one of the leading researchers of child and adolescent bipolar disorder, told *Psychiatric News* (Rosack, 2005, p. 3).

These conditions that can occur at the same time but don't have the same cause not only cloud diagnosis, but also complicate treatment and increase impairment. The authors of the 2005 *Treatment Guidelines* note that "comorbid conditions worsen the prognosis of BPD" (Kowatch et al., 2005, p. 226).

Attention deficit disorder is the most frequent comorbid condition, often presenting or being identified first. Chang and colleagues even suggest that "ADHD in children with strong family histories of BD [bipolar disorder] may be the first sign of a developing BD . . . a familial type of early-onset BD" (Chang, Steiner, & Ketter, 2003, p. 27f). Biederman (2006) also questions whether in some situations child mania may represent "a distinct subtype of either bipolar disorder or ADHD" (p. 282).

ADHD occurs more frequently with child rather than adolescent or adult onset bipolar disorder. Estimates of the number of bipolar children with ADHD run as high as 60 to 90 percent (Biederman, 2006). According to COBY data, there is a higher occurrence of ADHD in BP I and BP NOS than in BP II (Birmaher et al., 2006). Conversely, samples of children diagnosed with ADHD have been reported to have a low incidence of bipolar disorder (Post et al., 2004).

The potential coexistence of ADHD and bipolar disorder creates confusion, especially when deciding whether ADHD is comorbid or a differential diagnosis. ADHD itself also occurs with multiple comorbid disorders. The combination of ADHD and bipolar disorder can be more severe than either condition by itself. Biederman and others suggest that the simplest approach is to look at ADHD and bipolar symptoms that overlap and don't overlap.

Overlaps for ADHD: poor concentration, impulsivity, being talkative, psychomotor agitation, hyperactivity, and distraction.

Nonoverlaps for ADHD: elation, grandiosity, decreased *need* for sleep, hypersexuality, flight of ideas, suicidal ideation, hallucinations, extreme long-lasting tantrums (Biederman, 2006; Kowatch et al., 2005; Kupfer et al., 2002; Post et al., 2004).

Anxiety disorders are other conditions commonly comorbid with child and adolescent bipolar disorder. They also are often comorbid with ADHD. Rates of comorbid anxiety disorders in bipolar children and adolescents have been reported in a small number of studies, ranging from about 23 to 78 percent, depending upon types of bipolar conditions, diagnostic criteria, and ages. Among the most common co-occurring anxiety disorders reported are generalized anxiety disorder and separation anxiety disorder, OCD, specific phobias and panic disorder (Dickstein et al., 2005; Masi et al., 2001; Wagner, 2006).

A 17.5 month-year study by Masi and colleagues of 43 child and adolescent outpatients with *DSM-IV* BP I or II revealed that 76.5 percent had a comorbid anxiety disorder with OCD the most prevalent (44.2%; Masi et al., 2001). What may be most significant about comorbid anxiety disorders is that "the age at onset tends to precede the age at onset for bipolar disorder in children" (Wagner, 2006, p. 19).

Researchers have reported substantial rates of oppositional defiant disorder and smaller rates of conduct disorder among bipolar youths (Axelson et al., 2006; Tillman et al., 2005).

Classification, Assessment, and Diagnosis

How to classify child and early adolescent bipolar disorder has been at the nub of much of the controversy. So far the possibilities boil down to:

- *DSM-IV* criteria unmodified. The *DSM-IV* calls for three categories: bipolar I (mania and depression with mania lasting at least 1 week), bipolar II (hypomania and depression with the hypomanic episode lasting at least 4 days), and bipolar not otherwise specified (bipolar-type symptoms that don't meet full criteria for bipolar I or II; American Psychiatric Association, 1994).
- *DSM-IV* criteria modified in terms of the required duration of manic and hypomanic symptoms. Other modifications include using irritability alone as the required symptom for mania instead of using it along with elation and/or grandiosity.
- Consideration of a bipolar spectrum that may include bipolar I, bipolar II, bipolar not otherwise specified, cyclothymia, and a cyclothymic temperament.
- Consideration of alternate categories such as *cyclotaxia* or severe emotional dysregulation.
- Making a distinction between a bipolar condition and what might be considered multiple complex developmental disorder or multidimensionally impaired syndrome, *bad* ADHD, or aggressive disorders.

Cyclotaxia is a term Findling, Calabrese, Youngstrom, and colleagues have applied to a subsyndromal condition found in children and adolescents without BP I or II but whose parents or parent have bipolar disorder. Cyclotaxia is characterized by elevated moods accompanied by irritability and "rapid mood fluctuations" (Findling et al., 2005, p. 623).

NIMH recently used Emotional Dysregulation as a research criteria to describe the children and adolescents who don't meet narrow *DSM-IV* criteria but who have "chronic, nonepisodic irritability and hyperarousal" without elation or grandiosity and an abnormal mood of sadness or anger (Dickstein et al., 2005, p. 536). Carlson suggests that emotional dysregulation is at the heart of the problems experienced by youth with symptoms that meet modified bipolar criteria for mania. But she suggests that these symptoms might be "more accurately" associated with developmental delays and/or other risk factors (Carlson & Meyer, 2006, p. 959).

Soutullo and colleagues (2005) note that in Europe some children are diagnosed as having severe ADHD with "pronounced emotional dysregulation or ADHD with comorbid language disorders, perceptual difficulties or development coordination disorder that can be confused with mania because they are associated with irritability and severe impairment."

Bipolar I (58%) was the most common classification, followed by BP NOS (35%), followed by BP II (7%) for children and adolescents age 7 to 17, according to recent COBY data using *DSM-IV* criteria. The sample included 438 in- and outpatients at three university psychiatric centers. The mean age of onset was 9.0 (±4.1) for BP I, 11.0 (±3.4) for BP II, and 8.4 (±3.5) for BP NOS (Birmaher et al., 2006).

At this writing, there is no widely accepted definition of BP NOS in children and early adolescents. The 2000 Pediatric Bipolar Roundtable sponsored by NIMH (2001) suggested that "severely impaired children with mood disturbances who do not meet full criteria for BP-I or BP-II" who are "irritable and aggressive" be classified under the "working diagnosis" of BP NOS (p. 872). So far, the ongoing NIMH roundtables have not published a refinement of the 2000 Roundtable's working diagnosis.

The whole question of how to define BP NOS becomes important in terms of whether bipolar illness in children and adolescents will be looked at in narrow *DSM-IV* or broad bipolar spectrum terms.

The recent COBY data on conversion (see phenomenology section) from a less severe form of the illness to a more severe form of the illness supports the argument for looking at the pediatric illness as a bipolar spectrum, according to the COBY investigators.

The impact of childhood bipolar disorder adds to the argument for a broader definition. "The enduring and rapid changeability of symptoms in children and adolescents from very early in life and at crucial stages of their lives deprives them of the opportunity for normal emotional, cognitive and social development" (Birmaher et al., 2006, p. 182). Therefore, early identification and treatment of "BP spectrum disorders in children and adolescents" is important to reduce the "serious psychosocial morbidity that usually accompanies this illness" (Birmaher et al., 2006, p, 182). Yet if child and early adolescent BP NOS is defined too broadly it will include too many cases that are not related to the classic mania and depression found in adults. Carlson suggests that there is a heterogeneous juvenile group "with differing biological and environmental underpinnings, none of which are well understood. Based on a review of recent findings . . . although some of these children may ultimately merit a diagnosis of 'classic' bipolar illness, others may be on a pathway to chronic depression, . . . antisocial personality with mood symptoms . . . , and/or borderline personality disorder . . ." (Carlson & Meyer, 2006, p. 946).

There are several tools clinicians can use to identify and assess bipolar disorder in children and early adolescents.

Diagnostic checklists and screening instruments represent an efficient way to evaluate quickly whether symptoms need a more intensive review regarding possible bipolar diagnosis.

The widely used Achenbach Child Behavior Checklist (CBCL, 1991 and 2001) represents a way to take a quick snapshot of a child's functioning and highlight the possibility of a bipolar disorder. Elevated externalizing scores on the parent informant CBCL raise a flag regarding possible bipolar and other disorders. Even more strongly, low scores decrease the odds of a bipolar disorder. For a child 5 to 10 years old, a low T score would be less than 58, and for a child 11 to 17 it would be less than 54. A very high score would be 82 or more or 81 or more, respectively (Youngstrom et al., 2004).

Youngstrom suggests that the teacher informant version of the CBCL, the TRF, may not be useful because either a child doesn't display externalizing behavior in school or because he believes there is an inclination by teachers to attribute such behaviors to ADHD (Youngstrom & Youngstrom, 2005). However, Carlson (2005b) adds that the full Achenbach parent CBCL and teacher TRF can flag possible comorbidities, but that the CBCL and TRF should not be used for differential diagnosis.

Other parent rating scales that are more specific for mania can be used in place of the CBCL or as a follow-up to the CBCL where there are high externalizing scores. These include parent versions of the Young Mania Scale, the Child Mania Rating Scale, and the Parent General Behavior Inventory.

None of these screeners by themselves should be the basis for a bipolar diagnosis.

Interviews of both parents *and* children are key to assessment. Other adult informants who know the child well also can help illuminate the child's condition.

Parent interviews can help ascertain the essential spontaneous shift from a baseline behavior of the normal, usual self to manic and depressive behavior that is required to make a bipolar diagnosis. It is helpful to find out what alerted parents to the developing problem and how the child behaves at home, at school, and at play with peers. What is the child's current functioning and what was his or her worst and what was his or her best?

In the process of eliciting the child's history from conception to present day, including traumatic events, developing a timeline can be useful. That timeline should indicate onset and offset and duration of bipolar symptoms. It also should include BAMO (behavior, anxiety, mood, and other symptoms), according to the 2005 *Treatment Guidelines*.

Using the K-SADS-MRS (K-SADS Mania Rating Scale) is a way of adding some structure to the parent interview. A copy of the scale with advice on how to use it is in Appendix I of Kowatch and DelBello's 2006 article, "Pediatric Bipolar Disorder: Emerging Diagnostic and Treatment Approaches."

Child interviews may reveal information of which parents are unaware. In addition, getting the child's viewpoint can act as a check on parents' possible misinterpretations of behaviors, Geller suggests. She uses the example of a parent who thought a child had OCD because she seemed obsessed with making paper flowers constantly. It turned out that the girl wanted to sell paper flowers at school as a business, which was a child's version of a manic adult's decision to start a business that has little chance of success (Kupfer et al., 2002).

Findling argues that children find ways to tell a clinician what's wrong even though the child may not be upset about it. He describes the example of an irritable, manic 6-year-old who couldn't sit still because she said she feels like a bumblebee that is so angry it has to buzz around the room and sting people (Kupfer et al., 2002).

The benefit to interviewing parents first, according to Carlson, is that the child might have a different answer to a question. She then double checks whether the child's answer remains the same after being told what the parents said. Carlson then brings them all into the interview room to discuss the discrepancies (Carlson, 2005a).

Family histories of what sound like possible bipolar conditions can be another alert to clinicians to dig deeper.

A three-generation genogram is a tool that can not only record a mental health family tree but also can be used to ask parents questions, such as what were these relatives like and what was it like to grow up in that family, at school, and with friends. The combination may reveal psychiatric symptoms and possible disorders (Kowatch et al., 2005).

Since in past generations it was even more common for bipolar disorder to be unrecognized, it's important to go beyond questions regarding bipolar diagnoses. Geller suggests asking parents and families *way-of-life* questions. Examples of what she would ask are: "Has anyone in the family had multiple marriages before age 40?" "Has anyone started several different businesses without the knowledge or financial means to make them successful?" "Is anyone the life of the party needing little sleep?" (Kupfer et al., 2002, p. 5).

Carlson (2005a) proposes that "descriptions of behavior are often more informative than a diagnosis given by an unknown source" (p. 6). This approach helps avoid the misunderstanding created when a relative may have been given a bipolar diagnosis instead of a diagnosis with a poorer prognosis such as schizophrenia or antisocial personality disorder.

On the other hand, a relative may have been misdiagnosed as having schizophrenia when in reality he or she was experiencing the psychotic symptoms that sometimes can be part of bipolar disorder (Kupfer et al., 2002).

It also is important to look for descriptions of unipolar depression and its symptoms in family histories for two reasons:

1. The COBY phenomenology study found bipolar children were more often the offspring of depressed parents than bipolar parents (Axelson et al., 2006).

2. There is a possibility that bipolar disorder, particularly BP II, has been misdiagnosed as unipolar depression or its symptoms have been misinterpreted by family members as unipolar depression.

The lack of a family history, because of one of the previous factors does not rule out bipolar disorder. Nor does a family history of bipolar disorder clinch the diagnosis. As Carlson (2005b) warns, "At what point does one base treatment on family history rather than presenting symptoms?"

Gathering additional background in the form of school and medical records, including EEGs and neurological workups, as well as psychological and language testing can provide important context for evaluation. Some children with bipolar disorder and/or ADHD have learning disabilities, language problems, developmental disorders, or sleep apnea (Carlson, 2005a).

Diagnostic aids: Acronyms can help clinicians organize the information gathered previously and put it together with diagnostic criteria and the manic symptoms described in the phenomenology section in order to begin formulating a diagnosis. The two mnemonics recommended here are HIPERS and FIND. Carlson (2005a) suggests HIPERS:

H is for hyperactivity and high energy in goal-oriented and pleasure-seeking behavior.

I is for irritability, which usually for children is a short fuse or low boiling point.

P is for psychosis (grandiosity), which is most diagnostically useful when children know what reality is and then lose it during mania.

E is for elated mood, which is sometimes the most difficult to discern given the need to differentiate between euphoria or expansiveness and a normal mood or happiness.

R is for rapid speech, racing thoughts, and flights of ideas, can occur in other disorders.

S is for sleep need reduced.

FIND was first suggested by Mary A. Fristad, director of research and psychological services for Child and Adolescent Psychiatry at Ohio State University's College of Medicine, and modified by Kowatch and DelBello (Kowatch, 2006). They suggest that one way of looking at manic symptoms may be in terms of:

*F*requency: how often during a week do the symptoms occur?

*I*ntensity: does the severity of symptoms cause extreme disturbance in one domain or moderate dysfunction in two or more domains of functioning?

*N*umber: what is the total number of *DSM-IV* manic symptoms?

*D*uration: on a daily basis what is the average length of time a patient is manic or hypomanic?

FIND then can define a "clinically useful" but unvalidated threshold of severity that can be used to determine the presence of manic symptoms. It also is important to evaluate the context in which the symptoms occur in order to differentiate between normal behavior and, for example, pathological elation (Kowatch et al., 2005, p. 215). "Changes in mood functioning especially spontaneous mood swings that are unusual in their frequency intensity, or duration, heighten confidence in bipolar diagnosis" (Youngstrom et al., 2005, p. 438).

The 2005 *Treatment Guidelines* recommend that parents keep a log of the child's mood, energy, sleep, and unusual behavior for a 2-week period prior to their initial interview with clinicians.

Other diagnostic considerations: A rush to judgment may be a mistake in making a diagnosis of child or early adolescent bipolar disorder. Intakes often require more than one session and often, at most, bipolar disorder only may be ruled out at the end of intake. Youngstrom recommends "extending the window of assessment" in order to view mood functioning over a period of time, noting that "diagnoses are assembled out of combinations of mood episodes" (Youngstrom & Youngstrom, 2005, p. 238).

Mood charts can also play a part in the on-going assessment of bipolar disorders in children and early adolescents. They can help identify patterns of mood swings; severity and duration of depression and elation and sleep deprivation; and presence of comorbid symptoms such as anxiety. Several different models of life and mood charts are available online. Nonmedical clinicians can help families use them to track their children's symptoms and make more accurate reports to other treating professionals

Differential and comorbid diagnoses: Making differential diagnoses and being careful not to make a bipolar diagnosis based on symptoms of a comorbid condition are other factors that complicate assessment.

Some symptoms can turn out to represent conditions that many might not suspect could look like bipolar disorder. For example, the silliness or psychosocial problems found in childhood bipolar illness can send a clinician down the wrong track when these symptoms actually may represent Asperger or another pervasive developmental disorder. Reactive attachment disorder also can be confused with bipolar symptoms.

The obvious differential diagnosis is between unipolar depression and bipolar depression. Even if the final determination is unipolar depression, over time it's important to keep an eye out for the possible development of bipolar symptoms.

To make the careful differentiation between bipolar disorder and comorbid conditions, the 2005 *Treatment Guidelines* recommend assessing possibly comorbid illnesses individually. By stabilizing the mood first, as the *Guidelines* suggest, clinicians can determine if a condition is truly comorbid or somehow miscon-strued, Carlson explains. Truly comorbid conditions "only rarely . . . disappear when manic symptoms resolve" (Carlson, 2005a, p. 3).

The other side of that coin is that symptoms that have been attributed to mania may disappear when comorbidities are dealt with. "Much of what has been attributed to mania disappears when comorbidities are matched" (Carlson, 2005b, p. 337f).

Treatment

"Clinicians who treat children with bipolar disorder are in the unenviable posi-tion of having to make consequential decisions about clinical care without much data to inform them," says NIMH's Leibenluft (2006, p. 1129). The benefits of the flood of research about pediatric bipolar disorder over the last decade has been limited by conflicting definitions of bipolar classifications and different views of developmental considerations. There also is the question of whether some children brought into a large BP NOS tent aren't bipolar at all. Do they either have another condition altogether or prodromal symptoms that may lead to a later onset?

Determining which medications are effective for pediatric bipolar conditions has been hard because of the lack of random, double-blind, placebo-controlled studies. "Parents and clinicians can only be appalled by the contrast between the ample evidence documenting the severity of pediatric bipolar disorder and the paucity of controlled trials to guide its treatment," Leibenluft added (2006, p. 1129). But she noted that including children in a placebo-controlled trial might raise ethical issues.

Providers of psychosocial interventions until recently haven't had prime seat-ing at the case conference table in pediatric bipolar cases. The role of psychosocial interventions has not been supported by much research to provide empirical evidence of their effectiveness. That is changing as studies are now underway.

What follows is a short synthesis of clinical wisdom and research findings so far that provide some light in the dark alley of the bipolar world.

Medication

When there is an accurate diagnosis of child bipolar disorder, medication is just as essential for children as it is for bipolar adults. As Kowatch and Fristad (2006) put it, "Appropriate medication management is, no doubt, the *sine qua non* of successful intervention for children with bipolar disorders" (p. 224f). Successfully medicating pediatric bipolar disorder, however, is complicated by a number of different factors:

- Children do not necessarily react to the same medications the same way adults do.

- Only one medication, lithium, has been recommended by the U.S. Food and Drug Administration (FDA) for juvenile bipolar disorder, and then only for adolescents 13 and up. No medication has received an FDA recommendation for preadolescent bipolar disorder.

- There is a shortage of well-trained, experienced, and up-to-date practitioners who have mastered the art of medicating children with bipolar conditions.

There often is a significant time lag between when children experience the first symptoms of the bipolar spectrum and when they are diagnosed. In the interim, they may be misdiagnosed or diagnosed with a comorbid condition and receive medications that may precipitate or exacerbate bipolar symptoms. For example, an estimated 60 to 90 percent of children with bipolar disorder also have ADHD. Some experts contend that unless a child's mood is stabilized first stimulant medications for ADHD may ignite or worsen childhood mania. Others disagree and argue that SSRIs are the real culprits which kindle mania (Carlson, 2003).

Wozniak, Biederman, and Richards warned in 2001 that "in youth with bipolar disorder and comorbid ADHD, the sequence of treatments is critical: bipolar symptoms should be treated first and ADHD second" because of the need to have the protective properties of medications that stabilize mood before adding a stimulant (Biederman, 2006, p. 292). Consequently, some practitioners talk about an ABC approach to comorbid ADHD and bipolar disorder, where A indicates a mood stabilizer, B indicates SGA, and C indicates a stimulant.

While there has been some consensus on protocols (algorithms) for medicating BP I, there are no similar formal recommendations on what medications to use for childhood BP II or NOS. The two BP I algorithms published so far were put together in 2004 by a University of Illinois at Chicago group (Pavuluri, Henry, et al., 2004) and in 2005 by the working group of experts who wrote the *2005 Treatment Guidelines* (Kowatch et al., 2005). Medications in addition to lithium mentioned in these algorithms include Depakote, Tegretol, and second-generation antipsychotics, such as Risperdol, Zyprexa, and Seroquel.

Some research shows that monotherapy sometimes is not as effective in children as combination medication (Kowatch, 2006; Pavuluri, 2005). Finding the most beneficial medication regimen for a specific child sometimes can be like perfecting a sophisticated recipe. It calls for first A or B and if that doesn't work then C and then if that fails try A + B or A + C or B + C or E, F, or G, or in some combination with the previous A, B, and C. Moreover, all these changes take time.

For a parent praying for immediate results, such treatment plans may not sound very scientific. Consequently, that's why it's helpful for nonmedical members of a treatment team to be knowledgeable about medication. They can help parents monitor efficacy and side effects, encourage parents to contact the prescribing psychiatrist when important changes are occurring, and support the parents' hope that there is a right combination for their child.

While professionals strive for more pinpoint diagnoses, more effective medications, and stronger psychosocial supports, one key aspect of treatment remains in the hands of parents. That is adherence to the medication regimen. "[P]rescribing the right medicine is not enough," say Kowatch and Fristad (2006a, p. 225). They report studies that show only about 50 percent of children with all kinds of chronic health conditions adhere to treatment recommendations.

Kowatch and Fristad (2006) suggest that programs are needed to "teach children and their parents the components for treatment and the importance of medication adherence" (p. 225). "Adherence is especially important for children taking lithium," Findling reminds us, and "missing even a dose or two of lithium can be associated with the relapse of the illness" (Kupfer et al., 2002, p. 13).

Mood charts can aid children and parents in matching types, dosages, and administration times of medication with symptoms and side effects. When a patient sees a note about worse symptoms right next to a blank for not taken medication on that same day, it reinforces medication compliance. Clear plastic pillboxes can be a visual reminder of whether medication has been taken or not.

Psychosocial

Psychosocial treatment has gained new respect after being on the back streets of the bipolar world in earlier decades. All patients at Stanford University's Pediatric Bipolar Disorders Program receive both medication and psychotherapy, according to the program's director, Kiki Chang, MD. Medication alone is not enough, Chang adds (personal communication, August 31, 2006). Geller says that psychosocial treatment is "crucial" since "manic children have greater impairments in multiple areas" (Kupfer et al., 2002, p. 14).

Esposito-Smythers and colleagues (2006) point out that bipolar youths with comorbid conditions (and that may represent up to 80 percent of all bipolar youths) "may require more intensive treatment and exhibit a longer period from treatment onset to clinical remission" (p. 962).

The 2005 *Treatment Guidelines* recommend psychosocial treatment be considered for comorbid disorders because psychosocial therapy doesn't cause "mood dysregulation" and "can be used without risk of aggravating bipolar symptoms" (Kowatch et al., 2005, p. 227).

Again, it is helpful to work with psychologists, social workers, and other clinicians who are familiar with child bipolar disorder.

Psychoeducation

Parent training may be especially important where children and early adolescents have comorbid externalizing disorders because of the risk for "high family conflict and for low family cohesion" (Esposito-Smythers et al., 2006, p. 62).

Parents need education about bipolar disorder in childhood and support while clinicians are working with them to stabilize their child's mood and behavior.

Views of a child's bipolar condition may be skewed by parents' experience with adult relatives who were lucky enough to have quick results from the proper medications. Their bipolar children may be highly symptomatic for much longer than parents expect. Finding the right medication or medications may take multiple tries to get the right combination, Geller says (Kupfer et al., 2002).

In addition, childhood bipolar disorder is much more chronic and sometimes more severe than in adulthood. "The best that can be done for their child may be to make his or her highs less high, lows less low, and cycles less frequent. Healthy functioning, although the goal of treatment, may not be an immediate or easily gained outcome," Geller adds (Kupfer et al., 2002, p. 6).

As individuals, parents may wrestle with feelings of guilt about passing on the bipolar genes. Geller suggests, "These parents need to be given the opportunity to work through their guilt and to learn that people are not responsible for their genes" (Kupfer et al., 2002, p. 6). Gellar adds that grief counseling might also be part of family therapy if parents haven't mourned the loss of their hopes for a healthy child and to help them cope with a child with a possibly life-long illness.

Mood hygiene, often a major part of adult treatment, is rarely mentioned in articles about child bipolar disorder, but it may be important for children too. Parents are the ones in charge of mood hygiene for bipolar children. Clinicians should encourage parents whenever possible to:

- Prevent their children from being overstimulated for too long.
- Realize family and marital conflict or dramatic confrontations can be too stimulating.
- Establish a consistent bedtime and bedtime routine that helps a child wind down and have a child get sufficient sleep.
- Make sure they are adhering to their children's medication regimens.
- Talk to child and early adolescents about substance abuse and the risk it represents.
- Use mood charts to be able to track changes in mood states and the impact of incidents such as a lack of sleep or missing medication (Kowatch, 2006).

Parent support is another critical aspect of psychosocial treatment. The stress connected with having a bipolar child can be enormous. The stressors include lost income and financial hardship, exhaustion and weakened immune systems, post-traumatic stress disorders, accusations of poor parenting, and the breakup of marriages (Hellender, 2000; Hellender, Sisson, & Fristad, 2003).

Local parent support groups can make the difference between crumbling and coping. However, many parents can't make regularly scheduled meetings because they occur when they are still struggling to get their bipolar child to bed or they have no one to baby-sit.

Online support has advantages for many parents of bipolar children. "When you are in the middle of a crisis you can get online and get support. You can't wait to get support on Tuesdays at 7:00 P.M. Your crisis will probably be over," one participant in the Children Bipolar Foundation's (CABF) parent stress survey said. Others explained how internet interaction accommodates their lack of free time. "Most of our free time is in the middle of the night," said one mother. Another added, "I can make a cup of tea when the kids are in bed and feel a part of a support group" (Hellender et al., 2003).The CABF website (www.bpkids.com), which sponsors online support groups, chat groups, and message boards, is one of the largest of several childhood bipolar disorder websites on the internet. (For additional websites see the "Resources" section.)

Psychotherapy

Most child bipolar *psychotherapy* models follow family therapy and multifamily *group therapy* modalities, because the family unit is highly affected by a child with bipolar disorder. There is a high potential for conflict in these families. Research shows that children from intact, biological families, with high maternal warmth, patterns of positive interaction, and less dysfunction have improved outcomes (Emslie, Mayes, Laptook, & Batt, 2003; Kupfer et al., 2002).

Families play an important role in helping children manage their symptoms. "Parenting a child with early onset bipolar disorder takes special skills and education that are *not* taught in standard parenting books," Fristad and Goldberg Arnold (2003) explain. Parents need to know how their child cycles and "the biopsychosocial triggers that can ignite a child's episode" (p. 305).

Mary Fristad, PhD, and colleagues in Ohio and Mani Pavuluri, MD, and her University of Illinois at Chicago team have designed the two major family therapy protocols. Fristad and Goldberg Arnold also have modified their multi-family group model for individual family therapy. These family therapy programs generally include: psychoeducation, communication skills, anger and mood regulation skills, problem solving, advocacy for services, and ways for children to improve social skills and parents to lead more balanced lives (Fristad & Goldberg Arnold, 2003; Goldberg Arnold & Fristad, 2003; Pavuluri et al., 2005).

The Chicago model, called Rainbow Therapy, combines cognitive behavioral therapy and interpersonal psychotherapy techniques. Preliminary results of an outcome study for the Chicago model of child and family focused therapy showed "promise" for reducing symptoms of mania, depression, psychosis, and sleep disturbances in bipolar children (Pavuluri, Graczyk, et al., 2004, p. 536).

Goldberg Arnold and Fristad (2003) report improvements in parent-child relationships and children's perceptions of their parents in a group of 35 children and their parents who participated in a pilot study.

Ross Greene's approaches to explosive children represent another set of very useful techniques for working with subsyndromal and bipolar children and their families. Saying "no" or loudly confronting a bipolar child can be like wearing a red shirt when running with the bulls at Pamplona. Greene offers effective, gentler tactics that can be a replacement for or an adjunct to traditional cognitive-behavior therapy (Greene, 2001; Greene & Ablon, 2006).

Essentially, Greene's model includes several primary principals: lagging cognitive skills cause many problems; confronting a child during a meltdown (or rage attack) doesn't work and fuels the meltdown; and adults need to prioritize and address one issue at a time.

Individual psychotherapy also may help older children adjust to their condition and improve their self-esteem or deal with disorders comorbid to bipolar disorder, such as anxiety. Anxious bipolar kids may have cognitive distortions that frequently accompany anxiety and need to be addressed (Esposito-Smythers et al., 2006).

Education

Early onset bipolar disorder can create significant problems for children in school. These problems range from poor attention and concentration to difficulties with peers and social situations to lack of motivation. Irritability and rages or crying and sadness or agitation and anxiety may set them apart from their classmates. All of these difficulties can be exacerbated by side effects from medications or lack of sleep. Written expression, handwriting problems, speech and language disorders, verbal memory deficits and difficulties with math are frequently found in children with bipolar disorder (Fristad & Goldberg Arnold, 2003, 2004; Kowatch et al., 2005; Papolos & Papolos, 2006). The 2005 *Treatment Guidelines* note that children with bipolar disorder are "at increased risk for learning disorders" (Kowatch et al., 2005, p. 219).

In a small study of 56 pediatric bipolar patients who were medicated and unmedicated, neuropsychological testing results indicated that bipolar children especially have a hard time with attention, working memory, executive functioning, verbal learning, organization, and problem-solving skills (Pavuluri et al., 2006).

While these troubles may look like behavioral problems, neuropsychological testing, functional MRIs, and other neuroimaging studies are increasingly producing evidence of the biological basis for bipolar symptoms. Initial results show differences in the structure and functioning of the brains of small samples of children and adolescents with bipolar disorder (Blumberg et al., 2005; Chang et al., 2005; DelBello, Adler, & Strakowski, 2006).

Consequently, clinicians need to work with *schools*. Too often school personnel are bewildered by the emotional dysregulation, or socially inappropriate or withdrawn behavior, of children on the bipolar spectrum. Information about small details can make a difference in many situations. For example, one young, school-age, bipolar child became upset at school after being disciplined for asking to go to the bathroom too many times. No one understood that medication caused a need for frequent urination. In another case, a rapid-cycling early teen ended up in stress-laden and mania-worsening confrontations with high school teachers who didn't appreciate grandiose challenges to their teaching.

Here is a short list of steps to take and information to share with school personnel:

- Alert teachers to students' possibly oversensitive reaction to others. Explain what recent research has shown about bipolar children misinterpreting facial expressions.

- Alert teachers to any special needs students may have as result of medication (e.g., thirst, needing extra access to the bathroom).

- Alert teachers and school psychologists or social workers if a student is vulnerable to meltdowns and how best to handle them, possibly referring the school personnel to the sections on schools in Ross Greene's books (Greene, 2001; Greene & Ablon, 2006). The Juvenile Bipolar Research Foundation has excellent material for educators on its website (www.jbrf.com).

- Alert teachers and others to the type of variability in moods the child may experience and explain why. For example, a spell of giddiness and silliness may be biologically and not behaviorally driven. In addition, confronting an upset bipolar child usually is not useful. Discussing the unacceptability of meltdowns during a meltdown usually doesn't work. Afterward, when the child is calm it is much more possible to have a productive conversation.

- Make school staff aware of the fact that hypersexuality can develop as a symptom of the child's bipolar condition, so if a child displays that behavior at school no one will immediately jump to the conclusion that child abuse may be occurring at home.

- School personnel need to know that a student's variability in performance may be based on mood fluctuations.

Resources

Books for Professionals

Findling, R. L., Kowatch, R. L., & Post, R. M. (2003). *Pediatric bipolar disorder: A handbook for clinicians.* London: Martin Dunitz.

Geller, B., & DelBello, M. P. (Eds.). (2003). *Bipolar disorder in childhood and early adolescence.* New York: Guilford.

Greene, R. W., & Ablon, J. S. (2006). *Treating explosive kids: The collaborative problem-solving approach.* New York: Guilford.

Books for Parents

Birmaher, B. (2004). *New hope for children and teens with bipolar disorder.* New York: Three Rivers Press.

Fristad, M. A., & Goldberg Arnold, J. S. (2004). *Raising a moody child: How to cope with depression and bipolar disorder.* New York: Guilford.

Greene, R. W. (2001). *The explosive child.* New York: HarperCollins/Quill.

Papolos, D., & Papolos, J. (2006). *The bipolar child* (3rd ed.). New York: Broadway Books.

DVDs

Papolos, J. (2004) *Educating and nurturing the bipolar child.* Available at www.bipolarchild .com and through the Juvenile Bipolar Research Foundation (jbrf.org).

Organizations

The Child and Adolescent Bipolar Foundation (CABF): www.bpkids.org
Depression and Bipolar Support Alliance (DBSA)
The International Society for Bipolar Disorders (ISBD)
The Juvenile Bipolar Research Foundation (JBRF): www.jbrf.org
The National Alliance for the Mentally Ill (NAMI)

References

American Psychiatric Association. (1994). *Diagnostic and statistical manual of mental disorders, 4th edition (DSM-IV).* Washington, DC: Author.

Axelson, D., Birmaher, B., Strober, M., Gill, M.K., Valeri, S., Chiappetta, L., Ryan, N., Leonard, H., et al. (2006). Phenomenology of children and adolescents with bipolar spectrum disorders. *Archives of General Psychiatry, 63*(10), 1139–1148.

Biederman, J. (2006). Pediatric bipolar disorder: The promise of psychopharmacotherapy. In H. S. Akiskal & M. Tohen (Eds.), *Bipolar psychopharmacotherapy* (pp. 279–293). West Sussex, England: Wiley.

Birmaher, B., & Axelson, D. (2005). Bipolar in children and adolescents. In F. Goodwin & A. Marneros (Eds.), *Bipolar disorders: Mixed states, rapid cycling, and atypical* forms (pp. 237–251). Cambridge: Cambridge University Press.

Birmaher, B., Axelson, D., Strober, M., Gill, M. K., Valeri, S., Chiappetta, L., Ryan, N., Leonard, H., et al. (2006). Clinical course of children and adolescents with bipolar spectrum disorders. *Archives of General Psychiatry, 63*(2), 175–183.

Blumberg, H. P., Fredericks, C., Wang, F., Kalmar, J. H., Spencer, L., Papademetus, X., Pittman, B., & Martin, A. (2005). Preliminary evidence for persistent abnormalities in amygdala volumes in adolescents and young adults with bipolar disorder. *Bipolar Disorders, 7*(6), 570–576.

Canadian Broadcasting Corporation (CBC). (2006). Bipolar children often overlooked. Retrieved May 31, 2006, from www.cbc.ca/edmonton/story/print/ed-bipolar-2006 0532.

Carlson, G.A. (2003). Guest editorial: The bottom line. *Journal of Clinical Child and Adolescent Psychopharmacology* 13(2): 115-118.

Carlson, G. A. (2005a). Diagnosing bipolar disorders in children and adolescents. *Child & Adolescent Psychopharmacology News, 10*(2), 1–6.

Carlson, G. A. (2005b). Early onset bipolar disorder: Clinical and research considerations. *Journal of Clinical Child and Adolescent Psychology, 13*(2), 333–343.

Carlson, G. A., & Meyer, S. E. (2006). Phenomenology and diagnosis of bipolar disorder in children, adolescents, and adults: Complexities and development issues. *Development & Psychopathology, 18*(4), 939–969.

Chang, K., Steiner, H., & Ketter, T. (2003). Studies of offspring of parents with bipolar disorder. *American Journal of Medical Genetics, 123C*, 26–35.

Chang, K. D., Karchemskiy, A., Barnea-Goraly, N., Garrett, A., Smeonova, S., & Reiss, A. (2005). Reduced amygdalar gray matter volume in familial pediatric bipolar disorder. *Journal of Clinical Child & Adolescent Psychiatry, 44*(6), 565–573.

Child and Adolescent Bipolar Foundation. (2006). About pediatric bipolar disorder (timeline). Retrieved June 11, 2006, from www.bpkids.org.

Costello, E. J., Angold, A., Burns, B. J., Stangl, D. K., Tweed, L. Erkanli, A., & Worthman (1996). The Great Smokey Mountains study of youth: Goals, design, methods, and the prevalence of *DSM-III-R* disorders. *Archives of General Psychiatry, 53*(12), 1129–1136.

Craney, J. L., & Geller, B. (2003). A prepubertal and early adolescent bipolar I phenotype: Review of phenomenology and longitudinal course. *Bipolar Disorders, 5*, 243–256.

DelBello, M. P., Adler, C. M., & Strakowski S. M. (2006). The neurophysiology of childhood and adolescent bipolar disorder. *CNS Spectrum, 11*(4), 298–311.

Dickstein, D. P., Rich, B. A., Binstock, A. B., Pradella, A. G., Towbin, K. E., Pine, D. S., & Leibenluft, E. (2005). Comorbid anxiety in phenotypes of pediatric bipolar disorder. *Journal of Child and Adolescent Psychopharmacology, 15*(4), 534–538.

Emslie G., Mayes, T. L., Laptook, R. S. & Batt, M. (2003). Predictors of response to treatment in children and adolescents with mood disorders. *Psychiatric Clinics of North America, 26*(2), 435–456.

Esposito-Smythers, C., Birmaher, B., Valeri, S., Chiappetta, L., Hunt, J., Ryan, N., Axelson, D., Strober, M., et al. (2006). Child comorbidity, maternal mood disorder, and perceptions of family functioning among bipolar youth. *Journal of the American Academy of Child and Adolescent Psychiatry, 45*(8), 955–964.

Faedda, G. L., Baldessarini, R. J., Glovinsky, I. P., & Austin, N. B. (2004). Pediatric bipolar disorder: Phenomenology and course of illness. *Bipolar Disorders, 6*(4), 305–313.

Faraone, S. V., Althoff, R. R., Hudziak, J. J., Monuteaux, M., & Biederman, J. (2005). The CBCL predicts DSM bipolar disorder in children: A receiver operating characteristic curve analysis. *Bipolar Disorders, 7*(6), 518–524.

Findling R. L. (2005, June 17). Diagnostic issues and nosology–children. Presentation to the 6th International Conference Bipolar Conference, Pittsburgh, PA. (Video available at www.wpic.pitt.edu/stanley/6thbipconf/day2.htm)

Findling, R. L., Kowatch, R. A., & Post, R. M. (2003). *Pediatric bipolar disorder: A handbook for clinicians.* London: Martin Dunitz.

Findling, R. L., Youngstrom, E. A., McNamara, N. K., Stansbrey, R. J, Demeter, C. A., Bedoya, D., Kahana, S. Y., & Calabrese, J. R. (2005). Early symptoms of mania and the role of parental risk. *Bipolar Disorders, 7*(6), 623–634.

Fristad, M. A., & Goldberg Arnold, J. S. (2003). Family interventions for early onset bipolar disorder. In B. Geller & M. P. DelBello (Eds.), *Bipolar disorder in childhood and early adolescence* (pp. 295–313). New York: Guilford.

Fristad, M. A., & Goldberg Arnold, J. S. (2004). *Raising a moody child.* New York: Guilford.

Geller, B., Bolhofner, K., Craney, J. L., Williams, M., DelBello, M. P., & Gunderson, K.

(2000). Psychosocial functioning in prepubertal and early adolescent bipolar disorder phenotype. *Journal of the American Academy of Child and Adolescent Psychiatry, 39*(12), 1543–1548.

Geller, B., Fox, L. W., & Clark, K. A. (1994). Rate and predictors of prepubertal bipolarity during follow-up of 6- to 12-year old depressed children. *Journal of the American Academy of Child and Adolescent Psychiatry, 33*(4), 461–469.

Geller, B., & Tillman, R. (2004). Hypersexuality in children with mania: Differential diagnosis and clinical presentation. *Psychiatric Times, XXI*(October). Retrieved July, 1, 2006, from www.psychiatrictimes.com/article/print,jhml?articleID=175802492

Geller, B., Tillman, R., Craney, J. L., & Bolhofner, K. (2004). Four-year prospective outcome and natural history of mania in children with prepubertal and early adolescent bipolar disorder phenotype. *Archives of General Psychiatry, 61*(5), 459–467.

Glovinsky, I. (2002). A brief history of childhood-onset bipolar disorder through. *Child Adolescent Psychiatric Clinic of North America, 11*(3), 443–460.

Goldberg Arnold, J. S., & Fristad, M. A. (2003). Psychotherapy for children with bipolar disorder. In B. Geller & M. P. DelBello (Eds.), *Bipolar disorder in childhood and early adolescence* (pp. 272–293). New York: Guilford.

Goldstein, T. R., Birmaher, B., Axelson, D., Ryan, N. D., Strober, M. A., Gill, M. K., Valeri, S., et al. (2005). History of suicide attempts in pediatric bipolar disorder: Factors associated with increased risk. *Bipolar Disorders, 7*(6), 55–535.

Greene, R. W. (2001). *The explosive child.* New York: HarperCollins/Quill.

Greene, R. W., & Ablon, J. S. (2006). *Treating explosive kids: The collaborative problem-solving approach.* New York: Guilford.

Hellender, M. (2000). Easing the burden: Childhood-onset bipolar disorders and the Internet. *Child and Adolescent Bipolar Foundation White Paper,* May 15, 1–9.

Hellender, M., Sisson, D. P., & Fristad, M. A. (2003). Internet support for parents of children with early-onset bipolar disorder. In B. Geller & M. P. DelBello (Eds.), *Bipolar disorders in childhood and early adolescence* (pp. 314–329). New York: Guilford.

Hyman, S. E. (2000). Goals for research on bipolar disorder: The view from NIMH. *Biological Psychiatry, 48*(6), 436–441.

Kluger, J., & Song, S. (2002). Young and bipolar. *TIME, 160*(8), 38–46, 51.

Kowatch, R. A., & Fristad, M. A. (2006). Bipolar disorders. In R. T. Ammerman (Ed.), *Comprehensive handbook of personality & psychopathology, Vol. III: Child psychopathology* (pp. 217–232). New York: Wiley.

Kowatch, R. A., Fristad, M. A, Birmaher, B., Wagner, K., Findling, R. L., Hellender, M., et al. (2005). Treatment guidelines for children and adolescents with bipolar disorder: Child psychiatric workshop on bipolar disorder. *Journal of the American Academy of Child and Adolescent Psychiatry, 44*(3), 213–235.

Kraepelin, E. (1921). *Manic depressive insanity and paranoia.* Salem, NH: Ayer Company Publishers.

Kupfer, D. J., Findling, R. L., Geller, B., & Ghaemi, S. N. (2002). Treatment of bipolar disorder during childhood, adolescent and young adult years. *Audiograph Series: Journal of Clinical Psychiatry, 5*(5), 1–17.

Kyte, Z. A., & Carlson, G. A. (2006). Clinical and neuropsychological characteristics of child and adolescent bipolar disorder. *Psychological Medicine, 36*(9), 1197–1211.

Leibenluft, E. (2006). Flying almost blind [Editorial]. *American Journal of Psychiatry, 163*(7), 1129–1131.

Leibenluft, E., Charney, D. S., & Pine, D. S. (2003). Researching the pathophysiology of pediatric bipolar disorder. *Biological Psychiatry, 53,* 1009–1020.

Lewinsohn, P. M., Klein, D. K., & Seeley, J. R. (1995). Bipolar disorders in a community sample of older adolescents: Prevalence, phenomenology, comorbidity and course. *Journal of the American Academy of Child and Adolescent Psychiatry, 34*(4), 454–463.

Masi, G., Perugi, G., Toni, C., Millepiedi, S., Mucci, M., Bertini, N., & Akiskal, H. S. Obsessive-compulsive bipolar comorbidity: Focus on children and adolescents. *Journal of Affective Disorders, 78*(3), 175–182.

Masi, G., Toni, G., Perugi, G., Mucci, M., Millepiedi, S., & Akiskal, H. S. (2001). Anxiety disorders in children and adolescents with bipolar disorder: A neglected comorbidity. *Canadian Journal of Psychiatry, 46*(November), 797–802.

McClure, E., Treland, J. E., Snow, J., Schmajuk, M., Dickstein, D. P., Towbin, K. E., Charney, D. S., Pine, D. S., & Leinbenluft, E. (2005). Deficits in social cognition and response flexibility in pediatric bipolar disorder. *American Journal of Psychiatry, 162*(9), 1644–1651.

Mehl, R. C., O'Brien, L. M., Jones, J. H., Dreisbach, J. K., Mervis, C. B., & Gozal, D. (2006). Correlates of sleep and pediatric bipolar disorder. *Sleep, 29*(2), 192–197.

Miklowitz, D. J. (2002). *The bipolar survival guide.* New York: Guilford.

National Institute of Mental Health (NIMH). (2000). Child and adolescent bipolar disorder: An update from the National Institute of Mental Health [Fact sheet]. NIH Publication No. 00-4778. Bethesda, MD: Author.

National Institute of Mental Health (NIMH). (2001). National Institute of Mental Health research roundtable on prepubertal bipolar disorder. *Journal of the American Academy of Adolescent and Child Psychiatry, 40*(8), 871–878.

National Institute of Mental Health (NIMH). (2005). Mental illness exacts heavy toll, beginning in youth. Retrieved October 6, 2006, from nimh.nih.gov.

National Institute of Mental Health (NIMH). (2006a). Freedom of Information Act request. Retrieved September 6, 2006.

National Institute of Mental Health (NIMH). (2006b). Largest study to date on pediatric bipolar disorder describes disease characteristics and short-term outcomes. *Science Update.* Bethesda, MD: National Institute of Mental Health.

Papolos, D., & Papolos, J. (2006). *The bipolar child* (3rd ed.). New York: Broadway Books.

Pavuluri, M. N. (2005). Art and craft of pharmacotherapy in pbd: Problem solving in pediatric bipolar disorder. *Child and Adolescent Psychopharmacology News, 10*(8), 1–10.

Pavuluri, M. N., Birmaher, B., & Naylor, M.W. (2005). Pediatric bipolar disorder: A review of the past 10 years. *Journal of the American Academy of Child and Adolescent Psychiatry, 44*(9), 846–871.

Pavuluri, M. N., Graczyk, P. A., Henry, D. B., Carbray, J. A., Heidenreich, J., & Miklowitz, D. J. (2004b). Child-focused cognitive-behavioral therapy for pediatric bipolar disorder. *Journal of the American Academy of Child and Adolescent Psychiatry, 435,* 528–537.

Pavuluri, M. N., Henry, D. B., Devineni, B., Carbray, J. A., Naylor, M. W., & Janicak, P. G. (2004a). A pharmacotherapy algorithm for stabilization and maintenance of pediatric bipolar disorder. *Journal of the American Academy of Child and Adolescent Psychiatry, 43*(7), 850–867.

Pavuluri, M. N, & Naylor, M. W. (2005b). Multi-modal integrated treatment of youth with bipolar disorder. *Psychiatric Times, XXII*(6). Retrieved May 2006 from www.psychiatric times.com/print.jhtml?articleID=164303314.

Pavuluri, M. N., Schenkel, L. S., Aryal, S., Harral, E. M., Hill, S. K., Herbener, E. S., & Sweeney, J. A. (2006). Neurocognitive function in unmedicated manic andeuthymic pediatric bipolar patients. *American Journal of Psychiatry, 163*, 286–293.

Pederson, L. (2003, August 10). Offspring studies seek early markers: Interview with Kiki Chang, M.D. *CABF eBulletin: Newsletter of the Child & Adolescent Bipolar Foundation.* Retrieved August 28, 2006, from www.cabf.org.

Post, R. M., Chang, K. D., Findling, R. L., Geller, B., Kowatch, R., Kutcher, S. P., & Leverich, G. S. (2004). Prepubertal bipolar I disorder and bipolar NOS are separable from ADHD. *Journal of Clinical Psychiatry, 65*(7), 898–902.

Rao, U. (2003). Sleep and other biological rhythms. In B. Geller & M. P. DelBello (Eds.), *Bipolar disorder in childhood and early adolescence* (pp. 215–246). New York: Guilford.

Rich, B. A., & Vinton, D. T. (2006). Limbic hyperactivation during processing of neutral facial expressions in children with bipolar disorder. *Proceedings of the National Academy of Sciences, 103*(23), 8900–8905.

Rosack, J. (2005). Experts close to defining bipolar criteria in children. *Psychiatric News, 40*(23), 9.

Sadock, B. J., & Sadock, V. A. (2003). *Kaplan and Sadock's synopsis of psychiatry: Behavioral science/clinical psychiatry* (9th ed.). Philadelphia: Lippincott Williams & Wilkins.

Soutullo, C. A., Chang, K. D., Diez-Suarez, A., Figueroa-Quintana, A., Escamilla-Canales, I., Rapado-Castro, M., & Ortuno, F. (2005). Bipolar disorder in children and adolescents: International perspective on epidemiology and phenomenology. *Bipolar Disorders, 7*, 497–506.

Tillman, R., Geller, B., Grazier, J., Beringer, L., Zimerman, B., Klages, T., & Bolhofner, K. (2005). Children with prepubertal and early adolescent bipolar disorder phenotype from pediatric versus psychiatric facilities. *Journal of the American Academy of Child and Adolescent Psychiatry, 44*(8), 776–781.

Wagner, K. D. (2006). Bipolar disorder and comorbid anxiety disorders in children and adolescents. *Journal of Clinical Psychiatry, 67*(Suppl. 1), 16–20.

Wozniak, J., Biederman, J., Kiely, K., Ablon, J. S., Faraone, S. V., Mundy, E., & Mennin, D. (1995). Mania-like symptoms suggestive of childhood-onset bipolar disorder in clinically referred children. *Journal of the American Academy of Child and Adolescent Psychiatry, 34*(7), 867–876.

Youngstrom, E. A. & Duax, J. (2005a). Evidence-based assessment of pediatric bipolar disorder, part I: base rate and family history. *Journal of the American Academy of Child and Adolescent Psychiatry, 44*(7), 712–717.

Youngstrom, E. A., Findling, R. L., Calabrese, J. R., Gracious, B. L., Demeter, C., Bedoya, D. D., & Price, M. (2004). Comparing diagnostic accuracy of six potential screening instruments for bipolar disorder in youths aged 5 to 17 years. *Journal of Clinical and Adolescent Psychiatry, 43*(7), 847–858.

Youngstrom, E. A., Findling, R. L., Youngstrom, J. K., & Calabrese, J. R. (2005). Toward an evidence-based assessment of pediatric bipolar disorder. *Journal of Clinical Child and Adolescent Psychiatry, 34*(3), 433–448.

Youngstrom, E. A., & Youngstrom, J. K. (2005b). Evidence-based assessment of pediatric bipolar disorder: incorporating information from behavior checklists. *Journal of the American Academy of Child and Adolescent Psychiatry, 44*(8), 823–828.

Ziehen, T. (2004). Classic text no. 58: Theodor Ziehen on mania, melancholia and periodic psychoses in children. *History of Psychiatry, 15*(2), 213–226.

CHAPTER 12

Bipolar Disorder in Older Adults

Colin A. Depp, PhD

Introduction

The *graying* of the world's population is a continuing and unprecedented trend, meaning that a growing proportion of people with bipolar disorder will be older adults (Jeste et al., 1999). According to the U.S. Administration on Aging, for the first time in recorded history, the number of persons older than age 65 will outnumber children aged 0 to 14 by the year 2050 (Administration on Aging, 2006). The number of older persons with severe psychiatric disorders, including bipolar disorder, will double over the next several decades. Aging adds complexity to diagnosis and treatment of most psychiatric disorders, and bipolar disorder is no exception. This chapter will provide an overview of what is currently known about the bipolar-spectrum in older adults, and will offer suggestions for assessment and treatment.

Relative to other psychiatric disorders, such as later-life depression or schizophrenia, very little clinical research has been conducted on bipolar disorder in older adults (Charney et al., 2003). Most of what has been written about late-life bipolar disorder has derived from clinical observations or retrospective chart reviews of hospitalized older persons in a manic state (Depp & Jeste, 2004). Consequently, there are divergent views about what kinds of outcomes to expect as people age with bipolar disorder. Some early observers, including the preeminent psychiatrist Emil Kraepelin, proposed that *manic-depression* carried a reasonably good prognosis into later life, separating this disorder from the deterioration he observed in schizophrenia (Kraepelin, 1921). Several other authors have agreed that bipolar disorder may indeed *burn out* in later life (Blazer & Koenig, 1996). However, other researchers, basing their conclusions on the shrinking duration of interepisode recovery among many younger adults with bipolar disorder, posit that bipolar disorder follows a progressively declining course (Post et al., 1986). It is striking that so few of these observations have led to large-scale empirical studies to either confirm or disconfirm these hypotheses. Thus, clinicians should be aware that there is little data specific to late-life bipolar disorder to guide the treatment planning.

General Considerations in Older Adults

In working with older adults (i.e., people over the age of 60), with severe mental illnesses there are several general principles to keep in mind. First, aging brings heterogeneity in presentation, course, and outcome. For instance, an older person with bipolar disorder may have a long-term illness that he or she first experienced during adolescence or young adulthood (*early-onset*). Alternatively, he or she may have experienced de novo symptoms of mania or depression without ever displaying psychiatric symptoms before (*late onset*). Among these individuals, certain brain insults, such as a stroke or progressive dementias, may directly produce manic symptoms (*secondary mania*). Then again, he or she may have experienced a first episode of mania after many years of recurrent depression—an interesting group of patients that is often overlooked.

These multiple paths to late-life bipolar disorder are, in part, what drive the variability in levels of functioning and response to treatment in this population. Second, older adults often experience comorbid medical illnesses that can serve to complicate recognition of symptoms, as well as interact with treatment efficacy and tolerability. The same can be said for cognitive impairment, as often the primary determinant of functioning among elderly people is the degree to which cognitive abilities (e.g., memory) are intact in order to perform day-to-day tasks, over and above any psychiatric symptoms they may experience. Third, there are both unique barriers and strengths among older adults with severe mental illnesses. Older persons with mental illnesses face a *dual stigma* related to being both an aging individual and having a psychiatric disability. They often experience many practical barriers to accessing treatment (e.g., lack of transportation, losses in their social networks). On the other hand, older people who have lived with mental illnesses for a long time have often adapted to the illness, and some have found surprisingly effective methods of coping. Many no longer struggle with whether or not they have bipolar illness, and are thus more likely to adhere to treatment regimens. Overall, older adults with bipolar disorder are a unique and varied group, with special needs that lie at the cross-section of having a psychiatric disability and normal age-related changes. With these inherent factors in mind, we now turn to observations about the prevalence and presentation of late-life bipolar disorder.

How Common Is Later-Life Bipolar Disorder?

Estimates of the community prevalence of bipolar disorder among older adults are derived from community surveys, administrative databases, and large-scale mental health screening initiatives. The most commonly cited source for community prevalence is the Epidemiological Catchment Area (ECA) Survey, a large multisite study conducted in the 1980s (Regier et al., 1993). Using a structured diagnostic interview, the ECA provided an estimated prevalence of lifetime bipolar disorder in 0.4 percent among persons aged 45 to 64 and 0.1 percent among persons older than age 65 (compared to 1.4 percent among persons aged 18–44). Other community surveys provide estimates for the prevalence of bipolar disorder among persons older that range between 0.1 percent and 0.5 percent (Hirschfeld et al., 2003; Unutzer et al., 1998), all of which were lower than estimates for younger age groups. The apparent decline in prevalence is somewhat controversial (such as whether the data reflect a true decline in prevalence or limitations of assessment techniques), yet it should be noted that all psychiatric disorders, with the exception of dementia, show a similar rate of decline in prevalence into older age brackets. Within mental health settings such as inpatient facilities or outpatient clinics, bipolar disorder accounts for between 8 and 10 percent of all diagnoses among older adults (Depp & Jeste, 2004). Thus, available data indicate that community prevalence of bipolar disorder declines with age, but it remains a common diagnosis in settings where older adults are treated for psychiatric illnesses.

What Is the Clinical Presentation of Bipolar Disorder in Later Life?

In general, there are probably more similarities than differences in the kinds of symptoms older and younger persons with bipolar disorder display. Older persons can and do experience the full range of manic, mixed, or depressive symptoms that are the hallmark features of the disorder. However, there may be some positive trends that occur with aging. Older adults are more likely to have experienced onset of illness later in life. Therefore, they may have established educational, occupational, family, and financial resources that younger adults with bipolar disorder struggle to develop during the throes of their illness. There is some evidence that suggests that the severity of manic symptoms may lessen with age, identified in cross-sectional studies of people hospitalized for mania (Young & Falk, 1989). Furthermore, community-dwelling older adults report experiencing more depression- and mania-free days according to a large survey (Calabrese et al., 2003).

Compared to younger adults, it seems that older adults are far less likely to have met criteria for substance use or dependence within their lifetimes; prevalence for any substance use disorder among younger adults is about 60 percent, whereas among older adults estimates range from 20 to 30 percent (Cassidy et al., 2001). This may be partially attributable to demographic differences—older adults are more likely to be women, with a gender ratio of about 7 to 10 women, instead of 5 to 10 among younger adults. Substance abuse, as a rule, is among the most potent negative predictors of outcome in bipolar disorder. It is, however, important to note that substance misuse remains a common problem among older adults with bipolar disorder, and the consequences and interactions of substance use with medications may be greater (for example, older adults are less able to metabolize alcohol). Additionally, the discrepancies between younger and older persons may represent a cohort difference, and the *baby boom* generation will almost certainly have a greater history of exposure to illicit substances as they enter older age than the current cohort of older adults (Patterson & Jeste, 1999).

As stated earlier, older adults with bipolar disorder have special challenges that clinicians need to incorporate into their assessments and treatment planning. Among the most common factors in the treatment of older adults is medical comorbidity. The average person older than 65 has more than one chronic condition, and takes 5 to 10 medications (Hazzard et al., 2003). Particularly among older persons with bipolar disorder, the risk of diabetes and cardiovascular disease is several times higher than that among older adults without psychiatric illnesses (Kilbourne et al., 2004). There are a number of factors that may account for the higher prevalence of chronic medical conditions in late-life bipolar disorder, including poor health habits (e.g., smoking), diminished access to medical care, and medications with side effects (e.g., atypical antipsychotics). Clinicians must be prepared to consider drug-drug interactions (e.g., lithium and ACE inhibitors) when treating older adults with bipolar disorder and comorbid medical illnesses.

An emerging body of literature has provocatively identified cognitive impairments that appear to be stable in bipolar disorder, with deficits in verbal memory and complex mental functions (e.g., planning) apparent even during symptom-free periods (Bearden et al., 2001). The cause and course of these cognitive deficits await further study, however there is mounting evidence that these deficits accumulate over the course of the illnesses. Thus, older adults, particularly those with histories of multiple hospitalizations and more severe illness histories, may be most at risk for cognitive impairment. In one study, it was estimated that about 50 percent of persons older than age 60 display clinically significant cognitive impairment (Gildengers et al., 2004), several times the rate found among older adults without psychiatric illnesses. The reason to be so concerned about cognitive impairment is that, across psychiatric disorders in the elderly, these deficits are the single largest factor determining older people's capacity to reside independently. Additionally, older adults with bipolar disorder may also be at risk for social isolation (Beyer et al., 2003). The rate of divorce is high in bipolar disorder, and many patients may have small social networks or are estranged from their families. The combination of disability, cognitive impairment, and lack of reliable social support system could produce a need for multifaceted rehabilitative care and/or placement in an assistant living facility.

Are There Different *Subgroups* of Later-Life Bipolar Disorder?

It should be noted that, while there are older people with bipolar disorder who remain chronically ill and require assisted living, the great majority of older people with bipolar disorder reside in the community, and many function well on maintenance medication treatment. As stated earlier, the heterogeneity of outcome in bipolar disorder is substantial. One of the factors that has been theorized to account for this heterogeneity is age of onset of the illness. The cut-off between *early onset* and *late-onset* is often at age 50, but varies from study to study (Depp & Jeste, 2004). It has been suggested that late-onset patients more often have preserved social networks, lower family history of the illness, yet a greater likelihood of cerebrovascular changes that may coincide with illness onset. In contrast, early onset patients are more likely to have a family history of the illness (i.e., a higher genetic loading), and are more likely to experience poor outcome because of the cumulative effects of the illness. So far, data have not supported a sharp distinction in subgroups between early and late-onset patients in symptoms, functioning, or neuropsychological impairment. However, a higher rate of neurological comorbidity among the late-onset patients does seem to be a recurring finding (Depp & Jeste, 2004). There also appear to be a group of patients who are not truly *late-onset* in that they experience their first onset of mania after many years of recurrent depression. The reasons for the late emergence of mania, as well as the clinical features of this group, await further study. Of course, the *DSM-IV* distinguishes between bipolar disorder I and II, with the latter group having no history of full-blown mania. There is little, if any, data on the differences between these subtypes of bipolar disorder in older adults.

What Are the Steps in Assessment and Diagnosis?

Geriatric psychiatrists often need to collect a great deal more information than is typically part of a psychiatric interview. The first step is to obtain a thorough history of the illness. Older adults may be particularly reticent to discuss psychiatric symptoms and related issues, so a brief education framing mood disorders as treatable medical illnesses is often helpful. It is often necessary to gain information from reliable informants and/or medical records, particularly if cognitive impairment may be suspected. Among patients with bipolar disorder, using a life chart (placing episodes, hospitalizations, and life events on a written timeline) may be useful (Denicoff et al., 2002). In developing a life chart with patients and their family members, it is generally best to begin by discussing the most recent episode, and then starting from the beginning of the illness working forward in time.

Particularly in the case of a new-onset mood disorder, it is critical to rule out medical or medication-related causes of illness. Many medical illnesses or medications can mimic or produce depression, and some can even be associated with mania-like symptoms (e.g., hyperthyroidism, anti-depressants; Blazer, 2003). This process requires a complete physical examination, with associated laboratory tests. Late-onset mania, with no clinical history of affective disorder, may compel a clinician to obtain neuroimaging findings and/or neurological consultation.

In addition to screening for psychiatric symptoms and substance use (here the Mini-International Neuropsychiatric Interview [Sheehan et al., 1998] can be helpful), the assessment may also include measures of cognitive functioning, disability, and social support. Cognitive screening instruments that are easy to implement and that have adequate psychometric properties in older adults include the Mini-Mental State Examination (Folstein et al., 1975) and the Dementia Rating Scale (Gardner et al., 1981). Lists of adaptive abilities, such as activities of daily living (e.g., bathing, grooming) and instrumental activities of daily living (e.g., using the telephone), are freely available on the Internet. Obtaining an idea of the individual's social support system (or lack thereof) is crucial in determining who can be relied upon to support and help implement the treatment plan.

What Are the Basic Considerations in Medication Treatment for Older Adults with Bipolar Disorder?

Mood stabilizers are the mainstay of treatment for bipolar disorder at any age. However, the reader expecting results of randomized controlled trials (RCTs) of medications in older adults with bipolar disorder will be disappointed; to date there have been no such trials in older adults with this disorder. Therefore, what can be surmised about treatment of late-life bipolar disorder is derived from open-label quasiexperimental trials, extrapolations from RCTs in younger adults, and knowledge of the general principles of geriatric psychopharmacology (Young et al., 2004). Furthermore, the best data available are on the effectiveness of medications in reducing acute manic symptoms, with far less on the treatment of the depressive phase or on maintenance treatment.

In general, it is most important to know that older adults typically require much lower dosages of medications than do younger adults. They also, almost universally, are at higher risk for side effects and adverse events. Aging is associated with a reduced ability of the liver and kidneys to process medications; subsequently, medications have a longer half-life, and side effects emerge at lower dosages than they would among younger adults. As stated earlier, older adults, particularly people with bipolar disorder, are often taking a host of other medications to treat other medical illnesses. In addition, they often take over-the-counter medications and herbal remedies, which many physicians do not ask about, but that have significant effects on the efficacy and tolerability of medications. The often-stated rule of thumb for treating older adults with medications is to *start low and go slow.* The reader is advised to refer to geriatric medicine texts for more information on general principles of medication treatment in older adults (Hazzard et al., 2003).

Another general principle in treating older adults with bipolar disorder is, as stated by C. Everett Koop (former U.S. Surgeon General), "drugs don't work in those who don't take them." Nonadherence is a major issue across the life span in bipolar disorder, as approximately 40 percent of people affected do not take their medications as prescribed (Lingam & Scott, 2002). Medication nonadherence is a major risk factor for relapse, hospitalization, and higher healthcare costs. Thus, adherence to prescribed medications can be considered the *sixth vital sign* in bipolar disorder. Among older adults, some evidence would suggest that, despite having to take a great deal more medications than younger adults, adherence might be better. However, considering that nonadherence may be intentional (e.g., deliberately not taking medications due to lack of perceived need) or unintentional (e.g., forgetting to take medications), older adults may be at particular risk for unintentional nonadherence due to cognitive impairments and the large number of medications they are asked to take (Ayalon et al., 2005). A way of increasing the likelihood of adherence is to employ the Health Beliefs Model, which states (broadly) that (a) a person must understand what the medication they are prescribed is for, (b) believe it is important, and (c) remember to take it (Lacro et al., 2002). Thus, all patients should receive basic education about the purpose and instructions for medications, and should be made aware of the personal benefits and drawbacks to taking the medication. Among older adults, external aids such as reminders, pillboxes, and medication calendars are often essential tools to enhance adherence.

Which Medications Are Used?

Whereas lithium used to be the primary treatment for bipolar disorder, the medication options in this illness have expanded greatly over the past several decades. Classes of medications that are used include lithium, anticonvulsants, antipsychotics, antidepressants, and sedatives. These medications are sometimes prescribed as the sole medication to treat bipolar disorder, but more often nowadays, combination strategies are employed. The following is a brief overview of considerations of using these medications in older adults with bipolar disorder; comprehensive reviews on the pharmacology of late-life bipolar disorder have been published (Sajatovic, 2002; Young et al., 2004).

- *Lithium:* Lithium was the first medication approved by the U.S. Federal Drug Administration for bipolar disorder. The use of lithium in those older than age 60 has declined sharply over the past decade, a decline that has occurred in the absence of data (Shulman et al., 2003). The effectiveness of lithium in reducing acute mania has been examined in retrospective studies of older inpatients, with the majority of patients demonstrating clinical improvement. Challenges to lithium administration in older people include reduced renal clearance, which increases the half-life of lithium in the blood. Therefore, older people are at greater risk for elevated lithium levels, and subsequent toxicity. Furthermore, many medications interact with lithium, particularly the ACE inhibitors, anti-inflammatory agents, and diuretics. Tremor can be a troublesome side effect.

- *Valproate:* Valproic acid or divalproex sodium represents a common alternative to lithium in older people, generally viewed as having a better side effect profile than lithium. Valproate therapy does not appear to be affected by age-related changes in pharmacodynamics, as does lithium. Additionally, there are fewer drug-drug interactions than lithium. Side effects include sedation, tremor, and gastrointestinal effects.

- *Lamotrigine and topiramate:* Lamotrigine, and to a lesser extent, topiramate, are so-called *second-generation* mood stabilizers that have gained popularity in recent years. Lamotrigine may be particularly effective in the treatment of bipolar depression relative to other mood stabilizers, and there are few concerning side effects, making it an attractive agent among older adults. The risk of a serious rash is the greatest concern. Topiramate is used less often, possibility due to the potential for cognitive side effects.

- *Antipsychotics:* Both *typical* and *atypical* antipsychotics have a role in treating bipolar disorder, both in cases of psychotic mania and as augmentative or even as stand-alone agents. Among younger adults, there has been a recent accumulation of data in the use of atypical antipsychotics as monotherapy for the treatment of bipolar depression. A number of open trials have been reported in older adults, and in other late-life psychiatric disorders. In open trials, these agents are generally associated with reductions in mania. However, there are serious concerns about typical and atypical agents in older adults that warrant careful usage. Typical agents are used infrequently due to the high risk of tardive dyskinesia (TD), a side effect characterized by involuntary movements of the face, trunk, and limbs. Risk for TD increases linearly with age, and age is an independent risk for TD (Jeste, 2004). Atypical agents confer a much lower risk for TD in older adults, but recent reports suggest that they produce metabolic effects placing individuals at risk for diabetes and cerebrovascular disease. For elderly people with dementia, the U.S. Food and Drug Administration (2005) has issued several statements regarding these risks.

- *Antidepressants:* The use of antidepressants in bipolar disorder is controversial, primarily due to the risk of inducing mania. Nevertheless, a substantial percentage of patients are treated with antidepressants to augment mood stabilizers in the pursuit of reducing depression. Little is known about whether older adults are more or less at risk for antidepressant-induced mania, although there are case reports that antidepressant-associated mania can indeed occur in older people.

- *Other treatments:* The use of sedatives is common in inpatient settings to reduce acute manic states. Among older adults, these medications are quite commonly associated with orthostatic hypotension and increased risk of falls; therefore, they are best employed in controlled environments in circumstances of acute need in a time-limited fashion. Another treatment that is sometimes employed in bipolar depression is electroconvulsive therapy (ECT). Evidence from older patients with unipolar depression (including psychotic depression) suggests that ECT is surprisingly effective in reducing depression in a rapid manner, perhaps even more effective than it is among younger adults. However, there is often retrograde amnesia associated with ECT, which may be of particular concern among older adults.

In sum, although medications are generally an essential part of the picture in treating older people with bipolar disorder, the risks, interactions, and potential to do more harm than good is greater. Elderly people with bipolar disorder who are treated for multiple other conditions require a collaborative effort between psychiatric and medical care, and a balancing of risks and benefits with regard to symptom reduction and side effects.

What Is the Role of Psychotherapy in Late-Life Bipolar Disorder?

Psychotherapy as an adjunctive treatment is increasingly seen as a viable method of improving patients' chances of remaining euthymic and improving overall functioning (Scott & Colom, 2005). There are now several models of psychotherapy that have empirical support, among them are cognitive-behavioral therapy, psychoeducation, family therapy, and interpersonal and social rhythm therapy. None of these treatments have been adapted specifically for older adults, but older adults with other psychiatric illnesses often do respond well to psychotherapy when a few modifications are made. Adaptations for older adults may include holding briefer sessions, providing written review of session content to increase retention, and involving supportive persons in therapy (Arean et al., 2003). The psychotherapist may work with older adults to increase lifestyle regularity and sleep hygiene, adherence to medications, and identifying a reliable social network, all of which would occur in collaboration with other sources of care.

Because older adults with severe mental illnesses often have diverse needs, spanning financial, transportation, medical, and social realms, an important clinical task is to broker engagement with social service agencies serving seniors. Knowledge of community services is thus necessary. Given that social isolation is among the most potent predictors of recurring depression among older adults, mutual support organizations can be an incredible resource for people with bipolar disorder. The Depression and Bipolar Support Alliance (www.dbsalliance .org) and the National Alliance for Mental Illness (www.nami.org) are the largest such organizations, with thousands of chapters operating across the United States. Unfortunately, for reasons that are unknown, older adults typically underutilize mutual support groups.

Summary

In conclusion, older adults with bipolar disorder are a growing and diverse group that often has great psychiatric, medical, and psychosocial needs. Scientific studies have yet to fill the may gaps in information needed to describe these patients and to guide the optimal choices for their treatment. Clinicians who assess and treat older adults with bipolar disorder, particularly patients with medical comorbidities and/or with cognitive impairment, should gain a working familiarity with principles of geriatric medicine and psychiatry. Those working with older people should also be prepared to engage in a multidisciplinary approach to clinical management, combining medications and available forms of psychosocial rehabilitation. On a more optimistic note, clinicians should also note that the treatments that work in younger adults with bipolar disorder will likely work just as well in older adults, with a few adaptations and a careful approach. Finally, clinicians should be aware that people who have survived most of their lifetime with bipolar disorder often have much to teach others about how to successfully adapt to this devastating illness.

References

Administration on Aging. (2006). Available from http://www.aoa.gov/press/fact/pdf/fs _global_aging.pdf

Arean, P., Cook, B., Gallagher-Thompson, D., Hegel, M., Schulberg, H., & Schulz, R. (2003). Guidelines for conducting geropsychotherapy research. *American Journal of Geriatric Psychiatry, 11*(1), 9–16.

Ayalon, L., Arean, P., & Alvidrez, J. (2005). Adherence to antidepressant medications in black and Latino elderly patients. *American Journal of Geriatric Psychiatry, 13*(7), 572– 580.

Bearden, C. E., Hoffman, K. M., & Cannon, T. D. (2001). The neuropsychology and neuroanatomy of bipolar affective disorder: A critical review. *Bipolar Disorders, 3*(3), 106–150, 151–103.

Beyer, J., Kuchibhatia, M., Looney, C., Engstrom, E., Cassidy, F., Ranga, K., & Krishnan, R. (2003). Social support in elderly patients with bipolar disorder. *Bipolar Disorders, 5*, 22–27.

Blazer, D. (2003). Depression in late life: Review and commentary. *Journal of Gerontology, 58A*(3), 249–265.

Blazer, D., & Koenig, H. (1996). Mood disorders. In E. B. D. Blazer (Ed.), *Textbook of geriatric psychiatry* (pp. 241–269). Washington, DC: American Psychiatric Association Press.

Calabrese, J. R., Hirschfeld, R. M., Reed, M., Davies, M. A., Frye, M. A., Keck, P. E., et al. (2003). Impact of bipolar disorder on a U.S. community sample. *Journal of Clinical Psychiatry, 64*(4), 425–432.

Cassidy, F., Ahearn, E. P., & Carroll, B. J. (2001). Substance abuse in bipolar disorder. *Bipolar Disorders, 3*(4), 181–188.

Charney, D., Reynolds, C., Lewsi, L., Lebowitz, B., Sunderland, T., Alexopouls, A., et al. (2003). Depression and bipolar support alliance consensus on the unmet needs in diagnosis and treatment of mood disorders in late life. *Archives of General Psychiatry, 60,* 664–672.

Denicoff, K. D., Ali, S. O., Sollinger, A. B., Smith-Jackson, E. E., Leverich, G. S., & Post, R. M. (2002). Utility of the daily prospective National Institute of Mental Health Life-Chart Method (NIMH-LCM-P) ratings in clinical trials of bipolar disorder. *Depression Anxiety, 15*(1), 1–9.

Depp, C., & Jeste, D. V. (2004). Bipolar disorder in older adults: A critical review. *Bipolar Disorders, 6*(5), 343–367.

Folstein, M., Folstein, S., & McHugh, P. (1975). Mini-mental state. A practical method for grading the cognitive state of patients for the clinician. *Journal of Psychiatric Research, 12*(3), 189–198.

Gardner, R., Olivers-Munoz, S., FIsher, L., & Empting, L. (1981). Mattis dementia rating scale: Internal reliability using a diffusely impaired population. *Journal of Clinical Neuropsychology, 3,* 271–275.

Gildengers, A., Butters, M., Seligman, K., McShea, M., Miller, M., Mulsant, B., et al. (2004). Cognitive functioning in late-life bipolar disorder. *American Journal of Psychiatry, 161*(4), 736–738.

Hazzard, W., Blass, J., Halter, J., Ouslander, J., & Tinetti, M. (2003). *Principles of geriatric medicine and gerontology* (5th ed.). New York: McGraw-Hill.

Hirschfeld, R., Calabrese, J., Weisman, M., Reed, M., Davies, M., Frye, M., Keck, P., Lewis, L., McElroy, S., McNulty, J., & Wagner, K. (2003). Screening for bipolar disorder in the community. *Journal of Clinical Psychiatry, 64*(1), 53–59.

Jeste, D., Alexopoulos, G. S., Bartels, S. J., Cummings, J. L., Gallo, J. J., Gottlieb, G. L., et al. (1999). Consensus statement on the upcoming crisis in geriatric mental health: Research agenda for the next 2 decades. *Archives of General Psychiatry, 56*(9), 848–853.

Jeste, D. V. (2004). Tardive dyskinesia rates with atypical antipsychotics in older adults. *Journal of Clinical Psychiatry, 65*(Suppl. 9), 21–24.

Kilbourne, A. M., Cornelius, J. R., Han, X., Pincus, H. A., Shad, M., Salloum, I., et al. (2004). Burden of general medical conditions among individuals with bipolar disorder. *Bipolar Disorders, 6*(5), 368–373.

Kraepelin, E. (1921). *Manic-depressive insanity* (Trans. R. M. Barclay). New York: Arno Press.

Lacro, J. P., Dunn, L., Dolder, C., Leckband, S. G., & Jeste, D. V. (2002). Prevalence and risk factors for medication nonadherence in patients with schizophrenia: A comprehensive review of recent literature. *Journal of Clinical Psychiatry, 63*(10), 892–909.

Lingam, R., & Scott, J. (2002). Treatment non-adherence in affective disorders. *Acta Psychiatrica Scandinavica, 105*(3), 164–172.

Osterberg, L., & Blaschke, T. (2005). Adherence to medication. *New England Journal of Medicine, 353*(5), 487–497.

Patterson, T. L., & Jeste, D. V. (1999). The potential impact of the baby-boom generation on substance abuse among elderly persons. *Psychiatric Services, 50*(9), 1184–1188.

Post, R., Rubinow, D., & Ballenger, J. (1986). Conditioning and sensitisation in the longitudinal course of affective illness. *British Journal of Psychiatry, 149*, 191–201.

Regier, D., Narrow, W., Rae, D., et al. (1993). The de facto US mental and addictive disorders service system: Epidemiologic catchment area prospective 1-year prevalence rates of disorders and services. *Archives of General Psychiatry, 50*, 85–94.

Sajatovic, M. (2002). Treatment of bipolar disorder in older adults. *International Journal of Geriatric Psychiatry, 17*, 865–873.

Scott, J., & Colom, F. (2005). Psychosocial treatments for bipolar disorders. *Psychiatric Clinics of North America, 28*(2), 371–384.

Sheehan, D., Lecrubier, Y., Sheehan, P., & Amorim, J. (1998). The mini-international neuropsychiatric interview: The development and validation of a structured diagnostic psychiatric interview for the *DSM-IV* and ICD-10. *Journal of Clinical Psychiatry, 59*(20), 22–33.

Shulman, K., Rochon, P., Sykora, K., Anderson, G., Mamdani, M., Bronskill, S., et al. (2003). Changing prescription patterns for lithium and valproic acid in old age: Shifting practice without evidence. *British Medical Journal, 326*, 960–961.

Unutzer, J., Simon, G., Pabiniak, C., Bond, K., & Katon, W. (1998). The treated prevalence of bipolar disorder in a large staff-model HMO. *Psychiatric Services, 49*(8), 1072–1078.

U.S. Food and Drug Administration (FDA). (2005). Retrieved September 6, 2005, from http://www.fda.gov/cder/drug/infopage/antipsychotics/default.htm.

Young, R. C., & Falk, J. (1989). Age, manic psychopathology, and treatment response. *International Journal of Geriatric Psychiatry, 4*, 73–78.

Young, R. C., Gyulai, L., Mulsant, B., Flint, A., Beyer, J., Shulman, K., et al. (2004). Pharmacotherapy of bipolar disorder in old age: Review and recommendations. *American Journal of Geriatric Psychiatry, 12*(4), 342–357.

CHAPTER 13

A Multidimensional Approach to Helping Patients with Bipolar Disorder

The difficulties patients with bipolar disorder experience can often be addressed on several levels simultaneously: nutritional, biological, medical, pharmacologic, individual, couple/family, and group. All interventions aim at stabilizing the patients and the environments in which they function. Research indicates that combining specific forms of psychotherapy with medication produces better outcomes. There is also some evidence that combining nutritional and biological rhythm interventions with medication can enhance treatment results.

Patients should not attempt to self-treat with any of the following supplements or methods without first discussing them with their physician and therapist. The information provided for nutritional, biological rhythm, medical, and pharmacologic interventions are based on research described in the medical, psychiatric, and psychological literature. The citations for this information have been provided in previous chapters and will not be repeated here.

Basic Nutritional Support

There is some evidence that each of the nutrients listed in Table 13.1 may ease the symptoms of bipolar disorder. They are important for overall good health and are generally safe when used in moderation and are, with the exception of the omega-3 fatty acid EPA, inexpensive.

TABLE 13.1

Nutritional Supplements

- Multivitamin/mineral formula
- B complex (*only if adequate dosages are not available in the multi*)—preferably with at least some of vitamin B6 in the form of P5P
- Sublingual B12—preferably as methylcobalamin (oral B12 may by poorly absorbed)
- Folinic acid or Metafolin—folic acid may not be useful
- Magnesium—preferably in a form other than magnesium oxide (take RDA)
- Zinc
- One to two grams of EPA per day—elimination of trans fat and reduction of saturated fat and omega-6 intake is advisable

Biological Rhythms

It would be best for patients to maintain consistent work and activity schedules. Patients should be encouraged to consider seeking special accommodations at work to enhance stability and reduce stress, especially when first returning to work after a period of illness. The real key to stability for many patients is consistent sleep/wake times, even on weekends. Bed times and waking times should not be too late. In addition, patients should avoid exposure to late-night bright light and be sure to get at least some midday bright light. Patients should be urged to get into the habit of turning off the computer, TV, and any electronic device that emits light early in the evening. The bedroom should be as dark as possible. The windows should have room-darkening shades or opaque blinds. An eye mask should be used if the room is exposed to any remaining light or if the room faces the morning sun.

Patients should avoid caffeine, late-evening exercise, highly emotionally-charged discussions, and alcohol use. They should have a relaxing bedtime routine that can take place in dim light (listening to soothing music, the radio, or a recorded book, meditation). Reading would be okay if it is not too late at night and the light is not too bright. An air cleaner or white-noise machine can be used to help induce sleep.

Cognitive-behavioral approaches to insomnia can be helpful (Morin, 2004). First of all, patients should be helped to understand that occasional problems with sleep are not a catastrophe. Anxiety about not sleeping will only keep one awake. It is probably best if a clock is not visible in order to reduce preoccupation with the time. An alarm can be used if there is concern about oversleeping. It is best not to lie in bed for a long time thinking about problems or worrying about not sleeping. Patients might be advised that bedtime is for sleeping and not for problem solving. An overactive mind can be dealt with through distraction: thinking of pleasant things or concentrating on the natural rising and falling rhythm of the abdomen associated with breathing. Of course, unpleasant thoughts or concerns will return. As soon as the person becomes aware of them, he or she can gently shift attention back to pleasant thoughts or his or her breathing. If drowsiness is not felt within a reasonable period of time, then the person should get out of bed and not return until he or she feels sleepy. The same procedure can be used for middle-of-the night awakenings.

Patients can experiment with natural remedies for insomnia. Some people find herbal preparations such as valerian, hops, lemon balm, chamomile, and their combinations to be helpful. Others report that the amino acid GABA or the tryptophan-metabolite 5-HTP work for them.

Severe or prolonged insomnia or insomnia that is not responding to the measures previously discussed should be treated aggressively with medication. Some patients do well with benzodiazepines, although these drugs can be habit forming and addictive. Patients should anticipate they may have some temporary rebound insomnia when they discontinue these drugs after prolonged administration or the use of high doses. These drugs should be tapered off according to a physician's or nurse practitioner's instructions. New-generation hypnotic drugs like Ambien, Lunesta, or Rozerem can be considered. Lithium and divalproex (Depakote) may help when the entire daily dose is taken at bedtime. Seroquel is a very sedating atypical antipsychotic that also effectively treats mania and bipolar depression. Sedating antidepressant drugs such as trazadone (Desyrel), which are often prescribed for insomnia, should be avoided in bipolar patients. The availability of many other effective agents combined with the risk of adverse effects associated with antidepressants in patients with bipolar disorder make trazadone a poor choice. In addition, use of trazadone in men runs the risk of causing a dangerous, prolonged erection (priapism).

Exercise, particularly when done at the same time each day, can enhance the stability of biological rhythms and have antidepressant effects.

Medical

Medical disorders that can contribute to or cause symptoms of depression and mania are not rare. All clinicians must consider that patients may have an organic illness that is at least partially responsible for his or her symptoms. Physical examination, a medical history, and appropriate lab work are a must for all patients entering psychotherapy.

Common comorbid medical disorders, especially obesity, diabetes, sleep apnea, and cardiovascular disease, should be aggressively treated. If weight gain from medications cannot be controlled with diet and exercise, other measures should be taken. Topiramate or perhaps zonisamide can be prescribed or, if possible, the patient can be switched to a medication that does not cause as much weight gain. Patients and their physicians will have to discuss and weigh the risks of discontinuing an effective medication against the risks of weight gain.

Clinicians should suspect sleep apnea in middle-aged and older patients who are overweight and have high blood pressure, especially if they snore loudly. Untreated sleep apnea can lead to irritability and cognitive difficulties and be dangerous if left untreated.

Special attention needs to be paid to thyroid functioning in patients with treatment-resistant depression or rapid cycling. Family physicians, internists, and endocrinologists will often be satisfied with low normal thyroid functioning. For patients with bipolar disorder, low normal levels may not be optimal. Older women with residual depressive symptoms, fatigue, lethargy, and cognitive impairment, or with a family history of thyroid illness, may benefit from thyroid hormone supplementation. Some investigators and clinicians would add thyroid hormone regardless of the results of thyroid function tests in cases of treatment-resistant depression or rapid cycling.

Pharmacologic

Antidepressants should not be used initially in patients with bipolar depression or those of uncertain polarity, except perhaps in cases of severe, suicidal depression. Doing so often seems to start patients down a slippery slope of complicated and frustrating treatments. In patients who have been mistakenly treated with multiple antidepressants, clinicians should anticipate that the patient may have a less robust response to mood stabilizers and a more protracted course of treatment. Much of the chronic instability and treatment resistance seen in bipolar patients may be due not just to the nature of bipolar disorder but to the overzealous use of antidepressant medication. Bipolar patients who are on antidepressants and are rapid-cycling should be taken off these drugs. If a patient is on an antidepressant and has had a partial response but remains in a chronic, residually depressed state, the clinician can consider the addition of lithium. Or, the patient could be taken off the antidepressant and put on mood stabilizing medication and/or antipsychotics.

Individual

Temperament and Psychotherapy

Hagop Akiskal's revival of Kraepelin's ideas on the role temperament plays in psychopathology has a number of important implications for the conduct of individual psychotherapy. In Kraepelin's (1921) view, "peculiarities of the emotional life" (p. 118) are viewed as psychological epiphenomena of biologically-based temperament traits. For instance, someone who is sensitive, easily hurt, and anxious (a dysthymic or depressive temperament) will likely adapt to this temperament by becoming cautious, socially isolated, and risk aversive. That is, he or she will develop dependent and avoidant personality traits. What seem to be personality traits, can, in fact, be state-dependent phenomena. When an individual with a dysthymic temperament responds to medication, for instance, he or she may no longer feel so insecure, lacking in self-confidence, or fearful of rejection. As a result, he or she may be freed to take more risks, which may lead to greater career achievement or interpersonal satisfaction. These in turn may help to reduce depression.

It is often more helpful for the psychotherapist to approach a patient's difficulties from a temperamental or "wiring" point of view than a characterological one. The former exonerates the patient of blame or fault for his or her problems. The latter tends to prompt guilt and shame. The "wiring" perspective allows patients to separate themselves from the illness-related problems that plague them. It shifts focus from self-blame to learning tools to manage the problems associated with their wiring. In short, it helps protect self-esteem.

Family members sometimes express concern that this model strips patients of responsibility for their problems and allows them to use their illnesses as an excuse for unacceptable behavior or lack of effort. While this is a risk, patients are not required to be at fault to take responsibility for doing something about their illnesses. We don't blame people for having type 1 diabetes but we do expect them to take responsibility for managing it properly. Another implication of the temperament perspective for the conduct of psychotherapy is that temperament alters patients' perceptions. It causes them to overreact or react in idiosyncratic ways to unpleasant stimuli and stress. Perception of others' more positive traits may be blocked. In addition, tough problems may seem overwhelming and impossible to solve. As Kraepelin noted nearly a hundred years ago, depressive patients "in every occurrence feel the small disagreeables much more strongly than the elevating and satisfying aspects" (p. 119). He describes the way depressive thinking distorts perception by noting that "every moment of pleasure is embittered [to depressive individuals] by the recollection of gloomy hours, by self-reproaches, and still more glaringly portrayed fears for the future" (p. 119). Patients very often have no awareness of this distorting process, especially if it has been life long. (For them, there is no other way to see the world.) It is difficult for patients to grasp that their reactions are not due to the nature and intensity of a stressor alone. This is a perspective that has to be introduced gradually if the therapist does not want to seem insensitive to patients' distress.

The Diagnosis of Bipolar Illness

Individuals and couples often seek outpatient mental health treatment services from various nonmedically trained professionals for relationship problems or for painful emotional symptoms. These problems are frequently due, at least in part, to dysthymic, cyclothymic, irritable, or hyperthymic temperaments or to constellations of symptoms that meet diagnostic criteria for a major depressive episode or bipolar II illness. But these individuals and couples usually are not looking for and do not expect to be given a diagnostic label. Clinicians, especially social workers, psychologists, marriage counselors, and other nonmedically trained individuals must be careful to avoid premature discussion of diagnostic labels. This is especially the case with the diagnosis of bipolar disorder. Although there is now much less stigma attached to the diagnosis of depression, many patients still react to hearing a diagnosis of bipolar disorder with shock, disbelief, irritation, and dismay. It is narcissistically wounding and frightening to many, the equivalent of being certified as hopelessly crazy.

With some patients it is best to avoid using the bipolar label at all, simply explaining that they have a different kind of depression or a cycling kind of mood disorder. It is probably best to avoid getting hung-up on diagnostic labels in any case and to focus instead on the options available to help the patient.

Issues in the Early Phase of Individual Psychotherapy

Particularly with severely depressed patients, it is best to keep things simple early in therapy. Listening attentively, reflecting feelings, and getting to know the person and the important people in their lives is key. Guilt and shame can be reduced by pointing out that problems such as lethargy or irritability are symptoms of an illness, not reflections of character. Help the patient recognize his or her strengths. Depressed people forget they have them. Do not push for patients to make changes. If the patient does not have energy or hope, expecting too much too soon can often be counterproductive. In addition, bipolar patients often suffer from a number of cognitive difficulties including impairments in working memory, attention and concentration that may make it difficult for them to construct and implement plans for change (Torrent et al., 2006). Patients often achieve symptomatic remission long before they can achieve functional remission.

An analysis of data from patients treated in the National Institute of Mental Health's Treatment of Depression Collaborative Research Program found that patients with low social dysfunction did best in interpersonal psychotherapy and patients with low cognitive dysfunction did better in cognitive-behavior therapy (Sotsky et al., 1991). This suggests that therapists are more likely to be helpful working with patients' strengths rather than trying to get them to attack problems they may feel incapable of addressing or changing.

In-depth exploration of early traumatic experiences should probably be avoided in most cases. While many patients feel better with the emotional release that comes with openly sharing their pain with a warm and understanding therapist, others may be retraumatized.

Allow the patient to be sick. While it is true that depressed patients would probably feel better being more active, the therapist must often first deal with the patient's sense of guilt and shame about not being active. Patients are often very self-critical about their inactivity. Bipolar depression may makes it nearly impossible for patients to get themselves moving in the early stages of treatment.

Issues in the Middle Phase of Individual Psychotherapy

Mindfulness of Depressive Thinking and Rumination Therapists should consider helping their patients get a sense of when they are in the grip of depressive thinking. Combating depressive thinking either with rational disputing, distraction or with behavioral activation obviously begins with recognition of the problem.

Cognitive-behavioral therapists have cataloged and described characteristic cognitive distortions. They include all-or-nothing thinking ("I am a failure at everything I do."), disqualifying the positive ("Yes, I have a college degree but so do a lot of people. It means nothing."), catastrophizing ("It would be absolutely horrible if people saw that I was anxious."), and emotional reasoning ("I feel as if the future is hopeless, therefore it is."). Patients can learn to recognize these distortions as the first step in gaining some control over them. It is also critical that therapists familiarize themselves with the various types of cognitive distortions so they can quickly recognize them in their patients. Depressed patients' gloomy and pessimistic assessments can be so powerful and pervasive that therapists can be seduced into thinking things really are as bad as the patient portrays. This is particularly the case when, as is not uncommon, therapists themselves have struggled with depression.

Patients should be helped to recognize rumination and what sets it apart from adaptive mental rehearsal or problem solving. Rumination is a nonproductive and often painful process of brooding about one's faults, misfortunes, mistakes, or lack of future prospects. Patients may benefit from learning distraction through action or, as others have put it: Do, don't stew.

Behavioral Activation Colom and Vieta (2006) believe that "most of the targets of psychological treatment that may lead our patients to a good social, interpersonal and occupational functioning may only be reached once the patient is euthymic" (p. 338). As previously discussed, some patients should not be urged to make changes until they are feeling much better. However, if patients are only mildly to moderately ill, behavioral activation techniques may also move them towards euthymia. Even if activity does not bring euthymia, it may still improve the quality of life. Symptoms can be ignored to some extent and feelings do not necessarily have to dictate actions. This is akin to how some schizophrenic patients learn to pay less attention to auditory hallucinations as they struggle to recover.

Clinicians naturally tend to be on the look-out for ways in which their bipolar patients are actively self-destructive—spending money they do not have, sexual indiscretions, and abuse of alcohol and drugs, for example. But depressed bipolar patients can also be passively self-destructive in ways that can easily escape therapists' attention. Depressed bipolar patients may, for example, not pay their mortgage or car insurance or not seek medical attention when it is necessary.

Patients seem less inclined to mention these passively self-destructive actions to their therapists than the actively self-destructive ones. Therapists need to ask about them periodically.

Patients with bipolar depression frequently feel unmotivated. They often lack desire to do just about anything including getting out of bed. Sometimes they feel quite ashamed of this inactivity. (Never assume, however, that their assessment of how much they have accomplished is accurate. Sometimes, under the perceptual distortion that is characteristic of depressive thinking, they have actually gotten more done in a day than they realize.) On the one hand, they do not want to do anything but on the other hand they feel as if they should. Before they can be helped to overcome the motivational deficit, this internal conflict must be eased. Start by asking patients to think about the advantages of getting things done. Lead them toward the realization that being busy is better for no reason other than that it feels better than lying around ruminating about their problems. But, suggest they test this out for themselves by staying in bed one day and then doing some chores and pleasurable activities the next. For more on the treatment of depression with behavioral activation, readers are referred to Martell et al. (2001).

Medication Compliance If we expect patients to simply comply with our instructions about taking a particular medication, then we become as much a source of compliance problems as our patients. As Goodwin and Jamison (1990) note, compliance is as much a psychotherapeutic issue as it is a medical one. It is profoundly disturbing to many patients to be told that medication would help mental and emotional symptoms they believe should be under voluntary control. The depressed individual, already feeling beaten up by life and internal self-criticism, usually takes the news about medication as yet another punishing blow to his or her self-esteem. This tends to be especially true when it comes to taking mood-stabilizing and antipsychotic drugs. Until Prozac first came on the market in 1989, antidepressants were not something the average person had heard much about. There was a lot of stigma attached to depression and the use of medication. This is largely a thing of the past, at least in urban areas of the country. But the stigma attached to using mood stabilizers and antipsychotics is still substantial. Patients have many misconceptions about the use of these drugs including that they are used only by really crazy people or that they risk being turned into drug-dependent zombies. All these fears and misconceptions require exploration, education and time to work through.

After asking about side effects, a patient with bipolar illness nearly always asks how long he or she will need to take drugs. He or she usually has some idea of the answer to come. After answering the patient in whatever manner seems appropriate at the moment, a clinician can discuss problems the patient would like to target with medication and talk about how medication may help. The clinician might then say to the patient that he or she will decide for how long he or she takes medication.

Compliance issues arise with elements of psychosocial interventions as well as with medication. Interpersonal social rhythm therapy, family-focused treatment, cognitive-behavioral therapy, and behavioral activation all require that patients do something outside the office. This is the Achilles Heel of every psychotherapeutic method. Patients in clinical settings are much less likely to comply with homework assignments than patients in research settings, which is why methods that look so promising under controlled conditions are often much less effective in actual practice. Clinicians interested in learning tools for dealing with noncompliance issues in cognitive-behavioral practice, in particular, can consult Leahy, 2006.

Manic Defenses Psychodynamic principles for understanding and treating patients, especially those with serious psychiatric illnesses such as schizophrenia and manic-depressive illness, have lost their cachet. Although it would be foolish to limit psychotherapeutic work with bipolar patients to strictly psychodynamic interventions, it is an error to discard psychodynamic principles and techniques entirely. As Cookson and Ghalib (2005) note, a psychoanalytic perspective can be helpful in understanding the interpersonal dynamics of the bipolar patient. This is particularly true when it comes to understanding the dynamics of the patient's relationship with the therapist.

In interpersonal relationships, including the relationship with the therapist, hypomanic patients make use of the so-called manic defenses of omnipotent control and contempt. They do so in the service of avoiding feelings of guilt, vulnerability, and fears of abandonment. Carefree, euphoric hypomania and pressure of speech can be used to avoid depressive affect and true emotional contact with the therapist. Janowsky et al. (1974) in studying the "interpersonal maneuvers" (p. 250) of manic patients discovered that manic patients often manage to get clinicians caught up in intellectualized debates that help them avoid underlying feelings and emotional connection with their therapists. While hypomania serves to defend a bipolar patient against feelings of despair, helplessness, and low self-esteem, clinicians will also find that bipolar depressed patients' self-criticism, lack of self-confidence, and fears of disapproval often cover shame-provoking grandiosity. Bipolar depressed patients, who worry what others think of them, are sometimes secretly judgmental and harbor the feeling that they are actually superior to others.

Readers interested in the psychodynamic approach to depression and hypomania should consult Lewin (1950), Arieti and Bemporad (1993), Busch et al. (2004), and MacKinnon et al. (2006).

Couple/Family

The spouse of a bipolar patient can often feel as if he or she is being driven crazy. When depressed, the ill spouse may lie in bed or on a couch watching TV. He or she may not contribute anything to the upkeep of the home. He or she either withdraws or becomes very dependent on the well spouse for his or her basic needs. When manic, however, he or she may be nasty, critical, and emotionally unavailable. His or her spending habits may bring the family to the brink of financial ruin, he or she may be promiscuous, or he or she may become involved in using drugs. Understandably, the wife or husband of such an individual will feel frightened, worried for him or herself and the children, frustrated, enraged, and confused about what to do. The well spouse will likely intervene initially in ways that are aimed at bringing his or her spouse under control, but that inadvertently make the situation worse. This is especially the case when the spouse does not realize or refuses to believe that his or her husband or wife is ill and, to a large degree, unable to control his or her behavior.

In a study of 37 partners of bipolar patients, for instance, partners who believed that patients could control their behavior used strategies to influence behavior that added to the couple's problems (Lam et al., 2005). They may, for instance, engage in highly critical personal attacks (based as much, perhaps, on fear of the situation slipping out of control as frustration) that elicit defensive counterattacks or withdrawal from an irritably hypomanic individual. These behaviors may then prompt further attacks by the well spouse, leading to escalating arguments or further deterioration. Reversal of this pattern begins with acknowledgment of the well spouse's fear and frustration. The spouse is then helped to understand that the bipolar patient's behavior is not willfully chosen and does not reflect a lack of love or concern for family.

This is not to say that spouses need to excuse their bipolar husband's or wife's behavior, put up with abuse, or not expect their spouses to change or get help. It simply means that the spouse of the bipolar individual has to avoid the natural tendency to fight fire with fire. That will just ignite a conflagration.

What if the spouse denies he or she is ill and refuses to go for help? This is typical when the spouse is manic or hypomanic. The best time to suggest help is when the individual is depressed. In either case, he or she should appeal to his or her spouse's self-interest by pointing out he or she does not have to be in so much pain or feel so miserable. The husband or wife should learn as much as possible about the illness, so that he or she can gradually educate his or her spouse about the nature of the problem. This approach requires a great deal of patience but is generally more effective than nagging or threatening the individual.

Undiagnosed subthreshold irritable and cyclothymic temperaments may be an important and unrecognized factor in many marital conflicts. That is, one or both of the partners are moody, dissatisfied, irritable, or have explosive tempers, but they do not meet *DSM-IV* criteria for a major depressive episode or bipolar disorder. Lesser (1983) described seven patients with histories of hypomania whose presenting problem was marital conflict. Only one had previously been correctly diagnosed as bipolar.

Spouses with similar mood disorders or temperaments may tend to get married more often than one would expect by chance alone. Gershon et al. (1973)

described the concept of assortative mating. That is, the tendency for individuals with similar temperament dysregulations to marry each other. A meta-analysis with six controlled studies showed definite evidence for this process and indicated assortative mating is higher for individuals with bipolar disorder than for those with major depression (Mathews & Reus, 2001).

When both partners have highly reactive, irritable temperaments, it may be difficult to get them to learn and apply effective communication skills and rational problem-solving methods. Education about their temperaments may begin to allow them to get some distance from their emotions. However, the clinician needs to be cautious in bringing up this point of view. If done too quickly, partners may feel as if the clinician is insensitive to the emotional hardships they have to endure at the hands of their spouse.

The goal is to get each spouse to stay calm in the face of provocation. A husband with a highly reactive temperament, for instance, may feel quite justified in responding in kind to what he considers unfair hostility or criticism. This may be especially the case if the criticism leveled at him has some degree of truth to it. Sometimes a spouse's anger at his or her partner's irritability can be deflected from direct expression into a temporarily more adaptive passive-aggressive stance. This can be accomplished by pointing out the advantage to a spouse of staying in control: it highlights the other spouse's out-of-control behavior.

When the Patient Is an Adolescent or Adult Child

Staying calm in the face of provocation is not easy with irritable or explosive adolescents and young adults. This is particularly be the case for parents of bipolar patients, who themselves often have an irritable or explosive temperament, Putting together a parent who is stubborn and easily irritated with a child who has the same temperament is a recipe for child abuse or family violence. Interestingly, Goldstein et al. (2002) found that relatives who were critical, hostile, or overinvolved with their bipolar family member were *not* more likely to have *DSM* Axis I diagnoses or more mood and temperamental disturbances than those who were not critical or hostile. This is certainly not what one would expect based on what Kraepelin (1921) and scores of other clinicians have observed and documented about family members, what is known about the heritability of bipolar disorder, or the research on assortative mating. The researchers used self-report questionnaires to determine psychopathology and temperamental disturbances. One explanation for the counter-intuitive results may be that participants did not feel comfortable answering the questions openly.

Bipolar patients' demands and angry outbursts are often interpreted by family members as expressions of a willful disregard for the rights and feelings of others. This erroneous attribution of motive may prompt parents and siblings to react with angry criticism and character assassination, which only serves to heighten the emotional tension in the house and irritate the patient further.

Out of fear for their and their son or daughters' future, parents of adult children with bipolar disorder often try to get them to be more independent through nagging criticism. At the same time, they may inappropriately support their child's dependence on them by providing money or paying bills for which the adult child should be responsible. Sometimes parents have a paralyzing fear that if support is withdrawn the patient may do something criminal or become violent or suicidal. While such outcomes do occur and plans need to be made to address such possibilities, parents generally tend to overestimate the risk of such worst-case scenarios. They also tend to exaggerate the results of having the police or the courts involved. In short, they are convinced that the results of taking action would be catastrophic. At the same time, they often grossly underestimate the risks of not acting.

Parents of adult bipolar patients will often contact therapists to find out how to handle these individuals. This often happens after months and years of pushing the children to accept that they are ill and to seek help. Unfortunately, bipolar teens and young adults, especially males, often do not see a need for help and stubbornly refuse to get it. If they go for help, they are often very unwilling participants. Adolescent boys often seem to believe their only problem lies in their parents' irritating behavior. They figure that if mother and father would just stop bothering them, they would be fine and would not be so irritable. It is hard for them to conceive that they might also be irritated much of the time because they have an irritable temperament. Unfortunately, trying to help them understand and consider this alternative explanation often seems to irritate them even further.

To understand what might be most helpful in these situations, it is best to start with an understanding of what is not helpful: Confronting the individual with the fact that he or she is ill and needs help, or nagging, threatening, and criticizing him or her are probably worse than doing nothing. Such efforts create a great deal of tension and only serve to alienate the youngster from his or her parents. Parents should curb their efforts to mobilize, direct, orchestrate, or control the patient. Listening to the individual and finding out what is bothering him or her (as opposed to telling him or her how his or her behavior is bothering you), appealing to his or her self-interest in an effort to move him or her toward accepting help, identifying and supporting strengths, and providing encouragement for small steps are key. Teens and young adults are more likely to get help for a major psychiatric illness if they think there is something in it for them. So, for example, the adolescent or adult child can be told that he or she does not need to feel so depressed, unmotivated or have so little energy he or she can not get out of bed. These should be labeled as symptoms for which help is available. Families and therapists will find practical, detailed steps on how to approach patients from this perspective in Amador (2007). Finally, as Akiskal and Akiskal (2006) point out, it is important that families express warmth and caring for the patient to counterbalance their inevitable criticism and anger. Parents, especially fathers, must struggle to maintain a positive connection with their child. Failing to do so will make it much harder for parents to persuade their son or daughter to get help. Marital satisfaction in a couple with a child who is refusing help will be enhanced if the partners can avoid blaming each other for a child's problems and work together on a plan for dealing with him or her (Cook et al., 1992).

Groups and Beyond

Kessler et al. (2006) reported that bipolar disorder was associated with 65.5 and major depressive disorder with 27.2 lost workdays per ill worker per year. The higher productivity loss associated with bipolar disorder compared to major depressive disorder was due to more severe and persistent depressive episodes in those with bipolar disorder, rather than to manic and hypomanic episodes. The lethargy, lack of motivation, and inactivity characteristic of bipolar depression can breed demoralization, further depression, and lead to a spiraling down of functional abilities. Patients with significant functional impairment, particularly in their roles as workers, or those who have trouble getting out of bed and who lie about the house all day, should be strongly considered for intensive day treatment or partial hospitalization programs. These programs focus on activating patients in ways that can reverse demoralization and depression and prevent patients from becoming psychiatric invalids. Some young adult patients with bipolar illness have never left their parents' homes and function at very low levels vocationally. They would probably benefit from the services of vocational rehabilitation counselors who could provide supported employment placements.

Groups, both professionally lead and self-help support groups, can decrease the shame and stigma associated with bipolar illness. They can also reduce the social isolation many members of these families feel. Clinicians should keep in mind that family members need support in ways that therapists can not provide. Sharing the sorrow and the burden of having a disabled family member with others who are in the same position can be very healing and goes a long way toward reducing shame. Family members can be referred to multiple family groups provided by organizations such as the National Alliance for the Mentally Ill.

Finally, euthymic patients with bipolar illness who become involved in patients' rights movements and legislative advocacy can put their natural energy, passion, and often considerable interpersonal skill to good use. As long as they exercise caution about not overextending themselves and minimize the extent to which they might become embroiled in heated exchanges with other high-energy, driven people, these efforts can bring tremendous personal satisfaction while contributing to significant social change.

References

Akiskal, H. & Akiskal, K. (2006). Principles of caring for bipolar patients. In H. Akiskal & M. Tohen (Eds.), *Bipolar psychopharmacotherapy* (pp. 367–387). West Sussex, England: Wiley.

Amador, X. (2007). *I am not sick, I don't need help* (2nd ed.). Peconic, NY: Vida Press.

Arieti, S., & Bemporad, J. (1993). *Psychotherapy of severe and mild depression*. New York: Jason Aronson.

Busch, F., Rudden, M., & Shapiro, T. (2004). *Psychodynamic treatment of depression*. Washington, DC: APA Press.

Colom, F., & Vieta, E. (2006). The pivotal role of psychoeducation in the long-term treatment of bipolar disorder. In H. Akiskal & M. Tohen (Eds.), *Bipolar psychopharmacotherapy* (pp. 333–345). West Sussex, England: Wiley.

Cook, J. A., Hoffschmidt, S., Cohler, B. J., & Pickett, S. (1992). Marital satisfaction among parents of the severely mentally ill living in the community. *American Journal of Orthopsychiatry, 62*(4), 552–563.

Cookson, J., & Ghalib, S. (2005). The treatment of bipolar mixed states. In A. Marneros & F. Goodwin (Eds.), *Bipolar disorders: Mixed states, rapid cycling and atypical forms* (pp. 324–352). New York: Cambridge University Press.

Gershon, E. S., Dunner, D. L., Sturt, L., & Goodwin, F. K. (1973). Assortative mating in the affective disorders. *Biological Psychiatry, 7*(1), 63–74.

Goldstein, T. R., Miklowitz, D. J., & Richards, J. A. (2002). Expressed emotion attitudes and individual psychopathology among the relatives of bipolar patients. *Family Process, 41*(4), 645–657.

Goodwin, F., & Jamison, K. (1990). *Manic-depressive illness*. New York: Oxford University Press.

Janowsky, D. S., el-Yousef, M. K., & Davis, J. M. (1974). Interpersonal maneuvers of manic patients. *American Journal of Psychiatry, 131*(3), 250–255.

Kessler, R. C., Akiskal, H. S., Ames, M., Birnbaum, H., Greenberg, P., A, R. M., et al. (2006). Prevalence and effects of mood disorders on work performance in a nationally representative sample of U.S. workers. *American Journal of Psychiatry, 163*(9), 1561–1568.

Kraepelin, E. (1921). *Manic-depressive insanity and paranoia*. Salem, NH: Ayer Company.

Lam, D., Donaldson, C., Brown, Y., & Malliaris, Y. (2005). Burden and marital and sexual satisfaction in the partners of bipolar patients. *Bipolar Disorders, 7*(5), 431–440.

Leahy, R. (Ed.). (2006). *Roadblocks in cognitive-behavioral therapy: Transforming challenges into opportunities for change*. New York: Guilford.

Lesser, A. L. (1983). Hypomania and marital conflict. *Canadian Journal of Psychiatry, 28*(5), 362–366.

Lewin, B. (1950). *The psychoanalysis of elation*. New York: W.W. Norton.

MacKinnon, R., Michels, R., & Buckley, P. (2006). *The psychiatric interview in clinical practice* (2nd ed.). Washington, DC: APA Press.

Martell, C., Addis, M., Jascobson, N., & Addis, M. (2001). *Depression in context: Strategies for guided action*. New York: W.W. Norton.

Mathews, C. A., & Reus, V. I. (2001). Assortative mating in the affective disorders: A systematic review and meta-analysis. *Comprehensive Psychiatry, 42*(4), 257–262.

Morin, C. M. (2004). Cognitive-behavioral approaches to the treatment of insomnia. *Journal of Clinical Psychiatry, 65*(Suppl. 16), 33–40.

Sotsky, S. M., Glass, D. R., Shea, M. T., Pilkonis, P. A., Collins, J. F., Elkin, I., et al. (1991).

Patient predictors of response to psychotherapy and pharmacotherapy: Findings in the NIMH Treatment of Depression Collaborative Research Program. *American Journal of Psychiatry, 148*(8), 997–1008.

Torrent, C., Martinez-Aran, A., Daban, C., Sanchez-Moreno, J., Comes, M., Goikolea, J. M., et al. (2006). Cognitive impairment in bipolar II disorder. *British Journal of Psychiatry, 189,* 254–259.

A Remarkable Medicine Has Been Overlooked (Dreyfus), 144

Abbott Laboratories, 130, 137, 154, 155, 192

ABC approach to comorbid ADHD and bipolar disorder, 296

Abilify. See Aripiprazole (Abilify)

Achenbach Child Behavior Checklist (CBCL), 291

Achenbach Child Behavior Checklist, teacher informant version (CBCL TRF), 291

Acute dysphoric mania, 161

Administration on Aging, 309

Agranulocytosis, 141, 153, 154

Akathisia, 149, 150–151, 156, 157, 188, 199

Akiskal, H., 13, 19, 23, 44, 47, 72, 79, 135, 181, 324, 332

Akiskal, K., 332

Albanese, M., 97, 100

Alcohol abuse and dependence (AUD) in bipolar patients:
age of onset, 98–99
and suicide risk, 262
family history, 97–98
vs. in general population, 96
identifying AUD patients, 104–111
interviewing, 114–115
management of, 111–117
in older adults, 312
overview, 95–99
primary, 97
questions to identify AUD, 110–111
secondary, 97
stages of change, 112–113
treatment of, 117–118
women, 97

Alcohol Use Disorders Identification Test (AUDIT), 108

Algorithms, 163–164, 296

Alprazolam (Xanax), 104

Altshuler, L., 186, 187

American Association of Clinical Endocrinologists, 152

American Diabetes Association (ADA), 152

American Psychiatric Association, 17, 131, 152, 160, 164, 208, 280, 282, 284, 285, 289

Amlodipine (Norvasc), 158

Anabolic steroid abuse, vs. bipolar disorder, 60, 62, 64, 67

Anticonvulsants:
vs. antidepressants, 208
and bipolar depression, 181–182, 189, 191
and bipolar patients with substance abuse, 117–118
and eating disorders, 85
and ECT, 243
future of, 144–148, 195–198
and lithium, 135
and mania, 129, 131
and polypharmacy, 163
and rapid cycling, 162
and suicide risk, 188, 267
See also Carbamazepine (Tegretol); Divalproex sodium (Depakote); Felbamate (Felbatol); Gabapentin (Neurontin); Lamotrigine (Lamictal); Levetiracetam (Keppra); Phenytoin (Dilantin); Primidone (Mysoline); Tiagabine (Gabatril); Topiramate (Topamax); Zonisamide (Zonegran)

Antidepressants, treating bipolar depression with (*see* Bipolar depression, antidepressants)

Antiglucocorticoids, 201–202

Anxiety disorders and bipolar illnesses, 43, 80, 85–88, 147
in BP II patients, 24
in alcohol-dependent patients, 96–97
and levetiracetam, 147, 197
in pediatric bipolar disorder, 287, 288–289

Aretaeus of Cappadocia, 11, 275

Aripiprazole (Abilify), 150, 151, 152, 153, 156, 157, 158, 193, 200–201, 209

Arsenapine, 157

Artane. *See* Trihexyphenidyl (Artane)

AstraZeneca, 156, 198

Ativan. *See* Lorazepam (Ativan)

Atomoxetine (Strattera), 69

Attention-Deficit Hyperactivity Disorder (ADHD), 60, 67, 69, 84, 158, 247. *See also* Child and adolescent bipolar disorder, and ADHD

Atypical antipsychotic drugs:
  and bipolar depression,
    198–201, 209
  and older adults, 316
  overview, 149–150, 162,
    181–182
  problems associated with, 150
  under investigation, 157–158
  and suicide, 267
  and weight gain, 153
  See also Aripiprazole (Abilify);
    Clozapine (Clozaril);
    Olanzapine (Zyprexa);
    Olanzapine/Fluoxetine
    combination (Symbyax);
    Paliperidone ER (Invega);
    Quetiapine (Seroquel);
    Risperidone (Risperdal);
    Ziprasidone (Geodon)
Atypical depression, 18–19,
  43–45, 85, 184
Aura, 83
Axelson, D., 277, 279
Axis I and Axis II personality
  disorders, DSM-IV-TR demarcation of, 18

B vitamin supplementation,
  206–207, 242
Baillarger, Jules, 11
Ball, J., 233
Bauer, M., 234
Beck, A., 232
Benazzi, F., 44, 49, 72, 73
Benzodiazepine drugs, 104,
  158, 162, 245, 267, 323. See
  also Alprazolam (Xanax);
  Clonazepam (Klonopin);
  Lorazepam (Ativan)
Benztropine (Cogentin), 151
Biederman, J., 278, 280, 282,
  288, 296
Bifeprunox, 157, 158
Biocyclical rhythms, 322
Bipolar depression:
  age of onset, 45
  antidepressants
    and adverse effects, 180–182,
    187–191

and induced switch, 181,
  182–184, 185
vs. lithium, 181–182
long-term use, 186–187,
  190
MAOI antidepressants, 184
in older adults, 316–317
and relapse, 187, 190
response to antidepressants,
  50–54, 151
SSRI antidepressants,
  182–184, 186
use of, 179–182, 324
and atypical antipsychotics,
  198–201
atypical depression (see Atypical depression)
and behavioral activation,
  233–234
bright light therapy, 244
and B vitamin supplementation, 206–207
and bupropion (Wellbutrin),
  183–184, 209
and comorbid disorders,
  47–48
clinician's reaction to patient,
  39–41
course of, 45
depressive mixed states and,
  42–43
in DSM-IV-TR, 38
and duloxetine (Cymbalta),
  184–185
and experimental drugs,
  201–202
family history, 48–49
and folate deficiency,
  206–207
and homocysteine levels,
  206–207
inventories for diagnosis, 54
markers for, 53
mnemonic for, 54
and modafinil (Provigil), 201
nonpharmacologic treatment
  of, 242 (see also Nonpharmacologic approaches)
overview, 37–38

phenomenology, 38–39,
  41–44
premorbid history, 45–47
signs, 38–39
sleep-wake cycle manipulation, 245
and stimulants, 201
and suicide, 187–188 (see also
  Suicide risk)
symptom clusters, 41
symptoms, 41–44, 184
and thyroid augmentation,
  202–206, 209
treatment of, 191–207
treatment in outpatient settings, 207–209
and venlafaxine (Effexor), 184
and women, 27, 45, 251
See also Kraepelin, Emil
Bipolar diathesis, 19, 39, 43,
  79, 88, 189, 190, 195
Bipolar I disorder (BP I):
  and AUD, 98
  vs. BP II, 24
  in children and adolescents
    (see Child and early adoles-
    cent bipolar disorder)
  defined, 14–15
  in older adults (see Bipolar dis-
    order in older adults)
  overview, 20–22
  phenomenology of, 22
  psychosocial treatment of (see
    Psychosocial treatment)
  and suicide risk, 179
  symptoms, 21
  See also Bipolar depression;
    Bipolar illnesses; Mania;
    Mixed episodes; Rapid
    cycling
Bipolar II disorder (BP II):
  adult vs. children with, 23–24
  and atypical depression (see
    Bipolar depression)
  vs. BP I, 24
  in children and adolescents
    (see Child and early adoles-
    cent bipolar disorder)
  defined, 15

depression with cyclothymia, 23

depression with hypersomnia, 17, 43–44

family history, 24

and hypomania, 24

in older adults (*see* Bipolar disorder in older adults)

overview, 23–24

psychosocial treatment of (*see* Psychosocial treatment)

and suicide risk, 24, 49

symptoms, 23

See also Bipolar depression; Bipolar illnesses; Mania; Mixed episodes; Rapid cycling

Bipolar disorder not otherwise specified (BP NOS):

in children and adolescents (*see* Child and early adolescent bipolar disorder)

defined, 15

in older adults (*see* Bipolar disorder in older adults)

See also Bipolar depression; Bipolar illnesses; Mania; Mixed episodes; Rapid cycling

Bipolar disorder in older adults:

age of onset, 3310

assessment, 313–314

clinical presentation, 311–313

cognitive impairment, 312–313

considerations, 310

diagnosis, 314

medical comorbidity, 312

medical treatment of, 314–317

overview, 309–310, 318

prevalence, 311

psychotherapy, 317–318

subgroups of, 313

Bipolar Eating Disorders Scale (BEDS), 85

Bipolar illnesses:

and ADHD (*see* Attention-Deficit Hyperactivity Disorder[ADHD])

age of onset, 20, 45

vs. anabolic steroid abuse, 67

and antidepressants, 28–29, 324 (*see also* Bipolar depression, antidepressants)

antidepressant-induced hypomania, 51

and anxiety disorders, 85–88

atypical features of, 16–17, 87

typical antipsychotic drugs, 148–149

atypical forms of (no history of hypomania), 19

bipolar depression (*see* Bipolar depression)

and cardiovascular disease, 81–82

and childhood trauma, 70, 73–74, 87–88, 97

in children and adolescents (*see* Child and early adolescent bipolar disorder)

vs. cocaine abuse diagnosis, 65–66

comorbidity, list of, 80

course of, 21–22

and criminal history, 28

dark expressions of, 39–41

and dementia, 7, 37

depression as first episode, 20

and diabetes, 81–82

differential diagnosis, 60

and dissociative identity disorder, 70

vs. dissociative disorders, 69–71

DSM-IV-TR classifications, 14–19

and *DSM-IV-TR* Cluster B personality disorders, 84

vs. *DSM-IV-TR* Cluster B personality disorder diagnosis, 71–74

and eating disorders (*see* Eating disorders and bipolar illnesses)

and epilepsy (*see* Epilepsy and bipolar illnesses)

family history, 48–49

and gender differences, 27–28

history, 11–13

and impulse control disorders, 88–89

mania as first episode, 20

medical comorbidity, 80, 81–83

vs. medical illness diagnosis, 60–64, 66, 81–83

medical mimics, 65

vs. methamphetamine abuse diagnosis, 66–67

and migraines, 82–83

misdiagnosis of, xi–xii, 20

mixed first episode, 20

mood-congruent psychotic features, 15, 67

mood-incongruent psychotic features, 16, 67

multidimensional approach to, 321

adolescent/adult child, 331–333

biological rhythms, 322–323

couples, 329–331

family, 329–331

individual psychotherapy, 324–329

medical disorders, 323–324

nutritional support, 321–322

pharmacology, 324

support groups. 333

nonpharmacologic treatment of (*see* Nonpharmacologic approaches)

and obesity, 81–82

in older adults (*see* Bipolar disorder in older adults)

and personality disorders, 84

phenotypes, 21

postpartum onset of, 17, 29, 45

and PTSD, 87–88, 97, 100

vs. PTSD, 71

prognosis of, 21–22

proposed criteria for, 52

Bipolar illnesses (*continued*)
psychiatric comorbidity,
83–89
psychosocial treatment of (*see*
Psychosocial treatment)
psychotic features of, 15–16
seasonal pattern of, 17
vs. schizophrenia and
schizoaffective disorder
diagnosis, 67–68
and sleep apnea, 82
vs. stimulant-induced mania
diagnosis, 64–67
and substance abuse, 28, 48,
83–84 (*see also* Alcohol
abuse in bipolar patients;
Drug abuse in bipolar
patients)
sunny expressions of, 39–41
and thyroid disease, 83
true comorbidity vs. common
pathophysiology, 79
and Type A personality traits,
43
and women, 27–29, 45, 97,
100, 251–252
See also *Diagnostic and Statistical Manual of Mental Dis-
orders*, fourth edition, text
revision (*DSM-IV-TR*), and
bipolar illnesses
Bipolar Spectrum Diagnostic
Scale (BSDS), 54
Blonanserin (Lonasen), 157
Body dysmorphia, 85
Body-stuffing, 101. *See also*
Methamphetamine (MA)
abuse
Borderline Personality Disorder Severity Index, 143, 195
Borselli, Sergio, 136
Bright light therapy, 162, 181,
242, 243–244, 245, 246. *See
also* Dark therapy
Bucholz, K. K., 96
Buntinx, F., 107, 108, 109
Bupropion (Wellbutrin), 183–
184, 190, 196, 208, 209
Burdick, K. E., 202

Cade, John, 129
Caffeine, 22, 102, 162, 322
CAGE, 107–108, 109
Calabrese, J., 5, 131, 191
Calan. *See* Verapamil (Calan)
Calcium channel blockers,
158–159, 251. *See also*
Amlodipine (Norvasc);
Isradipine (DynaCirc);
Nimodipine (Nimotop);
Verapamil (Calan)
Camacho, A., 100
Canadian Broadcasting Corporation (CBC), 278
Canadian Network for Mood
and Anxiety Treatments
(CANMAT), 164
Cannabis Youth Treatment
(CYT) Study, 117
Cannabis. *See* Marijuana abuse
Carbamazepine (Tegretol), 159,
161, 162, 164, 183, 188, 296
and bipolar depression, 195
dosing, 140–141
drug interactions with, 140,
142
extended release (Equetro),
140, 195
food interactions with, 142
history of, 139–140
and intermittent explosive
disorder, 88
maintenance, 141–142
overdose, 142
overview, 139–140
preparations of, 141
side effects, 141
treatment of acute mania,
140, 195 (*see also* Mania)
See also Oxcarbazepine (Trileptil)
Carbohydrate-deficient transferrin (CDT), 109
Cardiovascular disease:
and atypical antipsychotics,
149, 151
and bipolar illness, 80, 81–82,
209, 312, 323
and essential fatty acids, 247

Carlson, Gabrielle A., 278, 281,
282, 288, 290, 291, 292,
293, 295, 296
Carlson, P. J., 201
Carraz, George, 136
Centers of Disease Control
(CDC), 262
Cephalon, 148
Chang, K., 163, 280, 288, 297
Child and Adolescent Bipolar
Foundation (CABF), 275,
302
Child and early adolescent
bipolar disorder:
and ADHD, 276–277,
287–288
BP I, 284–285
BP NOS, 279, 290–291
and child abuse, 70, 87, 301,
331
classification, 289–290
comorbid conditions,
287–289
cycling, 284–285
cyclotaxia, 289
and cyclothymia, 279, 289
defining, 290–291
diagnosis, 291–295
emotional dysregulation,
289–290
epidemiology, 277–280
hypersexuality, 284
medication for, 295–297
mixed mania, 284–286
mnemonics for, 293
overview, 275–277
phenomenology, 280–287
psychosocial treatment of,
297–301
suicide risk and BP II, 286
switching, 287
treatment of, 295
Child Mania Rating Scale,
291
Chlorpromazine (Thorazine),
129, 137, 148, 149, 154
Choline, 249. *See also* Fatty
acids, essential
Churchill, Winston, 104

Clarkin, J. F., 226

Clinical Global Impressions Scale for Bipolar Illness, Modified, 146, 196, 251

Clonazepam (Klonopin), 158, 245, 267

Clozapine (Clozaril), 81, 149, 151, 152, 153–154, 156, 267

Clozaril. See Clozapine (Clozaril)

Cocaine abuse, 60, 62, 63, 65–66, 80, 96, 99–100, 101, 116, 117, 262. See also Drug abuse in bipolar patients

Cogentin. See Benztropine (Cogentin)

Compliance, 132, 224, 227, 229, 328, 329

Cortisol, 201–202

Coryell, W., 23, 24,

Course and Outcome of Bipolar Youth (COBY) study, 277, 283, 284

Crack, 99, 101. See also Cocaine abuse

Craney, J. L., 279, 280, 281, 283, 284, 285, 286

Crowding of thoughts, 42

Crystal (methamphetamine hydrochloride), 66, 101. See also Methamphetamine (MA) abuse

Cyclotaxia, 289

Cyclothymia:
  in children and adolescents, 289
  and cocaine abuse, 100
  in DSM-III, 12
  overview, 14, 20, 25, 53
  psychosocial treatment of (see Psychosocial treatment)
  and thyroid disease, 83
  See also Bipolar depression; Bipolar illnesses; Child and early adolescent bipolar disorder; Cyclothymic temperament; Mania; Mixed episodes; Rapid cycling

Cyclothymic temperament:
  and BP II disorder, 23, 85, 165
  and depression, 72, 85, 165, 207, 326
  and personality disorders, 72–73, 79, 84
  and substance abuse, 84, 100
  in children and adolescents, 289
  in marital conflict, 330
  See also Cyclothymia

Cymbalta. See Duloxetine (Cymbalta)

Cyranowski, J., 87

Dark expressions of hypomania, 4, 39–41

Dark therapy, 8, 242, 244–245, 322

Delirium, 242

Delta-9-tetrahydrocannabinol (THC). See Marijuana abuse

Dementia praecox. See Schizophrenia

Dementia Rating Scale, 314

Depakene. See Valproic acid (Depakene)

Depakote. See Divalproex sodium (Depakote)

Department of Health and Human Services (DHHS), 262

Depersonalization, 70

Depression and Bipolar Support Alliance (DBSA), 235, 302, 318

Depressive personality disorder, 18

Derealization, 70

DHEA, 252

Diabetes and bipolar illnesses, 80, 81, 149, 151, 152, 312, 316, 323

Diagnostic and Statistical Manual of Mental Disorders, third edition (DSM-III), unipolar vs. bipolar disorder, 12

Diagnostic and Statistical Manual of Mental Disorders, fourth edition, text revision (DSM-IV-TR), and bipolar illnesses:
  and antidepressant-induced hypomania, 51
  bipolar disorder categories, 14–15
  cannabis abuse, 102
  in children and adolescents, 280, 284, 285
  Cluster B personality disorders, 71–74, 84
  demarcation of personality disorders, 18
  dissociative identity disorder, 69
  mood disorder specifiers, 15–17
  mood disorder symptoms, 15–17, 71–73
  mood episodes, 13–15
  problems with classifications, 17–19
  schizoaffective disorder, 68
  shortcomings of, 18

Diazepam (Valium), 104

Dilantin. See Phenytoin (Dilantin)

Dissociative Experiences Scale (DES), 70

Divalproex sodium (Depakote), 81, 88, 117–118, 129, 130, 131, 133, 140, 144, 145, 154, 155, 156, 160, 161, 182, 244, 252, 296
  and bipolar depression, 192–193, 209 (see also Bipolar depression)
  dosing, 137–138
  history of, 136–137
  maintenance, 138–139
  in older adults, 316
  overdose, 139
  side effects, 138, 139
  treatment of acute mania, 137–139
  and women, 138, 139

DMI pattern, 131
Docoahexaenoic acid (DHA).
    See Fatty acids, essential
"Dope-amax," 146, 197
Double-blind drug studies, 130
"Double-trouble meetings,"
    115
Dreyfus Fund, 144
Dreyfus, Jack, 144
Drug abuse in bipolar patients:
    vs. general population, 96
    stages of change, 112–113
    management of, 111–117
    in older adults, 312
    overview, 95–97, 99–104
    prescription drug abuse, 104
    and PTSD, 100
    treatment of, 117–118
    and suicide risk, 262
    women, 100
    See also Drug treatment studies
Drug treatment studies,
    130–131
Duloxetine (Cymbalta),
    184–185
DynaCirc. *See* Isradipine
    (DynaCirc)
Dysphoria:
    and antidepressants, 51, 185,
        190
    and substance abuse, 116
    See also Dysphoric mood
Dysphoric mood, 4, 39, 116,
    118, 165, 190. *See also* Dys-
    phoria
Dysthymia, 18, 25, 46, 53, 190,
    253, 284
Dystonia, 149

Eating disorders and bipolar
    illnesses, 7, 47–48, 53, 72,
    80, 84–85, 86, 147, 198,
    207, 209
Echo-planar magnetic reso-
    nance spectroscopic imag-
    ing (EP-MRSI), 243
Ecstasy, 102, 104
Effexor. *See* Venlafaxine (Ef-
    fexor)

Ehlers, C. L., 230
Eicosapentanoic acid (EPA).
    See Fatty acids, essential
Elan, 147, 197
Electroconvulsive therapy
    (ECT). *See* Nonpharmaco-
    logic approaches, electro-
    convulsive therapy (ECT)
El-Mallakh, R., 51, 190.
Eli Lily, 154
Emotional dysregulation,
    289–290
Epidemiological Catchment
    Area (ECA) Survey, 96, 311
Epilepsy and bipolar illnesses,
    48, 61, 62, 80, 82, 131, 139,
    193, 197
EPS. *See* Extrapyramidal symp-
    toms (EPS)
Equetro, 140, 141, 195. *See also*
    Carbamazepine (Tegretol)
Estradiol, 66, 251–252
Euphoric hypomania, 189, 329
Euphoric mania, 25, 131, 134,
    137, 142, 160, 163, 164,
    282
Euphoric mood, 14, 19, 39, 40,
    53, 64, 293
Euthymia, 17, 46, 51, 53, 98,
    204, 244, 327
Exercise, 253
Expressed emotion (EE),
    228–230
Extrapyramidal symptoms
    (EPS), 149, 150–151, 156,
    157, 188

Fagg, J., 263
Falret, Jean-Pierre, 11
Fatty acids, essential, 20, 136,
    151, 242, 246–249, 321
Fifth Annual Conference on
    Bipolar Disorder, 162
Findling, R. L., 289
Flight of ideas, 14, 39, 42, 54,
    69, 73, 283, 288
Folate, 63, 66, 133, 163, 206–
    207, 209, 242
Folie circulaire, 11

Folinic acid. *See* Folate
Frank, E., 230, 231
Freebase, 99. *See also* Cocaine
    abuse
Fristad, M. A., 281, 293, 295,
    297, 299
Fugue, 70

Gabapentin (Neurontin), 117,
    145–146, 196, 209
Gabitril. *See* Tiagabine (Gabi-
    tril)
Gamma-aminobutyric acid
    (GABA), 242, 252, 323
Gamma-glutamyltransferase
    (GGT), 109
Gangadhar, B. N., 253
Gelenberg, A., 191
Geller, B., 282, 283, 284, 285,
    287, 292, 298
Geodon. *See* Ziprasidone (Ge-
    odon)
Ghaemi, S., 38, 52, 135, 150,
    167, 181, 186, 190
Glaxo Smith Kline, 144, 193
Goldberg Arnold, J. S. 299
Glutamatergic neurotransmis-
    sion, 197
Goldstein, M. J., 228
Graying population, 309
"The great sleep," 43
Greene, R., 299-300
Grof, P., 163

Haldol. *See* Haloperidol (Hal-
    dol)
Haloperidol (Haldol), 144, 147,
    148, 149, 158, 200
Hamilton Rating Scales for
    Depression, 143, 194, 195,
    197, 200, 251
Hawton, K., 263
Health Beliefs Model, 315
Himmelhoch, J., 86, 134, 192
Hippocrates, 11
Hirschfield, R., 5
Homocysteine levels, 206–
    207
Hydrocodone (Norco), 104

Hypercortisolemia, 201–202

Hyperthymia, 47, 53, 208

Hyperthymic temperament, 19, 26, 40, 41, 47, 49, 52, 54, 84, 100, 103, 185, 207, 326

Hyperthyroidism, 62, 80, 83, 133, 203–205, 314

Hypomania, 4, 27, 40, 164, 181, 207, 225
antidepressant-induced, 51
atypical antipsychotic–induced, 150
and BP II disorder, 4
euphoric, 189, 329
and manic defenses, 329
nonpharmacologic treatment of, 242 (*see also* Nonpharmacologic approaches)
postnatal, 45
treatment of, 164–165
uncovering a history of, 46–47
See also Hypomanic episode; Mania

Hypomanic episode:
dark, 4
defined, 4, 14, 19
duration, 18
sunny, 4
See also Hypomania

Ice (methamphetamine hydrochloride), 101. *See also* Methamphetamine (MA) abuse

Iloperidone (Zomaril), 157

Impulse control disorders and bipolar illnesses, 13, 48, 49, 73, 79, 80, 88–89, 107, 207

Inderal. *See* Propranolol (Inderal)

Inositol, 242, 249–250

Intermittent explosive disorder, 48, 49, 69, 88, 282

International Society for Bipolar Disorders (ISBD), 302

Interpersonal Inventory, 230–231

Invega. *See* Paliperidone ER (Invega)

Isocarboxazid (Marplan), 184

Isradipine (DynaCirc), 158

Janssen, P., 148

Janssen Pharmaceuticals, 148, 156

Journal of the American Academy of Child and Adolescent Psychiatry, 276

Juvenile Bipolar Research Foundation (JBRF), 302

Karippot, A., 51, 180, 190

Keppra. *See* Levetiracetam (Keppra)

Kahlbaum, Karl Ludwig, 25

Kessing, I., 37, 83

Kessler, R., 333

Kim, E. Y., 228

Kleptomania and bipolar illnesses, 80, 85, 89

Klonopin. *See* Clonazepam (Klonopin)

Koop, C. E., 315

Kowatch, R. A., 281, 295, 297, 300

Kraepelin, Emil, xii, 11–12, 21, 25, 276, 278, 340–41, 331
and forms of psychosis, 67, 309
and spectrum model, 12
and subtypes of manic-depressive illness, 40–42
and temperament, 324, 325

K-SADS Mania Rating Scale (K-SADS-MRS), 291–292

Kyte, Z., 278

L-5-methyltetrahydrofolate. *See* Folate

La folie a double forme, 11

Labile mood, 39, 53

Lam, D., 233

Lambert, P., 136

Lamictal. *See* Lamotrigine (Lamictal)

Lamotrigine (Lamictal), 117, 130, 134, 144, 154, 193–195, 208–209, 316

Lecithin, 249. *See also* Fatty acids, essential

Leibenluft, E., 282, 295

Lejoyeux, M., 88, 107

Leonhard, Karl, 12

Levetiracetam (Keppra), 146–147, 197

Licarbazepine, 144

Life Goals Program, 234–235

Lincoln, Abraham, 44, 113

Lithium, 12, 81, 85, 89, 117, 129–136, 137, 138, 140, 141, 142, 143, 144, 145, 155, 156, 159, 160, 161, 164, 191–192, 226, 246
dosing, 132
drug interaction, 134–135
and ECT, 243
future of, 135–136
history of, 129, 154, 315
maintenance, 134–135
and older adults, 315–316
orotate, 252
preparations, 132
side effects, 132–134
and suicide risk, 132, 181, 192, 267
and thyroid augmentation, 205
toxicity, 133–134
treatment of acute mania, 131–136

Lithium orotate, 252

Lithium-induced nephrogenic diabetes insipidus, 133

Lonasen. *See* Blonanserin (Lonasen)

Lorazepam (Ativan), 104, 158

"Lying diseases," 64, 105

Magnesium, 251

Magnesium aspartate hydrochloride (Magnesiocard), 251

Magnesium oxide, 159

Major depressive episode, defined, 13

Mania:
acute dysphoric, 161
age of onset, 64
dark therapy, 244–245
euphoric (*see* Euphoric mania)
nonpharmacologic treatment
of, 242 (*see also* Nonpharmacologic approaches)
in older adults, 317
organic causes of, 62
polypharmacy, 162–163
secondary, 61, 310
stimulant-induced, 64–67,
201
pharmacologic treatment of,
160–164
treatment with atypical antipsychotics, 153–158
treatment with benzodiaz-
epine, 158
treatment with calcium channel blockers, 158–159
treatment with mexiletine
(Mexitil), 1560
treatment with opiates, 160
treatment with tamoxifen
(Nolvadex), 159–160
See also Hypomania
Manic episode, defined, 13–14
*Manic-Depressive Insanity and
Paranoia* (Kraepelin), 12,
276
Manji, G. S., 159
MAOIs (monoamine oxidase
inhibitors). *See* Atypical
depression; Phenelzine
(Nardil); Isocarboxazid
(Marplan); Selegiline
(Emsam)
Marijuana abuse, 102–103,
116–117. *See also* Drug
abuse in bipolar patients
Mean Montgomery Asberg De-
pression Rating Scale, 197
Marplan. *See* Isocarboxazid
(Marplan)
McBride, L., 234
Meclobomide, 86
Melatonin, 151, 242, 245

Melemis, S. M., 159
Memantine (Namenda), 202
Merck, 102
Metabolic syndrome, 81–82,
151–152, 161
Metafolin. *See* Folate
Meth, 100. *See also* Metham-
phetamine (MA) abuse
Methamphetamine (MA)
abuse, 66–67, 100–102. *See
also* Drug abuse in bipolar
patients
Methylenetetrahydrofolate
reductase (MTHFR),
206–207
Mexiletine (Mexitil), 160
Mexitil. *See* Mexiletine (Mexitil)
Mifepristone (Mifiprex),
201–202
Migraine headaches and bipolar illnesses, 82–83
Miklowitz, D., 228, 229
Miller, W., 114
Mini-International Neuropsychiatric Interview, 314
Mini-Mental State Examination, 314
Mirapex. *See* Pramipexole
(Mirapex)
Mirtazapine (Remeron), 151
Mixed states:
age of onset, 284–284
and antidepressants, 51
defined, 14, 18
depressive, 42
nonpharmacologic treatment
of, 242 (*see also* Nonpharmacologic approaches)
overview, 25–26
and substance abuse, 97
and thyroid dysfunction, 26
and women, 27–29
Modafinil (Provigil), 201
Montgomery Asberg Depres-
sion Rating Scale, 197
Mood Disorder Questionnaire
(MDQ), 54
Mood reactivity, 18

Mood-congruent psychotic
features of bipolar illnesses,
15, 67
Mood-incongruent psychotic
features of bipolar illnesses,
16, 67
*Motivational Interviewing:
Preparing People to Change*
(Miller & Rollnick), 114
Muller-Siechender, F., 200
Mysoline. *See* Primidone (My-
soline)

Naloxone, 160
Naltrexone (ReVia), 118
Namenda. *See* Memantine
(Namenda)
National Alliance for the
Mentally Ill (NAMI), 235,
302, 333
National Alliance for Mental
Illness, 318
National Depressive and Manic-
Depressive Association. *See*
Depression and Bipolar Sup-
port Alliance (DBSA)
National Epidemiologic Sur-
vey on Alcohol and Related
Conditions (NESARC), 95,
98, 103
National Institute of Mental
Health (NIMH), 69, 275,
277, 280, 287
National Institute of Mental
Health Treatment of De-
pression Collaborative Re-
search Program, 234, 326
National Institutes of Health
(NIH), 275
National Survey on Drug Use
and Health, 102
Neuroleptic Malignant Syn-
drome (NMS), 152–153
Neurontin. *See* Gabapentin
(Neurontin)
Nimodipine (Nimotop), 158,
159, 162, 251
Nimotop. *See* Nimodipine
(Nimotop)

Nolvadex. *See* Tamoxifen (Nolvadex)
Nonpharmacologic approaches:
as adjunctive treatments, 241
B vitamins (*see* B vitamin supplementation)
for bipolar depression, 242
bright light therapy, 243–244
dark therapy, 244–245
DHEA, 252
dietary amino acids and their metabolites, 250
electroconvulsive therapy (ECT), 241–243, 317
essential fatty acids, 246–249
exercise, 253
folate (*see* Folate)
homocysteine (*see* Homocysteine levels)
for hypomania, 242
inositol, 249–250
for mania, 242
magnesium, 251
for mixed states, 242
nutritional approaches, 252
qigong, 253
repetitive transcranial magnetic stimulation (rTMS), 243
reproductive hormones, 251–252
sleep-wake cycle manipulation, 245–246
vagus nerve stimulation (VNS), 243
vanadium, 252
vitamin D3, 251
yoga, 253
zinc, 251
Norco (hydrocodone), 104
North American Association for the Study of Obesity, 152
Norvasc. *See* Amlodipine (Norvasc)
Novartis, 139
Nutrition, 8, 252, 321–322

Obesity and bipolar illnesses, 81–82
Olanzapine (Zyprexa), 81, 130, 149, 150, 151, 153, 154–156, 160, 161, 198–200, 296
Olanzapine/Fluoxetine combination (Symbyax), 198, 199–200
Omega-3 fatty acids, 8, 20, 242, 246–249, 321
Opiate abuse, 96, 100
Opiates, 160
Ortho-McNeil, 146, 196
OtsukaAmerica, 157
Owens, D., 263
Oxcarbazepine (Trileptil), 143–144, 195
Oxycodone (Percodan), 104

Paliperidone ER (Invega), 156
Panic disorder, 96
Pankratz, V., 261
Parachuting, 101. *See also* Methamphetamine (MA) abuse
Parent General Behavior Inventory, 291
Parke-Davis, 145
Parkinsonism, 149
Paroxetine (Paxil), 182, 200, 209
Pediatric bipolar disorder. *See* Child and early adolescent bipolar disorder
Peirce, C. S., xii
Pentazocine, 160
Percodan (oxycodone), 104
Personality, 71
Pfizer, 145, 157, 196
Phenelzine (Nardil), 86
Phenylalanine, 250
Pies, Ronald, 55
Phelps, J. R., 190
Phenytoin (Dilantin), 144–145, 195–196
Phosphatidylcholine, 249
Phospholipids, 246
Physicians' Desk Reference, 154

Pindolol (Visken), 246
Pittsburgh Maintenance Therapies in Bipolar Disorder, 81
Placebo-controlled drug studies, 130–131
Polydipsia, 132
Polypharmacy, 162–163
Polyuria, 132
Postherpetic neuralgia, 145
Postnatal hypomania, 45
Postpartum psychosis, 29, 45, 251
Posttraumatic stress disorder, 71
Poverty of content, 39
Pramipexole (Mirapex), 202
Prepubertal early adolescent bipolar patients (PEA-BP), 281
Prescription drug abuse, 103–104
Pressure of speech, 39
Primary alcoholism in bipolar patients, 97–98. *See also* Alcohol abuse in bipolar patients
Primidone (Mysoline), 145
Prolactin, 156
Prolongation of the QT interval, 157
Propranolol (Inderal), 133
Prospective drug studies, 130–131
Protein kinase C (PKC), 159
Prozac, 51
Prozac "poop out," 52
Psychosocial treatment:
in children and adolescents (*see* Child and early adolescent bipolar disorder, psychosocial treatment of)
cognitive-behavioral therapy (CBT) and behavioral activation, 225, 226, 232–234
efficacy of, 236
family-focused treatment, 225, 228–230
integrated family and IPSRT, 232

Psychosocial treatment
  (*continued*)
interpersonal and social-
  rhythm therapy (IPSRT),
  225, 226, 230–232
vs. intensive clinical management (ICM), 231
Life Goals Program, 234–235
list of, 225
overview, 223–225
in practice, 235–237
psychoeducation, 225–227
self-help support groups, 235
structured forms of, 235
See Bipolar depression; Bipolar illnesses
Psychotic depression, 41, 48,
  52, 67

Qigong, 253
Quetiapine (Seroquel), 12, 117,
  150, 151, 153, 156–157,
  160, 182, 198–199, 296

Rainbow Therapy, 299
Randomized drug studies, 130
Rapid cycling:
  age of onset, 284–285
  and antidepressants, 51, 185,
    187, 188, 324
  and childhood abuse, 26
  dark therapy, 244–245
  defined, 16
  difficulty in treatment, 162
  and lithium, 131 (*see also*
    Lithium)
  and magnesium, 251
  in older adults (*see* Bipolar dis-
    order in older adults)
  overview, 26–27
  vs. posttraumatic stress disor-
    der, 71
  and substance abuse, 97
  and thyroid augmentation,
    205
  and thyroid dysfunction, 26
  and women, 26–29
  See also Bipolar illnesses

RAPS, 107–108
Remeron. *See* Mirtazapine
  (Remeron)
Repetitive transcranial mag-
  netic stimulation (rTMS),
  243
Reproductive hormones,
  251–252
Requip. *See* Ropinirole
  (Requip)
Retrograde amnesia, 317
ReVia (naltrexone), 118
Rilutek. *See* Riluzole (Rilutek)
Riluzole (Rilutek), 202
Risperdal. *See* Risperidone
  (Risperdal)
Risperdal Consta, 156. *See also*
  Risperidone (Risperdal)
Risperidone (Risperdal), 150,
  151, 153, 156, 160, 200,
  209, 296
Rollnick, S., 114
Ropinirole (Requip), 202
Royal Australian and New
  Zealand College of Psy-
  chiatrists Clinical Practice
  (RANZCP) Guidelines
  Team for Bipolar Disorder,
  164
RU-486. *See* Mifepristone (Mifi-
  prex)

SAMe, 250
Sanger, T., 155
Schindler, Walter, 140
Schizoaffective disorder, vs.
  bipolar disorder, 67–68
Schizophrenia, 67–68, 153, 158
Scott, J., 233
Seasonal affective disorder
  (SAD), 17, 45, 243–244
Secondary alcoholism in bipo-
  lar patients, 97–98. *See also*
  Alcohol abuse in bipolar
  patients
Secondary mania, 61
Sedatives and bipolar disorder
  in older adults, 317

Selective serotonin reuptake in-
  hibitors (SSRIs). *See* SSRIs
Selegiline (Emsam), 184
Seroquel. *See* Quetiapine (Sero-
  quel)
Sertraline (Zoloft), 184
Shire, 195
Simon, J.E., 234
Sixth International Confer-
  ence on Bipolar Disorder,
  282–283
Sleep apnea and bipolar ill-
  nesses, 82
Sleep-wake cycle manipulation,
  245–246
Social phobia, 96
Social Rhythm Metric, 231
Sodium valproate (Depakene
  syrup), 136. *See also* Dival-
  proex (Depakote)
Solvay Pharmaceuticals, 158
Spacebasing, 99. *See also* Co-
  caine abuse
Speed, 100. *See also* Metham-
  phetamine (MA) abuse
SSRIs (selective serotonin
  reuptake inhibitors), 51,
  182–184, 187–188. *See
  also* Citalopram (Celexa);
  Escitalopram (Lexapro);
  Fluoxetine (Prozac); Parox-
  etine (Paxil)
Status epilepticus, 148
Stevens-Johnson syndrome,
  194, 195
Strattera (atomoxetine), 69
Structural Clinical Interviews
  for *DSM-IV-TR* Axis I/II
  Disorders, 73, 89
Substance Abuse and Mental
  Health Services Adminis-
  tration, 117
Substance Abuse Subtle
  Screening Inventory
  (SASSI), 108–109
Suicide risk:
  in bipolar patients, 263–265
  management of, 266–268

in mood disorder patients, 262–263, 264
overview, 261
in pediatric bipolar patients, 286
and principles of psychotherapy, 268–269
short-term risk, 263
statistics, 262
Sunny expressions of depression, 4, 26, 28, 39–41, 63, 66, 80, 132, 133, 185, 204, 324
Systematic Treatment Enhancement Program for Bipolar Disorder (STEP-BD), 26, 27, 28, 69, 162, 181, 184, 188, 235, 236

T3 (triiodothyronine). *See* Thyroid augmentation and bipolar depression
T4 (thyroxine). *See* Thyroid augmentation and bipolar depression
Tachycardia, 154
Talwin, 160
Tamoxifen (Nolvadex), 159–160
Tardive dyskinesia (TD), 150, 151, 316
Tegretol. *See* Carbamazepine (Tegretol)
Temperament, 71
Testosterone, 252
Texas Implementation of Medication Algorithms (TIMA), 164
Thorazine. *See* Chlorpromazine (Thorazine)
Thyroid augmentation and bipolar depression, 202–206, 209
Thyroid disease and bipolar illnesses, 26, 28, 63, 66, 80, 83, 132, 133, 185, 204, 324
Thyrotoxicosis, 4. *See also* Hyperthyroidism

Tiagabine (Gabitril), 148
TICS (Two-Item Conjoint Screen), 107–108
Tillman, R., 284, 285
TIME magazine, 275
Tohen, M., 155, 161
Topamax. *See* Topiramate (Topamax)
Topiramate (Topamax), 85, 138, 146, 183, 196–197, 209, 316
Treatment guidelines, 163–164, 282, 291, 294, 297, 300
Treatment Guidelines for Children and Adolescents with Bipolar Disorder: Child Psychiatric Workgroup on Bipolar Disorder, 282, 291, 294, 297, 300
Trichotillomania and bipolar illnesses, 89
Trigeminal neuralgia, 139
Trihexyphenidyl (Artane), 151
Trinucleotide repeats (TNRs), 20
Tryptophan, 250
TSH (thyroid stimulating hormone). *See* Thyroid augmentation and bipolar depression
Turner, E. H., 244, 245
Typical antipsychotic drugs, 148–149. *See also* Atypical antipsychotic drugs
Tyrosine, 250

UCB, 146
Ultradian cycling, 16, 159, 285. *See also* Rapid cycling
Unipolar depression:
and behavioral activation, 233–234
clinician's reaction to patient, 39–41, 53
and comorbid disorders, 47–48, 53
course of, 45, 53
and inositol, 249–250

depressive mixed states and, 42–43
in *DSM-IV-TR*, 38
family history, 48–49, 53
markers for, 53
organic causes of, 63
overview, 37–38
phenomenology, 38–39, 41–44, 53
and phenylalanine, 250
premorbid history, 45–47, 53
vs. posttraumatic stress disorder, 71
response to antidepressants, 50–54
signs, 38–39
symptoms, 41–44, 53
typical symptoms, 43
and tyrosine, 250
and suicide risk, 263–265
See also Bipolar depression
U.S. Food and Drug Administration, 51, 316
U.S. National Comorbidity Survey, 86
U.S. National Epidemiologic Survey on Alcohol and Related Conditions, 85
U.S. Veterans Association, 234

Vagus nerve stimulation (VNS), 243
Valium (diazepam), 104
Valliant, G.E., 105, 107, 112, 114, 115, 118
Valnoctamide, 139
Valproate, 118, 136, 137, 144, 159, 161. *See also* Divalproex (Depakote)
Valproic acid (Depakene), 136, 137, 316. *See also* Divalproex (Depakote)
Valpromide, 136. *See also* Divalproex (Depakote)
Vanadium, 252
Venlafaxine (Effexor), 184, 187–188

Verapamil (Calan), 158–159, 251

Visken. *See* Pindolol (Visken)

Vitamin D3, 251

Wallace Laboratories, 197

Warner-Lambert, 145, 196

Wehr, T. A., 244,

Weissman, M., 5

Wellbutrin. *See* Bupropion (Wellbutrin)

Winokur, G., 48, 97, 100, 264

Wirz-Justice, A., 244

Wittgenstein, Ludwig, 67

Wozniak, J., 276

Xanax (alprazolam), 104

Yoga, 253

Young Mania Rating Scale (YMRS), 147, 154–155

Young Mania Scale, 291

Youngstrom, E.A., 279, 283, 289, 291, 294

Ziehen, T., 276

Zinc, 251

Ziprasidone (Geodon), 150, 151, 156, 157, 200–201

Zoloft. *See* Sertraline (Zoloft)

Zomaril. *See* Iloperidone (Zomaril)

Zonegran. *See* Zonisamide (Zonegran)

Zonisamide (Zonegran), 138, 147, 197–198, 209

Zyprexa. *See* Olanzapine (Zyprexa)

Zyprexa Zydis, 156. *See also* Olanzapine (Zyprexa)